New Perspectives on
MELVILLE

_____

to the memory of
my Mother

*

New Perspectives on
MELVILLE

EDITED BY
FAITH PULLIN

The Kent State
University
Press

*

Library of Congress Cataloging in Publication Data
Main entry under title:
New perspectives on Melville.
  Includes bibliographical references and index.
  1. Melville, Herman, 1819–1891—Criticism and
interpretation—Addresses, essays, lectures.
I. Pullin, Faith.
PS2387.N48   813'.3   78–16505
ISBN 0–87338–226–9

Published in the United States by
The Kent State University Press
Kent, Ohio 44242
Library of Congress Catalog Card No. 78–16505
ISBN 0–87338–226–9
Published simultaneously in the United Kingdom by
Edinburgh University Press

Contents

Preface

This collection of essays is designed to present a specifically Anglo-American view of Melville, and is not just another contribution to the Melville industry. For some time Melville's reputation was higher in Britain than in America, and he, himself, had a complex and ambivalent relationship with England,[1] its society and literature. In his own country, after the initial enthusiasm for his comparatively simple early works, Melville's reputation faded rapidly and he suffered years of neglect before his death. To such an extent that the New York *Commercial Advertiser*, in an article of 14 January 1886, claimed that 'although his early works are still popular, the author is generally supposed to be dead'.[2]

The resurrection of Melville's reputation had begun by the 1920s, and has continued until the present, with ever-increasing interest shown in his work by modern critics, so that he is generally considered to be the greatest writer America has produced.

The essays that follow have been written by British and American critics, not all of whom work primarily in the field of American literature. Six of the writers are British (Brian Higgins, Mrs Leavis, Robert Lee, Colin Manlove, Eric Mottram, Faith Pullin); and six are American (Richard Brodhead, Arnold Goldman, Harrison Hayford, Eric Homberger, Hershel Parker, Larzer Ziff). One essay, 'The Flawed Grandeur of Melville's *Pierre*', is a truly Anglo-American enterprise. What emerges from this Anglo-American confrontation with Melville is a predominant concern with Melville's attitudes to society and to language. The Melvillean concepts of nature and civilization are also canvassed. Melville's technical problems as a writer in nineteenth-century America are examined, as is the relationship of American writers to British culture. It is suggested that the wanderings of Melville's isolated protagonists betray a characteristic American tendency to refuse to be at home; or, rather, to refuse to accept any society that is less than ideal. Melville was appalled by the industrial poverty he saw in Liverpool, just as he was, in the end, appalled by the luxuriant paradise of Typee.

The collection contains, fittingly, a consideration of what Shakespeare meant to Melville, and to American society. Melville's response was complicated by the fact that Shakespeare was a representative of an aristocratic system, at variance with American democratic beliefs. But he was drawn to Shakespeare, both as a profound craftsman, and as a writer who, apparently, shared similar doubts about the value and status of human experience. Above all, he was attracted to Shakespeare because Shakespeare, like himself, was hesitant about stating truths and came upon them obliquely. In 'Hawthorne and His Mosses', Melville recorded his admiration for Shakespeare as the master of the 'great Art of Telling the Truth', but he does this 'covertly and by snatches' for, 'in this world of lies, Truth is forced to fly like a scared white doe in the woodlands; and only by cunning glimpses will she reveal herself'.[3] Melville occasionally made bitter reference to the fact that his contemporary audience was not interested in a writer telling the truth. In a letter to Hawthorne in June 1851, he wrote: 'Truth is the silliest thing under the sun. Try to get a living by the Truth – and go to the Soup Societies.'[4] Melville constantly returned to this problem of telling the truth, and the difficulty for the artist to express truth in words. In *Pierre*, he comments on the characteristic evasiveness of truth, and the near-impossibility of ever getting words to say exactly what you mean. In this despair over the failure of expression itself – this destructive lack of confidence in verbalization – Melville comes very close to the attitudes of modern writers; this, of course, is one of the reasons for his popularity today, since he appears to be expressing current nihilistic views, revealing a sense that the verbal artifact has failed, has been undermined from within.

In his introduction to *Pierre*, Henry Murray wrote: 'Perhaps the broadest generalization that can be made about Melville's different truths is that they are *all* culturally unacceptable'.[5] Obviously, Melville's sense of the essential blackness of human existence (his praise for Hawthorne for saying No! in thunder) runs counter to the transcendental optimism of his period. But in spite of his final sense that all human enterprises were doomed to failure, he did, to the end, believe in the possibility of community and fraternal co-operation. In fact, his last work, *Billy Budd*, encapsulates both his pessimism and his equally characteristic optimism. Billy Budd is an ideal figure, whom society cannot tolerate, but he serves, in the role of sacrificial victim, to inspire Captain Vere to an admirable, pragmatic justice – to an anguished respect for law and an ordered society. The characters of Billy and Vere refer back to Melville's earliest work, *Typee*, and, in this respect reveal Melville's achievement as unified. His fictional technique becomes more elaborate at the end of his career, but his usual preoccupations are already apparent in the reflective Tommo, who is, at this stage, an un-disciplined individualist, and the whole question of whether or not Typee is, in any real sense, an ideal society. Marnoo, in *Typee*, with his physical perfection and in his role as saviour, has much in common with Billy Budd. He is a tabooed native, who brings together the different communities on Typee; he is also the agent of Tommo's rescue. Melville describes him in the same terms that he is later to use of Billy. They are both Apollos, their faces being like the work of a Greek sculptor.[6]

Until recently, it has been difficult to assess accurately Mel-ville's status as a writer. There have been two major problems: one is the fact that his style appears, at times, wildly uncon-trolled, and is always extremely varied; the other problem has been expressed by Jay Leyda in the following statement: 'There is a link between Melville's experiences and his works, which are all a transmutation, to some degree, of a reality he had observed or lived'.[7]

Melville's lack of invention seemed a stumbling block, to himself, as well as to his critics. One difficulty in his later work was that he had used up the material provided by his early adventurous years. It has been hard for critics to categorize Melville's work. He is not a conventional novelist, and he is more interested in ideas than creative writers are ordinarily taken to be. His capacity for metaphysical speculation is often uncontrolled by the normal devices of fiction, and he often finds it impossible to create a form appropriate to his individual concerns. This has led contemporary critics to seize on Melville as a kind of post-modernist manqué; a tendency rightly dismissed by Robert Lee in his essay on *Moby-Dick*, in which he insists on Melville's preoccupation not only with thoughts but with things.

Melville himself was aware of a lack of aesthetic integration in his work. In a letter to Hawthorne he complains that his work is 'a final hash, and all my books are botches'. Brian Higgins and Hershel Parker comment perceptively on the 'botched' nature of *Pierre*. Their contention is that *Pierre* is really two books in one; the first, concerning an idealist trying to come to grips with the conventional world; the other, about Melville's own problems as a writer. However, they submit that, in spite of its lack of coherence, *Pierre* was 'the best psychological novel that had yet been written in English'.

Mrs Leavis's essay also deals with Melville's difficulties in trying to survive, literally and psychically, as a popular author in America. Her claim is that the work of the 1853–6 period should be recognized as superior, in quality and achievement, to his previous writings. Taking the story, *Cock-a-Doodle-Doo!*, as her focal point, she notes its incidental destruction of the Wordsworthian analogue, with its comparatively facile optimism. In spite of this, Melville uses the tale to register 'belief in the sustaining and revivifying power of art'. Mrs Leavis disputes Hawthorne's opinion about Melville's constitutional morbidity, and finds no evidence for this in the tales.

Melville's experience of his own society was a paradigm; he was the archetypal misunderstood artist, isolated and rejected. The (scandalous) subject-matter of *Pierre* caused such readers as he had to drop him, and, for the rest of his life, Melville was virtually without a significant audience. The books that gained recognition for him in terms of public esteem and financial reward were the very ones he had no longer any interest in writing.

How typical, in fact, is Melville of nineteenth-century American culture? How typically American is he? Perhaps what is essential to Melville is also essential to American attitudes in general. This is a kind of Manichaean combination of optimism and pessimism; what Richard Chase has called, 'a dialectic or continuing dialogue between the Yea-sayers and the Nay-sayers'.[8] Melville, in a sense, has no settled voice. He is

forever trying out alternatives. It may be this continuous movement of thought – this intense vitality – that makes him so
attractive to a British audience, conditioned to expect considered statement and perfection of form. Melville's, 'I try all
things; I achieve what I can' or 'God keep me from ever com-
pleting anything' are provocative and appealing to an audience
geared to the Great Tradition. It is the very openness and
experimental nature of Melville's method that compels.

What unites the essays in this volume is their empirical
approach and their close examination of texts. To return to the
association with Shakespeare, Melville, in many respects, works
in a manner that is diametrically opposed to the English writer;
Melville's entire mode is subjective and self-dramatizing,
whereas Shakespeare's is objective. This is one of the major
differences between English and American literature, and it is
brought out in this book. Melville is not a novelist in the Henry
James manner, but a writer of romance, making 'short, quick
probings at the very axis of reality'.

To the question, do we really need another book on Melville ?
this volume provides an affirmative answer. Scholars and
students will find, in the following pages, an examination of the
interrelation of British and American culture and society, and
an attempt to assess their mutual influence. The critics who have
written here have resolutely turned away from the fashionable
response and made a commitment to a deeper understanding of
Melville as an authentic American genius. To quote Melville
himself, 'To produce a mighty book, you must choose a mighty
theme'.

I wish to express my gratitude to the Newberry Library for a
Summer Fellowship; and to Harrison Hayford in Chicago, and
David Newton-de Molina in Edinburgh, for helpful
conversations about Melville, and this book.

Notes

1. See his *Journal of a Visit to London and the Continent 1849-50*, ed.
    Eleanor Melville Metcalf (Cambridge: Harvard University Press
    1948).

2. Quoted, Merton M. D. Sealts, Jr., *The Early Lives of Melville*
    (Madison: University of Wisconsin Press 1974) p. 24.

3. 'Hawthorne and His Mosses', *The Portable Melville*, ed. J. Leyda
    (London: Chatto and Windus 1952) p. 408.

4. *The Letters of Herman Melville*, ed. Merrell R. Davis and William
    H. Gilman (New Haven: Yale University Press 1960) p. 127.

5. Introduction to his edition of *Pierre* (New York: Hendricks
    House 1949) pp. xxix-xxx.

6. See E. S. Greja, *The Common Continent of Men; Racial Equality
    in the Writings of Herman Melville* (New York: Kennikat Press
    1974) p. 16.

7. Introduction, *The Portable Melville*, p. xi.

8. Introduction, *Melville* (Engelwood Cliffs, N.J.: Prentice-Hall
    1962) p. 3.

Melville's *Typee*:
The Failure of Eden

PERHAPS, to a sensitive imagination, those islands in
the middle of the Pacific are the most unbearable places
on earth.
D. H. Lawrence (Herman Melville's *Typee* & *Omoo*)

Typee, Melville's first work as a professional author, is not as
irrelevant to his later opus as it has usually been considered by
critics. In fact, it encapsulates and prefigures the major concerns
and biases of his later vision. What Melville is discovering in
Typee is what Milton Stern has called, 'his relationship to the
world';[1] his typical literary and philosophical preoccupations.
Typee is certainly not a simple travelogue, a picaresque South
Sea adventure, enjoyed, and, in some cases, endured, by a
narrator whose report is largely autobiographical. It is a symbolic narrative in which Melville delineates, in however preliminary a form, the basic inclinations of his thought. In no
sense is it a piece of juvenilia: Melville, in *Typee*, is the conscious
craftsman; the book, as with other later works of Melville,
inhabits the formal area which is only now being investigated by
critics – that area where fact and fiction are so closely allied as to
be indistinguishable.

Primarily, the book constitutes a rejection of primitivism.
Tommo, the narrator, enters an alien, physical world but is
unable to join it; his point of view is always that of the self-
conscious, rational and tormented nineteenth-century thinker.
Tommo observes a timeless world from the perspective of his
contemporary civilization. This juxtaposition inevitably involves a consideration of the question of what civilization
actually is. Melville obviously rejects the current views of his
own society of the irrefutable benefits of encroaching western
materialist society (a condemnation that predates Conrad's
annihilation of these same values in *Heart of Darkness* and

Nostromo). The main theme, then, of the novel, is the testing of
a Rousseauistic response to experience and the rejection of that
report, not simply on the part of Tommo as a 'sophisticated'
representative of an advanced society, but because it is inadequate in itself. The passivity of the inhabitants of this
Paradise is obviously as deeply offensive to Melville as it was to
Milton.[2] Perhaps one of the problems that Melville is grappling
with in *Typee* is the idea that any kind of society is bound to be
'evil'. It's the view expressed by Conrad in a letter to Cunninghame Graham in 1899: 'Le crime est une condition nécessaire
de l'existence organisée. La société est essentiellement crimin-
elle, – ou elle n'existerait pas.'[3] The fact that Typee is a relatively
simple society in its organization and customs distracts Melville
at first in his implied analysis of it. But, eventually, the simple
dichotomy between idyllic Typee and evil America is found to
be erroneous and irrelevant. Typee is a flawed Eden and one in
which Melville's critical consciousness can find no release and
no absolutes. There is no such thing as a pure state of nature:
Typee offers no prospect of regenerative salvation. Neither
Typee itself, nor the representative society of the *Dolly* provide
any solution to the questions about the nature of human society
that Melville raises in the book. Both reveal themselves as in
many respects corrupt, and deeply inadequate to human needs.
The limitations of life in Typee, paradoxically, come about
through the very communal nature of its society. A communality that attracts Tommo but equally frustrates him, immured as
he is in his solitary, individualistic consciousness. The ideal
society, in this case, ought to be found on the *Dolly* since the
ship provides a model of hierarchy and order and the opportunity for work (so essential to America's Puritan ethic). However, the social and legal abuses of life on that actual ship incapacitate her as any kind of model.

> In numberless instances had not only the implied but the
> specified conditions of the articles been violated on the
> part of the ship in which I served. The usage on board of
> her was tyrannical; the sick had been inhumanly neglected;
> the provisions had been doled out in scanty allowance; and
> her cruizes were unreasonably protracted. The captain was
> the author of these abuses; it was in vain to think that he
> would either remedy them, or alter his conduct, which was

> . . . arbitrary and violent in the extreme . . . , our crew was
> composed of a parcel of dastardly and mean-spirited
> wretches, divided among themselves, and only united in
> enduring without resistance the unmitigated tyranny of the
> captain.[4]

In addition, although the atrocities often enacted on Typee are
at first presented by Tommo as the natural reaction on the part
of the inhabitants to European treachery, it's clear that mutual
hatred and suspicion exist between the various tribal groups
themselves on the island:

> Owing to the mutual hostilities of the different tribes I have
> mentioned, the mountainous tracts which separate their
> respective territories remain altogether uninhabited; the
> natives invariably dwelling in the depths of the valleys, with
> a view of securing themselves from the predatory incursions
> of their enemies, who often lurk along their borders, ready
> to cut off any imprudent straggler, or make a descent upon
> the inmates of some sequestered habitation. I several
> times met with very aged men, who from this cause had
> never passed the confines of their native vale. (27)

Tommo himself is totally individualistic at this point; he leaves
the ship because he is unwilling to accept its lawlessness. Later,
he escapes from Typee since he can't tolerate the suffocating
luxuriousness of its life – and because he is un-free in an opposite
manner from the imprisonment he experienced on the ship. He
has no sense of the common good; he simply wishes to escape
from situations which he has chosen but which have become
oppressive to him. In this sense, Vere in *Billy Budd* is a chastened
and matured Tommo, who does his duty. Tommo, on the other
hand, merely uses Toby, first as a companion with whom to
escape; later as someone who can rescue him from what had
seemed a refuge. Toby is developed only schematically by
Melville as the foil to Tommo; as someone who takes easily to
the sensuous experiences in which Typee abounds, but who
makes no intellectual demands on his experience. Toby's dry
comments on Tommo's lack of physical expertise provide much
of the humour of the entry into Typee. But the humour itself
only highlights the essentially ominous quality of the experience. As has been pointed out by various critics, the question
whether the first inhabitants Tommo and Toby meet are Happar

(good) or Typee (bad) demonstrates Melville's characteristic sense of the ambivalent quality of experience. It is the same ambivalence that is at the centre of *The Encantadas*: 'the tortoise is both black and bright'.[5] Tommo is, of course, engaged in an elaborate attempt at escapism. The ship is an escape from the struggle for place, position and success in his native society. As an alien, he has a spurious status on Typee but he is without the human understanding of his companions as totally as he was on the ship. This is a symbolic prefiguring of Melville's own life in which he was misunderstood and seriously undervalued by both society and family. His art was the only recompense for this, and yet the profession of writer in nineteenth-century America meant that he could not write as he wanted and succeed: 'So far as I am individually concerned, & independent of my pocket, it is my earnest desire to write those sort of books which are said to "fail".'[6]

In view of the fact that, in Tommo, Melville is representing many of his own actual experiences in the South Seas, there is bound to be a large autobiographical element present in the novel; yet, Tommo stands not only for Melville but for a typical nineteenth-century intellectual / adventurer as unlike his shipmates as Melville himself obviously was. Conrad was in the same position, but his essentially sceptical response to experience, ('there are some things that do not bear too much looking into'), was deeply disturbing to Melville. In this event, the safety at which Tommo clutches in Typee is soon revealed to be deceptive and deeply ambiguous.

Throughout Melville's narrative, a factual, Crusoe-like surface covers an important symbolic substructure. The symbolic level works to support the concept of the essential ambiguity of experience and the deeply unsatisfying nature of human existence. In the beginning, the bay of Nukuheva appears as a vision of natural perfection.

> Nothing can exceed the imposing scenery of this bay. Viewed from our ship as she lay at anchor in the middle of the harbor, it presented the appearance of a vast natural amphitheatre in decay, and overgrown with vines, the deep glens that furrowed its sides appearing like enormous fissures caused by the ravages of time. Very often when lost in admiration at its beauty, I have experienced a pang of

regret that a scene so enchanting should be hidden from the world in these remote seas, and seldom meet the eyes of devoted lovers of nature. (24)

And yet, it is dangerous to take this beauty at its face value:

I had heard too of an English vessel that many years ago, after a weary cruize, sought to enter the bay of Nukuheva, and arriving within two or three miles of the land, was met by a large canoe filled with natives, who offered to lead the way to the place of their destination. The captain, unacquainted with the localities of the island, joyfully acceded to the proposition – the canoe paddled on and the ship followed. She was soon conducted to a beautiful inlet, and dropped her anchor in its waters beneath the shadows of the lofty shore. That same night the perfidious Typees, who had thus inveigled her into their fatal bay, flocked aboard the doomed vessel by hundreds, and at a given signal murdered every soul on board. (25)

Yet Melville's own attitude is ambivalent here. His prose operates on two distinct levels. On the one hand, he is expressing the concept of the duplicity of experience itself: on the other, he is concerned to attack the facile complacency of the view of his own century of the civilizing mission of the western, technologically advanced nations. The essentially punitive and exploitative nature of the European relationship to the South Seas is a point on which Melville insists (and develops at greater length in *Omoo*).

Melville's consideration of the nature of civilization is given visual content with the juxtaposing of the figures of the patriarch of Tior and the French admiral Du Petit Thouars. Here, Melville sets up a tableau which seems, superficially, to have an obvious meaning. But his following comment disturbs the clear reference of the picture and also disturbs the reader's common-sense view of things, disorienting him. As with the factual level of the story, beneath which exists a disconcerting conceptual stratum which undercuts its apparent optimism (Tommo suffers, but lives to tell the tale), so with this visual representation of an apparently self-evident truth:

The admiral came forward with head uncovered and extended hand, while the old king saluted him by a stately flourish of his weapon. The next moment they stood side

by side, these two extremes of the social scale, – the
polished, splendid Frenchman, and the poor tattooed
savage. (29)

Melville's comment is a conventional one on the 'immeasur-
able distance' between the two. The Frenchman being the
product of long centuries of progressive civilization and refinement, while the Marquesan 'has not advanced one step in the
career of improvement'. The comment that undercuts this
platitude concerns the nature of happiness, 'insensible as he is
to a thousand wants, and removed from harassing cares, may
not the savage be the happier man of the two?' This is the
question that forms the major part of the material of the book.
The answer, cumulative in nature and never explicitly stated,
is that neither of them are happy, and that happiness is not a
property of human life.

The isolation of Typee that Melville emphasises throughout
means that it can be used as a test-case for an examination of the
human condition. Activity is introduced into the narrative by
the movement of Tommo's mind, by his continual speculations
on the culture in which he finds himself and his (futile)
attempts to adjust himself to it mentally. This offsets the static
quality of the narrative. Melville's technique is highly pictorial
in nature. The juxtaposition of the patriarch and the French
admiral mentioned above, is set in a Douanier-Rousseau type
landscape which is the reverse of realistic: 'The umbrageous
shades where the interview took place – the glorious tropical
vegetation around – the picturesque grouping of the mingled
throng of soldiery and natives'.

The beauty of the island is always presented in visual terms.
Tommo instinctively withdraws and observes; he is the detached
observer whose function is to tell the story rather than to enter
into it and experience it as Toby does. It is for this reason that
Toby is allowed by the islanders to go – he is like them and therefore it is no conquest to convert him to their viewpoint of the
desirability of purely sensual happiness. Tommo is a renegade
who, in the end, lives only for escape from Eden. Not that
Tommo is unresponsive to the beauty of the island, but that,
finally, he is repelled by its easy luxuriance.

There are various set-pieces throughout the narrative. For
instance, the scene in which the young girls swim out to welcome

the *Dolly* in;[7] and yet the immediate contact between the two worlds is, as ever, the pollution of the welcomers. The overt sexuality of the girls' dances disturbs Tommo as much as it did Melville's contemporary audience: 'The varied dances of the Marquesan girls are beautiful in the extreme, but there is an abandoned voluptuousness in their character which I dare not attempt to describe' (15). In many respects, *Typee* has associations with *Robinson Crusoe* in the way in which both Melville and Defoe attempt to gain the readers' confidence by the manipulation of concrete detail. And yet, in both cases, what has most deeply affected readers is, of course, the symbolic content – the manner in which the isolated individual reacts to a situation of, possibly, permanent isolation. In the case both of Tommo and Crusoe there is no genuine attempt at adaptation. As Ian Watt has pointed out,[8] Crusoe simply seeks to re-establish the details of the society from which he has come, using objects which have conveniently been saved from the ship. Tommo isn't physically isolated (although he suffers a kind of double imprisonment, being kept against his will on an island) but he is obviously isolated psychically. In spite of the ministrations of Fayaway, he responds to the reference to 'home' and 'mother' which, naively expressed as it is, involves a recognition of the vital necessities of relating to one's own society and its emotional ties.

The early reviewers of *Typee* noted the similarity of Defoe's and Melville's methods; a reviewer in the London *Spectator* of 28 February 1846 made the following point, involving Melville's technique of heightening reality:

> Much of the book is not beyond the range of invention, especially by a person acquainted with the Islands, and with the fictions of De Foe; and we think that several things have been heightened for effect, if indeed this artistical principle does not pervade the work.[9]

To this may be added two comments by Melville himself, from *The Confidence-Man*:

> While to all fiction is allowed some play of invention, yet, fiction based on fact should never be contradictory to it.[10]
>
> . . . .
>
> And as, in real life, the proprieties will not allow people to act out themselves with that unreserve permitted to the stage; so, in books of fiction, they look not only for more

entertainment, but, at bottom, even for more reality, than
real life itself can show. Thus, though they want novelty,
they want nature, too; but nature unfettered, exhilarated,
in effect transformed.[11]

These two views on the necessary basis of fact in fiction, combined with a heightened reality, sum up Melville's method in
Typee. Although it was not till *The Confidence-Man* (1857) that
Melville actually enunciated this theory, it is in *Typee* that he
practises it; a remarkable achievement for a writer working on
his first book. Melville wrote *Typee* when he was twenty-five,
and was himself aware of his somewhat sudden access of
intellectual – and literary – maturity. As he wrote to Hawthorne,
while engaged on *Moby-Dick*, 'From my twenty-fifth year, I
date my life'.[12] The first publisher of *Typee*, John Murray,
insisted on Melville's adding more factual material about life on
the island to increase the authenticity of the novel; but this
material did not convince contemporary reviewers. The critical
controversy of the time concerning the facts of Melville's
experience in the Marquesas is similar to that aroused in 1977
by Alex Haley's *Roots*: one may answer these objections in the
same way, what is important is the symbolic quality of the
narrative, verisimilitude is more important than mere reporting.

As an anonymous reviewer wrote in the London *Critic* in
March 1846:

> The incidents, no doubt, are sometimes exaggerated, and
> the colouring is often overcharged, yet in the narrative
> generally there is a *vraisemblance* that cannot be feigned;
> for the minuteness, and novelty of the details, could only
> have been given by one who had before him nature for his
> model.[13]

What is striking about both *Typee* and *Robinson Crusoe* is the
way in which the symbolic undertones are fused with the very
physical quality of the narrative. Tommo describes, in close
detail, and with a Defoe-like pleasure in how things are done,
the manufacture of tappa:

> In the manufacture of the beautiful white tappa generally
> worn on the Marquesan Islands, the preliminary operation
> consists in gathering a certain quantity of the young
> branches of the cloth-tree. The exterior green bark being
> pulled off as worthless, there remains a slender fibrous

substance, which is carefully stripped from the stick, to which it closely adheres. When a sufficient quantity of it has been collected, the various strips are enveloped in a covering of large leaves, which the natives use precisely as we do wrapping-paper, and which are secured by a few turns of a line passed round them. The package is then laid in the bed of some running stream, with a heavy stone placed over it, to prevent its being swept away. After it has remained for two or three days in this state, it is drawn out, and exposed, for a short time, to the action of the air, every distinct piece being attentively inspected, with a view of ascertaining whether it has yet been sufficiently affected by the operation. This is repeated again and again, until the desired result is obtained. (147)

The text-book clarity of this style is in total contrast to the mixed tone of the prose in which it is embedded. Indeed, what distinguishes Melville's style in *Typee* is the very volatile changes of mood which the narrator reveals as he tells his story. For instance, the significant tableau of the indigenous ruler and the French Admiral is undercut by the humour with which Tommo mocks the scene itself and his own role in it as solemn observer: the passage ends with his memory of 'the golden-hued bunch of bananas that he held in his hand at the time, and of which I occasionally partook while making the aforesaid philosophical reflections'. The account of Kory-Kory's making fire in chapter 14 is very similar. What is presented by Melville in *Typee* is a series of animated tableaux; it is like being shown a collection of particularly rich and glamorous slides. But it is the narrator's voice that holds the attention, whether he is mocking himself and his own physical clumsiness in comparison with the more adept Toby, exclaiming at the horrors of colonialism, or responding to the perfection of the natural scene. Melville's method is one that is singularly mixed and, as such, is in line with his later works, *Mardi* (1849), *Moby-Dick* (1851) and *Pierre* (1852). There is little that is one-dimensional about *Typee*; the work has a smaller compass than those others in that it deals with a self-contained episode but it is no less rich technically. The following passage concerns an episode when the Typees hurry to sell their wares to boats on the beach:

> I could not but be entertained by the novel and animated
> sight which now met my view. One after another the
> natives crowded along the narrow path, laden with every
> variety of fruit. Here, you might have seen one who, after
> ineffectually endeavoring to persuade a surly porker to be
> conducted in leading strings, was obliged at last to seize
> the perverse animal in his arms, and carry him struggling
> against his naked breast, and squealing without inter-
> mission. There went two, who at a little distance might have
> been taken for the Hebrew spies, on their return to Moses
> with the goodly bunch of grapes. One trotted before the
> other at a distance of a couple of yards, while between them,
> from a pole resting on their shoulders, was suspended a
> huge cluster of bananas, which swayed to and fro with the
> rocking gait at which they proceeded. Here ran another,
> perspiring with his exertions, and bearing before him a
> quantity of cocoa-nuts, who, fearful of being too late,
> heeded not the fruit that dropped from his basket, and
> appeared solely intent upon reaching his destination, care-
> less how many of his cocoa-nuts kept company with him.
> (106–7)

This passage is very carefully controlled. Two initial points
are made and are carried through the whole piece; these are the
originality of the scene, and its vitality – the energy of the
exercise being so unusual with the native people that this, in
itself, produces a note of comedy. And yet, they are not of
course presenting their own produce; they have not created the
abundant fruit by labour since nothing has to be cultivated on
Typee. The pig becomes a recalcitrant child, refusing the
'leading strings', and incongruously clasped to the breast. The
biblical allusion in the next sentence distances the scene and
mplicitly comments on it. The bananas themselves become
animated, enlivened by their human transport system. Finally,
the ultimate absurdity comes in the confusion of means and
ends of the potential coconut vendor. The ironic tone here
serves to maintain in the reader an appreciative, but detached,
attitude. There is no attempt at involving him in the scene –
quite the reverse. Nor is there any hint of anything below the
surface; in fact, we are presented simply with surface and a
surface of lacquered brilliance. The natives are almost ridiculed,

but not quite, since they are simply exhibiting universal human traits, which can be treated with affection. And yet, as everywhere in the book, this passage is juxtaposed with, and receives its effect from, a following passage in which Tommo is deeply disturbed by the fact that Toby does not return. The ambiguous nature of all experience on the island is reinforced by this contrast. There are no answers to Tommo's questions, so he is tormented by doubt and fear: 'all their accounts were contradictory; one giving me to understand that Toby would be with me in a very short time; another that he did not know where he was; while a third, violently inveighing against him, assured me that he had stolen away, and would never come back'.[14]

What emerges from this is that there can never be any true sociality between Tommo and the natives. The idealized Fayaway is the only person who seems capable of understanding Tommo's crippling sense of alienation, cut off, as he is, from his own culture. Fayaway seems (unconvincingly) capable of an imaginative identification that Tommo himself admits is extraordinary in someone of her age and limited experience. It is through Fayaway that Melville is able to introduce the melancholy that typifies Tommo's response to his self-inflicted predicament. That Fayaway is a fantasy figure is betrayed by the easy sentimentality with which Tommo expresses her sense of his dilemma: 'she appeared to be conscious that there were ties rudely severed, which had once bound us to our homes; that there were sisters and brothers anxiously looking forward to our return, who were, perhaps, never more to behold us'. It is more credible and, pace Lawrence,[15] more moving, when the old chief Marheyo expresses his benevolent comprehension of the situation, at the time of Tommo's escape, in the words 'home' and 'mother'.

Typee is in some senses a comedy of manners. The first chapter sets the tone, with its episode of the Queen of Nukuheva and the French officers. This is a reported scene handled in a style of broad farce. But the naivety of the Queen is, in fact, touching rather than ridiculous; in her own terms, her behaviour is quite logical and reasonable. Melville here is employing a Swiftian type of satirical incongruity, similar to the dislocated expectations of Gulliver in various strange societies. The Queen is excited by the tattooing of an old sailor and proudly reveals her own:

the royal lady, eager to display the hieroglyphics on her own
sweet form, bent forward for a moment, and turning sharply
round, threw up the skirts of her mantle, and revealed a
sight from which the aghast Frenchmen retreated pre-
cipitately, and tumbling into their boat, fled the scene of so
shocking a catastrophe. (8)

This passage modulates into a breezy, jocular narrative of the
Dolly cruising on the Line.

The man at the wheel never vexed the old lady with any
superfluous steering, but comfortably adjusting his limbs
at the tiller, would doze away by the hour. True to her
work, the *Dolly* headed to her course, and like one of those
characters who always do best when let alone, she jogged on
her way like a veteran old sea-pacer as she was. (9)

The characterization of the *Dolly* as an 'old lady' who does
best left to her own devices, the total undercutting of any idea
of efficiency or of the ship as a working unit; her jogging, unsuit-
able for a ship and her age, all combine to create the impression
of successful amateur behaviour; the *Dolly* is the reverse of
stylish. This passage modulates into a description of the increasingly soporific effect of the South Seas. Significantly, all thought
is impossible; the crew are unable to think or act either –
'Reading was out of the question; take a book in your hand, and
you were asleep in an instant'. Tommo is thus put into a
receptive state to respond totally to the compelling sense
impressions the area provides. The passage that follows is comparable to those in *Moby-Dick* on the fascinating serenity of the
Pacific.

The sky presented a clear expanse of the most delicate blue,
except along the skirts of the horizon, where you might see
a thin drapery of pale clouds, which never varied their form
or color. The long, measured, dirge-like swell of the Pacific
came rolling along, with its surface broken by little tiny
waves, sparkling in the sunshine. Every now and then a
shoal of flying fish, scared from the water under the bows,
would leap into the air, and fall the next moment like a
shower of silver into the sea. Then you would see the
superb albicore, with his glittering sides, sailing aloft,
and often describing an arc in his descent, disappear on the
surface of the water. Far off, the lofty jet of the whale

might be seen, and nearer at hand the prowling shark, that villainous footpad of the seas, would come skulking along, and, at a wary distance, regard us with his evil eye. At times, some shapeless monster of the deep, floating on the surface, would, as we approached, sink slowly into the blue waters, and fade away from the sight. But the most impressive feature of the scene was the almost unbroken silence that reigned over sky and water. Scarcely a sound could be heard but the occasional breathing of the grampus, and the rippling at the cut-water. (10)

What is striking here is the ominous undertone beneath the surface charm. Everything is conducted in total silence, signifying the fact that, above all, this is an inhuman scene, or rather, a scene in which humanity has no place. The swell of the Pacific is 'dirgelike', the flying fish are scared by the passage of the ship, the prowling shark is 'villainous' and has an 'evil eye'. In spite of the humorous anthropomorphism of this, the point is made that the natural world is ambivalent and at times actively hostile.

The three passages quoted, although they span a chapter division, cohere, and typify Melville's achievement in what is by no means an apprentice work. The progress is from farcical anecdote, which nevertheless contains in itself a just appreciation of different manners and value systems (the French would have appeared equally ridiculous from a native viewpoint), to an introduction to the influence and novelty of the South Sea ethos. There follows a visual description of natural beauty, flawed by a sense of vague disquiet; and this constitutes a prefiguring of what the experience of life on Typee is to be.

Paradise itself is vitiated by the inescapable flaws of life; but a more grotesque and glaring flaw is apparent to Tommo as he arrives in the bay of Nukuheva:

No description can do justice to its beauty; but that beauty was lost to me then, and I saw nothing but the tri-colored flag of France trailing over the stern of six vessels, whose black hulls and bristling broadsides proclaimed their warlike character. (12)

This apparently remote retreat has already been infiltrated by Europe and taken possession of by the French. The link between the two worlds – and acceptable to neither – is the pilot who comes aboard the *Dolly*. The pilot is a disgraced English sailor, mistakenly employed by the French; his drunken antics are a suitable comment on the incongruity and ineffectuality of the Western presence in the South Seas. The immediate impact of the islanders themselves on the consciousness of Tommo causes him problems of interpretation:

> Such strange outcries and passionate gesticulations I never certainly heard or saw before. You would have thought the islanders were on the point of flying at one another's throats, whereas they were only amicably engaged in disentangling their boats. (13)

The first event that greets the crew is the welcoming swim of the young Marquesan girls out to the *Dolly*. This, in many ways, sums up the contradictory qualities of the Western / South Sea confrontation. Again, the visual picture is totally seductive – Tommo sees the girls as mermaids 'I watched the rising and sinking of their forms, and beheld the uplifted right arm bearing above the water the girdle of tappa, and their long dark hair trailing beside them as they swam'. The arrival of the Marquesan girls signifies the entry of sexuality into the sterile ship. Tommo is fascinated, but also repelled: 'not the feeblest barrier was interposed between the unholy passions of the crew and their unlimited gratification'. There is also the sense of a mutual contamination going on: in spite of Melville's facile diatribes inveighing against the 'vice' and 'ruin' inflicted upon the 'poor savages', what comes off the page is the fear with which the Europeans respond to the unconscious sensuality and physicality of the girls.

The superiority of Western technological civilization and Melville's self-conscious mockery of it ('four heavy, double-banked frigates and three corvettes to frighten a parcel of naked heathen into subjection! Sixty-eight pounders to demolish huts of cocoa-nut boughs, and Congreve rockets to set on fire a few canoe sheds') does not alter the fact that this equipment is useless against the real dangers the island contains; dangers that threaten the very consciousness and sanity of Western man who is unable to relate to what the nineteenth century, (but not Melville) would consider a more primitive mode of existence. The incongruity of applying the European way of life to the situation here is given visual expression by the hundred French soldiers who daily take part in military exercises. These exercises take on the impact of a theatrical performance intended to dazzle the locals; but they are impressed by the meaninglessness of the ritual, rather than the power of their conquerors. It may appear at this point that Melville is following those writers who set the customs of their own society in a foreign locale, to point up their essential stupidity or wickedness. This is not Melville's intention. French customs are suitable in France. The Marquesans have their own rituals of war, which are equally contemptible to the French. What Melville is advocating is cultural separation. The evil comes from domination, from the forcing of one set of mores on a situation where they are not relevant. The question Melville is examining here is, in what does civilized behaviour consist? There is no scale of values by which societies can be measured and awarded points for civilization. Melville doesn't take the easy way out, either, and simply invert the savage/civilization dichotomy. He makes a more sophisticated response than that: 'were civilization itself to be estimated by some of its results, it would seem perhaps better for what we call the barbarous part of the world to remain unchanged'.

Although Tommo has a companion in his discovery and investigation of Typee, they are really two isolates, associated not in friendship so much as in affinity; like other Melville protagonists, Toby is a doomed, compelled wanderer: 'he was one of that class of rovers you sometimes meet at sea who never reveal their origin, never allude to home, and go rambling over the world as if pursued by some mysterious fate they cannot possibly elude'. Toby is no Sancho Panza, 'no one ever saw Toby laugh'. His speciality is a kind of dry humour which in itself comments on the real horrors of their expedition. Their entry into the 'Happy Valley' becomes a kind of Pilgrim's Progress involving, from the very start, unexpected hindrances and difficulties. The first being the thicket of reeds which proved to be 'as tough and stubborn as so many rods of steel'. The effort of breaking through this barrier nearly exhausts the couple before they have even begun their journey – Tommo describes them as 'ensnared'. Many critics have noted the frequent references to *Paradise Lost* in the entry to Typee and here Tommo and Toby, the Satanic Whitemen, are described as gliding unseen across the ridge, 'much in the fashion of a

couple of serpents'. The Edenic quality of the natural scene is
stated explicitly by Melville as soon as Tommo and Toby begin
their attempt to descend into the valley; but it is a Paradise in
which man does not figure:

> The whole landscape seemed one unbroken solitude, the
> interior of the island having apparently been untenanted
> since the morning of the creation; and as we advanced
> through this wilderness, our voices sounded strangely in
> our ears, as though human accents had never before dis-
> turbed the fearful silence of the place, interrupted only by
> the low murmurings of distant waterfalls. (44)

The actual recounting of the process of traversing the terrain
reveals a Defoe-like interest in factuality. The details of the
descent from the ridges, the building of a shelter for the first
night, impel the reader's credence and, as with Crusoe, create
an admiration for human ingenuity as well as pleasure in finding
out how things are done. However overtly 'philosophical' Melville becomes in his later work, he never loses his concern with
real things.

The real dangers of Tommo's and Toby's situation are contrasted with the hyperbolic humour with which Toby deals
with them, while Tommo maintains a condescending and
incompetent calm:

> 'And what, in the name of caves and coal-holes, do you
> expect to find at the bottom of that gulf but a broken neck –
> why it looks blacker than our ship's hold, and the roar of
> those waterfalls down there would batter one's brains to
> pieces.'
>
> 'Oh, no, Toby,' I exclaimed, laughing; 'but there's some-
> thing to be seen here, that's plain, or there would have been
> no path, and I am resolved to find out what it is.' (44–5)

In spite of the mock-heroic quality of the description of the
physical unease of their first night, Melville is surely making a
serious point: the physical discomforts are dwelt on at great
length and the painfulness of their experience is out of all proportion to what has caused it. Guilt at the role of interloper, and
fear as to what they are to encounter obviously play a con-
tributory part:

> I have had many a ducking in the course of my life, and in
> general cared little about it; but the accumulated horrors

of that night, the deathlike coldness of the place, the
appalling darkness and the dismal sense of our forlorn
condition, almost unmanned me. (46)

Again, it is Toby's rage and fear, however carefully controlled
by irony, that express the emotional content of the situation:
when Tommo wakes him up, 'poor Toby lifted up his head, and
after a moment's pause said, in a husky voice, "Then shipmate,
my top lights have gone out, for it appears darker now with my
eyes open than it did when they were shut." ' Here, horror is
just below the surface ('my toplights have gone out'); immediately after this, Toby comments, 'It is an insult to a man to
suppose he could sleep in such an infernal place as this'. Tommo
also uses laughter as a way of dealing with difficulties, 'I recom-
mend all adventurous youths who abandon vessels in romantic
islands during the rainy season to provide themselves with
umbrellas'. At this point, Tommo develops the swelling in his
leg which almost incapacitates him in the future. It has been
observed by other commentators that the injury to Tommo's
leg comes and goes according to his rejection or acceptance of
life on the island. It significantly makes itself felt for the first
time just before he experiences the full impact of the island's
beauty:

Had a glimpse of the gardens of Paradise been revealed to
me I could scarcely have been more ravished with the
sight. . . .

Over all the landscape there reigned the most hushed
repose, which I almost feared to break lest, like the en-
chanted gardens in the fairy tale, a single syllable might
dissolve the spell. (49)

Doubt is the predominant sensation on Typee. As Tommo says,
'I saw everything, but could comprehend nothing' (177). The
very location of the valley is in doubt – when they finally manage
to descend will they find themselves among the Happars or the
Typees ? Tommo puts the situation in all its grim reality to
Toby:

When I reminded him that it was impossible for either of
us to know anything with certainty, and when I dwelt upon
the horrible fate we should encounter were we rashly to
descend into the valley, and discover too late the error we
had committed, he replied by detailing all the evils of our

present condition, and the sufferings we must undergo
should we continue to remain where we then were. (51)

The delusive quality of experience is apparent when Tommo
drinks the water of the stream at the bottom of the gorge.
Instead of the anticipated 'delicious sensation', the cold fluid
seems to freeze him and to cause 'deathlike chills'. The appalling
difficulties of their situation lead Toby to a reckless optimism;
he makes himself believe that it is impossible for the inhabitants
of such a lovely place to be anything else but good fellows. He
rushes forward in a reckless, transcendental fervour of optimism.
The nervous prose exactly parallels his inner agitation:

> Happar it is, for nothing else than Happar can it be. So
> glorious a valley – such forests of bread-fruit trees – such
> groves of cocoa-nut – such wildernesses of guava-bushes!
> Ah, shipmate! don't linger behind: in the name of all
> delightful fruits, I am dying to be at them. Come on, come
> on; shove ahead, there's a lively lad; never mind the rocks;
> kick them out of the way, as I do; and to-morrow, old
> fellow, take my word for it, we shall be in clover. (57)

Although their hardships were continually overcome, the
explorers gained no apparent sense of achievement from their
successes. After one of the most spectacular of them, Tommo
describes himself as 'cowering down to the earth under this
multiplication of hardships, and abandoning himself to frightful
anticipations of evil'. What seems to be implied here is that a
spiritual pilgrimage is being endured by the two, of far greater
intensity than the physical ills they experience, although those
ills are the spur to their psychic pain.

As usual with Melville in *Typee*, a significant point in the
narrative is stressed by means of a pictorial device; here, an
almost emblematic use of an Adam and Eve couple, the first
indigenous people that Toby and Tommo encounter:

> They were a boy and girl, slender and graceful, and com-
> pletely naked, with the exception of a slight girdle of bark,
> from which depended at opposite points two of the russet
> leaves of the bread-fruit tree. An arm of the boy, half
> screened from sight by her wild tresses, was thrown about
> the neck of the girl, while with the other he held one of her
> hands in his; and thus they stood together, their heads
> inclined forward, catching the faint noise we made in our

progress, and with one foot in advance, as if half inclined
to fly from our presence. (68)

Again, appearances are appallingly deceptive, since this
idyllic couple, caught in a posture as if on a frieze, are later to be
revealed as far from innocent; their reality is that of 'a couple of
wily young things'. The reception of Tommo and Toby into the
community of the Typees gives Melville scope for making use
of his intense interest in craft – in the way things are done (as in
the information about the techniques of whaling in *Moby-Dick*);
Melville delights in knowledge almost for its own sake. He
provides the reader with a sense of what it was like to be *there*,
on the island. After the first welcome, Chief Mehevi provides
the travellers with a calabash of poee-poee, the produce of the
breadfruit tree. Melville's explanation of the difficulties involved
in learning to eat this strange (to Westerners) substance is not
useless pedantry but an integral part of the narrative. The
reader experiences the novelty with Tommo and, like him,
learns to accept the food very quickly as an ordinary element of
diet. In spite of the friendly reception they have received,
Tommo continues to expect that appearance and reality will
prove total opposites; he goes further than this, to the extent of
fearing that the greater the friendliness, the more hostility it
actually conceals: 'Might it not be that beneath these fair
appearances the islanders covered some perfidious design, and
that their friendly reception of us might only precede some
horrible catastrophe ?' (76).

As Tommo becomes more acclimatized to this society, so the
factual element of the narrative becomes more prevalent. The
emotional tone has been set throughout the extended approach
to Typee (which takes five days). The interest of continually
new experiences distracts the explorers momentarily and
absorbs their attention, but beneath the surface of fact, the
symbolic meaning is still intimately concerned with emotions
of fear and despair. When Chief Mehevi revisits them in warrior
dress, a motif is introduced that becomes of great importance at
the end of the novel. This is the fact of tattoing. It had been
introduced as a humorous motif early on but finally becomes a
matter of fear to Tommo. He is afraid that he will be tattooed by
force and that this will finally incapacitate him for rejoining his
own society. And it is the tattooing of Kory-Kory (Tommo's

Man Friday) that makes him into an object to Tommo; in spite
of his admirable qualities, something not quite human:

> ... the entire body of my savage valet, covered all over with
> representations of birds and fishes, and a variety of most
> unaccountable-looking creatures, suggested to me the idea
> of a pictorial museum of natural history, or an illustrated
> copy of 'Goldsmith's Animated Nature'. (83)

Kory-Kory's father and mother take on the aspect of cari-
catures of common types in Western society. Again, the humour
has a serious underlying purpose. Melville is making the point
that human nature is universally the same. Fayaway is not disfigured by tattooing, being an unmarried girl. She, and the other
girls, exhibit the same tendencies as women everywhere, but
they wear flowers instead of jewels.

Following his typical method in the novel of juxtaposing
idyllic and terrifying episodes, so that the interpretation of
experience is always in doubt, Melville sets against the description of Tommo's first bath in the stream, the terrifying visit to
the Taboo Groves. Once again, tattooing is as an index of
horror – the bodies of the aged warriors there had become a dull
green colour – 'the hue which the tattooing gradually assumes as
the individual advances in age'. Time and tattooing had
destroyed any evidence of humanity in these creatures. Toby
expresses the fear of Tommo also when he imagines that they
have been brought there to be killed and then devoured by the
cannibals (Melville points out elsewhere that cannibalism was
practised by the Typees only on their enemies, dead in battle).
Instead they are roused to eat in the middle of the night and then
the question becomes not, are they going to be eaten, but what
are they being asked to eat. 'A baked baby, by the soul of Captain
Cook!' However, the Typees are revealed to have no ulterior
motives but merely wish to entertain their guests in the most
hospitable manner.

After the loss of Toby, Tommo is totally the prey of melancholy and depression since he must also try to disentangle the
motives of his companion for not returning. 'Yes, thought I,
gloomily, he has secured his own escape, and cares not what
calamity may befall his unfortunate comrade.' Paradoxically, it
is only when Tommo has his worst suspicions confirmed, (that
he is indeed a prisoner), that he becomes at all reconciled to his

situation. As he becomes more like the islanders, and refuses to speculate further about his situation, since speculation is useless, his leg begins to heal, as evidence of his psychic adjustment:

> Gradually I lost all knowledge of the regular recurrence of the days of the week, and sunk insensibly into that kind of apathy which ensues after some violent outbreak of despair. My limb suddenly healed, the swelling went down, the pain subsided, and I had every reason to suppose I should soon completely recover from the affliction that had so long tormented me. (123)

Tommo's acceptance of his captivity gives Melville space to develop the theoretical aspect of his narrative. The intellectual structure, of which his story is an illustration, is of the relativity of the concepts of civilization and culture. The first point is the conventional one of the happier life of the Polynesian; happier, because physically comfortable and happier, because less intellectual. It is a fallacy that any society, in whatever stage of development and organization, is happy. But Melville is concerned to attack the complacent idea of the West that its mission is a civilizing one; in fact, the mission is to dominate and thereby destroy the indigenous culture. It is the superimposing of one culture upon another by force that creates chaos and breakdown. And this superimposition comes out of the arrogant belief of Civilization that her way is superior.

Will the 'voluptuous Indian be happier,' asks Melville rhetorically, if Civilization 'cultivates his mind' and 'elevates his thoughts'? Diseased, starving and dying natives answer that question mutely. To describe the actions of Civilization at home, Melville coins the phrase 'civilized barbarity'. In his investigation of the real meaning of the term 'savage', Melville brings his argument to a comic apotheosis by recommending that four or five Marquesan Islanders be sent to the United States as missionaries. For the purposes of his argument, Melville then proceeds to a panegyric on the happiness of life in Typee. However, it is essentially an external view; Tommo is unable to speak the language with any facility, and, without words, he is in no position to pontificate on the lack of cares, griefs, troubles, or vexations in Typee. Human society cannot exist without tension and conflict, and if there was no money ('that root of all evil') there must have been a barter system, which would produce its own problems. In his satirical attacks on Western civilization, Melville intends to set up the Typees as participants in an ideal society (an ideal for which he was always searching and which provides the positive against which he measures his generally negative view of human life – thus saving himself from total scepticism). The ultimate statement of this position appears in chapter 27 in the following paragraph:

> During my whole stay on the island I never witnessed a single quarrel, nor anything that in the slightest degree approached even to a dispute. The natives appeared to form one household, whose members were bound together by the ties of strong affection. The love of kindred I did not so much perceive, for it seemed blended in the general love; and where all were treated as brothers and sisters, it was hard to tell who were actually related to each other by blood. (204)

Tommo is not really qualified to make such a statement, seductive though the observation may be; he is unable to converse in any significant way with the people and he is under constant surveillance. He sees what he is permitted to see. This statement of Melville's is a rhetorical device to support his argument, not an observation that arises naturally out of the material with which he and Tommo are dealing.

The central section of the novel is a factual kernel building up density and actuality in Tommo's perception of Typee society. Chapter 20 provides documentary evidence of a typical day in the life of the Marquesans. Chapter 24 is an extended exposition, in travelogue mode, of the Feast of the Calabashes. Melville makes a straightforward attack on the authenticity of earlier accounts. *His* sources were first hand; the accounts of others are distorted, in the case of the missionaries distorted by self-seeking. Melville's ironic comment is:

> Did not the sacred character of these persons render the purity of their intentions unquestionable, I should certainly be led to suppose that they had exaggerated the evils of Paganism, in order to enhance the merit of their own disinterested labors. (169)

Scientists are equally disingenuous in that they choose informants who tell them what they want to hear. Far from being the report of a rigorously conducted scientific investigation, the resultant book, if presented to the Marquesans themselves, 'would appear quite as wonderful to them as it does to the American public, and much more improbable'.

A focal point of this central section of the narrative is the varying reaction of Tommo and Kory-Kory to the mausoleum of the warrior chief. The effigy has a symbolic content to Tommo; perhaps because it is full of energy, of straining forward to some future goal; so different from the normal passive mode of the Marquesans, to many of whom, Tommo thinks, 'life is little else than an often interrupted and luxurious nap'. The dead chief's effigy is

> seated in the stern of a canoe, which was raised on a light frame a few inches above the level of the pi-pi.... The long leaves of the palmetto drooped over the eaves, and through them you saw the warrior holding his paddle with both hands in the act of rowing, leaning forward and inclining his head, as if eager to hurry on his voyage. (172)

The chief is paddling towards heaven; to Kory-Kory heaven is a heightened version of Typee. But, in spite of the attractions of this breadfruit heaven, Kory-Kory obviously prefers the commonsense reality he presently inhabits, thus manifesting a shrewdness that Tommo admires. Kory-Kory's vision is a totally materialist one; to Tommo the image obviously means something on a poetic level; the ultimate quest, the ultimate representation of the desire for escape from the present and the real. Tommo, being a thinker, at least embryonically, can't be content with mere empiricism.

Again, this relatively sombre and reflective passage is followed, in Melville's typical manner, by a scene, on the same kind of topic, but treated in terms of broad farce. This is the episode with the god Moa Artua, who is treated by his priest as though he were a ventriloquist's dummy; the priest is a juggler who performs sleight-of-hand tricks. Tommo's comment is: 'the whole of these proceedings were like those of a parcel of children playing with dolls and baby houses'. The juxtaposition of these passages again underlines the impossibility of ever being able to interpret events and customs in Typee. Tommo responds to available images such as the chief's effigy, but is then confused and repelled by its sequel. Tommo reacts against the lack of reverence with which the islanders treat their gods, yet, in so doing, he is revealing the same lack of imagination of which the missionaries are guilty; he is imposing his own cultural values on the Typees. The section on religion is summed up with Tommo's usual mockery – a device for dealing with a topic that can't be satisfactorily assessed: 'the tattooed clergy are altogether too light-hearted and lazy – and their flocks are going astray'. Yet the emotional impact of the Typees' religion continues to be felt in the reverberations of the evocative image of the chief.

The collision of the 'civilized' and 'savage' worlds will inevitably result in the destruction of the less developed. Part of the fascination of Typee for Melville comes of course from the fact that its existence as it is is doomed. 'Ill-fated people! I shudder when I think of the change a few years will produce in their paradisaical abode.' Melville warns that the Marquesans will suffer the same fate as the native Americans: 'The Anglo-Saxon hive have extirpated Paganism from the greater part of the North American continent; but with it they have likewise extirpated the greater portion of the Red race' (195).

One of the elements in Polynesian life that compels Tommo's admiration is its very communal nature; what Melville refers to as fraternal feeling. The ideal of brotherly love was one which Melville pursued all his life and, as mentioned above, the concept is one which has associated with it a high degree of optimism. Here, Tommo praises the unanimity of feeling the Typees displayed on every occasion: 'With them there hardly appeared to be any difference of opinion upon any subject whatever. They all thought and acted alike. . . . They showed this spirit of unanimity in every action of life: every thing was done in concert and good fellowship' (203).

However enviable this state might be in theory, it is obvious that in practice, Tommo would have found it suffocating. He is, in his actions and attitudes in the novel, an individualist par excellence. His very escape from the *Dolly* represents an inability to join his crew-mates in combined opposition to the captain; and he is to fail to join the community of Typee. It is the very isolation of Melville's protagonists, and of Melville himself, that makes society so appealing.

An oblique way of providing further evidence of the idyllic paradisial nature of life on Typee is given by Tommo's description of the birds and animals of the area; the dogs and the solitary Poe-like cat[16] are interlopers ('it was plain enough they did not feel at home in the vale – that they wished themselves well out of it'), and are therefore offensive to Tommo. But birds, lizards and insects are totally without fear of man.

It is with the reintroduction of the question of tattooing that the emotional pattern of the novel is once more made clear, after the discursive chapters of information and observation that have given weight and balance to the actual experience, on an every-day level, of Marquesan life. The tattoo signifies Tommo's sense of the real, unbridgeable gulf between the society of nature and his own. Although Melville sums up Tommo's apprehensions with an outrageous pun 'I should be disfigured in such a manner as never more to have the *face* to return to my countrymen', this is the nub of the whole issue. To be tattooed means to be a convert to the Typees' religion. It is immediately after this that Tommo's life becomes one of 'absolute wretched-ness'. His loneliness is complete: 'There was no one with whom I could freely converse; no one to whom I could communicate my thoughts; no one who could sympathise with my sufferings' (231).

At this point, significantly, his leg wound begins to trouble him again, stressing the fact that his adjustment to Typee has been fragile and temporary and has lasted only as long as his interest in the novelty of his new surroundings. From this point on, Tommo is desperate to escape and, as with the journey to the valley, his fear and physical unease are out of all proportion to what actually happens to him. He finally makes his escape by pretending that he still believes Toby to have returned. The determination of the Typees to retain him as a captive gives Tommo the strength to resist, since such a prospect has become terrible to him. Paradise has turned into hell, or at least, purgatory. Marheyo is the only islander equipped to understand Tommo's now frantic need to re-establish himself in his own society: 'He placed his arm upon my shoulder, and emphatically pronounced the only two English words I had taught him – 'Home' and 'Mother'. I at once understood what he meant, and eagerly expressed my thanks to him' (248).

Critics have noted the savagery with which Tommo finally secures his escape. Even in the rescue boat, he is not safe since he is pursued by the warrior Mow-Mow. Tommo strikes him with the boat-hook in the throat. Mow-Mow's ferocious expression is the lasting impression that Tommo takes away from Typee.

Melville rounds off his story with a final diatribe against the missionaries of the Sandwich Islands. And, a sequel is appended to the main narrative. Toby miraculously reappeared and, much to Melville's delight, corroborated the main events of the story,[17] thereby refuting those critics who had questioned its veracity; and (in the case of the British critics) the fact that *Typee* had been written by a common sailor.

Today, when literary categories are breaking down, it is easier to assess Melville's achievement in *Typee*. Is it novel or travel book; autobiography or anthropology? It is, in fact, an effective fusion of all these modes. The various devices used throughout are unified by Melville's adroit use of tone. The tall-tale, the element of broad farce, the underlying mockery, the interspersed sections of stasis and movement, whether mental agitation on Tommo's part, or actual event, the pretence of telling a simple tale, are all employed by a sophisticated literary intelligence. Melville's problem was more complex than Defoe's. His task was to deal with the fact that he had actually been in Typee personally. At times, Tommo is the narrator, at others, Melville is clearly making a direct statement to the reader. *Typee* is a seminal work of Melville's in that it initiates problems, both literary and intellectual that Melville was never really to solve, except perhaps in *Billy Budd*. Questions about the real meaning of civilization and community; the isolated, seeking life versus a reassuring, but stifling, communality. Above all, of the real meaning of human experience and its tragically ambiguous nature. What disconcerted Melville in the experience represented by *Typee* was his growing sense of the relativity of all social and cultural values.

Notes and References

I am indebted for the phrase 'The failure of Eden' and for many other insights, to Milton R. Stern in his chapter on *Typee* in *The Fine Hammered Steel of Herman Melville* (University of Illinois Press 1957) pp. 29-65.

1. cf. Stern: '*Typee* is the story of a man's discovery of his relationship to the world', p. 65.
2. Robert Stanton has dealt comprehensively with this topic in his

article, 'Typee and Milton; Paradise Well Lost', *Modern Language Notes*, LXXIV (May 1959) 407-11.

3. Letter to Cunninghame Graham, 8 February 1899, in *Life and Letters*, 2 vols (London 1927) I, 269.

4. *Typee: A Peep at Polynesian Life*, ed. Harrison Hayford, Hershel Parker and G. Thomas Tanselle (Evanston and Chicago: North-western University Press and the Newberry Library 1968) pp. 20-21. All future references are to this edition.

5. *The Encantadas*, ed. Harold Beaver (Penguin English Library edition 1967) p. 138.

6. Letter to Lemuel Shaw, 6 October 1849, in *The Letters of Herman Melville*, ed. Merrell R. Davis and William H. Gilman (New Haven: Yale University Press 1960) p. 92.

7. Incidentally, it seems unlikely that this actually happened since the log of the *Acushnet* records bad weather when the ship anchored. For an authoritative view of what is factual and what is not, in Melville's account, see C. R. Anderson: *Melville and the South Seas* (New York: Columbia University Press 1939). As the editors of the Northwestern-Newberry edition point out (p. 291), Melville probably used the following reference books: Reverend Charles S. Stewart, *A Visit to the South Seas, in the U.S. ship Vincennes, During the Years 1829 and 1830*; Captain David Porter, *Journal of a Cruise Made to the Pacific Ocean in the U.S. Frigate Essex*; William Ellis, *Polynesian Researches*; Georg H. von Langsdorff, *Voyages and Travels in Various Parts of the World*; and a summary of Pacific narratives entitled *Historical Account of the Circumnavigation of the Globe*.

8. *The Rise of the Novel* (Penguin edition 1956) chapter 3, p. 62.

9. From an unsigned review, London *Spectator*, 28 February 1846, quoted by Watson G. Branch: *Melville, The Critical Heritage* (Routledge and Kegan Paul 1974) p. 55.

10. *The Confidence-Man* (Signet edition 1964) p. 75.

11. ibid. p. 190.

12. *Letters*, p. 130. In the same letter, Melville expresses his horror at the thought that he will go down to posterity as the 'man who lived among the cannibals'.

13. Quoted Branch, p. 56.

14. Perhaps the most perceptive contemporary critic of *Typee* was Sophia Hawthorne. In a letter to her mother in 1850, she recorded the following impressions: 'It is a *true history*, yet how poetically told – the divine beauty of the scene, the lovely faces & forms – the peace & good will – & all this golden splendor & enchantment glowing before the dark refrain constantly brought as a background – the fear of being killed & eaten – the cannibalism in the olive tinted Apollos around him – the unfathomable mystery of their treatment of him.' Eleanor M. Metcalf, *Herman Melville: Cycle and Epicycle* (Cambridge, Mass. 1953) p. 91.

15. D. H. Lawrence, *Studies in Classic American Literature*: 'He even pined for Home and Mother, the two things he had run away from

as far as ships would carry him. HOME and MOTHER. The two
things that were his damnation. . . . When he really was Home
with Mother, he found it Purgatory.' (Penguin edition 1971)
pp. 144, 147.

16. 'I shall never forget the day that I was lying in the house about
noon, everybody else being fast asleep; and happening to raise
my eyes, met those of a big black spectral cat, which sat erect in
the doorway, looking at me with its frightful goggling green orbs.'
pp. 210-11.

17. 'Richard Tobias Greene, a Buffalo house and sign painter, (who)
announced through the local *Commercial Advertiser* of July 1 that
he was "the true and veritable 'Toby'" who would be "happy to
testify to the entire accuracy of the work, so long as I was with
Melville."' (Northwestern-Newberry edition) p. 287.

Mardi:
Creating the Creative

> I HAVE written independently *without Judgment* – I may
> write independently, & *with judgment* hereafter. – The
> Genius of Poetry must work out its own salvation in a
> man: It cannot be matured by law and precept, but by
> sensation & watchfulness in itself – That which is
> creative must create itself – In Endymion, I leaped
> headlong into the Sea, and thereby have become better
> acquainted with the Soundings, the quicksands, & the
> rocks, than if I had stayed upon the green shore, and
> piped a silly pipe, and took tea & comfortable advice. – I
> was never afraid of failure; for I would sooner fail than
> not be among the greatest.
>
> Keats to J. A. Hessey, 9 October 1818.

'If this book be meant as a pleasantry, the mirth has been oddly
left out – if as an allegory, the key of the casket is "buried in
ocean deep" – if as a romance, it fails from tediousness – if as a
prose-poem, it is chargeable with puerility.'[1] This is what the
reviewer of *The Athenæum* had to say about Melville's *Mardi*,
and his comments no doubt express the views of many intelligent
readers, both at the time of the book's appearance and since.
Even readers who are enthusiastic about *Mardi* tend to hedge
their praise with reservations – Melville's French admirer
Philarète Chasles, who judged it 'un des plus singuliers livres
qui aient paru depuis long-temps sur la face du globe', also
called it 'oeuvre inouie, digne d'un Rabelais sans gaieté, d'un
Cervantes sans grace, d'un Voltaire sans goût'; Hawthorne
wrote: '"Mardi" is a rich book, with depths here and there that
compel a man to swim for his life. It is so good that one scarcely
pardons the writer for not having brooded long over it, so as to
make it a great deal better.'[2]

Every unkind thing that has been said about *Mardi* is more
or less true. It is the loosest and baggiest of prose monsters, a
book that changes direction freely on its way it knows not where,

its ramblings held together only by the flimsy framework of a quest for an insubstantial maiden that would itself be completely forgotten if a boatload of phantom damsels did not appear every eighty pages or so to pelt the quester with symbolic flowers. The style of the book, with its addiction to bombast and the more mechanical sorts of poetic effects, is usually something to be endured, not enjoyed. Its metaphysical soarings, in which philosophical commonplaces are delivered as if they were newly discovered truths, are often enough to make a lover of Melville the deep diver blush. But the important thing is not that *Mardi* has flaws but that it has ones of such an order. The chaos of its narrative is not the petty fault of an author who has tried to make a work in a conventional form but failed for lack of skill, but the massive one of an author who has tried to construct a work in a radically new way. Similarly its more embarrassing passages of poetry and philosophy are products not of a simple stylistic or intellectual deficiency – the author of *Mardi* is obviously equipped to do many sorts of things well – but of the fact that Melville is straining after effects that are so grand in them, and so far beyond what he has the powers to achieve. What is remarkable about *Mardi* is not its specific virtues or defects but the boldness of its endeavour. Where did Melville find the confidence to depart so completely not just from his own earlier works but from any easily recognizable formal model? How could he have dared to go on working at a project that required him to live so far beyond his artistic means? Melville never was a cowardly author, but the writing of *Mardi* was little less than an exercise in sheer audacity.

As Merrell Davis has demonstrated, many of *Mardi*'s peculiarities are results of the peculiar way in which it was written.[3] Melville's letters show that after finishing *Omoo* he planned a third work that would continue the story of his South Seas adventures where *Omoo* left off. But a report from his publisher on the sales of his books discouraged him from attempting another work in the same format. This coincided with an event of the first importance in Melville's inner life, an explosion of consciousness touched off by his discovery of great literary works of the past (in early 1848 he began reading Rabelais, Montaigne, Sir Thomas Browne, and Coleridge, among others) and by what he later called the 'burst[ing] out

in himself' of a 'bottomless spring of original thought' (*P* 283).
The combination of pressure from without and the activation of
a powerful creative energy within him led to a series of changes
in the plan of the book he was at work on. A letter to his English
publisher, John Murray, on 1 January 1848, claims that 'the
book now in hand, clothes the whole subject in new attractions
& combines in one cluster all that is romantic, whimsical &
poetic in Polynusia'.[4] He is feeling his way toward a new mode
of composition, one less tied to documentary fact and actual
experience, but he has not yet made a complete break with his
earlier works – 'It is yet a continuous narrative', he hastens to
add. But when he writes to Murray again, on 25 March, this
break has been effected.

> I beleive that a letter I wrote you some time ago – I think
> my last but one – gave you to understand, or implied, that
> the work I then had in view was a bona-vide narrative of
> my adventures in the Pacific, continued from 'Omoo' – My
> object in now writing you – I should have done so ere this –
> is to inform you of a change in my determinations. To be
> blunt: the work I shall next publish will ⟨be⟩ in down-
> right earnest [be] a 'Romance of Polynisian Adventure'.

Melville goes on to explain here, as he does in the preface to
Mardi, that his chief motive for writing such a work is to show
readers who doubted the authenticity of *Typee* and *Omoo* that
'a *real* romance of mine . . . is made of different stuff altogether'.
But another inducement to change his plans, he continues, is
that Polynesia furnishes a rich poetic material

> which to bring out suitably, required only that play of
> freedom & invention accorded only to the Romancer &
> poet. – However, I thought, that I would postpone trying
> my hand at any thing fanciful of this sort, till some future
> day: tho' at times when in the mood I threw off occasional
> sketches applicable to such a work. – Well: proceeding in
> my narrative of *facts* I began to feel an incurible distaste
> for the same; & a longing to plume my pinions for a flight,
> & felt irked, cramped & fettered by plodding along with
> dull common places, – So suddenly standing [abandon-
> ing?] the thing alltogether, I went to work heart & soul
> at a romance which is now in fair progress, since I had
> worked at it under an earnest ardor. – Shout not, nor

exclaim "Pshaw! Puh!" – My romance I assure you is no
dish water nor its model borrowed from the Circulating
Library. It is something new I assure you, & original if
nothing more. But I can give you no adequate idea, of it.
You must see it for yourself. – Only forbear to prejudge it. –
It opens like a true narrative – like Omoo for example, on
ship board – & the romance & poetry of the thing thence
grow continually, till it becomes a story wild enough I
assure you & with a meaning too.[5]

This letter, surely one of the most extraordinary ever sent by
a young author to an established publisher, is a perfect expression of the audacity that brought *Mardi* into being. I got tired of
what I was doing, Melville tells Murray, so I decided to do
something else (without, of course, bothering to start the book
over); and if you don't think that's a proper way to compose a
book, you're wrong – 'My *instinct* is to out with the Romance, &
let me say that instincts are prophetic, & better than acquired
wisdom – which alludes remotely to your experience in literature as an eminent publisher'. As Melville tells the story,
having started writing a book like his earlier ones, he begins to
feel the stirring of an urge that cannot find expression in that
form. As he continues writing this urge becomes stronger and
stronger until it begins to generate fragments of a second work,
different in kind, alongside the first. Finally it becomes so
imperious that he can no longer resist it or channel it off; at this
point he discards his initial plans and allows this urge to take
over the writing of his book. The letter that chronicles this
usurpation marks a crucial turning point in Melville's career,
the moment at which he starts conceiving of his works not as a
record of preexisting experience – a narrative of *facts* – but as a
creative imaginative activity. His letter suggests that in its
change of design *Mardi* itself acts out this shift, that as one sort
of book displaces another in it it bursts the fetters of conventional form ('true narrative') and a reportorial tie to reality
('dull common place'), freeing the imagination to soar into
realms of beauty and strangeness.

Melville clearly feels that to be properly judged *Mardi* needs
to be taken on its own terms, seen as making its own formal
model rather than imitating an already available one, and that it
needs to be read as a metamorphosis, a growth through radical

changes of state. I am interested in trying to understand the strange thing that *Mardi* is, and also what it means for Melville to have undertaken such a work at this stage in his career; and it seems to me that Melville's directions to Murray point to the way in which the book should be approached. This is to pursue it through its changes – not to locate its chapters and sequences in relation to an externally established chronology, but to discover from within the book what sort of form it proposes for itself, and how this form evolves as the book unfolds.

As Melville's letters lead us to expect, the opening of *Mardi* does bear a direct resemblance to *Typee* and *Omoo*. Here again a sailor-narrator tells how he came to jump ship, with a companion, in search of adventure. He provides several reasons for his act, making sure that it seems plausibly motivated; he also provides a good deal of circumstantial information about nautical matters, taking care to locate his tale in a world that is solidly documented, if unfamiliar to us. But really *Mardi* is something quite different from *Typee* or *Omoo*, and it must be stressed that it is so from the first. While on watch in the masthead in the first chapter the narrator broods on the islands that lie westward in the Pacific, 'loosely laid down upon the charts, and invested with all the charms of dream-land', and that he will leave behind if he sails northward on the *Arcturion*.

> I cast my eyes downward to the brown planks of the dull, plodding ship, silent from stem to stern; then abroad.
>
> In the distance what visions were spread! The entire western horizon high piled with gold and crimson clouds; airy arches, domes, and minarets; as if the yellow, Moorish sun were setting behind some vast Alhambra. Vistas seemed leading to worlds beyond. To and fro, and all over the towers of this Nineveh in the sky, flew troops of birds. Watching them long, one crossed my sight, flew through a low arch, and was lost to view. My spirit must have sailed in with it; for directly, as in a trance, came upon me the cadence of mild billows laving a beach of shells, the waving of boughs, and the voices of maidens, and the lulled beatings of my own dissolved heart, all blended together. (7–8)

Shipboard life is a plodding affair, its very tedium heightening the lure for the narrator of what Ishmael calls the wonder world. Although he begins by thinking of this fascinating alternative in terms of actual Pacific islands, what attracts him quickly changes from an exotic location in the real geographical world to a vista in a world beyond, and from a place to be reached by physical travel to a state to be attained through the heightening of desire, ecstatic transformations of consciousness, and the flight of the visionary spirit. The narrator shares Melville's aversion to dull commonplaces; his adventure, like his creator's, defines itself as an imaginative flight into a romance world of expanded possibility.

What follows from this opening is a voyage not to strange lands but into strangeness itself. The narrative mode of *Mardi*'s opening phase has less in common with that of *Typee* than with that of Edgar Allan Poe's *Narrative of A. Gordon Pym*, which uses the format of the nautical adventure story to lead the reader on a magical mystery tour. The narrator's jumping ship, like Pym's running away from home, is presented not just as a rejection of a settled way of life but as a rejection of ordinary reality. His desertion is not just a lark but a knowing act of 'moral dereliction' (16) that is also an act of suicide, leaving him feeling like 'his own ghost unlawfully tenanting a defunct carcass' (29); like Pym denying his identity to his grandfather and descending into the coffin-like enclosure in the ship's hold, this narrator's adventure begins with a conscious rejection of the moral obligations of ordinary life and a willed dying to his own ordinary self. The chapters that follow, describing life on the ocean in an open boat and the sense of immobility and unreality induced by the calm, do not function simply as accounts of actual experience; like Pym's minute dissection of his feelings in the wildly accelerating boat or in the dark confinement of the hold, these are records of an extreme dislocation in the experience of space and time, a dislocation that is itself one of these characters' means for breaking out of ordinary reality. Similarly the chapters on sharks, swordfish, and marine phosphorescence are not merely informative; like Pym's discussions of the Galapagos turtle or the nests of penguins, they evoke a vision of nature as full of strange and alien forms. As nature becomes more marvellous in these books, marvels become more natural – the ship *Parki* in *Mardi*, like the ship of death in *Pym*, is experienced as a phantom craft; Samoa, like Dirk Peters, looks like a hitherto unknown form of human life.

The same patterns govern the actions of these books on their progress into strangeness. One of these patterns is the repeated overthrow of figures of authority. The narrator of *Mardi* gains through desertion the freedom from his captain's control that Pym gains through a mutinous rising of the crew of the *Grampus*. The massacre of the officers of the *Parki* by savages who have cunningly concealed their diabolical malice exactly repeats the fate of the captain and crew of Poe's ship *Jane Guy*. Another is a pattern of violation of taboos and sacred interdicts.[6] *Mardi* has nothing to match the cannibal episode in *Pym*, but its narrator's most pronounced trait is his urge to pry into what he has been warned away from. These two patterns come together in *Mardi* when, after the *Parki* episode, the narrator murders the priest and father Aleema, and, having been told 'that it would be profanation' (131), pierces the tent to seize the sacred maiden Yillah. In both books the violation of taboos and the destruction of authorities are the means by which the adventurer breaks into forbidden territory. The massacre of the crew of the *Jane Guy* and his disregard of the natives' dread of its sacredness bring Pym closer to the unutterable experience enshrouded by the Pole's white veil. By the same logic the conjunction of murder, sexual penetration, and profanation committed by the narrator of *Mardi* has as its immediate consequence the opening up before him of Mardi, the world beyond for which he sought.

The list of similarities between *Mardi* and the *Narrative of A. Gordon Pym* could be greatly extended, but these few examples suggest how like the books are in their procedures. What is important about this is not so much that it reveals particular debts on Melville's part as that it demonstrates what kind of a book Melville is writing in *Mardi*'s first fifty chapters – like Poe, he is using the form of the adventure narrative to conduct an exploration into other modes of reality. But, interestingly, when his book comes upon the islands of Mardi this seems to be as much a moment of discovery for the author as it is for his hero. The archipelago spreads before him a whole world of fictional possibilities, and at first he does not seem certain what he is going to do with them. He keeps alluding to Jarl, Samoa, and Yillah as if he thinks that his story's way might lie in continuing his narrator's earlier adventures; meanwhile he begins staging episodes on the island of Oro, and as it were testing what he can make of it. All at once he seems to see how he can go about exploiting Mardi in his book, and at this point he modifies his narrative in a drastic way. Samoa and Jarl become effectively invisible; Yillah vanishes, leaving the narrator to pursue her just half-heartedly enough to provide a pretext for a voyage; King Media, the historian Mohi, the philosopher Babbalanja, and the poet Yoomy join him for a tour through Mardi; then the narrator himself recedes, leaving the book to carry on not as the record of his adventures and speech but as a freewheeling island-hopping symposium.

The section of *Mardi* that follows takes as its model the anatomy form that Melville would have been familiar with in Swift and Rabelais.[7] As in the third book of *Gulliver's Travels* or the fourth book of *Pantagruel*, Melville's island voyaging permits him to people a world with shapes of his own invention. Some of these mirror features of the actual world more or less directly, as Pimminee reflects social affectation, or Maramma the collective blindness of institutional religion. Others seem completely unreal, wildly imaginative, until, as in a caricature, we recognize in their grotesque distortion a previously concealed feature of reality: the bloody war games through which the lords Hello and Piko maintain the population of Diranda in equilibrium thus bring into focus the nightmare of human destructiveness unleashed by a cynically calculated appeal to abstract values. But although the island voyage enables Melville to mirror actuality and to mock the lighter and graver follies of human behaviour, satire is only one ingredient of this part of the book, not the controlling intention. In the imagining of these islands the desire to expose specific abuses is subservient to the free play of fantastic invention. In any case the islands are surrounded by a sea of talk, insets in a never-adjourning colloquy that passes freely from poetic recitations to nonsense to philosophical speculations to celebrations of food and drink.

As Melville closes his Poe and opens his Rabelais the kind of book he is writing undergoes a radical shift. But it is also worth noting that the metaphysical adventure narrative in the manner of Poe and the Rabelaisian anatomy have similarities as narrative models. They are, thus, both episodic in structure. In the early parts of *Mardi* as in *Pym* ships appear out of nowhere and then vanish again, and the narrator goes through experiences which, although they are vividly real while they last, disappear without a trace when they are ended. The sequences of action simply succeed one another, without being caused by what came before them and without causing what comes after. The essence of organization of the anatomy, whether we see it in *Mardi* or in *Gargantua and Pantagruel* or in *The Tale of a Tub* or in *Tristram Shandy*, lies in the weakness of its narrative line, its failure to give the book's ramblings the coherence of motion directed to an end. Each island in Mardi is by definition a separate occasion for Melville, and each reopening of discussion offers him a chance to pursue a new topic. The result is that in both parts of his narrative Melville is remarkably free to project an imaginative possibility, toy with it, develop it further if he likes, and then drop it when he is tired of it, going on to project another without having to consult the requirements of an overall plan.

Not only do they emphasize the independence of parts over the coherence of a cumulative design; both of the forms Melville is working with also permit major structural modifications to be made while they go along. One of the most striking resemblances between *Mardi* and the *Narrative of A. Gordon Pym* is that in both of them characters and scenes that are distinctly defined at one moment undergo dreamlike metamorphoses at the next. In both books, for example, it is impossible to make the narrator compose into a consistent personality as, from chapter to chapter, he exhibits not only totally different amounts of knowledge and sensitivity but even totally different traits of character. This instability means that, while ostensibly pursuing the story of someone's adventures, the books actually keep revising the nature of their adventure – what is a dream voyage into mental darkness at one point becomes a white imperialist's voyage among primitive peoples at another, and so on. The anatomy form, in addition to encouraging frequent modulations of mode, also allows Melville to define and redefine the terms of his action while in the middle of it – it permits him thus to turn the visit to Mardi's islands into a tour of the contemporary social world, and then to continue it as such for twenty-five chapters, without violating the logic of the book. Both of the genres Melville employs in *Mardi* maximize the author's on-going freedom within his projected form. They require nothing

of him but that he improvise, that he keep making his book up
as it goes along.

After he has pursued his voyage through the countries of
Europe and the regions of the United States Melville again seems
uncertain what he is going to do next. At first he solves his
dilemma simply by carrying on with his device, extending his
tour through Asia, Africa, and the Middle East. But the tour is
yielding rapidly diminishing returns, and it is clear from its
accelerated pace that Melville has little interest in its continuation. Then he sees another way to solve his problem. He simply
puts his device aside and steps forward from behind his book's
action, addressing us now in his own voice:

> Oh, reader, list! I've chartless voyaged. With compass and
> the lead, we had not found these Mardian Isles. Those who
> boldly launch, cast off all cables. . . . Hug the shore, naught
> new is seen; and "Land ho!" at last was sung, when a new
> world was sought. (556)

What appears to happen here is that the breakdown of his
narrative device precipitates a moment of genuine self-
recognition for Melville. He begins with what sounds like an
explanation specifically of his present predicament – I don't
know where I'm going, I've been writing without a plan; his
blustering invocations of New World explorers sound like
pieces of bravado, attempts to present his directionlessness as a
sign of his courage. But having opened the subject, he now goes
on to define more and more precisely how his book came to be
written, and what it might mean to have written a book in this
way.

> And though essaying but a sportive sail, I was driven from
> my course, by a blast resistless; and ill-provided, young,
> and bowed to the brunt of things before my prime, still fly
> before the gale; – hard have I striven to keep stout heart.

> And if it harder be, than e'er before, to find new climes,
> when now our seas have oft been circled by ten thousand
> prows, – much more the glory!

> But this new world here sought, is stranger far than his,
> who stretched his vans from Palos. It is the world of mind;
> wherein the wanderer may gaze round, with more of
> wonder than Balboa's band roving through the golden
> Aztec glades.

But fiery yearnings their own phantom-future make, and
deem it present. So, if after all these fearful, fainting
trances, the verdict be, the golden haven was not gained; –
yet, in bold quest thereof, better to sink in boundless
deeps, than float on vulgar shoals; and give me, ye gods, an
utter wreck, if wreck I do. (557)

Here Melville brings to consciousness what he has been doing
in writing *Mardi*, and as he does so he redefines his book from
within one more time. He comes to see that its true action is not
his characters' adventures but his own creative process: that its
real voyage is the imaginative one he has undertaken in conceiving *Mardi*, that the real object of its quest is nothing his
characters seek but the mental world he himself discloses
through the act of creating his book.[8] His metaphors of exploration lose their initial defensiveness and develop into a fully
formed aesthetic of adventure, an aesthetic that validates his
audacity in writing *Mardi* as the boldness necessary for new
discovery, and that enables him to recognize the possibility of
the book's failure and to accept it as proof that its attempt was
bold enough.

After 'Sailing On' Melville continues with his symposium-
cruise, and at the end of the book he even reaches back to pick
up the thread of the narrator's progress through profanation
into strange new worlds. But it is hard not to feel that *Mardi*
reaches its real culmination in this chapter and the meditations
that follow from it. Subsequent discussions are increasingly
preoccupied with what Media calls 'the metaphysics of genius'
(559), and in Babbalanja's discourse on the poet Lombardo in
chapter 180 *Mardi* renews its consideration of itself as its
author's creation. The author who alluded to a blast resistless
that led him prematurely to attempt such a work becomes even
more candidly confessional here, taking us behind the curtain
to reveal the financial and family pressures that are driving him
to finish his book, and sharing what he has learned about the
genesis of works of art and the experience of inspiration in
composing it. He also formulates more clearly what the writing
of *Mardi* signifies. Babbalanja tells King Abrazza:

When Lombardo set about his work, he knew not what it
would become. He did not build himself in with plans; he
wrote right on; and so doing, got deeper and deeper into

himself; and like a resolute traveler, plunging through
baffling woods, at last was rewarded for his toils. 'In good
time,' saith he, in his autobiography, 'I came out into a
serene, sunny, ravishing region; full of sweet scents, singing
birds, wild plaints, roguish laughs, prophetic voices. Here
we are at last, then,' he cried; 'I have created the creative'.
(595)

Where in 'Sailing On' he implied that there is some connection
between chartless voyaging and coming upon new worlds of
mind, Melville sees much more clearly here how writing and
discovery are linked, and he is able to specify much more precisely what the 'world of mind' consists of. Writing spontaneously
and without plan is the means by which Lombardo blazes a trail
into the wilderness of his mind until, at its centre, he finds a
paradise within. This paradise is not so much a place as a deep
source of generative mental energy; and it is not something
already existing yet concealed but something that needs to be
brought into being. Through the act of writing, thus, Lombardo
creates the creative.

In this chapter the novel that unfolded without direction and
without a governing intention finds out where it was headed and
why it followed the course it did. The novel that revelled in
improvisation for five hundred pages discovers what improvisation is for – discovers that it is through the exercise of its freedom and invention, its unconstrained play of conception and
articulation, that the creative imagination brings itself into
being. Having, by means of it, created the creative, Lombardo
can discard his first writing and begin a work of greatness. In
the images of the chapter it is the trash that needed to be
removed from the mine for the ore of genius to be reached, the
callow form that the eagle had to pass through on its way to
attaining maturity and power. Melville is similarly detached
from his own writing in *Mardi*. Having lavished his inventive
energy on them he shows no further interest in the book's
individual episodes. He is the first to admit that it has deep
flaws – Hawthorne's assessment of *Mardi*, for instance, echoes
Melville's own, made in the book itself: ' "It has faults – all
mine; its merits all its own; – but I can toil no longer. . . . My
canvas was small," said [Lombardo]; "crowded out were hosts
of things that came last. But Fate is in it" ' (600–1). What

sustains his equanimity in the face of its faults is the fact that the aim implicit in the book is not the production of the perfect work Hawthorne has in mind. What he intends to achieve in writing it is not really to be understood at the level of the work itself at all. If Lombardo expresses Melville's thoughts, as there is every reason to assume he does, the value of *Mardi* for its author lies not in what it is but in what his composition of it could bring into being – his own mature creative self.

Melville consistently thinks of *Mardi* in terms of a future attainment that it points toward. Shortly after finishing it he writes to Evert Duyckinck:

> Would that a man could do something & then say – It is finished. – not that one thing only, but all others – that he has reached his uttermost, & can never exceed it. But live & push – tho' we put one leg forward ten miles – its no reason the other must lag behind – no, *that* must again distance the other . . .

The writing of *Mardi* is a step; even though he longs for it to be a final achievement he recognizes that it is truly only a stage in the ongoing process of realizing his creative potential. In a letter to *Mardi*'s English publisher, Richard Bentley, Melville speaks of the book in terms of germination and maturing: 'you know perhaps that there are goodly harvests which ripen late, especially when the grain is remarkably strong'. In another letter to Duyckinck he speaks of it in terms of education: 'I admit that I learn by experience & not by divine intuitions. Had I not written & published 'Mardi,' in all likelihood, I would not be as wise as I am now, or may be.'[9] We know, as Melville at this point could not, what the author of *Mardi* would go on to achieve. Since he himself conceives of it as pointing forward we might now look back at *Mardi* from Melville's later works, and try to discern what relation it actually has to what comes after it.

In terms of his career as a whole perhaps the most striking thing about *Mardi* is the emergence in it of the Melville who compulsively engages in ontological heroics. In *Mardi* Melville meets metaphysics and succumbs to its charms. The symposium format enables him to stage his first comedy of thought, to play with intellectual puzzles and explore the paradoxes of intellectual positions. The figure of Babbalanja embodies for the first time in Melville's fiction an obsession with cosmic riddles and a resolution to uncover 'that which is beneath the seeming' (352). Certainly one of the main functions of the anatomy form that he adopts midway through the book is that it permits him to speculate, with varying degrees of seriousness, on questions like what man is, what truth is, and what happens after death.

What Melville has to say about the problem of the universe in *Mardi* is often trite and naive. He is so excited by his discoveries for instance of how classical ethics prefigure Christian ones or of Hartley's distinction between the Necessitarian and the Fatalist that he presents them as unexampled profundities. Their sophomoric quality is not lessened by the style in which he carries out his investigations, a style that can sink to such lows as 'Are we angels, or dogs?' (433) or 'It hinges upon this: Have we angelic spirits?' (338). Above all there is a certain glibness about *Mardi*'s philosophizings. Its demonstration that the omnipresence of a good God is incompatible with the existence of evil comes across more as a clever logical trick than anything else. Statements like Babbalanja's 'truth is in things, and not in words' (283) or Media's 'final, last thoughts you mortals have none; nor can have' (370) are almost purely throwaway lines. The problem of evil, of the relation of knowledge to reality, of the impossibility of attaining final truth – Melville addresses them all in *Mardi*, but without yet being tasked and heaped by them. The result is that throughout the book ideas are simply tossed off by an author who does not suspect that what he says may be truer than he knows.

But even at their feeblest *Mardi*'s philosophical excursions are not without importance. In them Melville is appropriating a kingdom of thought. If he repeats ideas without having assimilated them, nevertheless *by* repeating them he begins to possess them, to make them his own. Thus as his writing proceeds his thought grows in depth. He keeps returning to subjects like the relation of belief to truth, considering it once in terms of religious belief, another time in terms of storytelling, another time in terms of our knowledge of the physical world – he never stops to treat it systematically, but with each return to it he extends the range of its implications. As he goes along ideas seem to be pressing up into his mind, making themselves felt in a number of places until finally, by grasping and articulating them, he brings them fully to the surface. Thus he discusses at one point how the alternating domination of his psyche by 'contrary impulses, over which he had not the faintest control' makes King Peepi incapable of 'moral obligation to virtue' (203); at another Babbalanja broaches a psychological theory based on demonic possession; at another the narrator, rapt in an ecstasy of inspiration, describes his mastery by 'this Dionysius that rides me' (368). All of these are partial versions of a notion that finally gets fully explored in chapter 143, where, discoursing on 'the incomprehensible stranger in me' (457), Babbalanja develops the idea that an instinctive, involuntary energy lies beneath the conscious rational self, governing and impelling it.

This notion is familiar from the works that follow *Mardi*. Babbalanja's 'one dark chamber in me is retained by the old mystery' (457) recalls Ishmael's allusion to an old State-secret kept at the bottom of the self, and his '[men] do not govern themselves, but are governed by their very natures' (457) is echoed by Ahab's discovery of his identity as a mysterious fatality in 'The Symphony'. His explanation of the priority of instinctive passions to the moral sense looks forward to Melville's study of the play of unconscious sexual impulses on the ethical consciousness in *Pierre*. *Mardi*'s treatment of belief and truth is similarly familiar: not only does it explore the involuted relations of truth, fiction, falsehood, trust, and doubt that will be pursued again in *The Confidence-Man*, but it also begins to establish the convertibility of frames of reference that makes that book possible – that it is with fiction as with religion is an idea already implicit in *Mardi*. Any reader of *Mardi* could extend the list of its thematic similarities to the books that follow it. This is the work in which Melville begins brooding on what will concern him in his major novels. But it is not just that his essential preoccupations are all present in *Mardi*. It is in this book that he generates his own themes, discovers and brings them to initial formulation. Finally the fact that *Mardi* lacks the sophistication or profundity of Melville's mature work seems less significant than the fact that it originates what they continue.

There is the same teasing likeness between the images of *Mardi* and those of Melville's later books as there is between their themes. This is Melville's description of Aleema:

The old priest, like a scroll of old parchment, covered all

over with hieroglyphical devices, harder to interpret, I'll
warrant, than any old Sanscrit manuscript. And upon his
broad brow, deep-graven in wrinkles, were characters still
more mysterious, which no Champollion nor gipsy could
have deciphered. (130)

It is impossible to read this without thinking of Queequeg's
tattooing, those 'hieroglyphical marks' in which a departed
seer 'had written out on his body a complete theory of the
heavens and the earth, and a mystical treatise on the art of
attaining truth . . . but whose mysteries not even himself could
read, though his own live heart beat against them' (*MD* 399).
It is echoed even more precisely by the end of the chapter 'The
Prairie' in *Moby-Dick*:

> Champollion deciphered the wrinkled granite hiero-
> glyphics. But there is no Champollion to decipher the
> Egypt of every man's and every being's face. Physiognomy,
> like every other human science, is but a passing fable. If
> then, Sir William Jones, who read in thirty languages,
> could not read the simplest peasant's face in its profounder
> and more subtle meanings, how many unlettered Ishmael
> hope to read the awful Chaldee of the Sperm Whale's
> brow? I but put that brow before you. Read it if you can.
> (*MD* 292–3)

To put it alongside these passages from *Moby-Dick* is to see
how undeveloped Melville's image is in *Mardi*. He has got so
far as to link Polynesian tattooing, wrinkles, hieroglyphics, and
the deciphering achievements of Champollion and Sir William
Jones, but he appears unaware of the symbolic content the
resultant image could carry – the undecipherable hieroglyph
has yet to become his preferred figure for a cosmic mystery that
invites but perpetually thwarts the human effort to solve it.
Describing a calm at sea in chapter 16 of *Mardi* Melville images
a process by which the totality of elements fuse with one another
to produce a nothingness, a 'blank', a 'vacuum', 'colorless', 'gray
chaos in conception' (48). We are on the verge, here, of *Moby-
Dick*'s 'colorless, all-color of atheism from which we shrink'
(*MD* 169); all that is missing is a perception of the metaphysical
condition such a fusion could symbolize. With these images as
with his philosophical throwaways Melville produces out of
nowhere something that will be saturated with significance in

his future work, but that has yet to acquire that significance.

How is it that 'The Prairie' manages so to intensify and extend the implications of the figure through which Aleema's brow is described in *Mardi*? Certainly part of the answer lies in Ishmael's (and the Melville of *Moby-Dick*'s) universalizing habit of mind. While *Mardi* keeps focussing on Aleema's face Ishmael moves from the whale's brow to 'every being's face', and from the face physically understood to the face 'in its profounder and more subtle meanings'. But this difference is itself a function of the different ways in which they handle figurative language. Melville's prose in *Mardi* keeps the image and the reality it describes rigidly separate. It isolates the precise points (like, harder, more) at which comparisons between the face and a scroll of mysterious writing are being established. Further, it establishes comparisons only between features the two already share – the face's lines already are hieroglyphical devices; it is not the analogy of the scroll that makes them so. In the passage from *Moby-Dick*, by contrast, analogy becomes a dynamic process, and a process of genuine transfiguration. Features associated with faces and features associated with writing continue to interfuse with one another. The result of this fusion is that each of these normally separate areas of experience provides a new idiom in which the other may be expressed (wrinkled granite hieroglyphics, the Egypt of the face, the awful Chaldee of the brow) and a new set of terms in which the other may be understood – here legibility or illegibility is not a property already possessed by the face but one it acquires by virtue of being conceived of in terms of language. The essential difference between the two passages is that in the one from *Moby-Dick* Melville commits himself to metaphor, allowing the play of figuration to generate meaning as it evolves.

Mardi is full of restricted images, images that have not undergone such a genuinely metaphorical development. King Uhia, a moody aspirer who lunges through the present toward future achievements and who feels intolerably confined by the limits reality imposes on his will, clearly prefigures Captain Ahab, as his perception of the human cost of his aspiration – 'Here am I vexed and tormented by ambition; no peace night nor day; my temples chafed sore by this cursed crown that I wear' (276) – looks forward to Ahab's in 'Sunset' and 'The Symphony'. But only when the crown and the experience of wearing it are imagined in an expanding series of particularized details, details that are allowed to stand for ambition's self-inflicted pain, will Uhia's lament open out into Ahab's 'Is, then, the crown too heavy that I wear ? . . . 'Tis iron – that I know – not gold. 'Tis split, too – that I feel; the jagged edge galls me so, my brain seems to beat against the solid metal' (*MD* 147). The ending of 'Sailing On' – 'yet, in bold quest thereof, better to sink in boundless deeps, than float on vulgar shoals' (557) – links pressing off into the ocean with heroic intellectual questing as Melville will again in 'The Lee Shore', and it even establishes the rhythms of 'The Lee Shore's' prose – 'so, better is it to perish in that howling infinite, than be ingloriously dashed upon the lee, even if that were safety!' (*MD* 97). The difference is not that 'The Lee Shore' celebrates such questing more ardently than 'Sailing On' but that, by allowing the opposition of sea and shore to develop itself ('the port is pitiful; in the port is safety, comfort, hearthstone . . .') and by allowing the figures thus generated to define the opposition between independence and spiritual timidity, it gives such questing an increasingly rich and precise content.

Many more examples could be added of images that are introduced in *Mardi* but only fully realized in Melville's later books – indeed almost every image central to his major work is present here in embryonic form. Really what is surprising is not that his later versions of these are richer but that so many of them are so exactly prefigured in this earlier book. And again, it is not just that Melville's personal symbolism is present in *Mardi*; what needs to be stressed is that in writing the book he is generating this symbolism, conceiving its figures, bringing them into focus, and beginning to explore what they might mean. Although he may not yet be fully aware of what they could signify, he is fashioning what has the capacity to carry significance. Although he has not yet connected his images with his metaphysical preoccupations, he is forging the means for their mature expression – what makes his later versions of *Mardi*'s philosophical insights original and profound is not an increase in their content as intellectual propositions but the dazzling metaphorical formulation Melville gives them, his expression of them through the very images we see him creating here. As he writes Melville is articulating his own mental world. In the process of composing *Mardi* he is conceiving ideas and images and partially unfolding their content; and what he does this with here is what he then possesses as the means for creating more fully developed work later.

We might look at one final example of how Melville works in *Mardi* and how what he writes here relates to his later writing. In chapter 180 Babbalanja explains that the opening of the artist's creative consciousness requires that he suffer:

> Woe it is, that reveals these things. He knows himself, and all that's in him, who knows adversity. To scale great heights, we must come out of lowermost depths. The way to heaven is through hell. We need fiery baptisms in the fiercest flames of our own bosoms. We must feel our hearts hot – hissing in us. And ere their fire is revealed, it must burn its way out of us; though it consume us and itself. Oh, sleek-cheeked Plenty! smiling at thine own dimples; – vain for thee to reach out after greatness. Turn! turn! from all your tiers of cushions of eider-down – turn! and be broken on the wheels of many woes. At white-heat, brand thyself; and count the scars, like old war-worn veterans, over camp-fires. Soft poet! brushing tears from lilies – this way! and howl in sackcloth and in ashes! Know, thou, that the lines that live are turned out of a furrowed brow. Oh! there is a fierce, a cannibal delight, in the grief that shrieks to multiply itself. That grief is miserly of its own; it pities all the happy.
> (594)

The relation of suffering to greatness is a new idea to Melville here, and this paragraph is not so much a statement of it as an attempt to grasp it. Melville thus keeps talking and talking, trying to express his conception one way, then another, then another. And by saying it over and over, he comes to find out more fully what it means. Certainly the ideas of the first three or four sentences are commonplace enough, but by repeating these commonplaces he begins to be able to go beyond them. Similarly the images in the opening sentences are the merest clichés, but having practised on them he begins to generate more daring and original ones; and it is by becoming more vitally metaphoric that the passage comes to give its conception a distinctive and memorable formulation. We can see here in little the process by which, through the act of writing, Melville acquires augmented powers of thought and expression. We may not feel that the passage is perfectly successful. It is repetitious, it is excessively rhetorical, its images are uneven in quality. But it contains the germ of what Melville does successfully else-where. In its weaving of an association between greatness, woe, a ravaging flame, and a fiery scar it prefigures the introduction of the scarred and branded Ahab in *Moby-Dick*, looking 'like a man cut away from the stake, when the fire has overrunningly wasted all the limbs without consuming them' (*MD* 109–10). Its explication of a wisdom that is woe prefigures Ishmael's meditations in 'The Try-Works', the conclusion of which, by reconceiving it in terms of the Catskill eagle, even manages to purge this passage's third sentence of its banality. And if Mel-ville is able to develop these images and ideas more successfully elsewhere, it is in part because he has already attempted them for the first time here.

So many passages in the later books resemble *Mardi* in some way as to suggest that Melville is rewriting rather than writing. As he comes to realize in it, the true significance of *Mardi* is that it is the first draft of all his subsequent works. Not a draft in the sense that it consciously undertakes to produce a rough version of a work whose subject or form is defined, however vaguely, in advance – as we have seen, Melville refuses to build himself in with plans, asserting his right to improvise without constraint. Rather, it is a draft in the sense that, without attempting to fore-see what it is a preparation for, it nevertheless gives initial formulation to the work that comes after it – without being directed toward any end, Melville's improvisational act generates themes, thoughts, characters, images, narrative forms, and stylistic features out of which other creations can then be made. In giving him the particular materials and skills that their composition required, and more generally in making him capable of conceiving and expressing them, the writing of *Mardi* made Melville the author who could then go on to write *Moby-Dick*, *Pierre*, and *The Confidence-Man*. To use Keats's words *Mardi* is the form in which the Genius of Poetry in Melville worked out its own salvation. Its spirited performance is the necessary prelude to the mature career of an author who always gained in power by exercising his power – who grew imaginative by exerting his invention, who grew profound by diving after deep thoughts, and who grew creative by engaging in the act of creation.

We have been considering how images and ideas that germinate in *Mardi* reappear in more fully developed forms in Melville's later novels. By way of an epilogue we might note that *Mardi*'s vision of the nature of its own creative act undergoes the same process of maturation. 'Sailing On' and Babbalanja's discourse on the poet Lombardo are the first drafts of the concluding sections of *Pierre*, the sections treating Pierre's experience as an immature author attempting a mature work. Melville's earlier descriptions of how he was blown off course by a blast resistless and how Lombardo was 'churned into consciousness' (593) are expanded into a full-scale analysis of how through 'a varied scope of reading' and the welling up of 'that bottomless spring of original thought which the occasion and time had caused to burst out in himself' Pierre is 'swayed to universality of thought' (*P* 283). The peculiar impulse of artistic confession, Melville's compulsion to push aside his narrative and share with us directly his personal experience as an author, reasserts itself here: *Pierre*'s comments on authors composing 'paltry and despicable' works, 'born of unwillingness and the bill of the baker' (*P* 258), repeat and elaborate on Babbalanja's description of Lombardo's anguished consciousness of his work's imperfections, a work undertaken through 'the necessity of bestirring himself to procure his yams' (592). Melville also returns to the notion of writing as an act of self-discovery and self-creation, expanding the story of Lombardo's creation of the creative into an even more detailed account of the symbiotic relation between verbal articulation and the generation of creative consciousness:

> that which now absorbs the time and the life of Pierre, is not the book, but the primitive elementalizing of the strange stuff, which in the act of attempting that book, has upheaved and upgushed in his soul. Two books are being writ; of which the world shall only see one, and that the bungled one. The larger book, and the infinitely better, is for Pierre's own private shelf. That it is, whose unfathomable cravings drink his blood; the other only demands his

ink. But circumstances have so decreed, that the one can
not be composed on the paper, but only as the other is writ
down in his soul. (*P* 304)

The amazing thing about *Mardi*'s concluding chapters is how
well Melville's creative self comes to understand its doings and
its needs in them. The wonder of these sections of *Pierre* is that,
over the space of only three years, that self has come to know
itself so much better – in terms of Melville's letter to Duyckinck
they are the twenty-mile step through which his other leg
catches up with and outdistances his first's ten-mile step. Thus
the Melville who so enthusiastically goes about furnishing *Mardi*
with what he is finding in books of literature and philosophy has
recognized, by the time he writes *Pierre*, that 'all mere reading is
apt to prove but an obstacle hard to overcome', that others'
works can only obstruct the author's imagination unless he uses
them 'simply [as] an exhilarative and provocative' to his own
'spontaneous creative thought' (*P* 283–4). Thus too the Melville who rejects all controls on the artist's work except that of
the 'one autocrat within – his crowned and sceptered instinct'
(597) has discovered, by the time of *Pierre*, the artist's need to
learn the discipline of a formal craft: however fine the marble
in his mental quarry, Melville writes there, if he is to make a
lasting work the young author 'must wholly quit . . . the quarry,
for awhile; and not only go forth, and get tools to use in the
quarry, but must go and thoroughly study architecture' (*P* 257).
Above all he recognizes in *Pierre* that the mental stride he took
in writing *Mardi* was not a completed movement but 'one of the
stages of the transition' (*P* 283) of his evolution, that in it he had
only initiated the process of discovering a world of mind.

If they reveal a growth of self-knowledge, Melville's rewrit-
ings of *Mardi* in *Pierre* also reveal a radical reversal of vision.
Thus, developing *Mardi*'s conceit that 'genius is full of trash'
(595), Melville writes in *Pierre*:

it is often to be observed, that as in digging for precious
metals in the mines, much earthy rubbish has first to be
troublesomely handled and thrown out; so, in digging in
one's soul for the fine gold of genius, much dullness and
common-place is first brought to light. Happy would it be,
if the man possessed in himself some receptacle for his own
rubbish of this sort; but he is like the occupant of a

dwelling, whose refuse can not be clapped into his own cellar, but must be deposited in the street before his own door, for the public functionaries to take care of. No common-place is ever effectually got rid of, except by essentially emptying one's self of it into a book; for once trapped in a book, then the book can be put into the fire, and all will be well. But they are not always put into the fire; and this accounts for the vast majority of miserable books over those of positive merit. (*P* 258)

Here again the production of inferior work is seen as a stage through which an author must pass on his way to producing superior work, but here this process has costs as well as gains. The trash through the writing of which genius evolves persists as an encumbrance to the emerging artist; by writing it he becomes implicated in producing the mediocre literature in which works of merit are smothered. The image of Lombardo going deeper and deeper into himself is revised even more drastically.

Yet now, forsooth, because Pierre began to see through the first superficiality of the world, he fondly weens he has come to the unlayered substance. But, far as any geologist has yet gone down into the world, it is found to consist of nothing but surface stratified on surface. To its axis, the world being nothing but superinduced superficies. By vast pains we mine into the pyramid; by horrible gropings we come to the central room; with joy we espy the sarcophagus; but we lift the lid – and no body is there! – appallingly vacant as vast is the soul of a man! (*P* 285)

Here the act of probing discloses not a paradise of creative fullness but the nightmare of a central emptiness.

In these passages we see Melville remaking *Mardi* into the vision of *Pierre*, the vision of the world as an imposture that every effort to escape only deepens one's involvement in. But the difference between these books is less a matter of their metaphysical stances than of their moods. *Pierre* is a book in which the creative impulse has lost faith in its own creativeness. Where *Mardi* images itself as a strong grain ripening into a rich harvest, *Pierre* is haunted by the spectacle of failed maturation – 'Oh God, that man should spoil and rust on the stalk, and be wilted and threshed ere the harvest

hath come!' (*P* 303). It is sobering to turn from *Mardi* to
Pierre, and to see how quickly Melville's sense of artistic
promise turns into despair. But to think of the two books
together is also to see more clearly the spirit in which *Mardi* is
made. Of all his works *Mardi* is the one in which Melville's
genius rejoices most unabashedly and unreservedly in its own
powers. As no other novel in the world quite does, *Mardi*
embodies the spectacle of a great author advancing, with perfect
confidence and good cheer, to greet his own mature creative
self.

Notes and References
Quotations from Melville's novels in this essay are followed by
page references in parentheses. Those without an initial abbrevia-
tion come from *Mardi*, those preceded by *MD* from *Moby-Dick*,
those preceded by *P* from *Pierre*. For my texts of *Mardi* and
Pierre I have used volumes 3 and 7 of the Northwestern-Newberry
Edition of *The Writings of Herman Melville*; for my text of *Moby-
Dick* I have used the Norton Critical Edition, edited by Harrison
Hayford and Hershel Parker (New York 1967).

1. Jay Leyda prints an extract from the review in *The Athenæum* in
    The Melville Log (New York: Harcourt, Brace, and Co. 1951)
    I, 293.
2. Chasles's comments on *Mardi*, from his essay on Melville in the
    Revue des Deux Mondes, and Hawthorne's, from a letter to Evert
    Duyckinck, are reprinted in ibid. pp. 304 and 391.
3. See Merrell R. Davis, *Melville's Mardi: A Chartless Voyage* (New
    Haven: Yale University Press 1952).
4. Herman Melville to John Murray, 1 January 1848, in *The Letters
    of Herman Melville*, ed. Merrell R. Davis and William H. Gilman
    (New Haven: Yale University Press 1960) p. 68.
5. Herman Melville to John Murray, 25 March 1848, in ibid. pp. 70-
    71.
6. On patterns of moral abdication and the crossing of ontological
    thresholds in *Mardi* see H. Bruce Franklin, *The Wake of the Gods:
    Melville's Mythology* (Stanford: Stanford University Press 1963)
    pp. 41-4, and John Seelye, *Melville: The Ironic Diagram* (Evans-
    ton: Northwestern University Press 1970) pp. 32-5. Seelye's
    whole discussion of *Mardi*, pp. 29-43, is interesting, and he is
    alert to the book's prefiguring of later works by Melville. Of the
    critics who argue that *Mardi* has a premeditated organizational
    design, Franklin's discussion, pp. 17-52, relating the book to Sir
    William Jones's categories of myth, seems to me by far the most
    illuminating; however, I think it is possible to agree that this
    structure is operating in the book without agreeing that it controls
    its whole design. Maxine Moore's argument for an astrological

design in *That Lonely Game: Melville, Mardi, and the Almanac* (Columbia, Mo.: University of Missouri Press 1975) combines curious erudition and wild invention in a way that recalls *Mardi* itself; but as a description of Melville's plan for the book it is unconvincing.

7. I take the term anatomy from Northrop Frye; see his discussion of this form in *Anatomy of Criticism* (1957; rpt. New York: Atheneum 1966) pp. 308-12. Melville's debt to Rabelais in *Mardi* is often noted – see for instance Newton Arvin, *Herman Melville* (New York: William Sloane Associates 1950) pp. 91-2. Less often considered is what it means for Melville to have adopted this of all models at this point in his career.

8. The best discussion of 'Sailing On' in particular and of the relation of the narrated voyage to Melville's act of conceiving *Mardi* in general is in Charles Feidelson, Jr., *Symbolism and American Literature* (Chicago: University of Chicago Press 1953) pp. 162-175.

9. Herman Melville to Evert Duyckinck, 5 April 1849; to Richard Bentley, 20 July 1849; and to Evert Duyckinck, 14 December 1849, in *Letters*, ed. Davis and Gilman, pp. 83, 87, and 96.

Shakespeare
and Melville's America

Among the letters of introduction Herman Melville took to England in 1849 was one addressed to Samuel Rogers from Edward Everett. 'I want him to see,' said Everett, 'a few of those choicest spirits, who even at the present day increase the pride which *we* feel in speaking the language of Shakespeare and Milton.'[1]

The 'we' can refer to Americans in general although Everett's underscoring also seems to give it a restricted reference to that class of New England gentlemen and scholars who saw themselves as the conscientious transmitters of high culture in the United States. Everett was the 'man of letters *par excellence*',[2] as Harriet Martineau observed more in scorn for his political pusillanimity than in praise of his writing, and his letter on Melville's behalf was an exercise in class comradeship. He had never met Melville but he was happy to oblige his friend Judge Lemuel Shaw and he could not but believe that the Judge's son-in-law, the brother of a former Secretary to the American Legation in Britain, and the author of two widely-read books was a very likely representative of the continuity that ran from the language of Shakespeare to the aspirations of America's best people.

Curiously, however, with respect to Shakespeare as well as in other respects equally unknown to Everett, Melville was an exception to the run of American authors. It was only in 1849, his thirtieth year and that year in which Everett wrote a letter for him, that Melville had begun to read Shakespeare's plays. Because he first encountered them as an adult who was himself an author rather than as a youth whose perceptions were dimmed by the pious aura in which school and home usually enveloped the plays, he detected in them a particular personality and a singular vision rather than a pageant of life. He responded as a fellow writer eager to learn craft as well as a maturing man with convictions and doubts about the human condition.

In his first amazement – 'Dolt & ass that I am I have lived

more than 29 years, & until a few days ago, never made close
acquaintance with the divine William' [3] – Melville summarily
dismissed conventional idolatry even whilst retaining the conventional 'divine'. When the editor of his edition claimed that
Shakespeare's powers were so superhuman that he attained his
ends 'without any throes or labor of the mind', Melville asked in
the margin, 'How know you that, sir'.[4] And when he read
another commentator who remarked that Shakespeare 'must
ever remain unapproachable', his flat reply was, 'Cant. No man
must ever remain unapproachable'.[5]

Abstracted, such an attitude borders on the ludicrously pre-
tentious, but in the context of Melville's career it appears to
quite different effect. Precisely because he saw Shakespeare as a
mortal who laboured for his effects and tailored his philosophy
to the conventionality of his audience, Melville took him as his
most reliable guide from 1849 through to his long silence. Those
writers who accepted Shakespeare's unapproachability alluded
to his plots and borrowed his phrases in pursuit of resonance.
Melville's view, however, led him to what can be likened to a
case study: here was the way toward the extension of fictional
form, the creation of original characters, and the employment
of the widest possible range of diction. Soliloquy rather than
allegory was the technique whereby psychological state was to
be dramatized.

Although he was unique among American novelists – and
perhaps among all novelists in English – in taking so many
lessons of craft from Shakespeare, however, Melville also
approached him in good part through assumptions, more
political than literary, that were common in his culture. What
had this man of an earlier century, another geographical world,
and an outdated social system to say that was appropriate in
America?

Such questions had a history at least as old as that of the
American republic, and one common answer to them was that
America validated Shakespeare. It is there, for example, in the
essay by Maurice Morgann, the man who was to be, ironically
in view of his remarks on Shakespeare and America, the
secretary of the British peace commission that negotiated the
end of the American revolution. Writing in 1777 in reaction
to Voltaire's opinion that Shakespeare was an uncultured

barbarian, Morgann said, 'When the hand of time shall have brushed off his present Editors and Commentators, and when the very name of *Voltaire* and even the memory of the language in which he has written, shall be no more, the Apalachian Mountains, the banks of the Ohio, and the plains of the Sciota shall resound with the accents of this Barbarian'.[6]

In paying back the French, Morgann was recklessly making a gift of Shakespeare to the Americans who were coming to believe not only that their increasing numbers spread his influence but that their very rudeness and vigour joined to the sublimity of their landscape fit them to be his finest audience. So Peter Markoe of Pennsylvania was quick to perceive that one of the spoils of the Revolution might well be Shakespeare himself, and published a poem in which he said:

Monopolizing Britain! boast no more
His genius to your narrow bounds confin'd;
Shakespeare's bold spirit seeks our western shore,
A gen'ral blessing for the world design'd,
And, emulous to form the rising age,
The noblest Bard demands the noblest Stage.[7]

Some fifty years later when the call for a truly American, American literature was heard far and wide in the land, then, to be sure, such guileless appropriation would not serve. But the force of the sentiment that Shakespeare's genius matched America's mountains rather than England's dells was felt widely even though it did not appear so crudely in the intellectual debates.

It is part, for example, of the extraordinary popularity of Shakespearean productions in the first half of the nineteenth century not only in the seaboard cities but on the fringes of the advancing population. There, for example, in the tragi-comic fortunes of the troupe of William Forbes, the impresario who in 1818 incredibly thought it worth the risk to follow the military forces of General Andrew Jackson into Eastern Florida, where they were pursuing the Seminole War, in order to put on Shakespeare's plays in one or another encampment.[8] It was there twenty years later in Texas where a one-time actor named Stanley rode 300 miles through the territory of hostile Comanches in order to persuade Joseph Jefferson and his mother to bring their company to the Mexican border in a Shakespeare play.[9] It was there in the Mississippi River villages of Mark Twain's boyhood as the Duke and the Dauphin illustrate.

These are among numerous examples which indicate that Shakespeare was America's favourite playwright, peculiarly dear to the frontier as well as to more civilized regions. Performances of his plays appeared to mean equal value given to each roared-out line, with little if any regard for proportion, symmetry, or interpretation of the whole. The frontier enthusiasm for spread-eagle screaming and violent action seems to have been well nourished by America's barn-storming Richards. Melville was contemptuous of those who adored Shakespeare for the 'rant, interlined by another hand',[10] and certainly Ahab's soliloquies are at the opposite extreme from such bombast for its own sake. Still, they do partake of the prevailing American habit of coupling scenes of natural vastness and terrifying peril with vaunting characters.

Against this popular sense of Shakespeare a more troubled, intellectual approach to him emerged in the course of the national debate on the nature of an American literature that was yet to be written. On one side were those who believed that American literature would best develop organically from its English roots and that the task of American literary men was to treat American themes in such a way as to link them with the best that had been said and thought in the Old World. Americans spoke the language of Shakespeare and this bound them to an essentially British outlook, as Edward Everett, for one, maintained.

On the other side were those who argued that literature as it was understood in the Old World was the institutional consequence of a hierarchical society. It depended ultimately on free time that the reading class procured through exploiting the mass of men. True democracy, making its first modern appearance on the American continent, meant not just a radically new kind of society but a radically different kind of literature. Walt Whitman wrote:

> Even Shakespeare, who so suffuses current letters and art (which indeed have in most degrees grown out of him,) belongs essentially to the buried past. Only he holds the proud distinction for certain important phases of that past, of being the loftiest of the singers life has yet given voice to. All, however, relate to and rest upon conditions,

standards, politics, sociologies, ranges of belief, that have been quite eliminated from the Eastern hemisphere, and never existed at all in the Western. As authoritative types of song they belong in America just about as much as the persons and institutes they depict.[11]

For Whitman democracy clearly meant the final destruction of feudalism, and this, in turn, meant that Shakespeare, seen as feudalism's last and greatest poet, had to be set aside in favour of the new songs of democracy. Other writers shared his view: Shakespeare was undeniably the greatest user of the common language and the greatest source of literary pleasure known to them, yet to yield to him was, they felt, to betray their mission to derive a literature from a new and democratic world.

Melville's enthusiasm for Shakespeare was strongly tempered by such considerations. He wrote Duyckinck that 'the muzzle which all men wore on their souls in the Elizabethan day' had been Shakespeare's also: 'I would to God Shakespeare had lived later, & promenaded in Broadway'.[12] He intensified this view in *Moby-Dick* when Ishmael, more self-consciously the writer of the narrative than at any other point in the novel, speaks of the lamentable literary necessity that requires a tragic dramatist to make his central characters men whose superiority is figured forth in the titles of noble lineage and bolstered by the superstition-linked vestments of office. They must be seen to assert their eminence by employing awe-inspiring devices however degrading to their integrity such theatricality may seem to the thoughtful. 'This it is,' says Ishmael, 'that for ever keeps God's true princes of the Empire from the world's hustings; and leaves the highest honors that this air can give, to those men who become famous more through their infinite inferiority to the choice hidden handful of the Divine Inert, than through their undoubted superiority over the dead level of the mass.'[13]

Charles Olson summed up Melville's attitude in this respect by saying, 'As the strongest social force America caused him to approach tragedy in terms of democracy'.[14] And he amplified this notion by saying that 'The crew is where what America stands for got into *Moby-Dick*. They're Melville's addition to tragedy as he took it from Shakespeare.'[15] This is so, and yet the matter is more complicated. Ahab, the figure most shaped by Shakespearian imperatives, is opposed to the Divine Inert in the

novel although until his mania came upon him he was, presumably, of that quality. Now, however, he would be a democrat
only among the gods. The crew can develop no representative of
a counterbalancing social principle, although the rudiments of
such development may occasionally be glimpsed in Starbuck, in
the freedom of the harpooneers, and in the broodings, rather
than the actions, of Ishmael.

Before Melville fell under Shakespeare's influence the Ahab-
figure was embedded in the crew rather than set against it.
Redburn tells us of the Yankee, Jackson, whose moral strength
was of heroic size albeit of diabolical application. He leaves us
room to speculate that Jackson's evil bent was imparted to him
by the social baffling of his powers because he was of common
origins. Relatively ignorant of Shakespeare, Redburn likens
Jackson to heroes drawn from other sources – Tiberius,
Napoleon, and Milton's Satan. After Melville's narrators had
taken Shakespeare's lesson, however, Jackson became Ahab and
was situated above the crew rather than secreted in its bowels.
But although Shakespeare led Melville to no central dramatic
function for the hero hidden among the commoners, Melville
was reluctant to relinquish him and he remains lurking about
the periphery of the narratives with nothing much to do within
the central plot. He is Mad Jack; he is Steelkilt; he might, perhaps, have been Bulkington. Until Billy Budd he is cramped for
scope, and, significantly, when he re-emerges translated into
Billy then Shakespeare no longer functions as a leading influence
on the technique of Melville's fiction.

In 1850, on the eve, as it were, of Moby-Dick, Melville con-
structed his fullest expository statement on Shakespeare. He was
led to it by his consideration of the 'blackness' of Hawthorne,
which, he felt, was the same as that 'against which Shakespeare
plays his grandest conceits, the things that have made for Shakespeare his loftiest but most circumscribed renown as the profoundest of thinkers'. Shaded characters and shaded sayings are
of the essence of this 'profoundest' Shakespeare: 'Through the
mouths of the dark characters . . . he craftily says, or sometimes
insinuates, the things which we feel to be so terrifically true
that it were all but madness for any good man, in his own proper
character, to utter, or even hint of them.'[16]

Melville anticipates the contention that to compare Hawthorne with Shakespeare is to make one's self ridiculous and warns that the view that Shakespeare is beyond comparison is a view that maligns mankind for the sake of one man: 'this absolute and unconditional adoration of Shakespeare', he says, has grown to the proportion of a religious superstition and must not be furthered by the American who is 'bound to carry republican progressiveness into Literature, as well as into Life'.[17] He echoes the sentiment of the Democratic politicians and their rhetoric of camaraderie when he adds, 'Believe me, my friends, that men not very much inferior to Shakespeare are this day being born on the banks of the Ohio'.[18] America, initiating a new era of human history and experiencing dews as fresh as those that wet Adam's feet in Eden, must dare to have its artists compared with Shakespeare. But unlike Whitman, Melville does not say that the American Shakespeare will have a new vision of man's spiritual condition. The similarity of Hawthorne's dark vision to Shakespeare's is what attracts him, and he himself, of course, was in the process of following it in his art far beyond the cautious Hawthorne. Democracy may work against the tragic conventions, but it does not mitigate the power of blackness which pre-exists political forms and is, for Melville, the essence of the human drama.

The contours of Shakespeare in *Moby-Dick* have been sketched by Charles Olson, 'What moves Melville is the stricken goodness of a Lear, a Gloucester, an Edgar, who in suffering feel and thus probe more closely to the truth'.[19] Olson is correct when he maintains that the 'Ahab-world' is finally closer to *Macbeth* than to *King Lear*: 'Ahab's tense and nervous speech is like Macbeth's, rather than Lear's';[20] Fedallah's prophecies function like those of the witches; Macbeth and Ahab share a hell of sleep-bursting dreams; and both suffer the torture of accelerating isolation from humanity.

To Olson's characterization must also be added a certain structural rhythm that Melville appears to have learned from *Macbeth*, one that permits the central character moments of objective recognition of the state of his mania so that even as villainies mount to the extent of the destruction of children (Macbeth's actions against Macduff's family; Ahab's refusal to aid the *Rachel*), the audience is unwilling to relinquish him to death until he himself signals his resignation (Macbeth's 'yellow leaf' speech; Ahab's musing on the eve of the chase: 'they have been making hay somewhere under the slopes of the Andes').[21]

Emerson was another American writer whom Melville dared to mention in the same context with Shakespeare. They are joined together as among the whales in the letter of 3 March 1849 to Duyckinck: 'I love all men who *dive*. Any fish can swim near the surface, but it takes a great whale to go down stairs five miles or more'.[22] A defence of Emerson precedes the image of the thought-diver and a qualification of the frankness of Shakespeare's utterances succeeds it.

When Emerson faced the problem of Shakespeare's usability in democratic America he moved toward a solution by first fragmenting him. 'It is easy to see,' he said, 'that what is best written or done by genius in the world, was no man's work, but came by wide social labor, when a thousand wrought like one, sharing the same impulse.'[23] Here Shakespeare is single only as a penman; the voices he records are those of all men speaking through him. Emerson's mental picture must have been of the thousands who laboured toward the unity of the great medieval cathedrals so that the architect was swallowed in the common enterprise.

Next, Emerson separated out that aspect of Shakespeare that was usable without prejudice to what he took to be the proper role of democratic literature. He said, 'Some able and appreciating critics think no criticism on Shakespeare valuable that does not rely purely on the dramatic merit; that he is falsely judged as poet and philosopher. I think as highly as these critics of his dramatic merit, but I still think it secondary.'[24] To be sure, more than a vestige of Puritan distrust of the players resides here. But the principal effect sought is the removal of what is truly Shakespearean from the specific form of the plays and the identification of it as a power that is independent of form. As pure flux, Shakespeare's poetic thought becomes accessible to all men regardless of their social condition, whereas if attention is given centrally to the way in which Shakespeare embodies his thoughts in dramatic structures then one has the Shakespeare who impedes democratic literature.

And so, finally, we have this praise of Shakespeare from Emerson:

He is like some saint whose history is to be rendered into all languages, into verse and prose, into songs and pictures, and cut up into proverbs; so that the occasion which gave the saint's meaning the form of a conversation, or of a prayer, or of a code of laws, is immaterial compared with the universality of its application. . . . He wrote the airs for all our modern music: he wrote the text of modern life; the text of manners: he drew the man of England and Europe; the father of the man in America; he drew the man, and described the day, and what is done in it. . . . The importance of this wisdom of life sinks the form, as of Drama or Epic, out of notice. 'Tis like making a question concerning the paper on which a king's message is written.[25]

In this apostrophe, Shakespeare, likened to a saint or a king, is finally most like the Holy Ghost. Released from the forms which sink from notice like a corpse descended into the grave, his disembodied spirit moves freely to inhabit where it will and pour vitality into radically different forms. It comes to the democratic artist the way grace comes to the humble believer.

This certainly is not Melville's Shakespeare because for Melville the formal Shakespeare is crucial if the lessons of the philosophical Shakespeare are to be applied by the creative artist. Moreover, the refinement of Shakespeare into a flux reinforces the vulgar notion of him as a deity unapproachable by mere man, albeit the undemocratic implications of the remark are avoided by Emerson who makes the flux the outlet of all men of Shakespeare's day rather than of one man. But Melville took inspiration and craft from Shakespeare precisely because he was single and limited. Where many admirers of the dramas did and still do feel authorial nonentity Melville felt a particular presence. When, in *The Confidence-Man*, he maintained that there could be but one original character to a work because the essence of originality is its capacity to shed light on the entire surrounding world so that two such lights would cancel one another,[26] he had Shakespeare's tragic heroes in mind, and, by extension, Shakespeare himself as the light-shedder of his era. Although like Emerson he placed enormous value on Shakespeare the philosopher, and, like Emerson again, sometimes recognized a Shakespeare apart from the surge of events upon the stage, he saw a quite different philosophy than did Emerson – one that asserted that the natural was real and powerfully creative rather than apparent and dependent upon the shaping force of the ideal.

Melville admired Emerson for all the disagreements he had with his philosophy and he paid him the arduous tribute of going through rather than around him when he did disagree. He emphatically branded as false Emerson's claim that man's 'ambition is exactly proportioned to his powers. The height of the pinnacle is determined by the breadth of the base'.[27] Ahab said no to this and Pierre added amen. How could one experience with Lear and with Hamlet, or with Edmund and with Timon, and so believe?

Comparison with Emerson does not so much point up Melville's superiority as a critic of Shakespeare as it serves to focus the particular aspects of Shakespeare's work that drew responses from him. However enfeebled Emerson's Shakespeare may finally seem, he is recognizable as the author of the entire canon. But Melville's Shakespeare wrote no history plays and no Roman plays. He wrote comedies only as an occasion to show forth cynics such as Jacques and Autolycus, and he took neither love nor sexual jealousy as major themes. *Romeo and Juliet* hovers over Pierre's doomed alliances, but not so closely as does Prince Hamlet in his perception that a man with troubles on his mind has better things to do than fret about his relations with women. Melville, in short, took his intensity from a narrowed focus on Shakespeare's blackness.

In the long silence that fell upon Melville after 1857, works by and about Shakespeare were among his favourite gifts to members of his family and Shakespeare figured memorably in one of his poems:

> No utter surprise can come to him,
>> Who reaches Shakespeare's core;
> That which we seek and shun is there –
>> Man's final lore.[28]

These lines were composed at the end of the Civil War by a man who had lived through that bloody time as he had lived through the ruin of his once considerable literary reputation. They are ambiguous, offering both consolation and self-reproach. When Melville returned to fiction in his final years, Milton, the Bible, and the French Wars, elements that figured in the fiction he

wrote prior to his discovery of Shakespeare in 1849, came to the
fore again and Shakespeare there was dimmed.

But before Melville walked into that silence he composed as
his final work *The Confidence-Man*, a novel which drew upon
Shakespeare in ways quite different from the already extensive
variations in the works that had preceded it. Its structure is
comic whereas that of *Moby-Dick* is tragic. But whereas *Moby-
Dick* drew upon specific tragic worlds such as those of *King Lear*
and *Macbeth*, and whereas *Pierre* drew upon the tragic world of
Hamlet, *The Confidence-Man* draws upon no specific comic
worlds of Shakespeare but reduces a number of Shakespeare's
tragic worlds to its bitter formulas. To be sure, one Shakespeare fable seems to dominate the others, that of *Timon*, but
the texture and rhythm of the novel are independent of its
texture and rhythm, as for example, *Moby-Dick* is not independent of those qualities in *Macbeth*.

Set upon a flat-bottomed boat gliding down the main line of
the American continent, always in sight of land and frequently
touching upon it, *The Confidence-Man* requires no lofty main
truck to offset the depth of its kelson. It consists almost exclus-
ively of talk – cosy chat, gruff bluster, impish extravaganza,
treacherous insinuation – all of it informal. Into and out of the
conversations slide the characters of Shakespeare, named or
alluded to, quoted or misquoted, as if they too shared the dead
level of humdrum motion toward a constant sameness that
prevails on the *Fidèle*. Goneril is now the name of a singularly
nasty American housewife, Timon is an ursine frontier loner,
and Polonius is talked over as if he were president of a wildcat
bank. There is no reference to the positions of Shakespeare's
characters within their own worlds, only to their attitudes
toward getting and spending. They are so many commercial
object lessons.

Among the vulgar, Melville had pointed out in his Hawthorne
review, Shakespeare was a deity. Now aboard the *Fidèle* the
Shakespearean canon is handled the way the Bible is: a commonly accepted account of the human condition that furnishes
a treasury of illustrations with which to lubricate the cogs of
conversation between strangers; a collection of ethical maxims
that are agreed to by all in the abstract but that yield contradictory meanings when pursued in the particular. As at times

Shakespeare and the Bible appear interchangeable with one another so at other times they appear interchangeable with the world of the *Fidèle*. No master lens can fix them in an unblurred relationship to one another, but the author of the drama does halt it at one point to contribute what he can to our clarification. By the time he does so, of course, many readers feel well justified in taking his as yet another confidence trick, but as other events in the novel have shown, one is not necessarily the worse off emotionally or intellectually for falling in with certain confidence games.

The author, who for convenience may be called Melville, raises the matter of what is involved in the requirement that fiction have a 'fidelity to real life', and since he has put us aboard the *Fidèle* we assume that he is talking about his work in particular as well as fiction in general. He sides, he says, with that class who take up novels or sit at a play desiring 'scenes different from those of the same old crowd round the custom-house counter, and same old dishes on the boarding-house table, with characters unlike those same old acquaintances they meet in the same old way every day in the same old street'.[29] Before we even arrive at fiction, then, Melville has created for us a singular fiction of what the real world is. Everyday reality is no larger than commercial transactions: the assessment of rates and payment of tariffs at the custom-house; the consumption of food directly billed to one's account at the boarding-house. There is, we may protest, also an everyday reality in which the principal business is not business and in which the ritual of taking food is conducted among those one loves without reference to cost and profit, but it is not only absent from *The Confidence-Man* it is absent from the everyday reality from which that novel's author departs.

The passage continues: 'And as, in real life, the proprieties will not allow people to act out themselves with the unreserve permitted to the stage; so, in books of fiction, they look not only for more entertainment, but, at bottom, even for more reality, than real life itself can show. Thus, though they want novelty, they want nature, too; but nature unfettered, exhilirated, in effect transformed.'

Since reality has already been established as singularly mean the fiction which unfetters nature would, one thinks, have

enormously wide scope, as wide as reality is narrow. But irony
is heaped on irony because the world of the *Fidèle* is concerned
only with everyday reality as Melville has characterized it and is
replete with tales of bankruptcy, blasted marriages, and children
out for rent on terms more favourable than machinery. Nature
has been fettered too long for it to leap into life when the
creative artist arrives with the key to the manacles.

But the confidential authorial explanation does not end without one further and more resonant hint. 'It is with fiction as with
religion;' Melville says, 'it should present another world, and
yet one to which we feel the tie.' Reality, layered between
religion and fiction, is inexpressible in its own terms; once it is
articulated in words it becomes either religion or fiction depending upon whether it is expressed in terms of the ideals which
justify it from above or the motives which it takes from nature.
The Bible is the supreme example of the world of religion,
Shakespeare's works of the world of fiction. But *The Confidence-
Man* in its deliberate interchanging of the two and its relentless
reduction of them to the level of the decks of the *Fidèle* in effect
denies them and in so doing denies the expressibility of life.
Silence is indeed descending upon its creator.

In the period of Melville's long fictional silence Walt Whitman looked at the troubled, alienated tribe of man and asked,
'What is this separate Nature so unnatural?'[30] His answer to
perplexity was progress and transcendence: seek meaning
beyond time and space, out, farther out, in the 'seas of God'.
Billy Budd, for all its difference, principally its insistence upon
pain and sacrifice, takes somewhat of the same direction. This
nature so unnatural – a depravity according to nature – wins on
the seas of man leaving Billy to gain his triumph on the seas of
God. Billy's world is the world of Edmund Burke, cautiously
confining social change to traditional ways, justly fearful of the
consequences of a violent challenge to established authority. It
is also the world of religion rather than of fiction as these were
characterized by Melville in *The Confidence-Man*. The long act
of Shakespeare's influence had closed.

Notes and References
1. Jay Leyda, *The Melville Log* (New York 1951) I, 312.
2. Harriet Martineau, *Autobiography* (London 1877) II, 63.

3. *The Letters of Herman Melville*, ed. Merrell R. Davis & William H. Gilman (New Haven 1960) p. 77.

4. *Log*, I, 289.

5. ibid. I, 363-4.

6. Henry N. Paul, 'Shakespeare in Philadelphia', *Proceedings of the American Philosophical Society* (1936) vol. LXXVI, p. 729.

7. Peter Markoe, 'The Tragic Genius of Shakespeare. An Ode', in *Miscellaneous Poems* (Philadelphia 1787) p. 27.

8. *The Autobiography of Joseph Jefferson*, ed. Alan S. Downer (Cambridge, Mass. 1964) pp. 49-50. The troupe was attacked by Indians, two actors were killed, and the properties seized. 'Several of the Indians were afterwards taken, and as they were robed and decked in the habiliments of *Othello*, *Hamlet*, and a host of other Shakespearean characters . . . their identity as the murderers was established.'

9. ibid. pp. 50-1.

10. Herman Melville, 'Hawthorne and His Mosses', *The Portable Melville*, ed. Jay Leyda (New York 1952) p. 407.

11. Walt Whitman, 'A Backward Glance O'er Travel'd Roads', *Complete Poetry and Selected Prose*, ed. James E. Miller, Jr. (Boston 1959) p. 448.

12. *Letters*, p. 79.

13. Herman Melville, *Moby-Dick*, ed. Charles Feidelson, Jr. (Indianapolis 1964) p. 198.

14. Charles Olson, *Call Me Ishmael* (San Francisco 1947) p. 69.

15. ibid.

16. 'Hawthorne and His Mosses', p. 407.

17. ibid. p. 409.

18. ibid.

19. *Call Me Ishmael*, pp. 50-1.

20. ibid. p. 54.

21. *Moby-Dick*, p. 685.

22. *Letters*, p. 79.

23. Ralph Waldo Emerson, 'Shakespeare; or The Poet', *Representative Men* (Boston 1884) pp. 190-1.

24. ibid. p. 200.

25. ibid. pp. 201-2.

26. See chapter 44.

27. William Braswell, 'Melville as a Critic of Emerson', *American Literature*, 9 (1937) 321. The Emerson quotation is from 'Spiritual Laws'.

28. Herman Melville, 'The Coming Storm', *Collected Poems*, ed. Howard P. Vincent (Chicago 1947) p. 94.

29. Herman Melville, *The Confidence-Man*, ed. Hershel Parker (New York 1971) pp. 157-8. Succeeding quotations follow immediately after.

30. 'Passage to India', l. 96.

Melville's
England

I

In *The Sketch Book of Geoffrey Crayon, Gent.*, Washington Irving fashioned a *persona* through whom he could effect an accommodation between the republic to which he owed allegiance and the English culture and literature he loved. His book was a pre-emptive defence against accusations of cultural toryism and his affirmative answer to the question whether an American, in 1820, could be both a democrat and an author – if to be an author meant retaining a connexion with the Ancestral Home and all its works.[1] *The Sketch Book* declares that the connexion can be and should be retained by authors who would thereby be loyal Americans and public benefactors, enriching the 'new' literature by preserving for it its primary tradition.

Irving endowed the sketchbook artist, Crayon, with an attachment to things English more naive and sentimental than his own, even encouraging us to view Crayon with detached amusement: in this way Irving distanced himself from his own anxieties and insecurities – was he himself unfit for life in the United States ? – and converted them into parable. Crayon has a nightmare of the deceased authors of the English tradition accusing him of wholesale plagiarism: Irving's sketch of this is a nicely calculated 'American' fable. Just as in 'Rip Van Winkle' he encodes a parable of the terms on which the pre-Revolutionary sensibility is accepted in post-Revolutionary America, so Irving accommodates the complementary difficulty, whether the American author is a legitimate inheritor of English culture, or only a sham. 'The anxiety of influence' has a full dress-rehearsal, and for a time threatens Geoffrey Crayon with non-entity.

But Irving secures his uneasy synthesis because Crayon, despite his insecurities, can find satisfactions and acceptance in England. He can find not only an England of the past – for example, Shakespeare's – to honour, but a past which lives into the present, and a valuable present as well. Irving takes pains to show that on occasion it is only Crayon who reveres that past – the English themselves are in danger of forgetting it, so its recovery advantages them as well as him – or that it is only available in an anachronistic setting, most notably Bracebridge Hall, which has preserved forms dying out elsewhere in the country. It is as though Irving's Crayon is the *last* American, as well as the first, who can build this particular bridge between England and the United States.

In his 'Historical Note' to Melville's *Redburn*, Hershel Parker describes *The Sketch Book* as a 'non-nautical source [or] analogue' for the novel, mentioning the resemblance between Crayon and Melville's narrator – 'the combination of sentimentality and gentle irony' – along with comparable episodes in both books.[2] While Parker does not claim the similarities amount to 'direct borrowing' (327), he suggests that,

> In view of [Melville's] habit of satirizing the authors of the books he was plundering, perhaps in gently satirizing the sentimentality of his narrator, Melville was also recognizing the limitations of the author he was to renounce the next year in his essay on Hawthorne's *Mosses From an Old Manse*. (328)

In 'Hawthorne and His Mosses', Melville is specifically discussing the matter of influence when he brings in Irving, and in particular the viability of cisatlantic models:

> that graceful writer, who perhaps of all Americans has received the most plaudits from his own country for his productions – that very popular and amiable writer, however good, and self-reliant in many things, perhaps owes his chief reputation to the self-acknowledged imitation of a foreign model, and to the studied avoidance of all topics but smooth ones. . . . Let us believe it, then, once for all, that there is no hope for us in these smooth, pleasing writers that know their powers. Without malice, but to speak the plain fact, they but furnish an appendix to Goldsmith, and other English authors. And we want no American Goldsmiths; nay, we want no American Miltons.[3]

Melville is not only renouncing Irving here, he is confirming an

exorcism that had begun in *Redburn* itself, though there inextricably involved with deference and condescension to
amiability, smoothness, and the need for 'plaudits'.[4] Apparently
undertaken almost as a direct admission that he had gotten off
the track of 'success' with *Mardi*, and as a means of beginning
over in the shoes of America's sole acknowledged Master,
Redburn had engaged *The Sketch Book* over the question of
England, the patrimony of America's culture, and the meaning
of an American's desire to retain or revive the connexion. Whatever Melville's original intentions, and they were probably very
mixed if not inchoate, his novel amounts to a significant revision
of Irving – testing, 'recognizing the limitations', and overturning
The Sketch Book. The process began Melville's preparation for
that definitive renunciation of 'success' in the ellipsis of the
passage just cited, where he announces, 'Failure is the true test
of greatness'. The necessary misinterpretation of Irving, as both
a real and a symbolic figure, contributed greatly to the clearing
of psychic space Melville needed in order to conceive and
execute *Moby-Dick*.

Wellingborough Redburn, though named for a Revolutionary
forebear, desires the repudiated fatherland as a sanctuary.
England represents for him – before he sees it – the recovery of
an imagined golden age of childhood, before his father died in
the collapse of his family fortunes. So desperate is the youth
that he is pictured, by his mature self (the narrator), as a kind of
wild man and near to psychological collapse. The humiliations
of the voyage out only increase that possibility of psychic dis-
integration: the disruption of every fantasy of revenge and
restitution only produces more global fantasies. The production
of the very guidebook his late father used in Liverpool appears
as the final term in a series, and by this point Redburn's
obsessive need to follow in Walter Redburn's exact footsteps is
the need for a magical ritual which will renovate and restore his
whole universe. It is as though he would become his father –
what his father was before his fall – and the English City will
become their Jerusalem: they will become one through it, and
all will be well.

It is a need the nakedness of which Irving never attributed to
Geoffrey Crayon, though he had himself the most painful and
wounding memories of the collapse of family fortunes. And the

restitution, so much more than Crayon required, was not to be given to young Redburn. Liverpool's landmarks are all gone, the life and culture in which his father participated, gone – either in reality (the dock, the hotel) or in terms of access (the reading-room and library to which Redburn is denied entrance). Redburn Sr. could dine with William Roscoe (144), the *Sketch Book*'s prime example of merchant, man of letters, and public benefactor. No such connexion is available to his son. Liverpool to Crayon was a model of what an American city might become; to Wellingborough Redburn it becomes a horror. Having discovered that the Liverpool of 1808 is no more, realising that he will never find his father, we might well expect him to break down altogether, so much has he invested in the search.

But he does not go under, and seems to survive at first by a certain naive and youthful quality, as though now that the terrible burden he had imposed upon himself is gone, he can become himself at last. What that self lacks is precisely the burden of ego, and so Wellingborough goes back to his ship, the other ships, the docks, and tells us what there is to be seen. These chapters, so much more in their placing than Melville's undigested travel notes, prepare Redburn for the experience of Launcelott's-Hey, for the registration of someone else's suffering, the desire to help somehow, its frustration where no man will take responsibility for any other, for the moral outrage. It is no wonder that Melville gives Redburn the relief of a single excursion into the countryside. But even here the old, constant pattern of desire and frustration is repeated: the 'old England, indeed! . . . found at last . . . in the country!' (209) becomes 'the forbidden Eden' through keep-off signs. The recurrence of Redburn's despair – 'It was too bad; too bitterly bad' (212) – is made worse by 'A sturdy farmer, with an alarming cudgel in his hand' who threatens to set 'Blucher' on the lad. But the episode ends happily, amusingly, sentimentally, when Redburn meets his 'three charmers, three Peris, three Houris!' and just about manages an invitation to tea. In truth, his farmhouse reception is more grudging than he can bear to admit, and he fantasises an acceptance he does not really achieve. (The fantasy apparently persists into his maturity, unless the narrator is being facetious when he claims 'to this day I live a bachelor on account of those ravishing charmers!' (215)) However disabused of the major misapprehension that through a reconnexion with England he can magically alter his condition, Redburn can perhaps only survive his disillusionment by imagining more satisfaction, Crayon-like, than he ought, by sentimentalization.

The episode of the 'ravishing charmers' is immediately succeeded by the introduction of Harry Bolton, young Redburn's *alter ego*. There is a logic to the novel which makes the appeal Harry has precisely attendant on the backsliding romanticisation: if Redburn can have that much of England, can he, perhaps vicariously, have more. Just as Redburn, born to democracy, has hankered after the superseded time, Harry Bolton is a born 'aristocrat' (even if his tales of aristocracy simply exploit class distinctions), who affects that he can 'precipitate himself upon the New World, and there carve out a fresh fortune' (218). But if Redburn can survive the sea and the cruel treatment of the sailors whom he 'loathed, detested, and hated' (52), Harry cannot. He tells Redburn, '*He could not go aloft*; his nerves would not hear of it' (255), and when he does, nevertheless, 'He came down pale as death':

> From that moment he never put foot in rattlin; never mounted above the bulwarks; and for the residue of the voyage, at least, became an altered person. (257)

'Perhaps,' says the narrator, as the crew jeer and jibe at Harry, 'his spirit, for the time, had been broken' (258).

Redburn is not so broken by the discovery that he cannot play the part he has imagined for himself. For one thing, he *can* survive on shipboard – which is why Melville gives us the return journey – can learn to function in a community which is neither democratic nor, despite the tyranny of Captain Riga, wholly autocratic. (In *White-Jacket* Melville would deepen the paradox of absolute rule in the service of a democracy.) Redburn can function physically, and can take a restorative pleasure in what he does and sees. He is sustained partly by mere powers of observation, most through observing the counter-career of Harry Bolton, who came on the scene purporting to have by birthright, and to scorn, what Redburn had so dearly wished for himself:[5]

> In vain did Bury, with all its fine old monastic attractions, lure him to abide on the beautiful banks of her Larke, and under the shadow of her stately and storied old Saxon tower.

By all my rare old historical associations, breathed Bury; by my Abbey-gate, that bears to this day the arms of Edward the Confessor ... by my Norman ruins, and by all the old abbots of Bury, do not, oh Harry! abandon me. (217)

Bury St Edmunds speaks with the accents of *The Sketch Book*. Redburn shares its wonderment at Harry's neurotic abandonment of home, and thus perhaps learns something about his own predicament.

Melville, however, by choosing to present his novel through the voice of Redburn in maturity, has left open the question of the completeness of Redburn's conversion. As with Dickens's Pip, there are hints that the experiences of a boy disillusioned over his expectations are never wholly to be surmounted. Though the events of the story occurred many years ago (200), the narrator is not at ease in the world. Superstitiously, if whimsically, he will not let his sisters restore the figurehead of the glass ship *La Reine* to its place: 'I will not have him put on his legs again, till I get on my own' (9). The novel has described a contrary process to that in Irving's book: it has discovered that there is *no* England for an American, that England is not the father of an American man, that its *uses* are all ironic – or ironic to a degree Melville would not attribute to Irving. For success had to involve cisatlantic accommodation, and the discovery that accommodation was not possible involves failure. From such a discovery there may be no complete recovery. Those unlucky enough to have caught the virus of need for patrimony may have ineluctable boundaries of spirit. They may survive only through qualities which are limited and limiting: their life-stories can no longer be 'smooth' or 'successful', 'however good, and self-reliant in many things'. Redburn's story is neither smooth nor successful: to follow in the steps of Geoffrey Crayon is a doomed enterprise, a desire to imitate 'a foreign model' – England, father, Irving – which cannot succeed. In becoming aware that it cannot, perhaps that it was wrong from the start, Redburn incurs our sympathy. Melville has created a *persona* to supplant and supersede Irving's Crayon – an angry, bitter, and cheated child – and a novel which offers a different and more critical view of the American's relation to English culture.

II

In 1849 Melville made his first trip back to England since the 1839 voyage which gave him the framework for *Redburn*. There he negotiated – successfully, but after very considerable difficulty – the sale of its successor, *White-Jacket*. The journey would also be, he hoped, a holiday after the labours of writing two books in less than a year. The stomach he had affected for that task in a letter to his English publisher Bentley shortly passed over into annoyance and even shame that in divesting himself of the *afflatus* of *Mardi* he had betrayed himself.[6] The mixture of his feelings can be gauged in his letter, written on the eve of sailing, to his father-in-law, whom he more usually reassured as to his material prospects as an author:

> no reputation that is gratifying to me, can possibly be achieved by either of these books. They are two *jobs*, which I have done for money – being forced to it, as other men are to sawing wood. And while I have felt obliged to refrain from writing the kind of book I would wish to; yet, in writing these two books, I have not repressed myself much – so far as *they* are concerned; but have spoken pretty much as I feel.[7]

The letter seems to say both that he *had* managed a synthesis of economic and artistic (emotional, spiritual) motives, and that he had *not*. Perhaps it is that while these are not 'the kind of books' he wishes to write, *Redburn* being in the mode of Irving's *Sketch Book*, he has in fact turned the mode to his purpose.

The scales of Melville's estimation of *Redburn* tip finally against the novel, however, on his arrival in London. He sees the English reviews, and despite their favourable notice, writes in his diary that the novel was not worth Blackwood's having 'waste[d] so many pages upon a thing, which I, the author, know to be trash, & wrote it to buy some tobacco with'.[8] A month later Melville wrote Evert Duyckinck that 'I hope I shall never write such a book again', and explained that 'with duns all round him . . . what can you expect of that poor devil [the author] ? – What but a beggarly "Redburn!"'[9] (How odd that Melville admits to more need in a letter, than in his private journal. Was it because his wife would read the journal ?)

Although Melville agreed the sale of *White-Jacket* to Bentley on the very next day (December 15), he 'irrevocably resolved' to return home: he felt he still could not afford to accept the Duke of Rutland's invitation to visit him at Belvoir Castle in January, however 'valuable' the experience would be as literary material:

> here I have before me an open prospect to get some curious ideas of a style of life, which in all probability I shall never have again. I should much like to know what the highest English aristocracy really & practically is. And the Duke of Rutland's cordial invitation to visit him at his Castle furnishes me with just the thing I want. If I do not go, I am confident that hereafter I shall upbraid myself for neglecting such an opportunity of procuring 'material'. And Allan [Melville] & others will account me a ninny.[10]

So perhaps feeling both *Redburn* and himself 'beggarly', on a 'Miserable rainy day', finding 'the British Museum – closed', Melville 'Looked over a lot of ancient maps of London. Bought one (A.D. 1766) for 3 & 6 pence. I want to use it in case I serve up the Revolutionary narrative of the beggar.'[11]

Melville's 1849 journal is filled with the record of publishers' rejections and London doors closed to him. Some doors, like the British Museum above, seem comically but symbolically shut. The comforts of the literary life of London are only minimally, and insufficiently available to him. It is a fitting climax to the sequence that, despite the sale of his novel, he decides he cannot take the 'material' advantage which he imagines the open portal of Belvoir holds for him, and that in the wake of his disappointment comes the first mention of a 'Revolutionary narrative' with a 'beggar' who will find no more reception in England than did Melville himself, and even less than Redburn. And when he did 'serve up' *Israel Potter* in 1854, he reached back to his journal for material reminding him of the blue-black infernal atmosphere of London as it appeared to him in 1849:

> While on one of the Bridges, the thought struck me again that a fine thing might be written about a Blue Monday in November London – a city of Dis (Dante's) – clouds of smoke – the damned &c. – coal barges – coaly waters, cast-iron Duke &c. – its marks are left upon you, &c. &c. &c.[12]

III

Of course the apparent downward spiral in which Melville was enmeshed between the composition of *Redburn* and December 1849, was arrested and reversed dramatically in the next autumn season which saw the recomposition of *Moby-Dick*. The reception of its successor, *Pierre*, however, may have left Melville in a state like that which came after *Mardi*. Once again he turned to the production of the supposedly marketable – this time to sketches and short stories – and once again he found that he could not guarantee his market. It is notable that during the time he thought he might, he dipped into his memory of the few spots of empathy and involvement in London which the 1849 trip had produced. To the theatre and its plebian crowd for 'The Two Temples', rejected because of the likely effect of the American sketch of the two on the pious sensibilities of certain readers. To the 'paradise of bachelors' experienced in that haunting idyll of male companionship. Even to the grossness of the Lord Mayor's banquet, whose 'crumbs' thrown to the poor are supposed to contrast unfavourably with the 'American Gothic' of rural poverty, but in their liveliness do not. Here the need for a qualified 'success', or at least economic survival, seems to have thrown Melville back upon just that literature which he had held to form 'an appendix to Goldsmith', sketches in the vein of the London excursions of Geoffrey Crayon, two of which, incidentally, had been added to the 1848 edition of *The Sketch Book*. In this mode 'Bartleby', though nominally set in lower New York, appears Melville's triumph, its dead-wall blankness owing something to his 1849 perception of London, as does the Dickensian law office of its setting. If it is strange to see reversion to a literary and social mode so categorically set aside in the flush of discovering Hawthorne's transcendence of it, it is noteworthy that the phase which had room for 'The Paradise of Bachelors . . .' could further those mirror-image lessons in *Redburn* by mapping London itself onto New York City.

Israel Potter: His Fifty Years of Exile plays a complex role in this new phase of Melville's career. As a speedily-executed serially-published work, it appears as much 'done for money' as those earlier 'two *jobs*'. *Putnam*'s ran the nine instalments along-side other Melville short tales, many, including the novel, anonymously or pseudonymously presented. Melville had promised to be on his best behaviour (as he had earlier promised Bentley), and to include 'nothing of any sort to shock the fastidious', a clear allusion to the editor's reception of 'The Two Temples'. 'It is adventure', he told Putnam.[13] Only, of course, at the most superficial level. *Israel Potter* is negatively picaresque, its *picaro* an often and progressively deflated figure who is thrust into mischance after mischance – a little like Henderson ('the Rain King') but without his stomach for disaster.

It seems odd on the surface that Melville did not retain the first-person narrative stance of Israel R. Potter's own memoir, the *Life and Remarkable Adventures . . .* of 1824. For in making a 'change in the grammatical person' away from that in which he had cast most of his fiction, Melville obviated the possibility that *his* Potter was a fraud with a story fabricated for gain. The possibility of imposture was an aspect Nathaniel Hawthorne reacted to when, in 'Consular Experiences', the opening section of *Our Old Home* (1863), he alluded to Melville's novel in a catalogue of the extraordinary tales to which he as consul had been obliged to give ear. Yet while the notion of an impostor cadging a passage to America held Hawthorne's attention – as confidence tricksters would shortly engage Melville's – he is even more captured by the idea that the story might be true, in which case 'The poor old fellow's story seemed to me almost as worthy of being chanted in immortal song as that of Odysseus or Evangeline'.[14] By taking the story as true, Melville had written his American mock-epic of Ulyssean wandering.

Hawthorne sketched the basis of his interest: how such an old man, twenty-seven years in England and unable to return to the United States, would lose 'in this long series of years, some of the distinctive characteristics of an American'. This is, however, just the contrary of Melville's equally 'true' American, instant volunteer for Bunker Hill and fired with Revolutionary ardour, who can *never* accommodate himself to his long years of exile. (Hawthorne too saw how his old petitioner's catchphrase, 'If I could only find myself in Ninety-second street, Philadelphia', kept him alive, 'his only locomotive impulse, and perhaps the sole principle of life that kept his blood from actual torpor'. But in a sketch he did not have to face the contradiction of obsession and Anglicisation.)

It is the peculiar tragedy of Melville's Israel Potter that his ingrained democratic instinct cannot accommodate itself to life in the unrevolutionised society. To be more accurate, it appears for a time that his democratic provincialism *is* to be educated into a paradoxical adaptability. If at first he cannot bring himself to address either Sir John Millet or George III (whose gardener he becomes) with their appropriate titles, he soon meets exemplary American heroes whose responses to the manners and arrangements of the Old World are very different. This is one function of the character of Benjamin Franklin which Melville developed from the merest mention in his source, and of John Paul Jones. Each in different ways presents Israel with the spectacle of an American who *can* function 'abroad'. Israel at first exercises a Yankee suspicion of both, Franklin for talking like the common man but arrogating to himself all the advantages of aristocracy, Jones for acting as flamboyantly as any aristocrat, punctilious in modes of address and salutation to nobility. Both win Israel's allegiance, and it seems right that they do so regardless of the 'confidence man' qualities they exhibit. For a time it looks as though Israel, under their tutelage, will actually 'succeed' as spy, patriot, even prisoner on the run. Franklin teaches him to combine suspicion and frankness, and Israel shows an apt pupil when, with secret messages screwed into his boot-heel, he wakes to find his boot being eased off by a fellow passenger. Paul Jones soon secures Israel's whole heart, and the union of the three is sealed when it is Israel who suggests the name of Jones's ship, the *Bon Homme Richard*.

But if the combination of serpent and dove is practically possible in Franklin, 'all over . . . of a piece', 'famous not less for the pastoral simplicity of his manners than for the politic grace of his mind . . . the deep worldly wisdom and polished Italian tact, gleaming under an air of Arcadian unaffectedness', it does not prove sustainable by the common man Israel.[15] If Franklin 'dressed his person as his periods', in 'linsey-woolsey', making his 'tattered wardrobe . . . famous throughout Europe', Israel Potter is forced through an extraordinary series of disguises by the whim of circumstance, sequentially hidden in the garb of a sailor, in the borrowed garments of Sir John Millet, Squire Woodcock, a scarecrow, a farmer, '&c. &c. &c'. John Paul Jones may 'strangely' couple 'regicidal daring . . . with octogenarian prudence . . . this combination of apparent incompatibilities' (ch. 16), but Israel gets few chances. We are soon to see how well Israel has learned his lessons, and of what advantage they are to him.

Accidentally stranded on the British warship Jones has engaged in battle, Israel spends a miserable night trying to avoid capture. It is the beginning of the novel's final phase: Israel is on his own now. Melville consistently uses the language of 'class' to bring home the symbolic – and humorous – import of Israel's inability to ingratiate himself: 'Jealous with the spirit of class, no social circle would receive him' (ch. 20). When even the *waisters*, 'the vilest caste of an armed ship's company, mere dregs and settlings', reject him, Israel has been 'Blackballed out of every club' possible. Finally, attempting to evade the direct questions of the officer-of-the-deck, Israel actually manages so to bemuse the officer as to avoid punishment: he is believed either loony or truthful in his claim not to recall the circumstances of his impressment, in any case a permitted exception. Allowed his freedom, though carried as inexorably into the land of bondage as Nigger Jim on the raft, Israel appears to have passed his first test. What awaits him ashore is his third exemplary 'American' model, Ethan Allen of Ticonderoga.

Allen is what Potter has so far avoided becoming for any period of time, a veritable prisoner in exile. Allen's method of dealing with his captors is stark, reiterated defiance. 'Ragged and handcuffed', refused honourable treatment as a captured officer, he taunts his captors 'with barbaric scorn' (ch. 21). Reminding his gaolers of Fort Ticonderoga at every turn, he brags of his and his 'nation's' heroism and loses no opportunity to denigrate 'Old England'. Despite his bravado, he can speak 'like an Ottoman' to the inquisitive ladies of Falmouth, who note that 'he talks like a beau in a parlour [to them], this wild, mossed American from the woods'. Allen charms the charmers, secures one's hand to kiss in exchange for a lock of matted hair, and eventually gains from her 'a bottle of good wine every day, and clean linen once a week'. Melville emphasises that the

character of Allen, like that of Franklin and Jones, is a 'combination', though perhaps more than theirs a synthesis denoting
the essentially 'American':

> Allen seems to have been a curious combination of a
> Hercules, a Joe Miller, a Bayard, and a Tom Hyer; had a
> person like the Belgian giants; mountain music in him like
> a Swiss; a heart plump as Cœur de Lion's. Though born in
> New England, he exhibited no trace of her character. He
> was frank, bluff, companionable as a Pagan, convivial, a
> Roman, hearty as a harvest. His spirit was essentially
> western; and herein is his particular Americanism; for the
> Western spirit is, or will yet be (for no other is, or can be),
> the true American one. (ch. 22)

In the event, Allen's defiance of his uniformed 'insulters'
mixed with 'Ottoman' courtesy for his British 'kind friends'
(ch. 21), a distinction he consciously and articulately maintains,
proves successful, Melville says:

> by his facetious scorn for scorn, under the extremest suffer-
> ings, he finally wrung repentant usage from his foes; and
> in the end, being liberated from his irons ... in due time, at
> New York [was] honorably included in a regular exchange
> of prisoners. (ch. 22)

The summary truncation of the latter portion of *Israel Potter*
is often remarked. It seems especially odd in the light of Melville's subtitle, 'His Fifty Years of Exile'. So far from seeing
Israel confront his fate at length, armed with the multiple
lessons in democratic conduct he has witnessed, we see only an
immediate and pronounced diminution of his force. His very
first encounter after fleeing imminent seizure at Falmouth
seems to rob him of vigour and intention. Working as a brick-
maker in the only too obviously titled chapter 'Israel in Egypt',

> hardly had he himself been a moulder [of bricks] three
> days, when his previous sedateness of concern at his
> unfortunate lot, began to conform to the reckless sort of
> half jolly despair expressed by the others. . . . 'What
> signifies who we be – dukes or ditchers?' thought the
> moulders: 'all is vanity and clay'. (ch. 23)

The clay-slapping process is an infernal parody of *Moby-Dick*'s
transcendental 'A Squeeze of the Hand' (ch. 94), only it is a
prolonged experience ('thirteen weary weeks'), and it appears

to rivet upon Israel a mood of sardonic hopelessness:

> Sometimes, lading out his dough, Israel could not but bethink him of what seemed enigmatic in his fate. He whom love of country made a hater of her foes – the foreigners among whom he now was thrown – he who, as soldier and sailor, had joined to kill, burn and destroy both them and theirs – here he was at last, serving that very people as a slave. . . . To think that he should be thus helping, with all his strength, to extend the walls of the Thebes of the oppressor, made him half mad. . . . But he drowned the thought by still more recklessly spattering with his ladle: 'What signifies who we be, or where we are, or what we do ? . . . All is vanity and clay'. (ch. 24)

Who can doubt Melville understood the psychology of the prisoner-of-war, the democrat encouraged into simple identifications – not those of his heroic exemplars – whom involvement with the life of the enemy overwhelms and casts into despair. Unprepared for exile 'in the English Egypt', the common democrat cannot rise to any philosophy of solace. Whether symbolically expressed or realistically induced by life in the brickworks, Israel's deflation presents the climax and conclusion of his spiritual career. Melville's stated reluctance to enlarge upon 'what befell Israel during his forty years' wanderings in the London deserts' (ch. 26) is logical because Israel's spiritual life is over. His subsequent existence is presented as posthumous.

Arrived in London, Israel's first sight of the 'City of Dis' (ch. 25) only confirms his despairing state, as Melville employs the emotional nadir of his 1849 diary to set Israel among 'that hereditary crowd – gulf-stream of humanity – which for continuous centuries, has never ceased pouring, like an endless shoal of herring, over London Bridge'. A ghost among those he sees as ghosts, Israel is entering Hell: 'As . . . midway, in a recess of the bridge, Israel surveyed them, various individual aspects all but frighted him . . . [O]ne after the other, they drifted by, uninvoked ghosts in Hades.' F. O. Matthiessen noted how both Melville and T. S. Eliot had reached back to Dante's *Inferno* for visions of London.[16] It is as processions of the Dead that both saw those crowds flowing over London Bridge – 'I had not thought death had undone so many'.

Hawthorne refrained from providing his aged petitioner with

more than alms, perhaps thinking of the end Melville gave
Israel Potter. Hawthorne noted,

> [I] dared not incur the moral responsibility of sending him
> across the sea, at his age, after so many years of exile, when
> the very tradition of him had passed away, to find his
> friends dead, or forgetful, or irretrievably vanished, and the
> whole country become more truly a foreign land to him
> than England was now. . . . In America, nothing awaited
> him but that worst form of disappointment. . . .[17]

In Melville's final chapter, Potter, at last revisiting just such
scenes, chances on 'a half-cord of stout hemlock',

> in a foregoing generation chopped and stacked up on the
> spot, against sledging-time, but . . . by subsequent over-
> sight, abandoned to oblivious decay – type now, as it stood
> there, of forever arrested intentions, and a long life still
> rotting in early mishap. (ch. 28)

Israel had stacked the wood himself. Jay Leyda cited Hawthorne's journal for 7 September 1850, as the source for this
passage, apparently under the impression that Melville was with
Hawthorne when the cut wood was chanced on, and perhaps
heard his reflection about it. In any case, Hawthorne had
reworked his impression into *The Blithedale Romance* (1852),
having Miles Coverdale, his narrator, imagine, on coming
across just such a 'green mound', 'the long-dead woodman, and
his long-dead wife and children, coming out of their chill graves,
and essaying to make a fire with this heap of mossy fuel!'[18]
(Coverdale is projecting his feelings about himself and the
Blithedale 'masqueraders' into his fantasy: it is strongly self-
revealing.) Melville would have been largely familiar, as well,
with the almost innumerable occasions in Hawthorne's fiction
where spiritual failure and displacement are accompanied by
gloom, despair, and feelings of *post mortem* or 'spectral' insub-
stantiality.[19] To be inauthentic, to lose heart, was for Hawthorne
to lose body as well, his central allegorical *topos*.

Melville sustains a funereal and posthumous character for
Potter throughout the final portion of the novel. The last chapter of all is aptly titled 'Requiescat in Pace'. Returned to America
on the anniversary of the birth of its independence, Potter witnesses the celebration from 'a mound in the graveyard', his 'true
"Potter's Field"', gazing towards the 'incipient monument' to

which Melville dedicated the novel. The moment equates the living corpse Potter, the Bunker Hill Monument, and Melville's novel, which the preface deprecatingly called 'something in the light of a dilapidated old tombstone retouched'. In more ways than one was Bunker Hill the tombstone of her native sons.

Melville's novel, like Hawthorne's glum expectation, revises the ending of Irving's 'Rip Van Winkle'. Though more deserving than Rip (who at best slept away the Revolution, but as likely slyly skulked off), Israel is afforded no place in the America to which he at length returns – no role as a licensed chronicler of 'old times' before the War, no solace, no pension. Not only has his democratic perseverance brought him no peace abroad, it is offered no recompense at home. And yet in truth that very perseverance was both the ground of his despair and had modulated into pitiable nostalgia and fantasy, 'a sort of hallucination' of youthful scenes the only 'alleviation' his psyche could create. Even marriage he viewed as an inexplicable hindrance to his plans to return: desperate as his circumstances are, from external causes (usually the ends of wars), there is no doubt he has no ability to make a life for himself where he is.

Having begun with a youth whose attachment to England was frustrated by external causes, Melville passed to reinventing a natural democrat who could not bring himself to function spiritually in that British context when chance thrusts him into it. Israel's failure, in part *personal*, an inflexibility and self-attributed despair, is also symbolic of a national potentiality, a tendency to refuse to be at home other than in the ideal place. The often-remarked and much analysed inability or unwillingness of Americans, American authors, and fictional characters to make a home within society is here made a social comment: the American Potter's inability to accommodate to non-democratic society is fed by his illusion that a life in America would have been wholly different. It was the last lesson that England, with which Melville had such an oblique but involved relationship, had to offer.

Notes and References

1. Debate about the necessity for a break with England in literary life had recently taken a strident tone. 'Our literary delinquency may principally be resolved into our dependence on English literature', wrote Walter Channing in 1815, in the second issue of the *North*

American Review. His essay, with other major documents of the debate on literary nationalism, is reprinted in Robert E. Spiller (ed.), *The American Literary Revolution* (New York: Anchor Books, Doubleday & Co., Inc. 1967). The sentence quoted is on pp. 123-4.

2. Hershel Parker, 'Historical Note', in *Redburn: His First Voyage, The Writings of Herman Melville*, 4, ed. Harrison Hayford, Hershel Parker, and G. Thomas Tanselle (Evanston and Chicago: Northwestern University Press and the Newberry Library 1969) p. 327. All references to *Redburn* are to this edition.

3. Herman Melville, 'Hawthorne and His Mosses', in R. W. B. Lewis (ed.), *Herman Melville* (New York: Dell Publishing Co., Inc. 1962) p. 58.

4. Parker (op. cit., pp. 327-8) notes Evert Duyckinck's diary entry of 31 July 1847: Melville 'is cheerful company [effaced: without being very [?] or original and models his writing evidently a great deal on Washington Irving.]' (Text, including material in square brackets, from Jay Leyda, *The Melville Log* (New York: Harcourt, Brace and Co. 1951) vol. I, p. 253). Melville knew that Irving had looked at *Typee* in proof and expressed what Leon Howard called 'confidence in its success' (*Herman Melville: A Biography* (Berkeley: University of California Press 1951) p. 96).

5. Also by the example of Jackson, the extreme version of the anger and hate Redburn has felt against everyone and everything he experienced as frustrating him.

6. Melville to Richard Bentley, 5 June 1849, *The Letters of Herman Melville*, ed. Merrell R. Davis and William H. Gilman (New Haven: Yale University Press 1960) p. 86. *Redburn* would be 'a plain, straightforward, amusing narrative of personal experience', that of 'the son of a gentleman on his first voyage', with 'no metaphysics, no conic-sections [a reference to *Mardi*], nothing but cakes & ale. . . .' What he writes, says Melville, 'I have almost wholly picked up by my own observations'.

7. Melville to Lemuel Shaw, 6 October 1849, in *Letters*, pp. 91-2. The letter continues, 'Being books, then, written in this way, my only desire for their "success" (as it is called) springs from my pocket, & not from my heart. So far as I am individually concerned, & independent of my pocket, it is my earnest desire to write those sort of books which are said to "fail".'

8. *Journal of a Visit to London and the Continent 1849-1850*, ed. Eleanor Melville Metcalf (London: Cohen & West, Ltd. 1949) p. 20.

9. Melville to Evert Duyckinck, 14 December 1849, in *Letters*, p. 95. The letter continues, 'And when he attempts anything higher – God help him save him! for it is not with a hollow purse as with a hollow balloon – for ⟨any⟩ a hollow purse makes the poet *sink* – witness "Mardi"' (pp. 95-6).

10. *Journal*, p. 64. Entry for 16 December 1849.

11. *Journal*, p. 66. Entry for 18 December 1849. 'Serve up' continues

and climaxes the imagery of food, one of the few positive images in the Journal, and one of the few solaces Melville had in London. Eleanor Melville Metcalf refers to this in her notes, as on p. 110. Here I sense a touch of the surly waiter as well as the calculating chef, Melville being on the serving not the receiving end.

12. *Journal*, p. 22. Entry for 9 November 1849.

13. *Letters*, p. 170.

14. Nathaniel Hawthorne, *Our Old Home*, Centenary Edition, vol. v (Ohio State University Press 1970) pp. 14-15.

15. *Israel Potter: His Fifty Years of Exile*, chapter 8. Since there is as yet no Northwestern-Newberry edition, I will cite all references to this novel only by chapters.

16. F. O. Matthiessen, *American Renaissance* (New York: Oxford University Press 1941) p. 400n.

17. *Our Old Home*, pp. 15

18. Nathaniel Hawthorne, *The Blithedale Romance*, Centenary Edition, vol. III (Ohio State University Press 1964) pp. 211-12. See Leyda, *The Melville Log*, vol. I, p. 394. In his journal Hawthorne 'Imagine[s] the long dead woodman, and his long dead wife and family, and one old man who was a little child when the wood was cut, coming back from their graves, and trying to make a fire with this mossy fuel'. *The American Notebooks*, Centenary Edition, vol. VIII (Ohio State University Press 1972) p. 297.

19. Not only does the assumption of sin in self or others produce this derealising effect, sometimes it is the thrusting or stepping out of place or office which so imperils the self. Contrariwise, Hawthorne can also see the reverse process in images of willed or accidental *return* to substantiality, as when, returned to private life, he feels his consular self to have been 'a sort of Double Ganger' (*Our Old Home*, p. 38).

Moby-Dick:
The Tale and the Telling

I

When Melville's friend, Evert Duyckinck, wrote up *Moby-Dick* as 'a most remarkable sea-dish', a work of 'divine impulses', for *The Literary World* in November 1851, he greeted the book with a degree of acclaim unusual for its time among American readers.[1] To the extent that Duyckinck thought Melville one of the 'nobler spirits', his judgement has proved prophetic. His notice, one of *Moby-Dick*'s first, and therefore obliged to make the critical running, recalls the warm-spiritedness of Melville's own 'Hawthorne and His Mosses', which had appeared in two parts in *The Literary World*'s columns the previous year. In expressing so generously his personal shock of recognition, Duyckinck deserves a respected place in the history of Melville's reputation. Confronted with as daunting and unusual a piece of new fiction as *Moby-Dick*, he showed himself marvellously able to grasp the size of Melville's achievement.

Yet in admiring so keenly, Duyckinck also chose to admonish. His critical sea-legs remained pretty steady and he spoke up with a number of reservations about *Moby-Dick*'s imaginative wholeness and integration. Tale and telling didn't entirely knit. However capacious Melville's imagination, he hadn't freed his narrative of snares and inconsistencies. What was fact, what fiction ? Did the cetology unhinge *Moby-Dick* and make it more an essay than a novel ? Had Melville fully blended his different styles, rhapsodic in one passage, full of 'minute observation' in the next ? These, and Duyckinck's other reservations, managed to anticipate much of the subsequent critical debate about *Moby-Dick*. But their implications for the balance of tale and telling, even yet, haven't been as fully explored as they might. They offer the departure-points for this essay.

Of the things Duyckinck felt 'reluctantly compelled to object

to', his Victorian flinch at the blasphemy of *Moby-Dick*'s conception – 'this piratical running down of creeds and opinions' –
won't long detain a modern reader honed on death-of-God
theology. His comments on *Moby-Dick* as literary form, however, sound at once pertinent and very modern. He writes 'It
becomes impossible to submit such books to a distinct classification as fact, fiction, or essay'. A later age might interpret this as
saying that *Moby-Dick* is a species of nineteenth-century
literary mixed media, an early version of the non-fictional novel,
or what Duyckinck calls 'an intellectual chowder of romance,
philosophy, natural history, fine writing, good feeling, bad sayings'. He speaks, too, of *Moby-Dick*'s 'German melodrama', its
attempted weave of 'the literal perils of the fishery' with 'extravagant daring speculation' and believes Melville too frequently
over-swayed by 'the run-a-muck style of Carlyle'. With a dis-
approving glance back to Melville's third book, he likens *Moby-
Dick* to *Mardi* 'in critical difficulty'. Given that he admired
Moby-Dick's grandeur, Duyckinck was far from writing mere
encomium.

In thinking that *Moby-Dick* lacked 'any distinct classification
of form' Duyckinck showed himself especially far-sighted.
Argument persists as to whether Melville wrote a *novel*, a prose
fiction comparable in kind and social concern with the line begun
by Fielding and Richardson and which evolves into the Great
Tradition of the English novel. Did not Melville rather create a
romance, of the kind adumbrated in the Custom House sketch
of *The Scarlet Letter* and in Hawthorne's other prefaces ? If so,
then *Moby-Dick* calls on a resonantly American narrative form
whose antecedents lie in the fiction of James Fenimore Cooper,
Charles Brockden Brown, and Edgar Allan Poe's *The Narrative
of Arthur Gordon Pym*. Or is *Moby-Dick* more a journal of ideas
than a fiction and only loosely tied to any notion of plot ? In other
words, influences like *The Anatomy of Melancholy* or *Sartor
Resartus* weigh heavier than any novel. And in a related classification, *Moby-Dick* has been thought to reveal Melville as an
encyclopaedist *manqué*. He writes as a not too ancient ex-
mariner home from the whaling grounds and compelled to list
his marvels for an assumedly incredulous wedding-guest reader.
Instead of a plot, an unfolding line of dramatic action, his text
grew into a swollen edifice of facts and catalogues and Whitman-

esque roll-calls. Un-believers, of course, have always argued that *Moby-Dick*'s true classification is that of Gothic. Melville mired himself in melodrama. His replay of the Byronic theme, full of strut and gesture, and enclosed within a fake metaphysics and rhetoric, takes *Moby-Dick* beyond all repair. If, as a narrative form, *Moby-Dick* appears more than most fictions to have resisted categorization, that hasn't, evidently, been to its advantage.

In the half-century since Melville's recovery in the 1920s, even enthusiastic readers of *Moby-Dick*, perhaps better versed than their predecessors in theories of literary genre and in analysing the rhetoric of fiction, have found themselves deflected, or at the very least disturbed, by the narrative's design. Their doubts resemble Duyckinck's. What price Melville's ventriloquism? Do Melville's sleights of hand, his antic digressions, neologisms and jokiness, really work? In essence, did Melville conceive his 'mighty theme' only to botch the telling? For readers who think *Moby-Dick*, in whatever degree, unable to come to imaginative order, even the international testimony of Melville's fellow writers to his story-telling powers – that of D.H.Lawrence, Pavese, Camus and Charles Olson comes strongly to mind – doesn't carry automatic authority.

Furthermore, the massive body of scholarship and exegesis which has accumulated around *Moby-Dick* since Raymond Weaver put together the Constable edition (1922–4) hasn't settled doubts about the knit of Melville's narrative. Much of the recent scholarly clutter and arcana reads like 'painstaking burrowing', to make over Melville's own phrase in 'Extracts'. Much of it doesn't proceed from any genuine critical point of view. The effect of interpretations which see less and less of the whole and which simply peck at the text has been to swell the columns of bibliographical reference and little more.

Obviously all has not been grey. Since the Melville industry got under way in the 1920s, there have been academic studies of profit and flair. Scrutiny of Melville's work habits and his letters, for instance, indices of an almost fevered intensity which seized him throughout 1850 and 1851, has helped in understanding the creative psychology which shaped *Moby-Dick*. Similarly, the copious biographical data, assembled most fully

by Jay Leyda in *The Melville Log* (1951) and by Leon Howard
in *Herman Melville: A Biography* (1951), have made available
in attractive form the means to see Melville in the context of a
life and its times as he wrote *Moby-Dick*. Then too, the compositional sequence of *Moby-Dick*, soon to be set out in detail in
the Northwestern-Newberry edition, a frequent source of
scholarly controversy and fraught with implications for how the
tale is told, has come to be better perceived. No longer can one
assume, all too uncritically, a 'two *Moby-Dicks*' theory of composition. Melville has also had his better critics. A serious
student of *Moby-Dick* wouldn't fail to acknowledge the range
of insights and understandings of the text advanced by names
like Leslie Fiedler, Newton Arvin, Richard Chase, Alfred
Kazin, Warner Berthoff, Ronald Mason, Daniel Hoffman, Leo
Marx, Merlin Bowen, Edgar Dryden, John Seelye and Bruce
Franklin, to offer one eminent post-war list. Further, after the
alarums and vexed first starts of the Constable and Hendricks
House editions, the emergence of a definitive edition under the
Northwestern-Newberry imprint, despite Edmund Wilson's
cavils in *The Fruits of the MLA* (1968), must surely be wel-
comed as evidence of scholarly health.

Scholarship has also borne down usefully on the crucial
impact of Hawthorne and Shakespeare on Melville in the
writing of *Moby-Dick*, debts and affinities which call to mind
the Wordsworth-Coleridge nexus or the T. S. Eliot-Ezra Pound
relationship at the time of 'The Waste Land'. 'Hawthorne And
His Mosses' not only reveals Melville's momentous discovery
of Shakespeare, it throws out important hints about what went
into *Moby-Dick*'s design from Hawthorne's tales. His Ethan
Brand no doubt provided one source for Ahab. But the review
also shows how Melville found himself re-thinking the formal
possibilities and strategies of fiction: emblem, language,
authorial tone. That story continues, in part, in Melville's
celebrated Agatha correspondence with Hawthorne.

Moby-Dick's non-literary sources have also been carefully
mapped. Among others, Howard Vincent in *The Trying-Out of*
Moby Dick (1949) took the measure of *Moby-Dick*'s borrowings
from Owen Chase's *Narrative . . . Of The Whale Ship Essex*
(1821), J. N. Reynolds' 'Mocha Dick' article in *The Knicker-*
bocker (May 1839), as well as the nautical 'ballast' Melville

culled from the naturalists and sea-experts Thomas Beale, William Scoresby Jr., J.Ross Browne and Frederick Bennett. The reader interested in *Moby-Dick*'s tissue of authenticating detail can only profit from reading in these sources. Equally, *Moby-Dick*'s more literary allusions and echoes have largely been traced to source. The overall list is daunting: the Bible, Montaigne, Burton, Milton, Dante, Cervantes, Shakespeare and his English contemporaries, Melville's fellow Victorians Emerson, Carlyle and Dickens, as well as Plato and the tradition of neo-Platonist thinkers. Despite surface appearances as an adventure-story, *Moby-Dick* calls on a wide range of literary antecedent. Both tale and telling in *Moby-Dick* assume a knowledge of, and fascination with, other forms of literature, high and popular.

Of late, it has appeared almost commonplace to see Melville, the Melville of *Moby-Dick* at least, locked inside one or another polemical schema. Since arriving in the classic pantheon of American Literature – Lewis Mumford's Golden Day or F.O. Matthiessen's American Renaissance – he has been a prime target for both the Freudians (Edwin Haviland Miller's recent *Melville: A Biography* (1975) returns to that approach) and Thirties-style Marxists. Critics drawing on insights from anthropology and with stakes in comparative-religious and myth and archetype criticism also have taken aim at *Moby-Dick*. More recently, structuralists of different shades, particularly in France, have sought to 'mathematize' Melville's text in a bid to elucidate its design. They have on occasion found congenial company in numerologists and cryptographers, several anxious to argue Melville's disguised allegiance to cabbalistic and American nineteenth-century masonic cults. More mainstream efforts, to greater critical profit in my view, have sought a pattern to Melville's journey-narratives. How did his earlier 'fictions of fact', *Typee*, *Omoo*, *Mardi*, *Redburn* and *White-Jacket*, prepare a way imaginatively for *Moby-Dick*? Tale and telling go on provoking inquiry.

And so, equally, persist the reservations about *Moby-Dick*'s imaginative means. Despite inventive theses about Melville's overall design and meanings, as well as the considerable source scholarship, he goes on being indicted, or scolded, for being too rhetorical by half, too prone to intrusive set-pieces. Duyckinck's notion of a narrative undecided on what to be – 'fact, fiction, or essay' – in one version or another gets invoked as clear evidence of weakness. By Jamesian criteria of form, Melville is judged a naif. As generally admiring, and discerning, a reader as R. W. B. Lewis, for example, is moved, finally, to write of *Moby-Dick* as 'a spectacular critical failure'.[2]

For those, and I include myself, who think *Moby-Dick* an imperial act of imagining, these charges have a habit of seeming churlish, or at least ungenerous, given the riches of the narrative. But one's pleasure in a narrative like *Moby-Dick* doesn't of itself make for a worked-through argument. *Moby-Dick* isn't free of fault, but I don't think Melville blundered, or even went significantly wrong, in his construction of the tale. However irritating his flaws, they don't make for 'spectacular critical failure'. Why, then, does the narrative imagination of *Moby-Dick* often fail to convince ?

Whichever way one comes at a final estimate of *Moby-Dick*, I suspect that, still, insufficient attention has gone into understanding *how* Melville first proposes to tell, then actually tells, his tale. For as much as *Moby-Dick* offers itself as high epic, it also functions as a wonderfully canny piece of self-knowing narration. Melville, I believe, in considerable degree, anticipated the objections of Duyckinck and his successors, to *Moby-Dick*'s apparent imprecision as literary kind and its allegedly 'run-a-muck' styles of disclosure. For *Moby-Dick* both tells a tale, and in ways which might strike us as radically contemporary, calls attention, throughout its length, to its own conception and modes of self-realization. It asks, in other words, to be thought of as 'a drama done', in the Epilogue's decisive phrase, and to be about the process of telling itself, the process of making a literary fiction. How, then, do these aspects of the book complement and serve each other ?

II

The interplay of tale with telling can usefully be brought into focus by contrasting two quotations. Placed alongside one another, they illuminate the kind of imaginative balance I believe Melville was working for in *Moby-Dick*. The first, from chapter 41, 'Moby Dick', gathers into a few lines the main elements of the tale, a plot-summary of sorts which offers a pause to gather breath, and take stock, amid the exciting sweep of the whale-hunt:

> Here, then, was this grey-headed, ungodly old man, chasing with curses a Job's whale round the world, at the head of a crew, too, made up of mongrel renegades, and castaways, and cannibals . . .[3]

The outward shape of *Moby-Dick* as tale, the contours of the narrative's dramatic action at least, lies precisely in an unfolding tension among these elements. In charting the *Pequod*'s search for the whale, the text of *Moby-Dick* takes us from Ishmael's spirited departure from New England, through Atlantic and Pacific fishing lanes, and into a head-on ritual of ocean search and destruction. Ahab's ungodly captaincy, his mongrel crew whom Melville elsewhere calls 'isolatoes federated along one keel', and the patience-defying white whale, move calculatedly one against the other. Melville's tale, neatly recapitulated in his summary, underpins the design of all *Moby-Dick*'s parts.

And the contours of the hunt round the Cape of Good Hope and on into Pacific waters Melville fills up busily, in almost Homeric fullness. At each turn the reader meets the authentic smack and texture of whaling life. Sea and spray, try-works, blubber, work-tools and songs, the whole powerful and diverse activity of men bound to manage a whaleship as a historic human livelihood, grows and swells at each outward thrust of the *Pequod*. The tale binds and organizes Melville's narrative, not always in an explicit way, but subtly, suggestively. However much Melville makes us wait on, or diverts us, or beguiles us down one corridor of thought then another, the movement forward and out which will bring whaleship into direct clash with the whale, remains palpably there. Gam by gam, ceremony by ceremony, digression by digression, the tale relies upon, and is tied to, the rhythm of the dramatic fable. The tale, despite those who adulate Melville mainly for his 'thought', is never lost. If it grows subdued in *Moby-Dick*'s middle stretches, it encloses the 'thought', being vitally in play at the narrative's beginning and end.

Indeed, as a journey-out, the tale imposes an almost geometric check upon *Moby-Dick*'s metaphoric and philosophical journeys-out. As Melville's telling takes us deeper into the recesses of self and the equivocal realms of myth and language, his basic tale keeps us properly mindful of whaling as a human drama. The chase after this Job's whale, for all its cosmic suggestions, refers us first to human dimensions of risk and challenge. The busyness aboard the *Pequod* is, first of all, *human* busyness, the vitality of men seen first hand by the author at work on a whaleship. In other words, before we can allow the *Pequod* to enter our readerly imaginations as a species of *Flying Dutchman*, a mythy world-ship launched as in dream after world-truths, we need Melville's reminder (issued probably as much to himself as the reader) that this journey-out is indeed the 'WHALING VOYAGE BY ONE ISHMAEL' promised in chapter 1, 'Loomings'. Beguiling as are Melville's ways of telling, especially his enormously playful sleights-of-hand and spirals of wit, the tale as necessary frame for *Moby-Dick*'s larger concerns, stays firmly girdered in place.

In insisting upon Melville's tale in *Moby-Dick*, it is possible to overstress, however. Certain readers, in arguing the strengths of the chase and its spectacular *dénouement*, have found it necessary to censor Melville's telling as over-literary and mannerist. His asides, jokes, the intimacy of tone assumed by the narrative's voices, the nudges and coaxings thrown out to the reader, even the equivocal characters and the objects in their world, come to be thought evidence of an impatient, heated imagination. Melville, runs the argument, couldn't leave his tale alone, but had to fuss and bother. Where *Moby-Dick* speaks in the voice of Carlyleian declamation, or reworked Shakespeare, or the mock-scholar of 'Etymology' or 'Cetology', this ventriloquism depends on means which fail to connect. Melville's telling ill-serves the tale.

For readers who don't take their preference for the tale to these lengths, but who still think the elements which make up the tale best capture Melville's art, he reads at his strongest when evoking an Atlantic sea-port, or developing the rituals and argot of whaling itself. He appeals, by this standard, as the voice of a man of the sea rather than a man of letters. His text is seen to capture the hard press upon muscle and bone of whaling dangers and stress. He writes especially to this kind of admiring readership when depicting the sailing-out, the routines of first catching, then melting down and processing whales for oil.

The world as live business and graft presses close, for instance, when Ishmael signs up for his 'three hundredth lay'. However much Melville renders the scene as an occasion for comedy with Peleg and Bildad, whaling is linked to a wider market system of investments and profit. And even though, in 'Loomings', *Moby-Dick* proposes to take off through 'great flood-gates' into 'a wonder-world' (16) (this passage I shall come back to), Melville's first chapters assure the reader bent primarily upon hearing a sea-tale, that Ishmael ships out from a real enough world of dockside taverns, of men returning, and re-signing, for further ocean voyages. The talk, as given in the sea-stretches of *Moby-Dick*, is thus the talk of a community of workers, of men bound together, often literally, in the experience and crafts of the sea. Their supper is shared clam-chowder; their weapons the harpoon and whaling knife; their chapels the memorials to comrades lost at sea; their art etched on whale-bone and tooth. Against every risk and danger, they ship out time and again into fresh sea-dangers like masons of a given mystery. As a tale, *Moby-Dick* doesn't fail to call on the quick and the living.

Where better does *Moby-Dick* put the felt drama of whaling life onto its pages than in its concluding scenes? From the moment Daggoo shouts 'It is Moby Dick!' (446), one recognizes a coalescing of all the previous elements which have gone into the tale. The tale's outward movement, which begins with the *Pequod*'s departure from Nantucket at the turn of a New Year, and moves through graphic scenes of storm and typhoon, and which embraces Ahab's baptism of the harpoons (ch. 36) and the exuberant three-day chase (ch. 133ff), rises finally to an awesome and utterly organic conclusion. The narrative invites a recollection of Lear facing out the storm on the Heath. Ahab, Melville's nineteenth-century branded Cain, with his Manichean Parsee crew, his *Pequod* isolates and Pip, his Holy Fool, at last faces head on the monster which he has made his secret sharer, the white whale. Melville orchestrates the whale's cunning fury and assault into cathartic high drama. His writing marvellously engraves the vital nervousness of the attacks, the pounding of spray and splintered wood. These final scenes of suicidal hubris – Ahab bent upon puncturing the blank white wall of the whale's forehead – amount to the necessary crescendo of the tale. We can see as a whole the price of Ahab's ignoring the weave of prophecy and omen, especially the nine encounters with other whaling ships, the 'gams', and bear witness, with Ishmael, to the price of so monstrous an impatience. In this powerful last confrontation, the narrative gathers its energies into one. The drama has been seen to be done. We have before us the conclusion of the tale.

III

My second quotation brings up sharply the question of Melville's ways of telling in *Moby-Dick*. In his chapter 'Cetology', he makes considerable play of his difficulties in classifying different whales. In a passage which recalls Duyckinck's worries about *Moby-Dick* as literary kind, he writes:

> It is some systematized exhibition of the whale in his broad genera, that I would fain put before you. Yet it is no easy task. The classification of the constituents of a chaos, nothing less is here essayed. (116-17)

This notion of classifying a chaos, of eliciting patterns of order and sequence from apparent disorder, implies problems of an epistemological and literary scale far greater than the classification of mere whales. Throughout *Moby-Dick*, Melville harnesses his telling to the difficulty of 'classifying' all kinds of facts and objects. *Moby-Dick* makes recurring use of lists, catalogues, systems of language and myth, sermons, affidavits, quotations and prophecies, some mock, others real, which balance off like elements in an intricate mosaic. Just as a catalogue of whales, offered as if they were books, invites contemplation of the ways we fictionalize fact for zoological convenience, so Melville invites his reader to regard his narrative as an extended run of fictionalized facts. *Moby-Dick* offers, in just the way Melville's cetological categories offer, a 'systematized exhibition'. His telling, so richly duplicitous in its means, directs us towards that 'exhibition'.

Throughout *Moby-Dick*, Melville juxtaposes different ways of seeing, different ways of classifying, different ways of telling. He seems to suggest that, like the chaos of the ocean's whale species, the materials of his own book need to be seen through eyes conscious that the means of classifying things changes them. 'Cetology' is not the only section of *Moby-Dick* which shows how difficult it can be to see clearly and whole in the matter of whales. In 'Etymology' and 'Extracts', then later 'The Whiteness of the Whale' (ch. 42) and 'The Honor and Glory of Whaling' (ch. 82), he enlarges on the ways whales have been classified – as biology, semantics, literary imagery and allusion, as religious and classical myth. Melville's telling insists on the partialness of most vision. His narrative relies on telling which, time and again, asks us to reconsider what we think we have seen.

This process of relative definition and mutually poised classification needs emphasizing for it guides us in the ways of Melville's telling. 'Etymology' registers semantic variants and spellings of the word whale. 'Extracts' provides an extensive list of whaling references and tropes. 'Cetology' allows Melville to play naturalist and mock-encyclopaedist. 'The Whiteness of the Whale' amounts to a stunning compendium of myth and colour systems, a *symboliste* tract or poem. 'The Honor and Glory of Whaling' looks for images of the whale in myths of Perseus, St George, Hercules, Jonah and Vishnoo. These 'classifications', when taken with Melville's other whale classifications – in whale songs, choric speculations by the crew, in stories within stories like the *Town-Ho* episode, in the whole run of anecdotes and folkloric and phallic jokes like 'The Cassock', in the references to whale paintings and sculpture (chs 55–7), and in the Homeric and Biblical analogues developed in sequences like 'Knights and Squires' (chs 26–7) – underscore the fictiveness of almost every system of reference in *Moby-Dick*.

Whether classified in lists of different languages, or anatomically as in chapters like 'The Blanket' or 'The Nut', or in the pseudo-book categories of 'Cetology', or through the elusive schemae of different sacred and religious myths, the whale in *Moby-Dick* provides a continuous source of definition.[4] Each of these definitions, of necessity, can be only partial and provisional. By counterposing differing registers of definition, Melville dramatizes how classifications of the whale – and by implication true definitions of Reality – become at once absolute and relative. *Moby-Dick*'s classifications, and the telling which 'exhibits' them, amount to fictions, notes towards an ordering epistemology. So elastic in its telling and in the play of definitions, *Moby-Dick* builds these different fictions of order into a multi-layered whole, a narrative of interlocking and inter-balancing classifications.

Melville tells his tale in such a way that particular classifications which on first view seem stable, or accurate, frequently begin to turn dubious, shape-shifting, suggesting more a *trompe d'oeil* than truth. The white whale itself, for example, *Moby-Dick*'s determining centre and point of reference, Melville depicts as a protean compound of fact and rumour, literal mammalian bulk and at the same time an expression of 'half-formed foetal suggestions' (156). If it swims the sea as the brute monster which has unlimbed Ahab and taken off the arm of Captain Boomer of the *Samuel Enderby*, it swims also as a creature of dream and reverie, the phantom spirit-spout (ch. 51) which so entranced Sophia Hawthorne when she read *Moby-Dick*. The aggregate of all the different attempts at definition, the whale is never finally defined. Even after the destruction of the *Pequod*, its colours and direction of purpose remain as hooded as they were suggested to be in 'Loomings' (Ishmael speaks there of 'a grand hooded phantom' p. 16). Masked and elusive to the end, enclosed as much as ever within myth and superstition, its ropes trail beckoningly for the next Ahab, the next Pierre. Melville's white whale, like Hester Prynne's A, and Poe's raven, functions both as fact and fiction.

If Melville's telling works to make the reader see the tentativeness of classification, it does so especially in respect to the human presences in *Moby-Dick*. The depiction of Queequeg, for instance, is a masterly example of the art of narrative duplicity. Ostensibly a Pacific islander and harpooner, he in 'fact' comes from 'Kokovoko, an island far away to the West and South. It is not down in any map; true places never are' (56). With his War and Peace tomahawk pipe, his chess-board tattoo, his beaver headgear and topsy-turvey way of dressing and washing (34-5), he might just as easily be a Plains Indian, a sea-rover, or a frontiersman. In another view, Ishmael provocatively calls him 'George Washington cannibalistically developed' (52). To Captain Peleg, in a comedy of name-calling, he seems to be 'Hedgehog' or 'Quohog' (84). Later, in his Highlands costume, he can strike the eye as a displaced Scotsman. His paganism out-

Christians the Christianity of New England's true believers, especially when he saves the passenger who has mocked him. His worship of Yojo, his diminutive black phallic god, parallels and comically subverts, the rituals of Ishmael's native Presbyterianism. Melville's telling again works to make us see double.

Queequeg's doubleness, or perhaps multiplicity of identity, re-emerges in his coffin scene (ch. 110). Having had his life-buoy hearse made up by the carpenter, he devotes himself to transforming it into a sacred totem to his own history and culture:

> Many spare hours he spent, in carving the lid with all manner of grotesque figures and drawings; and it seemed that hereby he was striving, in his rude way, to copy parts of the twisted tattooing on his body. And this tattooing, had been the work of a departed prophet and seer of his island, who, by those hieroglyphic marks, had written out on his body a complete theory of the heavens and the earth, and a mystical treatise on the art of attaining truth; so that Queequeg in his own proper person was a riddle to unfold; a wondrous work in one volume; but whose mysteries not even himself could read, though his own live heart beat against them; and these mysteries were therefore destined in the end to moulder away with the living parchment whereon they were inscribed, and so be unsolved to the last. (399)

Queequeg functions as a 'text', a hieroglyphic and polymorphous instance of what, in *The Confidence-Man*, Melville calls 'that multiform pilgrim species, man'. He is 'a wondrous work in one volume', the bearer of 'a mystical treatise on the art of attaining truth', appropriately compositional metaphors for a personified example of the human mystery. As 'living parchment', 'a riddle to unfold', Queequeg embodies the textual spirit of *Moby-Dick* itself.

The process of inviting the reader to see doubly, or in multiples, dilates and extends throughout the narrative. In Fedallah, and his Parsee comrades, the *Pequod*'s crew see ghostly counterparts, shadowy second selves. Fedallah is thought at one point to have a tail. Throughout *Moby-Dick*, Melville develops similarly interlocking tiers of superstition, gloom, things and people half-seen. With Ishmael we stumble into a cloudy vision of Hell at the Black revivalist church, The Trap. Elijah issues masked and equivocal warnings ('Very dim, very dim' p. 91) about Ahab and the *Pequod*. From the plague-laden *Jeroboam* the Shaker prophet Gabriel, an archangel turned manic and shrill, shrieks out his admonitions. The *Jeroboam* is but one of several ships which bear omens of disaster. On the journey-out the *Pequod*'s crew witness fallen speaking trumpets, coffins and hearses, and letters to the dead. The *Pequod* must double as a death-ship (its name is taken from a massacred Algonquian Indian tribe) and a perfectly live ship of fools. In Melville's telling of the tale, night blends mistily into day, things seen in open sea with others seen as nightmare and dream.

Just as the whale, and figures like Queequeg, Fedallah and Elijah, are presented equivocally, so the 'objects' and things which fill out *Moby-Dick*'s imaginative world call on the reader's second sight. For facts in *Moby-Dick* frequently dissolve into fictions. Reciprocally fictions enclose, and function as, facts. 'Nothing exists in itself' (55) says Ishmael lying in bed along-side Queequeg. The observation might easily gloss Melville's way of presenting objects in *Moby-Dick*. Almost all of them are offered in the text in such a way as to suggest larger connections, coiled possibilities of meaning. At one level they give the show of fact and bind down the metaphysics and fantasy of the journey-out. At another, they build into Melville's 'wonder-world', his *symboliste* universe of daring, transcendent affinities. To see Melville's objects whole in *Moby-Dick* needs both the reader's outer and inner eye. The telling, as always, works doubly.

Take, first, the picture encountered in the Spouter Inn. Seemingly of 'unaccountable masses of shades and shadows' (20), it eventually yields the 'meaning' of a whale impaled upon a Cape-Horner during a hurricane. Working through the picture's age-darkened *chiaroscuro*, Ishmael thinks it in turn 'chaos bewitched', 'the Black Sea in a midnight gale', 'the unnatural combat of the four primal elements', 'a blasted heath', 'a Hyperborean winter scene' and 'the breaking-up of the ice-bound stream of time' (20). This remarkable paradigm of per-ceptions, each a vivid act of associative interpretation, con-ditions the reader to a process of seeing. The oil-painting, 'a marvellous painting' (20) and a 'boggy, soggy, squitchy picture truly' (20), in this respect resembles *Moby-Dick* in small. To see the design behind Melville's telling, to hear the full play of his authorial voices, requires vigilant attention, a suppleness of response. Precisely with that in mind Ishmael says of the picture and its meanings:

> in the unequal cross-lights by which you viewed it, it was only by diligent study and a series of systematic visits to it, and careful inquiry of the neighbors, that you could any way arrive at an understanding of its purpose. (20)

It is Melville's telling which has created the need for such 'diligent study' of both picture and text.

The picture also acts to introduce the Spouter Inn, a literal tavern, but also a kind of surreal ante-room to the House of Fiction ahead. With Ishmael inside the Inn, Melville puts before the reader a magic palace décor of whale trophies and 'dusty rarities' (21). The Spouter Inn bears a marked resemblance to Hawthorne's living-room as he describes it in *The Scarlet Letter*'s Custom House sketch. The Inn's eerie atmosphere, its oscillating half-colours and shades, like Hawthorne's room, derives from similar 'magic moonshine'.[5] The Inn, and the room, are both places where facts can turn fictional, where truth can lie, where stories can be situated 'somewhere between the real world and fairyland'. Both the whaling picture, and the Inn, we see through Melville's wholly equivocal, and mediating, telling.

In like manner, the *Pequod* (ch. 16) appears, on first view, 'a thing of trophies' (67), 'a cannibal of a craft' (67). Its eclectic design leads Ishmael to observe 'You may have seen many a quaint craft in your day . . . but you never saw such a rare old craft as this same rare old *Pequod*' (67). Ishmael describes the craft in terms of a French grenadier's complexion, Cologne Cathedral, Icelandic heraldry, an Ethiopian Emperor, a whale ('her unpanelled, open bulwarks were garnished like one continuous jaw') and an Indian outpost (68). Half-whaler, half an anthropomorphic sea-beast, the *Pequod* is made from timber, ropes, whale-bone and sail taken from all parts of the globe, a modern *narrenschiff*. Again, seeing approximates to a process of weaving all the boat's associated possibilities of meaning into a provisional whole.

The list of duplicitous objects runs on, of course, served and glossed by Melville's resourceful telling. Those which stand out haven't wanted for critical attention: the mat woven by Ishmael and Queequeg (ch. 47), one of a cluster of items which call into play an imagery of fibres, lines and stitching and which, in a typical sleight-of-hand, turns into a conceit about Free Will, Fate and Chance; the monkey-rope (ch. 72) binding Ishmael umbilically to Queequeg and a means of illuminating the human nexus; the heads of the Sperm and Right Whales (chs 74–5), Melville's image of Stoicism and Platonism held in equipose; the Fast and Loose Fish (ch. 89) embodying in one angle of vision 'the great globe itself', and in another, the reader of *Moby-Dick*; and the Tranque whale in 'A Bower in the Arsacides' (ch. 102), among several things a tapestry of the weave of Life and Death and a satire on spurious and inefficient ways of measuring and classifying reality.

Most crucially, Melville offers the golden doubloon for contemplation. Of all *Moby-Dick*'s duplicitous objects, the doubloon is perhaps the most important. Melville again organizes his telling to keep the reader alert, receptive to nuance and counterfeit meanings. The doubloon is first nailed up by Ahab as 'the whale's talisman'. Made at the world's meridian in Ecuador, and embossed in the zodiac, yet another classification of the universe, at once the philosopher's stone and a Shield of Achilles, it is also coin of the realm, like all literal money a paradoxically symbolic means of exchange, here useable for the purchase of cigars. Once Ahab and the crew have spoken out their various interpretations – the three mates, Queequeg, Fedallah, the Manxman, et al – Pip, in his gibbering but sane dementia, suggests in an old joke that the coin is 'the ship's navel', the screw which holds everything together. In seeking to unravel the significance of the three hills on the doubloon, topped in turn by a crowing cock, a flame and a tower, the crew can only 'look'. Melville puts before us, in fact, a very zodiac of interpretations: Ahab's solipsistic vision, Starbuck's Christian outlook, Stubb's almanack readings, Flask's comic empiricism, Fedallah's manicheanism, and Queequeg's phallic bafflement. Pip alone is left to conjugate the verb 'to look'.

'Looking' as against 'seeing' – Melville's telling works to point to that essential contrast. The doubloon, like the Black Church,

the 'boggy, soggy, squitchy picture', the spectral Elijah, like
Queequeg and Fedallah, and like the white whale whose talisman it is, cannot yield to the single interpretation. It deceives
any single pair of eyes. Classification again becomes a slippery,
sliding exercise. The crew's looking, but not seeing whole,
underlines once more how an object classified one way, changes
when that classification gives way to another. As if to enact his
own uncertainty principle for the reader, Melville renders each
crew member's perception, absolute in itself, not only as
changing the object of perception, but as contributing to a con-
tinuum of perceptions, each in parallel with, and frequently
countermanding the other. Once more Melville's telling imposes upon the reader the burden of saying what is there to be
seen.

In this regard Ahab's classification of the whale is particularly
instructive. He defines the doubloon solipsistically: 'The firm
tower, that is Ahab; the volcano, that is Ahab; the courageous,
the undaunted, and victorious fowl, that, too, is Ahab; all are
Ahab . . .' (359). His vision of the white whale, just like his way
of regarding the doubloon, defines him. In his pain and delirium,
he has dreamed up his own whale, whatever Moby Dick's
objective reality. That whale, the creature of his Frankenstein-
ian imagining, turns back on him, a nightmare transferred
parasitically from dream to reality. From Fedallah he takes false
comfort about the means of his own death. He believes fiction
(410), confusing it with fact. Like Macbeth committed to the
prophecy of the three witches about Birnam Wood, he goes to
his death tricked by prophecy, following his own Parsee shaman,
roped to the whale, and 'seeing', for the first time, the two hearses
as foretold. The pursued has trapped the pursuer. Fiction has
turned fact and facts have proved fictions. And so, in overall
degree, turns the imagined world as told by Melville in *Moby-
Dick*. Its meanings, locked inside layers of classification or
fictionalized fact, dissemble brilliantly. Just as the tale must be
seen to be done, so the telling requires our closest attentions of
eye and ear.

IV

Where certain readers have overstressed their allegiance to the tale, others overstress an allegiance to Melville's telling in *Moby-Dick*. For these readers, often exercised on the French *nouveau roman* and accompanying formalist theory, as well as on carefully selective readings of post-Modernist American fiction, the telling in itself becomes the be-all and end-all of the text. Melville is confidently appropriated for a prophet of literary post-Modernism, a forerunner of what Richard Poirier has called 'the performing self', a writer in search of 'a world else-where' and obsessed, above all else, with 'pure style'[6] and the sheer possibilities of fabulation. Such readers have to play down the vital density of real things in Melville's narrative, his insistence upon a ground-base of objective and human reality. In despite of this human realm and his literal points-of-departure, the very dimensions of 'ballast' Melville himself insisted upon, his name is bracketed with those of Joyce, Nabokov and Borges as a great anti-mimetic writer. Latterly, Thomas Pynchon, John Barth and William Gaddis have been added to the tally. Melville's fragmentation, real or imagined, is immediately thought worthy of applause. His doublings-back of style and form, the authorial circlings and gyrations, the refusal of an instantly recognizable narrative rhythm, are honoured as anticipating expression of the post-Modern temper. Yet this line of assimilation, and the accompanying admiration for his powers of fabulation and alleged habits of compositional self-display, does considerable injustice to the breadth not only of his own achievement, but that of his 'successors'.

To insist upon either the tale or the telling too emphatically risks responding to Melville's imagination only in part. His extraordinary feat lies in dressing the tale inside the telling. Assuredly, the narrative displays a consciousness of its own devising. This is so whether we settle upon Ishmael as pseudo-nymous narrator speaking in tones which range from whimsey to high seriousness, or upon *Moby-Dick*'s self-referring hints about writing, or upon the interplay of myths and ways of classifying the world which make *Moby-Dick* so treacherously difficult to interpret. Melville's telling encompasses Ishmael's jokes and asides, his buoyant habits of digression and tom-foolery. Right through to the Epilogue, the book remains just that, a book, a self-aware narrative made up of narrator, point of view, a knowing tone, and a full play of equivocation and plural meanings. As a tale, *Moby-Dick* cannot function without its teller. And that teller is Melville, working only in part through his designated spokesman, Ishmael.

And assuredly, also, *Moby-Dick* is no exercise in mere telling, however companionable the feats of authorial voice. For all the resources brought into play in the telling, *Moby-Dick* does indeed function as a 'drama done', or a drama on its way to being done. But, especially once Ahab has entered the story, one can't pretend that *Moby-Dick* amounts wholly to a tale of the whaling fisheries. Each of the cetological chapters has been processed, carefully textured by an awareness of how objects, facts, particulars, might be made over into more metaphoric properties. These sections, like the adventurely elements which make up the dramatic fable, help to convey the physical girth and dimensions of *Moby-Dick*'s world. Their equivocations and ambiguities, however, also serve the deeper meanings of the journey out, the larger implications of the search for the white whale. Thinking of *Moby-Dick* as tale, which undoubtedly needs to be done, doesn't respond in full to Melville's narrative.

In truth, does not the tale in *Moby-Dick* work with, and within, the telling? We listen neither to wholly self-reflexive fiction, nor to wholly objectified narration. Melville uses something of both. My argument would be that, for the purposes of reading and understanding his singular creation, *Moby-Dick*, Melville proposed his own rules and regulations.

In 'Etymology', Melville speaks of the word whale deriving from other words meaning 'rolling' and 'wallowing' (1). He might well have thought *Moby-Dick* a narrative in which meanings and classifications of reality revolve – or roll and wallow – before the reader. The design of the narrative is certainly circular. Tale and telling turn, then re-turn. Just as the chapter 'Cetology' uses books to classify whales, so *Moby-Dick* classifies 'the constituents of a chaos' in a book. Whales can be seen as books, books whales. Would not a narrative of revolving forms and meanings, of revolving facts and fictions, tale and telling, largely by-pass Duyckinck's worry about *Moby-Dick*'s own lack of 'a distinct classification'?

Melville offers a guiding clue to his imaginative procedures in *Moby-Dick*, as pointed as the term 'Inside Narrative', *Billy Budd*'s half-title. In 'The Honor and Glory of Whaling' he

writes: 'There are some enterprises in which a careful disorderliness is the true method' (304). That disorderliness, so
often misconstrued as slackness, but so carefully ordered, I
believe, into the book's 'true method', should be weighed carefully. It locates, with great precision, the relationship of tale
with telling in *Moby-Dick*.

V

To underline and explore that relationship yet further, I need
to consider *Moby-Dick* from two further emphases. Firstly, how
does the reader enter the text? What does Melville actually
create within his 'Etymology'-'Extracts'-'Loomings' axis?
Secondly, is there a pattern to Melville's references to writing,
or at least his consciousness of imagining and shaping 'texts', in
Moby-Dick? What is the impact of constantly being exposed to
such sub-texts?

The authorial presence which signals itself on almost every
page of *Moby-Dick* does so most potently at the very outset of
the tale. In the 'Etymology' component of the 'Etymology'-
'Extracts'-'Loomings' axis, an 'I', possibly an omniscient
narrator, or Ishmael, or a yet other voice, conjures up 'a late
consumptive usher' (1), to provide a list of whale etymologies.
For the most part, they tend to get passed straight over. Do they
bear upon the incoming text, or play no better part than finicky
curtain-raisers to the main event? Taken with 'Extracts' and
'Loomings', they invite the reader, I suggest, to confront *Moby-
Dick* as co-creator with the author, to become an accomplice in
telling the tale and working out the meanings of the journey to
be told. Melville's etymologies yield a beginning set of clues to
his overall methods of narration.

Yet 'Etymology' is not actually the first item in *Moby-Dick*.
In the Hayford-Parker Norton Critical Edition, the most
authoritative text pending issue of the Northwestern-Newberry
Moby-Dick, working from the first English edition of *The
Whale*, the editors include on their title-page Milton's rendering
of Leviathan in *Paradise Lost*:

There Leviathan,
Hugest of living creatures, in the deep
Stretch'd like a promontory sleeps or swims,

And seems a moving land; and at his gills
Draws in, and at his breath spouts out a sea.

Milton's conception of Leviathan relies upon antithetical images: a moving land drawing in, then spouting a sea. The quotation captures vividly enough the living and breathing rhythm of a whale. It also adapts marvellously to *Moby-Dick* as artifact. In a similar rhythmic motion, *Moby-Dick* draws in its eclectic materials, then spouts a text. That assimilative and regurgitative process also yields a sea, more accurately a sea-narrative, of allusion and wide-ranging meanings. (In chapter 85, 'The Fountain', which deals ostensibly with the whale's spout, Melville suggests that the whale's breathing can yield a spout which if approached too closely 'will blind you' p. 313).

From so apt, and suggestive a quotation (it was removed in later American editions of *Moby-Dick*), Melville then moves on, after dedicating the book to Hawthorne and listing his chapter-headings, to 'Etymology', a compendium of whale words as registered through time and space. The list begins with Hebrew, first of tongues, and ends with Erromangoan, a New Hebrides pidgin Melville first makes mention of in *Omoo*.

Our supplier in all this is a now extinct usher, a teacher summoned from the past by the narrator's necromancy, who was 'consumed' precisely by his interest in the grammar of things, that is his interest in the origin of words and meanings and their relationship one to another. In 'seeing him now', Melville, or the narrative 'I', in part creates a *persona* whose 'exhaustion' in having dwelt upon the names of things and having sought to understand how meaning can be expressed, anticipates Ishmael's lonely witness to the quest of Ahab and the *Pequod*. The usher also forewarns the reader that he, too, might risk exhaustion in seeking to understand and express the world's conflicting grammars and etymologies.

A love 'of old lexicons and grammars', emblematizes the love, compulsion might be a better word, of all seekers after definitive explanation of the world's truths and words. The usher's 'queer handkerchief', made up of 'all the gay flags of all the known nations of the world' (1) expresses the universality of this search for truth. Is he not 'reminded of his mortality' precisely by the awareness that universal systems of accurate reference fail to make themselves available ? He seeks to understand the meanings and structure of the world's syntax, and this anticipates Ish-mael's, and by implication our, efforts to classify the realms of non-self and Other. How do we register an understanding of the true syntax and organization of an ambiguous and protean uni-verse ? Does not Melville invite our recognition of an affinity with his emaciated usher, his prototypal Bartleby, dusting and attend-ing grammars in the hope that they encode universal truths ?

The quotation which then follows, from Richard Hackluyt, another species of explorer, confers more warnings upon the reader, and upon anyone who seeks to instruct in truth. He states that in missing out the letter 'h' from the word whale, one 'delivers that which is not true'. The 'h', the sound which aspirates or breathes life into 'whale', if left out, mis-spells a word, but more crucially, leaves out the very life of the creature itself. To enter into a living, breathing relationship with the whale, and with all it embodies – the world and its ambiguous texts – we must learn how to spell accurately. Melville, I take it, is asking whether, in mis-spelling the name of the whale, we understand a metaphor of how we can mis-spell the world and its meanings. Like consumed ushers, are we fated to 'survive' only among fugitive meanings, among words which mis-represent the living vitality of things, which have become dead letters or mis-spelt names ? Are we bound always to issue words and names of 'that which is not true' ? How, indeed, do we find the words of truth ? *Moby-Dick*, at most points in the narrative, directs its energies at the gaps between sign and signal, object and name.

From Hackluyt, Melville turns to two dictionary etymologies of 'whale', first from Webster's, then Richardson's. Both under-score the sense of words only approximating to what they name, to the 'truth' of things. From Webster's we gather that 'this animal is named from roundness or rolling; for in Dan. *hvalt* is arched or vaulted' (1). From Richardson's we learn that 'whale' derives from '*Walw-ian*, to roll, to wallow' (1). The suggestion that a whale embodies high-reaching architecture ('arches' and 'vaults'), and that it 'rolls' and 'wallows', surely bears directly upon the experience of reading *Moby-Dick*. It, too, has a structure of arches and vaults. It, too, rolls and wallows. Its words dazzle, and turn elusive and equivocal. It, too, depicts journeys-out and journeys-in. In Hamlet's words, it too is 'very like a whale', circular in style and movement, unreceptive to firm or absolute definition.

The whale-words which Melville gathers into a list, beginning from the Hebrew and moving through to Erromangoan, make for a further, if somewhat studied, parody of other processes of definition. Even allowing that Melville got some of the originals wrong by error (the Hebrew is slightly askew, as are the Greek and Anglo-Saxon), the point of the list is to mock our expectations of ever assigning exact, or correct, etymologies and words to the whale. As with the picture in the Spouter Inn, or Queequeg's pipe, or the doubloon, as we define the world and its objects, so we define ourselves. We manage, at best, only *approximate* signs for what we wish to signify, for all language works metaphorically. And as we move down the list, from Hebrew to Greek and Latin, and on to modern tongues, through semantic and etymological space as it were, we arrive at 'Erromangoan' whose term for whale is 'Pehee-Nuee-Nuee', a kind of baby-talk (perhaps sounding slightly off-colour to Victorian ears ?) which in its very saying seems to mock efforts at precision. Part of becoming co-partners in securing right names for the whale involves sharing in the larger task of securing a stable, and accurate, nomenclature for all of reality's truths. We are bound, as in all language, to have to compromise with linguistic 'fictions'. *Moby-Dick* provides a narrative frame for such fictions. And it demands our participation and collaboration as readers in both writing the text and eliciting its meanings.

In 'Erromangoan', a name ripe with comic possibility and ambiguity, Melville cites from a language which, though it exists in fact, appears to embody, or at least half-evoke, various possible puns – 'errare-man-go' – for instance. It functions, in part, as a joke-term, a word of play, a gesture at meaning in which meaning has reverted to onomatopoeic sound and little more. For in tracking down the whale, the very centre of *Moby-Dick*, has not Melville launched Ahab and the *Pequod* on a quest to name *all* meanings ? The white whale, especially as evoked in 'The Whiteness of the Whale' (ch. 42), for Ahab, for Ishmael and indeed, for the *Pequod*'s 'Anacharsis Clootz deputation' (108) of mankind, acts as a grand constellation of meanings, none of which in itself can amount to the whole account. 'Etymology' cannot satisfy wholly. Nor can the 'Extracts' which follow. Nor can the meanings imputed to the doubloon, the whale's talisman, by each crew-member in turn. Nor can the mock-scholarly definitions put forward in 'Cetology'. We are left, finally, with the all-colour, no-colour white mass, roped like Ahab to its pulpy and ambiguous meanings. If one side of us goes down with Ahab trapped to the whale's body, demanding absolute truths and absolute definitions and absolute accuracies of word, another part, the Ishmael part, has to settle for something less.[7] Ishmael's survival suggests we settle for more provisional words, that quests for definition be left alone, and that we take our bearings and meanings guardedly inside a vortex (see 470). To an extent, we remain Erromangoans of necessity, 'delivering that which is not true' in all our words. As a writer of fiction, Melville formalizes the condition and invites us to share his fictions of fact.

VI

The 'I' who introduces the 'late consumptive usher' also acts as a 'commentator' on the 'sub-sub-librarian', to whose labours we are indebted, apparently, for 'Extracts'. Yet another explorer of 'what has been promiscuously said, thought, fancied, and sung of Leviathan' (2), he, too, functions as a *persona* through whom the reader becomes involved in further quests for definition of the whale. Like his co-eval, the 'usher', under Melville's guiding pen, he also plays the part of a Bartlebyesque scrivener, a 'poor devil' from a 'hopeless, sallow tribe' of librarians. Just as he does in 'Etymology', Melville invests his sketch of the Sub-Sub with a subtle texture of double-meanings and lexical playfulness, inviting again the imaginative, and equally playful, collaboration of the reader.

Firstly, 'Sub-Sub', another of Melville's echoic or onomato-poeic concoctions, embodies a process of 'diving', going below. One is reminded of Melville's encomium on Emerson, a writer he otherwise thought largely deceived in his deciphering of the world's codes, in a letter to Evert Duyckinck: 'I love all men who *dive*'. This Sub-Sub pre-figures Ishmael, and all others, who think by diving they will secure the truth. For their pains, as Melville says of Emerson in his letter, at best they will re-surface with 'blood shot' eyes.[8] Uncannily, the Sub-Sub might be said to pre-figure Melville himself, also a bookish man and a journeyer through 'the long Vaticans and street-stalls of the earth' (2), also a writer-diver whose assembling of references and allusions 'to please the world' would go largely 'thankless' after *Moby-Dick* was published. As a librarian of sorts, a user and assimilator of others' books at least, Melville foresaw how a writer could be treated as pariah, a 'painstaking burrower' whose burrowings, and their ways of being expressed in fiction, would pass unattended, un-deciphered. The rewards for such a writer, as for the Sub-Sub, by way of belated compensation, might eventually be a heaven of fellow-isolates, Bartlebies finally come to glory, displacing the 'long-pampered Gabriel, Michael, and Raphael' (2).

More important, however, than the *persona* of the Sub-Sub, are Melville's observations on the Extracts themselves: 'You must not, in every case at least, take the higgledy-piggledy whale statements, however authentic, in these extracts, for veritable gospel cetology' (2). If the 'Extracts' amount to 'higgledy-piggledy' statements, just so the text of *Moby-Dick*. Its method of making 'statements' will, also, to a conscious and finely-judged degree, be 'higgledy-piggledy'. When Melville jostles the reader's elbow by terming the whale 'Pehee-Nuee-Nuee' in Erromangoan pidgin, or describes the Spouter Inn whale picture as 'boggy, soggy, squitchy . . . enough to drive a nervous man distracted' (20), or uses Pip to joke about the doubloon as 'the ship's navel' and as a source of conflicting meanings, is he not, quite emphatically, asking for collaboration in the making of definition ? And whatever definitions of the whale we can come up with, singly or in response to Melville's suggestions, are they not, too, bound to be 'higgledy-piggledy' ? Seeing the picture 'truly' almost suggests an impossibility. Art for Melville, and one can draw supporting evidence from chapters 14, 33, and 44 of *The Confidence-Man* (1857), doesn't state truth. Art speaks the truth tentatively, slyly, calling on masks of equivocation and ambiguity. Melville's mature narratives, most especially *The Confidence-Man* itself, the tales he wrote in the 1850s and *Billy Budd*, call just so upon slippery schemes of language and design to convey truth as coiled and equivocal. Melville designed his narratives, at risk of being damned for seeming inconsistencies of form, as 'higgledy-piggledy'.

Moby-Dick doesn't operate, any more than 'Extracts' as 'veritable gospel cetology'. In getting the *Pequod*, and the reader, into confrontation with the whale as a source of meanings and definitions, Melville resorts time and again to 'higgledy-piggledy whale statements'. His narrative method embodies the meaning of his tale. To insist upon unequivocal and seamless narrative, a narrative of things and episodes told as 'gospel', seriously misconstrues *Moby-Dick*'s 'careful disorder'.

The 'Extracts' themselves begin with a reference to Genesis and 'great whales' (2) and end with a reference to 'the rare old Whale', 'King of the boundless sea' (11). The whale swims before the reader in a sea of print – in the Bible, the great travel and exploration narratives, Shakespeare, Milton, Dryden, Natural Histories, Whaling and nautical studies – in volumes as practical as McCulloch's *Commercial Dictionary* (10) and in a volume as elusive as '"Something" unpublished' (10). In that "Something", Melville refers to a 'mystic North-West Passage', a hitherto unrevealed sea-corridor to the whaling grounds. The 'Extracts', like Melville's 'Etymology', offer a sea-corridor into *Moby-Dick*. Seeking out the whale in 'Extracts', through libraries and works of imagination and reference, in dictionaries and travel-books, can act as preparation for seeking out the truths of Melville's own "Something", his own travel and whale-book, *Moby-Dick*. We ship out, as readers, both into the tale and into the telling.

VII

'Call me Ishmael' (12) – Melville's brisk and stirring imperative which opens *Moby-Dick*'s first chapter installs a pseudonymous narrator, *par excellence*. Named for the classic Biblical outcast, and first of a cluster of suggestive Biblical names, his *persona* contributes to the narrative another masked presence, in the line of the consumptive usher and the pale Sub-Sub. Ishmael, from the outset, identifies himself as a man of contraries. Prone on the one hand to the 'hypos' (12), to self-destructive urges, he insists on himself, too, as a species of *homo ludens*. He speaks a language of rich ambivalence, of quick-witted asides. This story, he asserts, will be his story and, so his winkings, beckonings and signals to the reader suggest, ours.

Ishmael's touch is that of the illusionist. Quickly, and with enormous fertility of reference, he offers a world of things seen and seeable. Against sea-scape he invokes landscape. Against pictures of land and prairie, he counterposes water and oceans. For every invitation he issues to envision *things* however, he invites a consciousness of words, of print, rhetorical digression and talk.

Hence, the chapter-title under which he asks to be called Ishmael, appropriately, is called, 'Loomings'. It serves to suggest attempted 'seeing', a perspective ahead of misty foresight. In 'Going Aboard', twenty chapters later, Ishmael says of his arrival at dockside with Queequeg before they board the *Pequod* 'It was nearly six o'clock, but only grey imperfect misty dawn, when we drew nigh the wharf' (90). 'Loomings' also anticipates the loom of words ahead. Loom imagery, allusion to the making of tapestries real and imagined, recurs in the text. The Mat-Weaving scene (ch. 47) offers a crucial instance. The Great Weaver God is referred to several times (as in 'The Bower in the Arsacides' p. 374) and Mapple's Sermon draws on images of 'strands' and 'fibres' to drive home its lesson on Jonah. *Moby-Dick* as a whole makes knowing use of references to stitching, patching, seaming. The force of these allusions and images, which have origins in *Redburn* and *White-Jacket*, lies in alerting the reader to how 'texts', be they sermons, systems of religious myth, acts of advocacy or documentation, or a whaling epic, get 'woven'.

Another implication of Ishmael's opening use of the imperative voice is that so direct a mode of address sets up, immediately, a powerful sense of an 'I' and a 'you'. Just as the monkey-rope binds Ishmael to Queequeg ('an elongated Siamese ligature united us. Queequeg was my own inseparable twin brother' p. 271), so Ishmael tries to bind himself to the reader. Narrator and reader become paired travellers, kinsmen in imagination. Ishmael cajoles, lectures, asks approval and sanction. Whether the tone is breezy, or rueful, or mischievous, he asks – this, or this, is so, isn't it? He tries, almost always, to invite sympathy for his difficulties in telling the tale. In 'The Whiteness of the Whale', he sounds almost plaintive: "But how can I hope to explain myself here; and yet, in some dim, random way, explain myself I must, else all these chapters might be naught' (163). In 'The Advocate' (ch. 24), he assumes the role of professional persuader, a rhetorician, taking his aim directly at his landsman-reader:

> As Queequeg and I are now fairly embarked in this business of whaling; and as this business of whaling has somehow come to be regarded among landsmen as a rather unpoetical and disreputable pursuit; therefore, I am all anxiety to convince ye, ye landsmen, of the injustice hereby done to us hunters of whales. (98)

In 'Loomings', immediately having identified himself, Ishmael creates a lively collage of pictures and images, from vistas of wharfs and coffin-warehouses to rows of men water-gazing, from 'the Prairies in June' (13) to Rockaway Beach (13). Just as landsmen take to the water's edge, compelled to gaze narcissistically into the watery mirrors of truth, so the reader 'takes to sea' with them. Ishmael assumes, almost insists upon, a jointness of interest in casting free of home and land in order to explore ocean selves. His clusters of interlinking imagery – the undulant sea, dreaminess, oceanic longings for travel and self-escape – beckon seductively, or more strongly seek to compel. His way of speaking, at one turn soft and coaxing, at the next garrulous and cheerfully knock-about, invites, even command-eers us into the text. The tale lies ahead. We must participate in the telling.

Ishmael's imperiousness of tone, anticipating his way of speaking in 'The Advocate', is strongly marked in the following passage from 'Loomings':

> What of it, if some old hunks of a sea-captain orders me to get a broom and sweep down the decks? What does that indignity amount to, weighed, I mean, in the scales of the New Testament? Do you think the archangel Gabriel thinks anything the less of me, because I promptly and respectfully obey that old hunks in that particular instance? Who aint a slave? Tell me that. (15)

His questions sound almost rhetorical. They assume an audience but not a voiced set of answers. We are bound to work with Ishmael's imagination, his lines of questioning. His questions assume our interest. We have to loosen up, expect neither entertainment nor instruction, but to work for our literary supper. Each of Ishmael's questions serves to provoke, to invite participation. His puzzlements become ours. His humour and whimsey seek to embrace us. We, too, must make order and meaning of this 'journey-out'. Rather boldly, he makes an early assumption of intimacy when he indulges a sly allusion to human wind, to a fart. 'Head winds are far more prevalent than winds from astern . . .' (15) begins the section. The effect is to test, to make sure we are listening, and yet to make us congenial, to amuse and divert.

In a similar gesture, he invites consideration of how we our-selves might have thought up a tale to tell, and of how it might have been told. He does so through an invitation to 'set type', as it were. He lists three theatre-programme notes, or cosmic newspaper-headlines, the first an 'Election', the second his own 'whaling voyage', the third 'a bloody battle' (16). In a possible echo of Wordsworth deciding in *The Prelude*, Book 1, which story he might narrate, Ishmael decides that 'the invisible police officer of the Fates' (15) commanded him to tell his whaling story. He mocks any idea of representing a 'free' agent. He speaks of 'performing a part', like the actor he in fact is, being manipulated by an invisible author, Herman Melville.

As actor, Ishmael plays his part to the full. He minces, affects, shouts, intimidates, struts, and above all, in 'Loomings', he aims to tantalize. Using language appropriate to a dream-voyage, he summons his reader to join him in visiting places remote and forbidden as well as places of ocean fact '. . . but as for me, I am tormented with an everlasting itch for things remote. I love to sail forbidden seas, and land on barbarous coasts' (16). Ishmael's itch surely becomes the reader's. Who would not be called to forbidden seas, barbary, things remote? Ishmael's travel, however, is also self-travel, the interior journey back into childhood dream and reverie. The reader's physical appetite is aroused; as is his imaginative need for beyondness, for journeying across watery space.

'Loomings' also, as suggested earlier, points to Melville's means of telling the tale of this journey-out. *Moby-Dick* will be woven into being, a double-stranded weave like Mapple's sermon and the *Pequod*'s mats. Not inappropriately, therefore, Melville stuffs both weave and weaving into Ishmael's carpet-bag (the title of chapter 2) as the journey begins for 'Cape Horn and the Pacific' and for imaginative domains far beyond.

We are led, thus, into 'Loomings's' last paragraph:

> By reason of these things, then, the whaling voyage was
> welcome; the great flood-gates of the wonder-world swung
> open, and in the wild conceits that swayed me to my pur-
> pose, two and two there floated into my inmost soul, end-
> less processions of the whale, and, midmost of them all, one
> grand hooded phantom, like a snow hill in the air. (16)

In passing out through 'flood-gates' not merely into the world,
but the 'wonder-world', Ishmael registers the doubleness of the
now begun sea-narrative. At one level, he will leave land aboard
a literal whaler. At the level of 'wonder', his journey will pass
into transcendent worlds of dream and fantasy. His craft and
fellow crew-members are to become argonauts of sea-myth.
Most things and objects in *Moby-Dick* will 'float' before Ishmael,
and through him the reader, 'two and two', especially the hooded
white whale.

Truths in *Moby-Dick* are narrated to play double, to dazzle
and disconcert. They hover behind Melville's deceptive layers
of mask and emblem. If the text ostensibly tells of whaling as
epic adventure, it doubles as a narrative of 'wild conceits' and
'classified' meanings, in all a two-fold and heraldic story.[9] We
listen to the tale, wedding-guests entranced by the composite
Ancient Mariner voice of *Moby-Dick*, but gradually must
assume a part in the responsibility for telling and understanding
the story. Under Melville's rules of the game, the reader plays
map-reader and map-maker. Melville's 'Etymology'-'Extracts'-
'Loomings' so tries to educate the reader in his obligations to
both tale and telling.

VIII

In the Doubloon scene, once Ahab and Starbuck have interpreted the Ecuadorian coin, in a typical Melvilleian transfer of
authorial voice, the narrative is put into the hands of Stubb.
First, he offers his own version of the doubloon and then, in
turn, he glosses each of the other readings. He also makes two
observations on the interpretations unfolding before him which
give concentrated expression to the self-referring quality of
Moby-Dick as a whole. They describe not merely the interpreting of the doubloon, but the way Melville looks to the reader to

collaborate with the writer in making sense of the text. Working from his almanack of 'signs and wonders' (360), Stubb tries to construe for himself the zodiac engravings on the doubloon, only to remark: 'you books must know your places. You'll do to give us the bare words and facts, but we come in to supply the thought' (360–1). And a moment later, as Queequeg is about to look 'to the vicinity of his thigh' for a clue to understanding the doubloon's implied connections between fire and phallus, he observes: 'There's another rendering now; but still one text. All sorts of men in one kind of world, you see' (362).

Moby-Dick, a narrative text woven of many sub-texts, similarly offers its meanings to the reader and invites, in turn, the reader's 'renderings'. The text's words and facts might appear deceptively 'bare', but given Melville's authorial finesse and the collaborative efforts he invites from the reader to 'come in to supply the thought', they knit into larger patterns of organized meaning. These acts of invitation to weave words and sub-texts into an imaginative whole bear directly on how *Moby-Dick* is told.

Moby-Dick alludes to its own provenance in assorted ways, sometimes quite explicitly, at other points through careful innuendo and implication. Throughout the narrative many kinds of text are referred to, some which are crucial to *Moby-Dick*'s internal structure like the two sermons, or the various prophecies, or the 'texts' of the doubloon or the Spouter Inn picture, others which refer more clearly to texts outside the narrative like last wills and testaments, books of nautical law, or missionary tracts of the kind left by Captain Bildad on the *Pequod*. In arguing for Melville's sureness and subtlety of narrative direction in *Moby-Dick*, I think it necessary first to pause over the clearly self-referring passages, then to explore the links of these inside texts with the text as a whole as well as one to another, and finally to consider Melville's references to 'outside' texts which he uses as a further source of allusion and comparison.

IX

The best-known of *Moby-Dick*'s self-referring passages I have already given: 'There are some enterprises in which a careful

disorderliness is the true method' (304). Almost as celebrated is
the opening sentence of chapter 63, 'The Crotch': 'Out of the
trunk, the branches grow; out of them, the twigs. So, in pro-
ductive subjects, grow the chapters' (246). Both observations,
offered as single-sentence paragraphs, bear upon the organic
form, and conception, of *Moby-Dick*. And they might be read
profitably with a string of Melvilleian asides, each also seemingly
made *inter alia*, remarks like the following from 'Cetology':

> My object here is simply to project the draught of a
> systematization of cetology. I am the architect, not the
> builder. (118)

or the notable sentence which concludes the same chapter:

> God keep me from ever completing anything. This whole
> book is but a draught – nay, but the draught of a draught.
> Oh, Time, Strength, Cash, and Patience! (128)

or Melville's way of introducing chapter 45, 'The Affidavit', in
which he tenders 'proof' for his whale-story:

> I care not to perform this part of my task methodically; but
> shall be content to produce the desired impression by
> separate citations of items, practically or reliably known to
> me as a whaleman; and from these citations, I take it – the
> conclusion aimed at will naturally follow of itself. (175)

or his challenge to the reader to decipher the 'text' written on the
whale's 'mystical brow' in chapter 79, 'The Prairie', in which he
says of his own efforts: 'I try all things; I achieve what I can'
(291); or, finally, his wonderfully comic nudge to the reader in
chapter 104, 'The Fossil Whale', about the scope and necessary
formal elasticity of his own narrative:

> One often hears of writers that rise and swell with their
> subject, though it may seem but an ordinary one. How,
> then, with me, writing of this Leviathan? Unconsciously
> my chirography expands into placard capitals. Give me a
> condor's quill! Give me Vesuvius' crater for an inkstand!
> Friends, hold my arms! For in the mere act of penning my
> thoughts of this Leviathan, they weary me, and make me
> faint with their outreaching comprehensiveness of sweep,
> as if to include the whole circle of the sciences, and all the
> generations of whales, men, and mastodons, past, present,
> and to come, with all the revolving panoramas of empire on
> earth, and throughout the whole universe, not excluding

its suburbs. Such, and so magnifying, is the virtue of a
large and liberal theme! We expand to its bulk. To produce
a mighty book, you must choose a mighty theme. (379)

Through these intervening asides and nudges, Melville
nimbly keeps an alert reader up to the mark about *Moby-Dick*'s
ways of telling. They link one to another by their buoyancy,
their authorly intimacy, and by insisting we remember that we
are witnesses to actual composition, to a text under process of
being imagined and told. Far from intruding in unnecessary
fashion, they go to the essence for Melville's telling. They too
serve, and gloss, the tale.[10]

With these asides in mind as a kind of authorial toning of the
narrative, and there are many more than I have listed,[11] one can
move logically to *Moby-Dick*'s allusions to other kinds of
writing and text-making. These, also, bear on the narrative at
large in the manner of intersecting planes within a geometric
construct. Perhaps, first, it should be noticed that *Moby-Dick* is
bounded by two species of sub-text, the 'Etymology'-'Extracts'
sequences which embody multiple ways of definition-making,
and the Epilogue, a peroration deeply encrusted in myth, and
spoken by Ishmael as the sole survivor of an epic quest after
final meanings. Between these textual points of entry and exit,
Melville situates a run of strategically inserted texts-in-small.

As pre-eminent as any are the two sermons preached by
Father Mapple and the *Pequod*'s black cook, Fleece (chs 9 and
64). Each sermon draws on a context purposely suggestive of
larger meanings. Ishmael leads the reader into Mapple's sermon
via three epitaphs, themselves funeral texts, 'bleak tablets' which
are 'steadfastly eyed' by 'silent islands of men and women' under
a 'muffled silence' (39). Inspired by this mortuary, and the
sober reverie about him, and soon to 'eye' his own killer whale,
Ishmael works up a sermon of sorts of his own on the integrity of
the human soul in the face of death, a text woven as much from
bravado as religious conviction.

He then 'reads' Mapple's pulpit, another of Melville's
protean whaling objects. Mounted by a ship-ladder of rope,
prow-like in shape, panelled 'in the likeness of a ship's bluff
bows' (43), the pulpit functions as both ship and lectern. As
usual, in pushing the reader towards a wider sighting than that
which first meets the eye, Ishmael makes an appeal to the trans-

forming powers of imaginative vision. Of the spiritual 'Quebec' (43) enwalling Mapple as he preaches in splendid self-isolation, he observes '. . . it must symbolize something unseen. Can it be, then, that by that act of physical isolation, he signifies his spiritual withdrawal for the time, from all outward worldly ties and connexions?' (43). Of the Bible resting upon a scroll 'fashioned after a ship's fiddle-headed beak' (43), he asks, in similar vein: 'What could be more full of meaning?' (43). This typical coaxing guides the reader to the compounded meanings present in the sermon.

Just as inside the Spouter Inn, Ishmael met with a picture, so the pulpit is backed by 'a large painting', this one 'representing a gallant ship beating against a terrible storm off a lee coast of black rocks and snowy breakers' (43). For Ishmael, it seems clearly an allegory of hope amid ocean peril, although other readings would not only be possible, but appropriate. Relatively, however, it reads clearly compared with the more thickly double-skeined meanings of the sermon.

Mapple works from a text which embodies a 'two-stranded lesson'. The Book of Jonah, 'one of the smallest strands in the mighty cable of the Scriptures' (45), at once 'pregnant' and 'full of meaning', in Mapple's purpose, yields at least two sets of meanings: it provides a language and sea-frame for the sermon appropriate to his audience, and it yields powerful orthodox Calvinist lessons on the nature of 'the living God'. For the narrative at large, however, it supplies strands and echoes which will reverberate throughout. The contrast of Delight with Woe, for instance, points to the meetings of the *Pequod* first with the self-delighted *Bachelor*, then the dolorous *Rachel* and inversely-named *Delight*. Jonah's paradoxical flight into bondage has a parallel in the nature of Ahab's pursuit of his whale. And the story of Jonah's whale metamorphosing into a prison-universe matches in kind the story of *Moby-Dick*'s white whale. Even Mapple's insistence, as the 'annointed pilot-prophet' (50), that the sermoniser never deviate from speaking Truth, is mirrored in Ahab's belief that he alone, a sovereign self *par excellence*, can strike through to Truth's absolute realities. In both its means and its various messages, Father Mapple's sermon offers yet one more double text.

Just so Fleece's address to the sharks in the aftermath of pre-

paring Stubb's whale-steak supper; Fleece is made to preach a
mock-sermon, a parody Sambo piece of black pulpit oratory. In
calling upon the sharks to 'gobern their woracity', Fleece not
only behaves true to his name in fleecing the sermon of its
customary solemnity, he 'acts out', or cooks, his words. He
might indeed be a first shy at Black Guinea of *The Confidence-
Man*. From inside Fleece's 'puttin' on Ole Massa' voice, at least,
Melville plays off injunctions to Christian charity and self-
restraint against a savage, unheeding ocean congregation. The
same kind of parodic energy which feeds into Guinea's 'game of
charity' aboard the *Fidèle*, and into the Liverpool land-shark
scenes of *Redburn*, feeds into Fleece's sermon. Stubb goes on to
tell Fleece to get re-born as a cook, then mocks his vision of a
pentecostal Heaven. His own supper, almost if not quite his
last, suggests a final communion. And Fleece, fed up with the
whole shenanegans, offers a benediction which turns into a
curse, in direct contrast with Mapple's silent blessing. To the
sharks he says: 'Cussed fellow-critters! Kick up de damndest
row as ever you can; fill your dam' bellies till dey bust – and den
die' (252); and to the departing Stubb: 'Wish, by gor! whale eat
him, 'stead of him eat whale. I'm bressed if he ain't more of a
shark dan Massa Shark hisself' (254). The paradoxes are again
plentiful. Cannibalism mixes with communion; charity with
hate; blessings with curses. Sea-sharks lurk inside the human
form. The hunter turns hunted, and the eaten consumes.
Another of Melville's texts-within-a-text speaks doubly.

Moby-Dick's interior sermon-texts are not all laid out at
lengths similar to the addresses by Mapple and Fleece. Yet the
narrative abounds in them. Just as, in chapter 44, 'The Chart',
Melville speaks of the *Pequod*'s pursuing a 'devious zig-zag
world-circle' (174), so his text zig-zags, equally deviously,
through sea-lanes of narrative. Melville's textual self-references,
in effect, act as beacons. They show him at once conscious of,
and firmly in charge of, the imaginative direction of his tale. A
number of such references I have already given, the allusion in
'Loomings', for example, to the three 'theatre-bill' notations
(16), which sets Ishmael's whaling journey amid other possible
tales for the telling. One could re-mention the hieroglyphics
upon Queequeg's body (28–9), and his coffin (399), which
contribute to a constellation of codes, cyphers, systems of

language and myth in *Moby-Dick*.

In chapter 79, 'The Prairie', to develop one notable instance, Melville purports to tackle the whale's 'mystical brow' (292), speaking of its wrinkles as a species of language. His interest moves on to the undecipherability of the human face. And in the transition from whale's brow to human form, he invokes the name of the greatest of Sanskrit and Asiatic scholars:

> If then, Sir William Jones, who read in thirty languages, could not read the simplest peasant's face in its profounder and more subtle meanings, how may unlettered Ishmael hope to read the awful Chaldee of the Sperm whale's brow? I put that brow before you. Read it if you can. (292–3)

Reading the brow, reading 'Erromangoan', or 'Chaldee', or the simplest peasant's face, again underscores Melville's belief in the plural lines of meaning extractable from any given text. It bears very directly upon how we read the fictional languages, and 'inside' texts, of *Moby-Dick*. The reader picks up a challenge to read the brow in rather the way he accepts the challenge of *Moby-Dick* as narrative.

X

As with Melville's whaling 'objects' and 'inside' texts, the list of seemingly 'outside' texts referred to in *Moby-Dick* runs to great length and variety. Captain Bildad, as the *Pequod* is about to sail, fumbles in his pockets to produce 'a bundle of tracts' (85), richly comic pieces of preachment given the context, especially when handed to an uncomprehending Queequeg, tracts which proffer only a single register of truth, here Calvinist. In fact, they smack of the same double-talk which marks Captain Bildad's farewell text to the crew: 'Don't whale it too much a' Lord's days, men; but don't miss a fair chance either, that's rejecting Heaven's good gifts' (96). To equally unheeded effect as these tracts and farewell speeches are the Isaac Watts hymnals left at each berth by Aunt Charity. If the *Pequod*'s owners attempt to speak in the register of a single truth, Elijah, to be followed by Gabriel and Fedallah, by contrast, issue polymorphous prophecies, which Ishmael glosses as 'ambiguous, half-hinting, half-revealing, shrouded sort of talk' (88), and in which meanings turn inside out and 'very dim' (91). In another textual feint, in 'Cetology', Melville borrows a catalogue system of Folios, Octavos and Duodecimos to classify his whales, sea-creatures expressed as textual hierarchy (120).

Similarly, the reader is referred to diaries, particularly Owen Chase's in 'The Affidavit'; to last testaments as in chapter 49 'The Hyena', perhaps the most sardonic chapter in *Moby-Dick* in which Ishmael writes a will to the ironically silent, sly, howl of the hyena at his whaling fate; to the sacred texts of Vishnoo, Eastern Books of Revelation (306) which match *Moby-Dick*'s ample references to the Western Judaeo-Christian Testaments; to treatises, whether on genealogy as in 'Etymology' (1) and chapter 82, 'The Honor and Glory of Whaling', or sea-law as in chapter 89, 'Fast Fish and Loose Fish', or of a more jocular cast like Ishmael's 'little treatise on Eternity' (313), or his treatise on royal fish in chapter 90, 'Heads or Tails', where the humour re-plays the sexual double-talk of 'The Cassock'. Melville also takes several comic digs at the treatises of William Scoresby, especially in chapter 65, 'The Whale as a Dish', chapter 92, 'Ambergris', and chapter 101, 'The Decanter'. Another treatise, on 'the art of attaining truth', is thought by Ishmael to lie inside the hieroglyphics of Queequeg's coffin (399).

Tracts, prophecies, catalogues, diaries, Holy Writ, treatises, affidavits, volumes of law and genealogy, all act as variations of text. Others from *Moby-Dick* can easily be added: almanacks of the kind used by Stubb to interpret the language of the zodiac engraved on the doubloon (360); dissertations, especially chapter 104 'The Fossil Whale', where Melville explicitly terms Leviathan a 'text' (378) and asserts that the whale can only properly be 'treated of in imperial folio' (378); baptisms, not least Ahab's crucial 'Ego non baptizo . . .' (404); cryptic messages as in the reference to the Book of Daniel's 'Mene, Mene, Tekel, Upharsin' (415); oaths, especially those extracted by Ahab from the crew; and the new dictionary entries proposed by Melville, 'gam' (206–7), 'quoin' (286) and 'gallied' (322), single-word texts now available for use in future narratives. One might further invoke Melville's false textual authorities (*Moby-Dick* has no shortage of legitimate authorities): the 'old writer' who composed a commentary on Euroclydon and 'of whose works I possess the only copy extant' (19); 'my late royal friend

Tranquo, king of Tranque, one of the Arsacides' (373), the
literary custodian of a South Seas museum whose prize exhibit
is a whale skeleton; and the figures Melville invents in the image
of William Scoresby, author of *Journal of a Voyage to the
Northern Whale Fishery* (1823), among other books, and at
whom *Moby-Dick* takes frequent satiric aim, Captain Sleet,
Fogo Von Slack, Dr Snodhead and Zogranda. *Moby-Dick* uses
each and all of these textual elements as species of imaginative
self-referencing. They can give the reader, especially if taken
up in the playful spirit offered, ways of seeing how the overall
text incorporates, and subtly marks its own literary kind by,
lesser-scale textual allusion. To one degree or another, like the
'inside texts', they signal *Moby-Dick*'s imaginative habits as
narrative, and enact, in small, the telling of the larger tale.

XI

In arguing for the sophistication of Melville's telling in *Moby-
Dick*, one further habit deserves an emphasis, that is his awareness of how the transmission of a text can alter its meaning and
feel. Three examples, in ascending order of seriousness, will
underline the point. In 'A Bower in the Arsacides', Melville's
chapter-length satire on 'admeasurement' of the whale, he
rounds out his observations with the following:

> The skeleton dimensions I shall . . . set down are copied
> verbatim from my right arm, where I had them tattooed;
> as in my wild wanderings at that period, there was no other
> secure way of preserving such valuable statistics. But as I
> was crowded for space, and wished the other parts of my
> body to remain a blank page for a poem I was then com-
> posing – at least, what untattooed parts might remain – I
> did not trouble myself with the odd inches; nor, indeed,
> should inches at all enter into a congenial admeasurement
> of the whale. (376)

Apart from the evident good humour of this paragraph, it says
a good deal about the process of bringing a text into being. The
author's body, as it were, absorbs facts, registers them at levels
beyond the visceral, then keeps them engraved in outline upon
pulse and skin. In the matter of measuring, or telling of, this
particular Tranque Leviathan from the Arsacides, Ishmael

reinvokes the sight from 'rough notes' tattooed upon his right arm. His text thus tells literally of himself as much as the whale, the end-product of a mode of transmission which might cause the reader to think upon what is being tattooed into his own awareness.

In the Doubloon scene (ch. 99), the narration begins in Ishmael's voice, reporting in sequence the voices of Ahab, Starbuck, then Stubb. He, in turn, assumes charge of the unfolding tableau, and reports the responses to the coin of Flask, then the Manxman, Queequeg, Fedallah and Pip, glossing each as it is spoken. Melville thus creates a composite layering of voices and interpretations, a weave of response and commentary. The doubloon's possibilities of meaning are shown to rise and accrete with each interpreting consciousness, and to extend out even further, in the commentary first of Ishmael, then Stubb. The reader, in his turn, will bring one more level of commentary to the whole talismanic operation. If the doubloon is one of *Moby-Dick*'s vital 'inside' texts, its 'telling', also, speaks vitally to *Moby-Dick*'s overall telling.

In chapter 54, 'The Town-Ho', Melville again offers an 'inside' narrative, almost explicitly so, since it was printed as a separate story in *Harper's New Monthly Magazine* (October 1851), and in two other journals, as *Moby-Dick* was coming from the press. The *Town-Ho*'s tale of Radney, Steelkilt and the white whale is 'inside' to the extent that it tells one story within *Moby-Dick*'s larger story, but also 'inside' in that it is kept from Ahab and the mates, thereby heightening the suspense of the *Pequod*'s approaching final catastrophe. Its mode of transmission again bears directly upon the telling-at-large of *Moby-Dick*.

The *Town-Ho*, named for a whaling cry, is homeward bound, in direct contrast with the *Pequod*, still upon a journey-out. Its story of meeting the whale, and of Steelkilt's insurrection and the demise of Radney, not only provides another 'gam' text (the second in fact of the nine), it begins as 'the private property' (208) of three white sailors, 'confederated' with an otherwise Polynesian crew, who tell it to Tashtego to oaths of secrecy. He, in turn, rambles in his sleep, 'and revealed so much of it in that way, that when he was wakened he could not well withhold the rest' (208). From there, Ishmael reassumes the narrative, offering this cryptic comment on the story's double meanings: 'Interweaving in its proper place this darker thread with the story as publicly narrated on the ship, the whole of this strange affair I now proceed to put on lasting record' (208).

Ishmael, 'for my humor sake' (208), retells the 'lasting record' of the story as he once rendered it to 'a lounging circle of Spanish friends' (208) in The Golden Inn at Lima. His telling thus passes the story to yet one further tier of narrative 'inside-ness'. In the course of the telling, he is interrupted a half-dozen times, asked to define words like 'Lakeman' (209) and 'Canal-lers' (214), to listen to jibes about priests, sin, Venice and Lima (214–15), a body of associations Melville returns to powerfully in 'Benito Cereno', and to receive encouragements of drink and applause as the story builds to a conclusion. Finally, he feels moved to appeal to an ultimate text in proving the truthfulness of his tale. He swears upon 'a copy of the Holy Evangelists' (224), a sacramental and duplicitous swearing, in effect, to the truth of yet another of Melville's inside fictions. Transmitting a text, 'telling' as it were, plays an equal part with the tale in hand. The Town-Ho's story embodies telling, in imaginative liveliness and subtlety of kind, which reflects, once more, the telling of Moby-Dick at large.

XII

Having begun with Evert Duyckinck's remarks on Moby-Dick, I want to return to his Literary World review. From the outset, Duyckinck detected a double-weave in Moby-Dick, but believed it for the most part a weakness. He felt, as have many succeeding critics, that Melville hadn't blended tale with telling, that Moby-Dick was two, if not three, books unevenly rolled into one. 'Vivid narration', 'strong powers', 'freshness of perception', even Melville's 'divine impulses', he was prepared to allow, but he couldn't bring himself to think Moby-Dick an imaginative whole.

In refocussing attention on Moby-Dick's 'vivid narration', my contention has been that Melville didn't cavalierly plunge into his tale, but tried for telling which, by its flexibility and utterly careful disorderliness, routed most seeming by-paths back into a central narrative track. Melville's telling reveals a conscious maker of narrative, but not one self-conscious to the point of empty mannerism. His *tale* reveals an author who knew the human compass first-hand, and only from there was prepared to step boldly towards metaphysics and beyondness.

Tale and telling, if not undeviatingly put to the service of one another in *Moby-Dick*, blend and intertwine sufficiently to rescue the book from often routine charges of failure in formal wholeness. When Melville wrote to Hawthorne proposing he work up the Agatha materials into a new story, he spoke of 'a skeleton of actual reality to build about with fulness & veins & beauty'.[12] The phrase offers a wholly appropriate gauge for *Moby-Dick*. Clearly, it doesn't want for 'actual reality' or 'fulness'. Its beauty, doubtless, will remain a relative perception. But the 'veins' in *Moby-Dick*, 'built about' with such canny purpose and skill, if the line of my considerations in this essay has been at all apt, are what make it imaginatively the larger sum of both tale and telling.

Notes and References

1. Evert A. Duyckinck: 'Melville's *Moby-Dick; or The Whale*', New York *Literary World* (two notices), 15 November and 22 November 1851. In thinking Duyckinck anticipated the terms of *Moby-Dick*'s subsequent reputation, I have relied on Hugh W. Hetherington: *Melville's Reviewers British and American 1846-1891* (University of North Carolina Press 1961) and two collections of critical reviews: Hershel Parker (ed.) *The Recognition of Herman Melville* (University of Michigan Press 1967) and Hershel Parker and Harrison Hayford (eds) *Moby-Dick as Doubloon* (New York 1970). I would like to express my gratitude to the Newberry Library for a Summer Fellowship while writing this essay. I also owe great thanks to the following: Professors Harrison Hayford and Walter B. Scott of Northwestern University, Mr Brian Higgins of the University of Illinois, Mr Henry Claridge of the University of Kent and Dr Bernard Mosher.

2. *Herman Melville: Stories, Poems and Letters* (New York: Dell Publishing Company 1967) introduction p. 7. I should add that Mr Lewis's introduction is one I greatly admire.

3. *Moby-Dick*, Norton Critical Edition, ed. Harrison Hayford and Hershel Parker (New York 1967) p. 162. All quotations and references are to this edition. Unless otherwise stated references are to page.

4. In an introduction to the Everyman Edition of *Moby-Dick* (London: J. M. Dent & Sons 1975) p. xii, I have suggested that 'The whale, which is *Moby-Dick*'s central and organizing point of reference, is not the symbol of any one thing – death, American

capitalism, evil have been the most commonly ventured – but a reflection of the many, often competing, meanings we project upon the world.'

5. *The Scarlet Letter*, Centenary Edition (Ohio State University Press 1962) p. 36.

6. I am borrowing terms from two books by Richard Poirier here: *A World Elsewhere: The Place of Style in American Literature* (New York: Oxford University Press 1966) and *The Performing Self: Compositions and Decompositions in the Languages of Contemporary Life* (New York: Oxford University Press 1971).

7. Alfred Kazin, in an introduction to *Israel Potter* (New York: Warner Books 1974), writes: 'Melville's heroes are mostly himself under various disguises (he was complicated enough to be both Ishmael and Ahab) . . .' p. 5.

8. Letter to Evert Duyckinck, 3 March 1849, in *The Letters of Herman Melville*, ed. Merrell R. Davis and William H. Gilman (New Haven: Yale University Press 1960) p. 79.

9. Lawrence Durrell in *The Alexandrian Quartet* (1957-60) develops an interestingly similar preoccupation with a heraldic universe.

10. An article which touches on a number of the issues raised in this essay is Edward Rosenberry: '*Moby-Dick*, Epic Romance', *College Literature*, vol. II, no. 3 (Fall 1975) pp. 155-70, especially section VI. Mr Rosenberry's insights into what he calls Melville's 'analogical technique' strike me as eminently just, but I don't agree with his view that 'Melville talks often and at length about his "mighty theme" in *Moby-Dick*, but only twice, in short, isolated sentences, does he allude to the structure of his book' (p. 169).

11. One general comment Melville offers on the kind of vision he is seeking to embody in the telling of *Moby-Dick* appears in chapter 85, 'The Fountain': 'My dear sir, in this world it is not so easy to settle these plain things. I have ever found your plain things the knottiest of all' (p. 312).

12. Letter to Hawthorne, 13 August 1852, in *The Letters of Herman Melville*, p. 157.

Unnecessary Duplicates:
A Key to the Writing of *Moby-Dick*

THE lock contains no key. Hearing him foolishly fumbling there, the Captain laughs lowly to himself. Chap. 9.

I

Melville introduces the *Pequod*'s carpenter by remarking that
if you seat yourself 'sultanically' among the moons of Saturn
'high abstracted man alone' seems 'a wonder, a grandeur, and
a woe' but that from the same viewpoint 'mankind in mass' for
the most part seem 'a mob of unnecessary duplicates' (ch. 107).
Something of the same sort can be said about two such ways of
looking at *Moby-Dick*. From an integrative critical viewpoint
the book gives a unified impression of wonder, grandeur, and
tragic woe. But on close scrutiny many of its compositional
elements seem, in ordinary fictional terms, to be 'a mob of
unnecessary duplicates'. You could call both views 'sultanically'
elevated, since each is way outside any view mundane readers
are likely to take of the book. In this essay I am going, arbitrarily
enough, to disregard the integrative view and take the second
way of looking at it. First I'll point out the curious pattern of
duplicates I see in it, and then I'll go on to use this pattern as
evidence for a major hypothesis I'll offer about Melville's shift-
ing intentions for some of the central characters in *Moby-Dick*
as it developed through several phases during the year and a half
he was writing it. I believe these duplicates give us a new key, to
add to the several we already have, to fumble with (let's hope
not altogether foolishly) as we keep trying to open some of the
interlocked complications of the book's genesis, to which there
is no master key we know of.

Duplicates begin at once. It takes not one but two chapters to
do the narrative job of getting Ishmael started out to see the
watery part of the world on his first whaling voyage. Chapter 1

loses narrative headway after its third sentence, so that chapter 2 must duplicate its job and start him again, as he stuffs a shirt or two in his bag and sets out for a whaling port, New Bedford. But at once there's another duplicate; he tells us he won't sail from that first port but from a second, Nantucket. Moreover, since at New Bedford he misses the Nantucket boat and it's Saturday night he must spend not one but two nights and the intervening Sunday there, getting no closer to a whaleship. The job of the rest of chapter 2 is to deal with his problem of finding an inn. Presumably the inn, like the whole chapter, serves the book's larger fictional purpose of illustrating the whaleman's world as a tyro encounters it; but presenting two whaling ports entails presenting two inns – duplicates breed duplicates. Why need we be shown the whaleman's shore life via *two* inns, one at New Bedford run by an officious humorous landlord, and a second at Nantucket run by an officious humourless landlady? Seeking a suitable inn, Ishmael passes up a couple of 'too expensive and jolly' ones and blunders into and out of a Negro church before he manages to select the Spouter-Inn.

The first of the two problems in the Spouter-Inn (ch. 3) is for Ishmael to find a sleeping-place there. And he finds duplicates, not one place but two, and goes to bed twice, first on a cold narrow bench alone, then in a warm prodigious bed with a harpooneer bedfellow. Why both?

The chapter's second problem is the larger narrative job of introducing an experienced whaleman to become tyro Ishmael's comrade and probably also his mentor in 'this business of whaling'. But the chapter proceeds to introduce not one but two such characters, first Bulkington, then Queequeg – duplicates. Bulkington enters the inn with the *Grampus* crew, just landed from a three years' whaling voyage; he is a 'huge favorite' with the crew and evidently an experienced whaleman. Ishmael describes Bulkington, he says, because he'll be a shipmate – only to explain in an immediate parenthesis and metaphor that he won't: 'This man interested me at once; and since the sea-gods had ordained that he should soon become my shipmate (though but a sleeping-partner one, so far as this narrative is concerned), I will here venture upon a little description of him.' After a portentous description of Bulkington in romantic-heroic terms he is said to slip away unobserved, and we are told 'I saw no more of him till he became my comrade on the sea'. The word 'comrade' applied to Bulkington here is a noteworthy one; it postulates a special personal relationship transcending that of a mere 'shipmate', and later in the book Ishmael applies the word in the singular to only one man, not to Bulkington but to Queequeg (chs 13, 18, 72). At once Bulkington slips away, is missing from the following shore chapters, is seen once more as the ship puts out to sea, and then is altogether absent from the book. Thus he sets a pattern of 'hiding out' that is to be duplicated by several characters who are themselves duplicates. But, oddly, the bulk of chapter 3 is then given over to the spun-out practical-joke introduction of a duplicate comrade.

This duplicate is a second experienced whaleman, a harpooneer, who is missing (a second 'hide out') until near the chapter's end; there, after 'second thoughts' on the part of both landlord and Ishmael, he's accepted as the tyro's literal 'sleeping-partner' that Saturday night. And in the course of Sunday evening, after Ishmael sallies out twice, first for a morning sightseeing stroll then to visit the Whaleman's Chapel and hear Father Mapple's sermon, Queequeg further becomes Ishmael's 'bosom-friend' and is a second time his sleeping-partner. He resolves to accompany Ishmael on his whaling voyage and share his every hap. Ishmael tells us, 'To all this I joyously assented; for besides the affection I now felt for Queequeg, he was an experienced harpooneer, and as such, could not fail to be of great usefulness to one, who, like me, was wholly ignorant of the mysteries of whaling . . .' (chs 4–12).

Monday morning, in chapter 13, Ishmael sets off with Queequeg – 'my comrade' as he twice calls him – for Nantucket, to the second whaling port, second inn, second dominating keeper, and even two chowders. The next problem, in chapter 16, is for them to choose a ship and sign aboard. Ishmael had 'not a little relied upon Queequeg's sagacity to point out the whaler best fitted' for their voyage, and certainly Queequeg's novelistic job, as experienced-whaleman mentor, should be to 'be of great usefulness'. Nevertheless, he declares he can't do so, reassigns the job to his little god Yojo, and 'hides out' a second time. Consequently, since he doesn't accompany Ishmael to the docks, not one but two signing-aboard scenes must be presented, first one for Ishmael then another for

Queequeg; that is, duplicate chapters (16, 18) must be devoted to business that might have been economically accomplished in a single one.

So tyro Ishmael goes alone and himself decides on the *Pequod* – or duplicates Yojo's pre-decision. In chapter 16, 'The Ship', in which he does so, duplications continue. First, there are duplications with respect to the ship herself. For some of the *Pequod*'s attractive peculiarities are specified here in particulars that are later to be negated by discrepant duplicate specifications. Here, for example, she's said to have 'unpanelled, open bulwarks' all round; but later, off the Cape of Good Hope, the crew seek shelter from the heavy seas 'along the bulwarks in the waist', which must, therefore, be panelled ones (ch. 51), Here, again (as in chapters 96, 123) she's said to sport instead of a turnstile wheel 'a tiller . . . curiously carved from the long narrow lower jaw of her hereditary foe'; but twice later she's given a wheel with spokes (chs 61, 118).

Besides these minor duplications in the ship's details, there are at once major duplicates among characters associated with her, notably in her having not one but three 'captains'. For as Ishmael first goes aboard the *Pequod*, who's in charge ? Not, as might be expected, just one agent, owner, or captain to sign him on, but two – both retired Quaker captains who are also the two chief owners, Peleg and Bildad. And – though it's old Captain Peleg who has served for years on the Indian-named ship, who sits in a 'wigwam' of whalebone on her deck, and who has, we're told, done the curious whalebone carving work that dresses her in 'barbaric' apparel – it turns out to be not Peleg but still a third duplicate old Quaker captain, Ahab, who is to be her actual captain in command on the upcoming voyage and who (not Peleg) possesses the most striking piece of whalebone carving, a 'barbaric white leg' which 'had at sea been fashioned from the polished bone of the sperm whale's jaw' (ch. 28). But this third duplicate captain is not to be seen until days after the ship sails; he's said to be sick (like Bulkington and Queequeg he 'hides out'), and so his appearance will require a later separate chapter (ch. 28). The two old Quaker captains who do appear in chapter 16, Peleg and Bildad, so overlap in fictional uses that they may seem to be duplicates as indistinguishable as Rosenkranz and Guildenstern, though they are given individualizing peculiarities. Peleg is a profane 'blusterer' while Bildad is a quiet, pious canter who solemnly declares his fear that impenitent Peleg's leaky conscience will sink him 'foundering down to the fiery pit'. Peleg angrily rejects Bildad's prophecy, rephrasing it in plain English: 'Fiery pit! fiery pit! ye insult me, man; past all natural bearing, ye insult me. It's an all-fired outrage to tell any human creature that he's bound to hell'. But, as it turns out, it is not the first captain, Peleg, with his mild everyday profanities, but the third captain, Ahab, with his outraged sense of the insults and indignities heaped upon the human creature, and with his major blasphemies, who is the one indeed 'bound to hell' and who drives the *Pequod* and all her crew (save one) to 'sink to hell' (ch. 135).

And very soon further duplications of characters follow, centering upon the role of prophet of Ahab's fate. Bildad's prophecy here in chapter 16 makes him the first of seven duplicate prophets, all of whom take up in their various direct or indirect ways the burden of Christian Bildad's initial prediction of a profane captain's hell-bound career (though not Peleg's, it turns out, but Ahab's). After Bildad, these prophets are, in order, three who are introduced ashore – 'the old squaw, Tistig, at Gay-head' (ch. 16); an old sailor, Elijah (chs 19, 21); the Parsee Fedallah (who's hiding out in chapter 21); and two more who are introduced at sea, upon Ahab's first appearance, in chapter 28: 'Tashtego's senior, an old Gay-Head Indian among the crew', and 'a grey Manxman . . ., an old sepulchral man'. To these six prophets closely associated with Ahab on shore or ship can be added a seventh encountered on another ship, the crazy Shaker Gabriel, who also warns Ahab to 'beware of the blasphemer's end!' and prophesies, 'thou art soon going that way' (ch. 71).

Among these prophets along Ahab's hell-bound route the most curiously conspicuous duplicates are three Gay-Head Indians (the book uses the place name in several forms as quoted here). The first, the old squaw Tistig, is followed in prophetic role by the old Gay-Head Indian crewman, 'Tashtego's senior', and both of these Gay-Headers know circumstances of Ahab's birth and speak portentously about his career. The old crewman appears only once, and two of the three items of Ahab's history he gives out are later contradicted by discrepant duplicate information: 'Aye, he was dismasted off Japan,' he volunteers, 'but like his dismasted craft, he shipped another mast without coming home for it. He has a quiver of 'em' – whereas later it's established that it was on the equator (and not off Japan) that Moby Dick took off Ahab's leg (ch. 130), and also shown that Ahab has no quiver of extras but must order a new one to be made by the carpenter when his original one is wrenched (chs 106, 108). This old Indian crewman, 'Tashtego's senior', never reappears, but his prophetic role is duplicated by Tashtego, 'an unmixed Indian from Gay Head' (ch. 27) who is prominent as one of the *Pequod*'s three pagan harpooneers. 'To look at the tawny brawn of his lithe snaky limbs, you would almost have credited the superstitions of some of the earlier Puritans, and half believed this wild Indian to be a son of the Prince of the Powers of the Air' (ch. 27). It is Tashtego, this third Gay-Head Indian, who at the masthead sights and sings out for the *Pequod*'s first whale and in doing so is described as like a prophet or seer:

> High aloft in the cross-trees was that mad Gay-Header, Tashtego. . . . As he stood hovering over you half suspended in air, so wildly and eagerly peering towards the horizon, you would have thought him some prophet or seer beholding the shadows of Fate, and by those wild cries announcing their coming. (ch. 47)

Months later, when Moby Dick is sighted for the first time, it is Tashtego again at the masthead who 'saw him at almost the same instant that Captain Ahab did' and cried out – just missing award of the doubloon (ch. 133). And on the final day, in the moments of Ahab's fated end when the unanimous prophecy of all these duplicate prophets is fulfilled, it is for some reason the red Indian Tashtego who at Ahab's command is nailing Ahab's red flag of no-surrender to the mast of the fated *Pequod* during the moments when she must 'sink to hell' (ch. 135).

As for the other two prophets introduced ashore before the ship sails, Elijah, though 'crazy', is a true prophet, an 'old sailor chap' who has sailed under Ahab and calls him 'Old Thunder'; he reveals to Ishmael and Queequeg some hints of Ahab's character and history, and warns them of the soul-peril of shipping on the *Pequod* – 'that ship' – with him. Elijah also hints the existence of Ahab's false prophet-companion,

Fedallah, the Parsee of vague East Indian or else devilish origin, whom Ahab smuggles aboard along with his oriental four-man duplicate boat-crew, to 'hide out' below until the first lowering (ch. 48). Why all these seven duplicate prophets?

At long last chapter 22 gets the *Pequod* hauled out from the Nantucket wharf. The twenty-one shore chapters have already taken up about a fifth of the book – surely a disproportionate share – before the whaling voyage begins, before Ishmael sees anything of the watery part of the world, before the book's tragic protagonist appears, and before its plot and Ahab's mighty antagonist are revealed. There have been two narrative starts, two whaling ports, two inns (and two chowders), two innkeepers, two beds and goings-to-bed, two comrades (one dismissed already), two signings-aboard, two Quaker captain-owners and a third Quaker captain-in-command, four (of an eventual seven) prophets, four hide-outs, and an extra boat-crew. No wonder it has taken so much space, with so much duplication already! Did Melville think the book itself had to be stocked with duplicates just as the *Pequod* had to be provided with 'spare boats, spare spars, and spare lines and harpoons, and spare everythings, almost, but a spare Captain and duplicate ship'? (ch. 20).

Nor does this space-demanding pattern of duplicates cease when the ship has left the wharf. As the *Pequod* is worked out of Nantucket harbour into the open sea, not just one pilot but two are aboard. What need two? Again it is those two old Quaker owner-captains (the ship's commanding Quaker captain, Ahab, still hides out in his cabin); both of them are 'going it with a high hand on the quarter-deck, just as if they were to be joint-commanders at sea, as well as to all appearances in port'. Captain Peleg's first order is one that Captain Ahab significantly duplicates fourteen chapters later, to open the 'Quarter-Deck' scene (ch. 36). Peleg's is an order that by usage a captain would give his mate soon after such a ship got under way – 'Call all hands, then. Muster 'em aft here. . . .' This order customarily initiated one or two routines neither of which follows Peleg's order here. On an actual voyage the crew thus mustered aft might be harangued by the captain, who would lay down the purpose of the voyage, the crew's duties, and his own policies; and the mates would choose up men for their watches. (For accounts see Melville's own *Redburn*, or R. H. Dana's *Two Years Before the Mast*, J. N. Reynolds' 'Mocha Dick', and J. Ross Browne's *Etchings of a Whaling Cruise* – works Melville knew and used in writing *Moby-Dick*.) In *Moby-Dick*, however, the all-hands sequence does not get played out normally but is curiously split in two after the duplicate orders in chapters 22 and 36. Profane Captain Peleg (standing in here for Captain Ahab) begins it with his first order to the mate, 'Well, call all hands, then. Muster 'em aft here – blast 'em!' But Peleg, it turns out, doesn't want them all aft for either of the usual routines just mentioned; no, what he wants done there by the 'sons of bachelors' is only to have his whalebone tent struck – scarcely a duty requiring all hands. Apparently something went askew in Peleg's – or Melville's – orders. (Peleg's next order, however, is a proper one, actually requiring all hands, though for duty forward not aft: 'Man the capstan! Blood and thunder! – jump!' This is the order to raise the anchor, an order, indeed, that normally came *before* the order to muster, lest the crew might sober up and desert before the ship got under way.) On the *Pequod*, Captain Ahab's duplicate muster order comes after the ship has been at sea for many days, with the mates and crew doing their regular duties, though, as was just pointed out, no account of choosing up watches (indeed nothing in detail about deck or forecastle life at all) has been given before Captain Ahab, at last out of hiding, appears above hatches (ch. 28). When Ahab 'impulsively' orders the mate to send everybody aft, Starbuck is said to be 'astonished at an order seldom or never given on ship-board except in some extraordinary case' (chs 46, 36). True enough, at *that* stage of a voyage. But what then ensues on the quarterdeck is, in form, one part of the long-overdue normal follow-up of Peleg's order days ago – the captain's harangue to the crew about the voyage's purpose and his own policies – though in *content*, as Starbuck sees and the narrator tells us, Ahab's 'prime but private purpose', is a mad usurpation of any proper purpose and policy. In sum, Melville has his duplicate captains give duplicate muster orders; Peleg's is too early (in harbour) and is not followed by either customary routine; while Ahab's is fourteen chapters too late (at sea) and is followed by a customary but subverted routine. It's as if Ahab took up right where Peleg left off.

And this duplication of orders is not the only or most significant duplication that occurs in the Christmas-day departure
chapter. While profane Peleg rips and swears astern at the crew
'in the most frightful manner', Ishmael pauses in his efforts at
the capstan forward to think of the perils he and Queequeg are
running 'in starting on the voyage with such a devil for a pilot' –
though even a tyro whaleman should realize that a *pilot*, soon
to go ashore, could offer them no peril on the voyage itself. Then
Ishmael feels a 'sudden sharp poke in my rear' and is horrified
to see Captain Peleg 'withdrawing his leg' from 'my immediate
vicinity'. And he remarks, 'That was my first kick'. Yes, but it's
not the first we've heard of Peleg's leg, or the last we'll hear of a
kick from a captain. There's in fact some confused duplication
of legs and kicks on the *Pequod*. Already in the first signing-
aboard scene (ch. 16) Peleg has for some reason called Ishmael's
special attention to his leg though apparently it's just a normal
leg, Ahab's being the only remarkable one, of whalebone:
'Dost see that leg? – I'll take that leg away from thy stern, if ever
thou talkest of the marchant service to me again.' So sure
enough, though for another offence, here at up-anchor time
Peleg does kick Ishmael with 'that leg'. It's Ishmael's 'first kick',
as he says; and, though this expression implies more kicks, it's
also his last kick and indeed anybody's last actual kick of the
voyage, apart from those Peleg gives in 'using his leg very
freely' as the anchor is being raised. Yet, more kicks and kicking
soon do follow, but only in a reported dream, including a dream-
kick from a captain with a more noteworthy leg than Peleg's.
The recipient this time is not Ishmael (a common sailor) but
Stubb (an officer – who sounds like a duplicate of the Ishmael of
chapter 1) in his 'Queen Mab' dream of his own kicking a
pyramid, of being invited to kick a merman's marlinspike-
bristling rump, and of having been kicked by Ahab's ivory leg,
and in his wide-awake rationalizing of his wisdom in not kicking
back (ch. 31). Duplicate legs-and-kicking galore!

In the course of chapter 22 the *Pequod* at last gains an offing
in the wintry Atlantic, and the duplicate pilot-captains (the
swearing-kicking fearsome Quaker 'devil' Peleg with 'that leg'
and the pious Quaker prophet Bildad) both say their reluctant
farewells to the ship and both drop into the pilot boat to go
ashore, leaving the third and still hidden-out duplicate Quaker

captain, the soon-to-be-revealed Satanic Ahab, in command for the voyage.

The *Pequod* is at sea. But the book's duplicative treatment of three central and closely related novelistic jobs still confronts us with questions we might suppose Melville should have settled by this point. These are questions as to its narrator and narrative point-of-view, its protagonist or hero, and the over-all shape of its narrative line – its action or plot. For each of these questions, however, we have already been offered, or are about to be given, several duplicate answers. Nor do duplications of other kinds cease in the sea chapters. I'll leave readers the pleasure of compiling their own lists. Some duplicates are not obvious but no one will overlook the series of deaths and averted near-deaths (I think of it as the 'man-overboard' pattern); or the closely related series of rescues and redeemings by Queequeg already begun ashore; or the series of ship-meetings, sometimes miscalled gams; or the *Pequod*'s final three-day trio of encounters with tragic-hero Ahab's great antagonist; or the duplicate names of that antagonist, the 'White Whale' some call 'Moby Dick'; or the book's own successive duplicate titles, *The Whale* and *Moby-Dick*. But the ones I have just listed in the shore-narrative – taken with the sea-narrative matters they implicate – already give me more duplicates than I can deal with in this essay. As a key, they give me enough, as I try to account for them, to give rise to my major hypothesis about a part of the genetic history of some of the book's characters.

II

Among the duplicate characters, Bulkington and Queequeg are the best pair to begin with, because it's so obvious which of them came first, and because our seeing the compositional ways Melville handled this pair leads us on, by a somewhat devious path, to see the ways he handled the other major duplicate characters, and thus to my major hypothesis. My line of reasoning about the composition stages is simple enough, but since it has to work backwards from what's in the printed book to earlier inferred stages, it will be easier to follow if I list the stages here by numbers and use them all along in my discussion. I provisionally distinguish three stages through which Melville's shore-narrative must have gone – I mean just with respect to this pair of alternate comrades, not to its whole writing history. Stage 1 included neither Bulkington nor Queequeg; Stage 2 added Bulkington; Stage 3 dismissed Bulkington and added Queequeg, ending up as the version printed. All three probably included substages.

In the finished book, Bulkington, unlike any of the other duplicate characters, sticks out as vestigial because in the two early passages that he enters (chs 3, 23) he is assigned the dual roles of comrade and truth-seeker, but is not developed later in either role; indeed, in both passages Melville explicitly dismisses him from appearing in any role at all in the ensuing narrative. The explanation of this anomalous assignment-dismissal procedure must be that two compositional stages are involved in the passages as they stand, that at the earlier (Stage 2) Melville intended him to play these roles but then at the later (Stage 3) changed his intention and revised the passages to dismiss him from both roles, yet for some reason did not discard him, or the passages, altogether.

Not only is Bulkington vestigial, he is one of our duplicates – in chapter 3 he and Queequeg pair in the one-man role of narrator's comrade. Again, the explanation must be that two composition stages are involved. Bulkington must have been either Melville's earlier or his later intended choice for the comrade role; and it is easy to see that he was earlier (Stage 2) than Queequeg, since it was he whom Melville (Stage 3) dismissed and Queequeg whom he kept and developed in this and other chapters.

So far I've distinguished Stages 2 and 3 and in a moment I'll distinguish the still earlier Stage 1, at which Melville had not yet got around to assigning the narrator any companion at all. First, however, I want to look more closely at Stage 2, to see what Melville did and didn't have in his shore-narrative about these two characters at that time. We have just seen that in it Bulkington, not Queequeg, was to be the narrator's comrade; so Bulkington was there, but we must infer that Queequeg wasn't. Bulkington was there, presumably, in only the same two passages he occupies in chapters 3 and 23 of the book – meaning those passages as they stood before Melville made the later (Stage 3) revisions by which he dismissed him, from one of them by the curious 'sleeping-partner' parenthesis, and from the other by the two-and-a-half new or recast paragraphs in which he managed both to bury and to praise him.

Well then, at Stage 2, as in the book, Bulkington entered the shore-narrative in the four-paragraph episode in which the narrator reports his coming into the Spouter-Inn with the *Grampus* crew, describes him (because he later became a ship-mate), and says he slipped out pursued by the crew and wasn't seen again by the narrator 'till he became my comrade on the sea'. That last clause tells us Bulkington left the shore-narrative then and there and played no further part in it; and I see no good reason to suppose he ever did so. But what about Bulkington at sea? Had Melville already written – or did he later write – any passages for him there? I mean, aside from his standing at the helm (in Stage 2, as now) when the *Pequod* thrust off. Of course he now doesn't appear in the sea-narrative, and so far I can identify only one passage I think Melville wrote for him in it. But I can see further passages Melville *may* have written for him; and I have my major hypothesis to offer in due course about Melville's intentions, when I take up what I believe he did at Stage 3 with the two roles he had assigned at Stage 2 to Bulkington as comrade and as truth-seeker.

Let me regress from Stage 2 for a moment to distinguish Stage 1, the earliest narrative stage I infer from the duplicates I am considering here. In Stage 1, I infer that Melville had in hand a first-person shore-narrative in which Bulkington played no part at all. In it, Melville had evidently not yet assigned his narrator a comrade for the voyage (and possibly not yet the name Ishmael). Since Queequeg, as we've seen, wasn't yet present in Stage 2, he can't have been in this earlier stage either. Bulkington's absence at Stage 1 is inferred from the two compositional procedures by which, in the four-paragraph *Grampus*-crew episode, Melville simultaneously introduced him into and got him right off the Spouter-Inn scene. Clearly, Melville (at Stage 2) inserted that episode into an already-written sequence (first procedure). It is detachable, unintegrated with anything that precedes or follows, a patch designed to introduce Bulkington as the narrator's prospective comrade (though the dramatic whaling-life vignette that encapsules him yields a surplus illustrative value). At the same time, the transparent purpose

served by Melville's ending it with Bulkington's disappearance
and the narrator's statement (second procedure) that 'I saw no
more of him till he became my comrade on the sea' (i.e. with
what I've called Bulkington's 'hiding out') was to spare Melville
the necessity of incorporating Bulkington more thoroughly into
his existing shore-narrative (of Stage 1). Furthermore, that
second compositional procedure seems to me to explain the
pattern of 'hide outs' by duplicate characters to which I have
called attention: of Bulkington, Queequeg, Ahab, and Fedallah
with his boat-crew. Each of them, I am saying, was occasioned
by Melville's procedure of inserting the character at an early
point (or points) into an already-written narrative, and by his
then sparing himself the revisional work of writing the character
into further passages of that existing narrative by instead supply-
ing some rationalization for the character's not appearing in it
but in effect 'hiding out'. Sometimes, however, Melville chose
(notably in the case of Queequeg) to write and insert entirely
new passages about the character. I believe some of the book's
most awkward anomalies were induced and some of its best
passages inspired in just these ways.

Now I return to the matter of Queequeg's absence from
Stage 2 and of what its lean narrative was like then without him;
after that I'll go on to the meatier matter of just how much more
was involved when Melville was introducing and developing
him at Stage 3.

As readers of *Moby-Dick* we may not care much that the
vestigial Bulkington was no more important in the Stage 2 shore
scenes than he is now; but as readers we do care a great deal
about Queequeg, so long known to us in his central, even
indispensable, role that we assume Melville must have conceived him as the narrator's comrade from the time he first set
pen to paper to write the book. So it's startling to realize, following my line of reasoning, that at Stage 2 Queequeg can't have
played any part at all in the shore-narrative. The reason he can't
have done so is that his *only* shore role even now is the integral
one of narrator's comrade – the role which at that stage Melville
had assigned to Bulkington. Well, what can that Stage 2 narrative have been like without him? Can it have stood in anything
like its printed form without the extended passages in which
Queequeg is so important? Surprisingly, it can, though much

abridged. For the most part we can excise him simply by bracketing whatever involves him. (That is to say, conversely, during Stage 3 Melville inserted whatever now involves him, with very little *rewriting*, though a fair amount of new writing, including several new chapters.) And to me at least, the excision of Queequeg from the shore-chapters seems to demonstrate that the curious pattern of duplicates did result, as I'm suggesting, from separate composition stages. For with that excision many of the duplicates in these chapters disappear: the two comrades, two sleeping places (and 'second thoughts'), two signing-aboard scenes – each of these pairs shrinks to a single member. Not only do these duplications disappear, but, of course, so do the wonderful Queequeg matters that swell the number of shore-narrative passages so disproportionately before the narrator finally gets to sea.

Let's follow the book's shore chapters in detail to see what was and wasn't there at Stage 2, judging simply by what's left after excision of the Queequeg (Stage 3) materials. In the Stage 2 Spouter-Inn passage (now in chapter 3) Melville solved each of its two narrative problems – of a sleeping-place and a comrade – only once, not twice (by duplicates) as at Stage 3. When the narrator asked Peter Coffin for a room the landlord simply told him there was 'not a bed unoccupied'. The narrator responded, 'I'll try the bench here'. And after a supper in an adjoining room cold as Iceland, and the landlord's futile attempt to plane the bench smooth, he spent a drafty night on it, in the winter cold that afflicts him throughout the shore and early sea chapters. So much for the sleeping problem. At Stage 2 Melville handled the second problem more simply. He supplied a comrade by inserting the four-paragraph irruption of the *Grampus* crew with the momentary glimpse it gave the narrator of Bulkington, his comrade-to-be, who slipped away leaving him companionless for the rest of the shore-narrative, to reappear at the *Pequod*'s helm in a scene presumably written at Stage 2.

What our excision of Queequeg reveals as not yet present at Stage 2 is of course – besides Queequeg himself – what's now the warm comic heart of the Spouter-Inn chapter, the whole business set off by the landlord's 'second thoughts' practical joke of offering tyro Ishmael half of a harpooneer's blanket. That is, Ishmael's own series of 'second thoughts' – first reluctantly agreeing, then changing his mind and trying the bench, then changing his mind again and consenting to share the harpooneer's bed, then his strange meeting and sensible accept-ance of the cannibal, followed by his warm night's sleep. All this, it would seem, was Melville's brilliant comic elaboration by which he wrote the 'hidden-out' Queequeg into the bare Stage 2 narrative he had written earlier for his cold and alienated narrator.

Next morning, at Stage 2, the companionless narrator woke up, breakfasted alone, and strolled alone to see the New Bedford street sights; perhaps he sallied out again to the Chapel alone, as the sky 'changed from clear, sunny cold, to driving sleet and mist', to hear Father Mapple's sermon alone, like the other solitary worshippers. (But more likely the duplicate sally, the Chapel and sermon episode, was inserted at Stage 3.) The only important Stage 3 Queequeg matter that this sequence (now in chapters 4–9) lacked was the whole of chapter 4, where Ishmael wakes up caught in the 'comical predicament' of his sleeping-partner's 'bridegroom clasp', and Queequeg dresses first in his own outlandish way. Elsewhere Melville brought Queequeg into the sequence with only slight revisions and minor insertions: in the first three paragraphs and the last one of chapter 5; in the discrepant reference to him in the first sentence of chapter 6; and in the three adjacent sentences in chapter 7 that briefly and rather implausibly bring the pagan (who's 'given up' on Christians) into the Chapel.

In the remaining shore-narrative at Stage 2, the narrator sailed to Nantucket alone, stayed and ate alone at Mrs Hussey's, signed aboard the *Pequod* alone (as he now does). He encoun-tered Elijah alone. And he sailed alone. A possibility I cannot pursue here is suggested by some of the duplicates I have pointed out: the two whaling ports, two inns, two innkeepers. Perhaps at a very early stage the narrator went to and sailed from only one port, New Bedford. Bulkington's appearing there then popping up on a Nantucket ship might suggest this. But it's an intricate problem. Can the ship – or its earlier duplicate – with all or any of its duplicate captains have at first been from New Bedford? Similarly, can the duplicate prophet Elijah (whose Biblical name, at least, seems dependent on Ahab) have been generated somewhere in the process that induced Ahab's series of prophets ? As I have remarked, there were probably substages within the three stages I have needed to distinguish here, perhaps other major stages as well.

As from earlier chapters, Queequeg can be readily excised from the present chapters 10–21. Since he is undetachably central to chapters 10, 11, 12, where his bosom-friendship with Ishmael develops, these chapters belong to Stage 3. The same is true of much of chapter 13, 'Wheelbarrow', with Queequeg's anecdote in comparative anthropology and his rescue of the bumpkin, though its paragraphs 5, 6, and part of 7 may have been part of the Stage 1 narrative. Chapter 14, 'Nantucket', has no reference to Queequeg (nor does it have the narrative mode or dramatized first-person narrator after its first sentence, and in this, like its twin chapter 6 on New Bedford, it anticipates the imminent fictional truancy of the companions). Queequeg is easily removed from chapter 15, 'Chowder', by bracketing a few phrases and sentences, changing the first-person plural pronouns to singular, and cutting out the byplay with Mrs Hussey about his harpoon. The sequence of chapters 16–18 shows Melville engaging in a compositional procedure we've already observed. I think he already had written at Stage 1 the scene of the narrator's signing aboard the *Pequod*. Rather than revise it to include Queequeg, what he did, I think, was to write a new passage (the first two and a half paragraphs of chapter 16) in which he provided reasons why Queequeg could not 'be of great usefulness' and choose their ship as he should do in his role of experienced-whaleman mentor: Queequeg assigns Yojo that job and also 'hides out' (a second time) for his 24-hour Ramadan. This procedure kept him out of chapter 16, where Melville might have managed to have him too sign aboard; and it motivated the two fine new comic chapters 17–18, about Queequeg's Ramadan and signing-aboard. From chapters 19–22, Queequeg is again easily removed by cutting out or changing the few words here and there by which Melville (at Stage 3) established his presence. The thematic common denominator of Melville's additions occasioned by his introduction of Queequeg is the contrast of savage and civilized, pagan and Christian; their cumulative effect is an eclectic enrichment of the religious dimensions of the book's world.

So much for the lean narrative of Stage 2 and the startling but

negative matter of Queequeg's absence from it. Now I'll move
further into the positive matter of just how much more was
involved for his central characters while Melville was introducing Queequeg into Bulkington's vacated place as Ishmael's
comrade at Stage 3. Above, I called this a 'meatier' matter; and
so it was, because it was part of a larger process in which Melville
was doing far more than fleshing out the then lean shore-
narrative by importing an exotic new comrade and the newly-
written passages about him which were not present at Stage 2,
when even Bulkington was barely there.

III

The larger process in which Melville was engaged at this point
was a multiple reassignment of roles among four of his central
characters. I even dare surmise this was the decisive turning-
point in their genetic development, and in the definition of the
narrator himself. What I've called the major hypothesis of this
essay is my formulation of the several interconnected reassignments involved. I'll state the hypothesis now, in two different
perspectives, in advance of my presentation of the specific compositional evidence by which I'll later support it. Because up to
here I've approached the hypothesis piecemeal, through Melville's treatment of Bulkington and Queequeg, I'll state it first
in that perspective.

At Stage 3 of his shore-narrative Melville decided to dismiss
Bulkington from his dual role of comrade and of truth-seeker,
and from any active role in the narrative. He reassigned Bulkington's comrade role to Queequeg, as we've just seen. And he also,
I now add, made two further closely-related reassignments
which involved two more characters. He reassigned Bulkington's truth-seeker role to a newly-invented character (who was
even more startlingly absent – in the book 'hiding out' – up to
this point) – Ahab. He simultaneously reassigned to Ahab the
sea-role of captain of the *Pequod*, taking that commanding role
away from the captain who had first held it – Peleg – and
reducing Peleg thus to his present shore role as her 'captain'
without command, retired chief-mate, and duplicate part-
owner and pilot. The narrator, too, was redefined in the
reassignment of his comrades.

Now I'll restate the hypothesis from a second perspective (with recognizable reference to the pattern of duplicates I have summarized but still without detailed compositional evidence). The hypothesis is this. Four central characters of *Moby-Dick* were involved, at this crucial stage of the book's development, in a multiple reassignment of roles, which also redefined a fifth, the narrator. (By a 'role' I mean intentions Melville had projected for a character, some of which were actually written but some were still only in his mind, though signalled in what he had written.) In the process of reassignment, each of the four became in certain ways a duplicate; but while two of them gained and consequently became major characters, two of them lost and became to a degree vestigial – 'unnecessary duplicates'.

The two gainers were Queequeg and Ahab – and, coincidentally, Ishmael himself. Queequeg, up to this point, had not been brought into the shore-narrative; but in its continuation in the already-written sea-narrative he by then was one of the three harpooneers, and was (then as now) usually named and presented there not singly but linked with the other two, though in several passages he already played a separate role and was sometimes individually characterized. Queequeg received from Bulkington at Stage 3 of the shore-narrative the role of Ishmael's comrade; but Melville made him a quite different comrade from what Bulkington would have been, by not assigning him as well the alienated, aggressive component implicit in Bulkington's romantic, truth-seeking role. Instead, Queequeg embodied a reconciling principle. While he brought over with him from the sea-narrative the aggressive filed teeth of a cannibal and the harpoon of a whaleman, he brought also a noble savage's 'calm self-collectedness of simplicity', a tranquil piety, and a capacity for bosom-friendship. His tomahawk-pipe shows the union in him of war and peace. Whereas Bulkington, that unresting voyager (in 'the deep shadows' of whose eyes 'floated some reminiscences that did not seem to give him much joy'), as a comrade would have engaged and heightened Ishmael's own alienated and aggressive tendencies (even while ennobling them), Queequeg caused him to feel 'a melting in me'. 'No more my splintered heart and maddened hand were turned against the wolfish world. This soothing savage had redeemed it' (ch. 10). Queequeg's pagan warmth softened and assuaged the

aggressive disaffection from cold Christendom that had driven
Ishmael, as a 'substitute for pistol and ball', to take to the ship
in midwinter – and did so even before he had found and signed
aboard the vindictive *Pequod*! Thus Melville's substitution of
Queequeg for Bulkington as the narrator's comrade signalized,
or perhaps even precipitated, a reorientation in Ishmael's
psychology. And this reorientation was explicitly defined and
delimited by Melville's elaboration of the new shore-narrative
episodes, told by Ishmael in his own individualized first-person,
that dramatize the terms of their likewise individualized bosom-
friendship. So Ishmael, too, as an emergently defined fictional
character, was a gainer from the reassignment of comrades. At
least he gained in the shore segment of the narrative, where
Melville elaborated his relationship with Queequeg; however,
in the already-written episodes of its sea segment that bring
Queequeg and the narrator together Melville did not fully carry
through the elaboration of their relationship.

The second (not to count Ishmael), and of course even
greater, gainer by the reassignments was Ahab. Up to this
decisive point Ahab had simply not existed at all as a character
in either the shore or the sea segment of Melville's earlier narrative, but only in large fractions of the potential roles Melville
had so far assigned to two other characters, Bulkington and
Peleg. (You could say that these fractions of Bulkington and
Peleg went into the initial making of Ahab.) From Bulkington,
Ahab received the projected role of heroic truth-seeker, with its
Gothic and Romantic penumbra of 'noble' traits and its
inherent alienated, aggressive component. Possibly he was also
given by revision some passages Melville had already written
for Bulkington. Just possibly, too, Ahab's quest of the White
Whale was to have been Bulkington's – I am not yet sure. From
Peleg, on the other hand, Ahab received (purged of original
comic overtones) the role of ungodly Quaker commanding
captain of the whalebone-apparelled, Indian-named, vindictive
Pequod; along with the whalebone leg (and whalebone stool?);
probably the attendant old Gay-Head devil-associated Indian
prophet who gets so duplicated as the narrative goes on; and
(if it had indeed been Peleg's not Bulkington's) the hell-bound,
devil-involved, vindictive quest of the particular whale who had
taken off his fleshly leg, very likely the White Whale some call

Moby Dick. So Ahab was, as Peleg aptly said, 'something like me – only there's a good deal more of him'.

The two losers by Melville's reassignments were Bulkington and Peleg. Bulkington's loss was in fact fatal: while in a spiritual sense you could say he 'became' the god-like Ahab in his apotheosis, in the quite literal sense he became only the vestigial description and eulogy which make clear Melville's original intention for his character before reassigning both his roles. One role, as Ishmael's comrade, went to Queequeg (but, as I've said, without its aggressive component). If, as seems likely, Bulkington was also projected to be a harpooneer, perhaps that role too was quite early transferred to Queequeg in the sea-narrative, where some significant passages suggest he was not originally conceived as one. The second loser was Peleg; he is quasi-vestigial, if not unnecessary, because Melville gave his original role as *Pequod*'s sea-commander to Ahab along with his whale-bone appurtenances. Peleg lost to Ahab his whalebone leg (probably his fleshly one was lost, like the *Pequod*'s masts, 'off Japan', just as the no doubt well-informed old Gay-Head Indian said). And so he lost by transfer to Ahab the self-pitying epithet 'a poor pegging lubber'. Also, probably, along with 'that leg' and epithet Peleg lost one letter from his original name (I dare say it): Pegleg – too homely and comic a sailor soubriquet to reassign to the lofty and tragic new captain, to whom Melville gave a Biblical name that 'the old squaw Tistig, at Gay-head', said 'would somehow prove prophetic' (ch. 16). But even so Peleg as a duplicate retains vestiges of all these; he is still 'Captain' Peleg, in half-command of the *Pequod* in dock and in getting her to sea and ordering all hands about. It is still he who did the whalebone carving-work for the ship; who was aboard her (though as mate under Ahab, not captain himself) in that dismasting typhoon off Japan; who has 'that leg' (now of restored flesh – possibly his only gain!) with which he threatens and delivers kicks; and who, despite now having both good legs, does his mildly comic 'roaring' (and perhaps 'hobbling'), 'clattering' about the decks, and profane swearing (including the epithet 'thunder'); and who still has his prophet, Bildad, to tell him he's hell-bound, and also his Indian-named ship *Pequod* and his 'wigwam' as links to Indians, and is himself still a 'devil'.

There, in duplicate summary, is my major hypothesis. Now I pick up my line of reasoning upon the compositional evidence that suggested and supports it, with Bulkington's quietus. Melville carried out his Stage 3 decision to remove Bulkington from both of his roles simply by inserting into the already-written sentence that makes him the narrator's 'shipmate' (at Stage 2) the contradictory parenthesis '(though but a sleeping-partner one, so far as this narrative is concerned)'. Did the metaphor suggest the literal 'sleeping-partner' sequence that introduced his replacement? He also at this time revised the first sea episode, where Bulkington appears at the *Pequod*'s helm, and with a eulogy but no epitaph made that 'six-inch chapter' his 'stoneless grave'. (And thereby too he made Bulkington the first of the duplicate 'man-overboard' casualties who mark the wake of Melville's compositional voyage.) Just why Melville kept these two vestiges of Bulkington rather than discard him altogether one can only guess, and I have now no guess to offer, beyond the humdrum one that Melville, like lesser writers, found it hard to throw away good words he had written.

Bulkington is disposed of in chapter 23, and Ishmael opens chapter 24 saying, 'Queequeg and I are now fairly embarked in this business of whaling'. But no sooner is this said than – in the very same sentence – two abrupt and linked shifts occur: in narrative voice and in presentation of the Ishmael-Queequeg relationship. Not only does the voice of tyro Ishmael give way to the (duplicate) voice of a veteran and sometimes omniscient whaleman who is only putatively the same tyro Ishmael grown older (several duplicate voices can be distinguished within that unsingle voice, among them Herman Melville's own). Suddenly, also, the narrative mode gives way to the argumentative and expository, and the presentation no longer focuses closely on the experiences of tyro Ishmael and his harpooneer-mentor and comrade Queequeg. From now on the tyro voice is heard only intermittently, in sporadic episodes; and few episodes show the pair engaged in either comradeship or pupil-teacher relationships. Even in those episodes where both Ishmael and Queequeg are included by name or inference they are usually not brought together in any personal interchange – they just don't seem to be aware of each other. Surely, this abrupt double shift, of narrative voice and of presentational focus, between the shore and sea segments of the book is fictionally the most curious oddity among many in *Moby-Dick*. What is the explanation ?

On the face of it, one might guess that Melville lost either his interest in the comradeship or his technical control of the materials. Another explanation is more circumstantially genetic. The few scholars who have theorized about the book's genesis have thought, as I do, that it is possible to distinguish various parts of the book as written earlier or later in the course of its composition, that its pages were not necessarily written, by any means, in the order in which they now stand. Whatever their more specific theories may be, however, these scholars have all thought that the shore-narrative, with the Ishmael-Queequeg comradeship, belongs to the earliest distinguishable writing stage. Nobody has seen a means of distinguishing stages within its development as regards Ishmael and Queequeg, as I have just done, though they have seen that anticipatory refer-ences to Ahab were inserted. Nor has anybody tried to explain the abrupt double shift between the two parts of the book by hypothesizing that some of the veteran-narrator passages and Ishmael-Queequeg passages in the sea segment were written before not after the relevant tyro-narrator passages in the shore segment, as I am now doing.

But the fact is that the truancy both of the tyro-narrator and of the close comrades (hard on the heels of Bulkington's dis-appearance) can most plausibly be explained this way. As for Queequeg, the infrequency and spareness of his involvement with Ishmael in the sea chapters means not that Melville lost interest in developing their comradeship, but that, by and large, those passages as they touch on the pair had already been written, before not after, those relevant passages in the shore chapters which include Queequeg and develop their comrade-ship in detail. Melville certainly made some appropriate revisions and numerous brief insertions in the earlier-written sea-narrative but did not carry through into it the detailed elaboration by which, as I have argued, he had incorporated Queequeg into the shore-narrative. What Melville lost, I venture, was not interest but 'Time, Strength, Cash, and Patience' – maybe heart, too – for continuing the job: near the end of it, in June 1851, he wrote Hawthorne, 'What's the use of elaborating what, in its very essence, is so short-lived as a modern book ?'

When Melville imported cannibal Queequeg at Stage 3 into the shore segment of his narrative, he did not invent him at that point as a new character. For Queequeg, as I shall now argue, already had a place in the sea segment of the narrative, from an earlier stage, though not as the narrator's comrade. Examination of compositional details in three scenes involving Ishmael and Queequeg strongly supports this conclusion. The first is representative, the other two central to my argument.

The scene I've taken as 'representative', the mat-making passage in chapter 47, is the first in which Ishmael and Queequeg are brought together since just before the ship sailed, twenty-six chapters back, in chapter 21, where Ishmael expostulated with Queequeg for sitting on a sleeping rigger's 'face'. In the intervening chapters, Queequeg is 'there' in these ways: he is mentioned only once, misnamed by Peleg, in the departure scene, chapter 22; he and Ishmael are named together in the first sentence of chapter 24, and Queequeg is named once in a later paragraph but isn't there; Queequeg's selection as Starbuck's harpooneer is reported in two brief sentences of chapter 27; he's discrepantly grouped with the other barbaric harpooneers, but not named, in chapter 28; he's named, and shown eating in the officers' cabin with the two other savage harpooneers in chapter 34, but Ishmael isn't there, unless by implication he, 'like any mere sailor', can see him through the cabin skylight; he's named casually once in chapter 35 when Ishmael says that he might 'have a chat with Queequeg, or any one else off duty'; he's one of the three harpooneers in Ahab's quarter-deck ritual in chapter 36, where Ishmael is only inferentially present; he's missing from the forecastle midnight roysterings (ch. 40), though the stage directions call for 'Harpooneers'; and he next is named in Ishmael's company in the mat-making passage. This chapter sequence just summarized illustrates Melville's technique of introducing Queequeg's name, without really building him into scenes, and they seem more likely to have been written before than after the shore Ishmael-Queequeg scenes – otherwise there's no reason Melville shouldn't more often have engaged Ishmael and Queequeg in them somehow. And so it goes through the rest of the book. I must ask readers to check for themselves exactly how, in compositional terms, Melville established Queequeg's existence, presence, actions, and only occasionally his involvement with Ishmael.

In the mat-making passage, Ishmael is acting as 'the attendant or page' of Queequeg in weaving a sword-mat for 'our boat'. Perhaps this fits the forecast tyro-mentor relationship well enough, though nothing is said of Queequeg's teaching, or Ishmael's learning, anything – they are just doing it, which suggests that Melville hadn't yet thought of their special mentor-pupil relation when he wrote it. Moreover, no personal interaction of any sort is worded; on the contrary, 'each silent sailor' acts on his own, Queequeg 'idly looking off upon the water', Ishmael weaving his own analogical thoughts. Queequeg is not personalized by so much as one word; in fact only his name, given four times, and his usual epithet the 'savage' (shared with the two other pagan harpooneers) attach him to the passage. Another shipmate – say Bulkington – would do as well, which is to say the passage can have been reassigned to Queequeg by changing these few words from an earlier named or unnamed incumbent. I keep pointing out how inorganically present Queequeg is all along, first to call attention to Melville's relative lack of concern about him, in his special comrade-mentor relation to Ishmael; second, to show the possibility that at a quite early stage Melville wrote many such passages without any particular or individualized characters in mind, and only later assigned names and did more or less 'elaborating'. In the process he may have reassigned roles. I entertain seriously the possibility that earlier Bulkington indeed occupied some of Queequeg's present name slots, so to speak, and was a harpooneer, and I am considering the possibility that some of Ahab's may have been reassigned from Bulkington. I am calling this mat-making passage 'representative' because what is true of its handling of Queequeg simply by name, with no individual detail, turns out, upon examination, to be characteristic of many passages that stick in our minds as presenting the two in a comradely relationship, which in fact nothing in the passage really establishes. Again, I must ask readers to check for themselves.

Two further Queequeg passages, however, are crucial to my argument from compositional detail. On inspection significant details of their wording show pretty conclusively that Melville wrote them before not after he wrote the shore-narrative chapters in which he developed their bosom-friendship.

The monkey-rope episode (ch. 72) is one of those frequent passages where Melville dramatizes his initially present-tense exposition of a whaling routine by attaching it to a particular occasion and to named characters of the *Pequod*'s voyage. Here, as often, the expository mode and purpose come foremost, and the named characters play their part in the scene primarily by virtue of their shipboard station and only secondarily in ways calling on their individual traits (so that Melville might easily have assigned the name of another character of the same station). Here, Queequeg, 'whose duty it was, as harpooneer', was overboard upon the whale's back; Ishmael, 'being the savage's bowsman, that is, the person who pulled the bow-oar in his boat', had the duty of safeguarding his movements by means of the monkey-rope which was attached to both of them. The scene specifies no particular qualities of Queequeg. He is the 'savage' and repeatedly 'poor' Queequeg, like 'poor' Tashtego in the scene of his falling into the whale's head (ch. 78). His special relationship to Ishmael is specified by epithets at two points: the first reference is 'my particular friend Queequeg whose duty it was, as harpooneer . . .'; the second is 'my dear comrade and twin-brother, thought I'. A third reference is Ishmael's comment on Queequeg's Highland costume, a shirt and socks, '. . . in which to my eyes, at least, he appeared to uncommon advantage . . .'. In the light of what follows, I argue that Melville later inserted 'my particular friend' and 'my dear comrade', perhaps as well the third reference quoted, and added the comic dramatic scene with Stubb at the end. The third reference does not necessarily presuppose the bosom-friendship, however, and may have been original in the passage. Nothing else in that scene of the chapter is written in a way that presumes or requires the pair to be comrades already. Indeed, the central monkey-rope metaphor, and the way Melville has Ishmael apply it, makes that prior-established bosom-friendship highly unlikely. Furthermore it suggests the likelihood that it was his writing of this scene and this metaphor that opened to Melville the possibility of making the pair bosom-friends in the shore sequence when he removed Bulkington from the comrade role. As Ishmael states his perilous monkey-rope attachment to

Queequeg, he develops it into a metaphor: 'So that for better or for worse, we two, for the time, were wedded'. To me it is not conceivable that Melville could write 'for the time, we were wedded' – especially the phrase '*for the time*' – if he had already written the shore chapters in which he dramatized the bosom-friendship of Queequeg and Ishmael, starting off with Quee-queg's declaration, 'Henceforth we were married'. 'Hence-forth', not 'for the time'. Could Melville have forgotten he'd written – if in fact he had – the paragraph in which Ishmael and Queequeg are compared to 'man and wife', ending with the sentence, 'Thus, then, in our hearts' honeymoon, lay I and Queequeg – a cosy, loving pair'? (ch. 10). And the comic anticipatory marital imagery of chapter 4? And Ishmael's declaration, 'From that hour I clove to Queequeg like a barnacle'? (ch. 13). Nor is that all that's askew in this monkey-rope passage. It goes on from the 'wedded' metaphor to, 'So, then, an elongated Siamese ligature united us. Queequeg was my own inseparable twin brother', and twice repeats the twin figure. If this figure in itself is not incongruous enough with the 'wedded' image, surely its re-insistence that the mere monkey-rope was what tied the pair together, at this late point – weeks, and chapters, after their New Bedford union – thickens the unlikelihood that Melville had already provided that union. No, I must conclude, Melville had not yet written those earlier passages or yet conceived the bosom-friendship they establish.

My third Queequeg scene, on Queequeg in his coffin (ch. 110), is the most telling in its compositional betrayals. Most glaringly, though his bosom-friend is dying, Ishmael is not placed bodily on the scene at all, or even represented as having witnessed it. The focus is not once that of a first-person participating narrator. The pair's special relationship is sig-nalled at only two points, one of eight words early in the chapter, one of a single word near its end. The first is in the single-sentence second paragraph that effects a transition between the expository first and third paragraphs about the process of breaking out leaky casks and Queequeg's catching a fever while performing his routine duties on them in the hold as a har-pooneer. (The chapter thus has the same compositional struc-ture, and I think genetic pattern, as 'The Monkey-Rope'.) The sentence reads: 'Now, at this time it was that my poor pagan companion, and fast bosom-friend, Queequeg, was seized with a fever, which brought him nigh to his endless end.' The double epithet and the pronoun 'my' that tie Queequeg to Ishmael here were patently inserted. The epithets' content is contradicted by the whole chapter's detached (though sentimental) omniscient presentation of the death scene. At the second point that ties the (elsewhere) 'cosy, loving pair' the tie is effected in the next-to-last paragraph, when the crisis has passed, by the single word 'my' in 'So, in good time my Queequeg gained strength' – again a patently inserted word. The sentence could do better without it, because 'my' makes an even more abrupt and gratuitous break in point-of-view than the first 'my' above. The absence of Ishmael from the side of his 'fast bosom-friend' is made still more glaring by further compositional details. We are told, 'Not a man of the crew but gave him up'. (Not even 'We all. . . .') Including Ishmael? Did *he* have feelings about it? Why not say so? Then Queequeg has some dying wishes. He wants someone to get him a coffin made. Does he call his 'fast bosom-friend'? No: 'He called one to him . . ., and taking his hand', made his first request – made it of some indefinite 'one'! And the request was transmitted not even by this indefinite 'one' but simply 'was made known aft' in agentless passive voice. When Queequeg is satisfied with his coffin, he tells an indefinite 'one', again, his second dying request – not Ishmael, who should be the only 'one' to rummage his bag on such an errand; no, he 'told one to go to his bag and bring out his little god, Yojo'. Throughout the chapter Queequeg is repeatedly called 'poor' Queequeg, 'savage', 'pagan', 'waning savage', etc., with no word of a more intimate feeling than pity and awe. Even a barnacle would feel more affection and cleave closer! The point of view shifts about (but is never first-person) from that of a disembodied third-person observer into several sentences of close focus on Queequeg's eyes and facial expression observed by a disembodied 'you' (four times), who 'sat by his side', and who fuses into an omniscient sententious authorial 'us' ('let us say'), and declares selfconsciously that 'only an author from the dead' could adequately tell Queequeg's expression. Well, Melville's handling of point-of-view is often wayward enough; but he could scarcely have handled it this way in Queequeg's dying scene had he already written the foregoing shore scenes that bound them as bosom-friends.

A further glaring inconsistency throughout chapter 110 directs me to a new area of genetic questions and possibilities, one which I've hinted in my hypothesis but which I can't do more than outline. It concerns Queequeg as harpooneer and the whole unexplored topic of the role of harpooneers in the book. As noted, Queequeg is a harpooneer in the chapter's third paragraph. In its middle he gets assistance (in a series of passive constructions, not from Ishmael) in stocking his coffin-canoe with his needs for his eternal voyage, including the iron part of his harpoon; and also at its end, 'poising a harpoon', he said he was fit for a fight. So he's a harpooneer at three spots. But the glaring discrepancy is that Melville has gone out of his way in 'The Specksynder' (ch. 33) to establish the social status of the harpooneer, entailing where he is quartered: 'The grand political maxim of the sea demands, that he should nominally live apart from the men before the mast, and be in some way distinguished as their professional superior; though always, by them, familiarly regarded as their social equal.' A grand distinction, he goes on, 'drawn between officer and man at sea, is this – the first lives aft, the last forward', and in most American whalers 'the harpooneers are lodged in the after part of the ship' and so 'take their meals in the captain's cabin, and sleep in a place indirectly communicating with it'. Why then, does Melville – who has properly shown him and the two other pagan harpooneers eating in the captain's cabin, in chapter 34 – show the dying Queequeg, throughout chapter 110, quartered *forward, in the crew's forecastle* ? The carpenter is twice said to go 'forward' to the forecastle about his coffin, and Starbuck looked 'down the scuttle' at Queequeg in his coffin. Oddly, it is one of the book's very few forecastle scenes, and dying in it is a harpooneer who belongs aft. (He's also – contrary to whaleship usage – in a hammock; but so are several others, including Ahab and Stubb.) Did Queequeg, at the time Melville wrote his dying scene (at least that layer of it) *belong* in the forecastle, because he was then a common sailor, not yet a harpooneer ? This is only the first of many questions the book's compositional details arouse about its harpooneers. Why are there a number of mis-assignments of harpooneers to the wrong mates' boats ? Did Melville nod, or are they vestigial ? Why do so many chapters

focus on the harpooneer and harpoon? Why did Melville
describe his work in progress to his English publisher in late
June 1850, as 'illustrated by the author's own personal experience, of two years & more, as a harpooneer'? (As to his own
career it was a gross exaggeration; but perhaps this book was to
be set up as if that were true.) Such questions suggest a genetic
phase of *Moby-Dick* when Melville was projecting a book that
would focus both its narrative line and its whaling activities on
the harpooneers. And even, it could be, on a harpooneer hero –
on Bulkington, whom he intended to be Ishmael's comrade at
sea, before he substituted the harpooneer Queequeg. In the
opening three paragraphs of 'The Specksynder' (ch. 33), Melville carefully established the harpooneer class of officers as
intermediary between crewmen and officers; the harpooner is
in a sense both and thus provides a social bridge between them.
Fictionally, in these three paragraphs Melville was preparing
the way for some narrative situation that was to follow. But
nothing does follow from it. The chapter in its fourth paragraph
drops the harpooneers altogether and with a shaky transition
via the topic of officer-crew relations is soon discussing Ahab's
relations with his crew, in highly exalted terms. Some ill-spliced
genetic seam divides the chapter into two ill-matched parts. The
Specksynder-harpooneer is displaced by the captain: perhaps
Bulkington by Ahab? Its first part is the one passage (to which
I referred some pages above) that I can now identify as one I
think Melville wrote for Bulkington. My suspicion is that these
opening paragraphs were setting up Bulkington, Ishmael's
comrade-to-be, for a role which involved his harpooneer status
between officers and men. If so, several inferences follow. If
Bulkington as harpooneer was to be the book's heroic figure,
Ishmael as his comrade would have been personally close to the
action and the main actor, whereas now he has no plausible close
access to Ahab – one reason for the book's curious hiatus in
point-of-view, and for the veteran-narrator's (putatively
Ishmael's) reporting various matters he could know nothing
about. As I've said, I think that Bulkington, in Melville's mind,
outgrew his station, 'becoming', in his heroic role, Ahab. For if
Bulkington was a heroic harpooneer, at what was his harpoon,
in more than a routine whaleman's way, to be pointed? At the
White Whale some call Moby Dick? Was that whale among the

'reminiscences that did not seem to give him much joy'?
(ch. 3).

But here two trains of my present speculations collide. For
my hypothesis, as summarized, points also to Captain Peleg as
the duplicate who may have yielded to Ahab in that hell-bound
devil-guided quest.

In conclusion, two of Captain Peleg's shore chapters require
brief examination to show the compositional signs they betray –
apart from what's on the face of matters I've already catalogued –
for my notion that as a duplicate Peleg is the vestige of the
Pequod's original commanding captain, a large fraction of whom
Melville reassigned to Ahab. I need not discuss the first, 'The
Ship', (ch. 16) in detail. I think my summary of its duplicates
reveals the pattern that suggests Captain Ahab was grafted into
the chapter. (Other scholars, using other keys, are in consensus.)
I suggest only that readers try the experiment of bracketing out
all that refers to Ahab and then looking at the literal words left,
to see their changed significance when taken to apply to Peleg:
for example, Bildad's first answer to Ishmael's inquiry whether
he's captain of the *Pequod*; and the way 'that leg' of Peleg's may
have been whalebone; and how his remarks and 'hearty grief'
originally could refer to his *own* (not Ahab's) loss of a leg to
'the monstrousest parmacetty that ever chipped a boat'; and
so on.

With the hypothesis that Peleg was originally captain, and
Ahab nonexistent, readers should continue the bracketing
experiment with 'Merry Christmas' (ch. 22). To me its compositional oddities seem enough proof in themselves that at
some earlier composition stage Peleg actually sailed on this
voyage as the ship's captain. Ishmael would more justifiably fear
'such a devil' as *captain* than as 'pilot' (for Melville a one-word
substitution there). Ahab's later supplanting Peleg would have
called for only simple revisions in this earlier already-written
episode. Ahab's 'hiding out' (as earlier and later) – now an
effective device of suspense rationalized by his moody sickness –
would be genetically explained by his then non-existence. The
four brief direct references to him are local and dissect out
neatly. The one indirect reference to Ahab (as an old shipmate
of Bildad) would originally in fact have applied even better to
Peleg ('in which an old shipmate sailed as captain; a man almost

as old as he'), for nowhere else is it said that Bildad and Ahab were old shipmates – whereas Bildad and Peleg are so described in chapters 16 and 22. Peleg's part in the chapter is just what it would be, except for his farewells and leaving the ship at the end. The few revisional words tying Peleg to the stay-at-home role would be simple to insert ('with Peleg'; 'the two pilots'; etc.). Bracketing out the two words 'both dropt' from the passage where both Peleg and Bildad now go over into the pilot boat, leaves the context a perfect statement, as is the whole scene, of Bildad's being the only one who's to go ashore, while Peleg is to go with the ship. Most conclusively, the paragraph about the two captains' reactions at leaving-time is so written that it would make more sense (cutting out references to Peleg's going) if Bildad alone, not Peleg as well, were leaving. The first sentence joins them, but at once moves back, awkwardly, to Bildad alone and develops only his (not Peleg's) feelings: 'It was curious . . . how Peleg and Bildad were affected at this juncture, especially Captain Bildad'. Bildad acts for all the world as if he's giving Peleg a *goodbye* handshake and taking a last (for three years) long look at him by holding up the lantern: '. . . poor old Bildad lingered long; . . . convulsively grasped stout Peleg by the hand, and holding up a lantern, for a moment stood gazing heroically in his face. . . .' Why does he do that, if they are not separating? 'As for Peleg himself' [why 'himself'?], his less emotional behaviour fits that of the person going the voyage though 'there was a tear twinkling in his eye when the lantern came too near'. Apart from the easily adjustable farewells to the mates the rest of Peleg's words and actions fit perfectly the situation of his urging Bildad to stop talking and leave them: '"Come, come, Captain Bildad; stop palavering, – away!" and with that, Peleg hurried him over the side and [both dropt] into the boat'.

Remaining questions are large, my answers uncertain. As to Queequeg's place in the harpooneer mixups, I can only suspect that in his earliest appearances in Melville's sea-narrative he was not yet a harpooneer. Similar discrepancies suggest that Tashtego too may not have originally been a harpooneer. (For example, in the first paragraph of 'The Town-Ho's Story' – chapter 54 – he's sleeping forward with the crew.) At some stage, perhaps, Melville conceived the schematic trio of pagan harpooneers and promoted Queequeg and Tashtego, already existing crewmen, into these roles. If so, perhaps it was from Bulkington that Queequeg took over his (you'd think inseparable) harpoon, along with the comrade role ? Wasn't Tashtego, the wild Indian harpooneer, generated (by adding the possessive and the word 'senior' to the name 'Tashtego' in his epithet 'Tashtego's senior' ?) from the 'old Gay-Head Indian' prophet, who thus became vestigial in his one appearance while the thus-created Tashtego took over his name and Indian-devil role as Ahab's (Peleg's ?) original accompanying prophet and his original series of masthead prophetic assignments, a role to be duplicated by all those other prophets, notably Fedallah ? More conjectures than I can now resolve.

Finally, if Peleg was to sail as the *Pequod*'s captain, what of Ahab ? Simple: he didn't yet exist; he was invented later. Then conversely, with the invention of Ahab what was Melville to do with the original captain ? Drown him ? (Perhaps; I mean, he could have worked him into the remarkable 'man overboard' series of duplicate deaths and near deaths that, like the so-called 'gams', punctuate the voyage.) Melville's actual solution was to demote and retire him. This solution had the advantage of not requiring Melville to throw away but only to adapt the lively chapters built around him and Bildad. Did the newly created 'grand, ungodly, god-like man', Captain Ahab – who had still further developments to undergo – take up his vengeful quest of the White Whale from this quasi-comic old Quaker 'devil' Captain Peleg, along with his ship – or from the truth-seeking Bulkington ? I cannot now tell. And that is only the most pressing of my unanswered questions and loose ends.

IV

Maybe scholarly prudence should have kept me from offering with such apparent confidence this sketch of what I think was a crucial phase in the writing of *Moby-Dick*. Still, I am confident that the unnecessary duplicates do give us a new key to Melville's work on the book. I'm not committed to my hypothesis in detail, and likely enough before it is printed will have reformulated it in some ways. Its essentials, I think, don't conflict with those of the more comprehensive theories already offered by Leon Howard, George Stewart, Howard P. Vincent, James

Barbour, and others, who have used different keys, and I believe it can be synthesized with theirs to improve our understanding. All of us must go on with our fumbling – with any combination of keys we can find – at what I've called the interlocked complications of the book's genesis.

Melville wrote a great book. In writing it he worked hard at the job, and during the year and a half his work went on he said so in various ways, both in his letters and in the book itself. Often he identified his writer's job with those of many common workmen, from cooks to ditchers. He introduced his carpenter with remarks I quoted at the beginning. As the carpenter, having made Ahab a duplicate ivory leg, is commanded in chapter 126 to rework the unnecessary coffin he made for Queequeg into its duplicate, the life-buoy that saves Ishmael, and grumbles over his job, isn't Melville describing and grumbling over his own reworking of *Moby-Dick* ?

> Are all my pains to go for nothing with that coffin ? And now I'm ordered to make a life-buoy of it. It's like turning an old coat; going to bring the flesh on the other side now. I don't like this cobbling sort of business – I don't like it at all; it's undignified; it's not my place. Let tinkers' brats do tinkerings; we are their betters. I like to take in hand none but clean, virgin, fair-and-square mathematical jobs, something that regularly begins at the beginning, and is at the middle when midway, and comes to an end at the conclusion; not a cobbler's job, that's at an end in the middle, and at the beginning at the end.

Note of Acknowledgment

Leon Howard, to whom this essay is offered in professional homage and affectionate friendship, initiated nearly forty years ago our scholarly study of the genesis of *Moby-Dick*, and he has done more than anyone else over the years to advance our understanding of it. George Stewart, Howard P. Vincent, and James Barbour, among others, have made distinguished contributions. In this undocumented essay, none of their works needed to be cited specifically, but I wrote it with their approaches, theories, and discoveries in mind and could not have developed the hypothesis I sketch here without them. I gratefully acknowledge my conscious and unconscious debts to them. Since my approach in the essay happens to be through close examination of compositional peculiarities in the book, with little recourse to outside evidence, the approach used up to now chiefly by George Stewart, I am most immediately indebted to his work. My assumptions about Melville's compositional procedures draw confidence from my own close textual study of *Moby-Dick*, with Hershel Parker and G. Thomas Tanselle, and especially, with Merton M. Sealts, Jr, of his semi-final draft manuscript of *Billy Budd, Sailor*, where similar procedures are demonstrable.

The Flawed Grandeur of
Melville's *Pierre*

Pierre was not conceived as a lesser effort, a pot-boiler like *Redburn*, which Melville disparaged as something he wrote to buy tobacco with. Judging from his response to Hawthorne's praise of *Moby-Dick* in mid-November, 1851, Melville intended his next book to be as much grander than his last as the legendary Krakens are bigger than whales.[1] Never a novelist or romancer within the ordinary definitions, Melville in *Moby-Dick* had attempted to convert the whaling narrative, a flourishing division of nautical literature, into a vehicle for the philosophical and psychological speculations a pondering man like him was compelled toward. *Pierre* is his comparable attempt to convert the gothic romance (in one of its late permutations as sensational fiction primarily for female readers) into a vehicle for his psychological and philosophical speculations (now in this order of importance). The technical sea-knots he untied in *Moby-Dick* are grappled with again in the lacy toils of *Pierre*. In the earlier book, certain obligatory scenes, the staple of any whaling story, had to be converted into chapters which would retain their sturdy informativeness while advancing Melville's higher purposes. At best, as in 'The Try-Works', routine exposition was transformed into intense philosophical drama. Much the same way, Melville in *Pierre* inherited a Gothic toybox stuffed almost as full as Poe's with mysterious family relationships, enigmatical recollections of long-past events, suspenseful unravelling of dark, long-kept secrets, and landscapes symbolical of mental states, but once again in the best passages the trivial subgenre bore up under the weight of intense psychological and philosophical drama.

While *Moby-Dick* succeeded for many of its first readers, even if only as a reliable source of cetological information, *Pierre* failed disastrously on all levels. Yet Melville's basic preoccupations and aesthetic strategies are almost identical in both, except that in *Pierre* he shifted considerably from metaphysics toward psychology. Many of the themes of *Moby-Dick* recur, among them the determinant power of wayward moods over human destiny and the tragic necessity that loftier souls hurl themselves against the unresponsive gods in order to assert their own godhood; many of the images recur, especially the sliding, gliding aboriginal phantoms which link Fedallah and Isabel as embodiments of the Unconscious.[2] Stirred by these or other powerful elements, whether or not related to *Moby-Dick*, the best readers of *Pierre* have paid tribute to the heroic intellectual tasks Melville undertook in it. Yet of them only E. L. Grant Watson thought those heroic tasks had been successfully accomplished,[3] while others more often admired the endeavour, whatever they construed it to be, but praised only one aspect or another of the performance. This critical ambivalence toward *Pierre* is captured in the concluding assessment of the Historical Note in the Northwestern-Newberry Edition: 'none of Melville's other "secondary" works has so regularly evoked from its most thorough critics the sense that they are in the presence of grandeur, however flawed'.[4] But scholars and critics have not been able to define the precise nature of the book's grandeur or the precise nature of the flaws which prevent it from being the masterpiece which *Moby-Dick* indisputably is. The problem of how *Pierre* fails can be answered only by rigorous attention to both biographical and aesthetic evidence. Our answers derived from documentary evidence are presented elsewhere; here we focus on evidence from within the book itself.[5]

To understand Melville's achievements and failures in *Pierre*, especially the unusual complexity of its plottedness, the air it initially breathes of being all worked out in advance, requires going backwards beyond *Moby-Dick*. Though real-life adventure dictated the simple, suspenseful outline of *Typee*, the book is marred by confusing shifts in narrative attitude, and several late-written chapters betray Melville's pragmatic necessity to overlay useful information onto his slim set of personal actions and perceptions. *Omoo* is much more of a piece, but its secure point of view does not wholly disguise the tinkering process by which Melville added chapters or parts of chapters as he gained access to certain sourcebooks or became absorbed with a particular topic. The first chapters of *Mardi* reveal far greater literary control than *Typee* and *Omoo*, but much of the book is notoriously 'chartless'. Far from being written consecutively according to a well-designed plan, the book reflects Melville's altering interests, as when the lengthy section of political satire was plumped down into a manuscript already thought of as completed. The latter half of *Redburn* is less unified than the first, despite the power of individual scenes. Most critics agree that an alteration in the point of view blurs the distance between Melville and his narrator and between the narrator and his younger self. As with *Mardi*, Melville seems to have drafted an ending of *Redburn* before inserting lengthy sections of new material, possibly even adding a major character. In *White-Jacket* Melville skilfully deals out through the book little sets of chapters concerning the Jacket, flogging, places visited or passed in the voyage, and chapters anatomizing the man-of-war and its inhabitants. His narrator this time is close enough akin to himself to speak the most profound thoughts Melville could think on subjects such as human societies, and even shares his own lesser crotchets and compulsions. Still more ambitious than *White-Jacket*, with epic and tragic drama the models rather than a somewhat perfunctorily allegorical anatomy, *Moby-Dick* triumphs over its grabbag qualities. Melville's narrator is once again all but indistinguishable from the author in his patterns of thought, and as much more complex than White Jacket as Melville himself had become during the intervening year or two. Still, Melville's letters to Hawthorne show that however strong the 'pervading thought that impelled the book', the completion of *Moby-Dick* involved last-minute patchwork. After the first half or so had gone to press, chapters or parts of chapters were inserted here and there in the latter parts of the manuscript. Unlike his first three books, *Moby-Dick* triumphantly sustains its power to the end. By *Moby-Dick*, however, an ominous pattern had emerged: when Melville failed, it was not at the outset of a book, but later on, when the initial impulse had faded.

We are convinced that in *Pierre* Melville knew what he wanted to do when he set out to write and that for many chapters (and entire 'Books') he did very much what he had planned, exhibiting an intellectual power and artistic control which before this he had manifested only in *Moby-Dick*. Leon Howard thought that *Pierre* was 'possibly the most carefully planned' of all Melville's novels, even though he also thought that Melville's attitude toward his plot changed after the eighth Book and that he subsequently made unexpected enlargements.[6] But we believe the evidence shows that what changed first was not Melville's attitude toward his plot but toward his literary career: his unsuccessful efforts to peddle his manuscript on the good terms he had previously enjoyed coincided with his reading some of the most condemnatory reviews of *Moby-Dick*, so that he had good reason to feel that his career might well be brought to an abrupt end. Swiftly reconceiving the plot, Melville used the unfinished manuscript as an outlet for his all-absorbing pre-occupation with authorship, not only introducing unplanned-for elements but also condensing or otherwise altering parts already written or projected. Still, signs of Melville's careful planning undeniably remain evident everywhere throughout the first half of *Pierre* and survive even later, especially at the level of plot details, just where he had never manifested anything approaching a compulsive tidiness.[7] A few awkwardnesses can be adduced,[8] but by and large the plotting in *Pierre* (at least in the first half) is intricate and accurate, and of a novelistic kind new to Melville. To the end of Book XIV, 'The Journey and the Pamphlet', action taking place in the novel's present occupies just four days, with Pierre and his companions leaving Saddle Meadows early on the morning of the fifth; lengthy flashbacks to different periods in the past illuminate and explain develop-ments in the present. Care in plotting is also obvious – indeed, deliberately overobvious – both in the elaborate predictions of events to come and in the complex set of cross references which lace parts of the book together.

The predictions come thick and fast at the outset, where one would expect them if they were going to come at all. We are led to expect that the lives of Pierre and his mother will divide (5), and that after Pierre's interior development he will not prize his ancestry so much (6). His aspirations clearly will be thwarted by Time (8), and his 'special family distinction' will be important to his singularly developed character and life career (12). Fate will very likely knock him off his pedestal (12), he will become philosophical (13), and will become a thoroughgoing democrat, even a Radical one (13). The predictions continue: Nature will

prove ambiguous to Pierre in the end (13); Lucy will long afterwards experience far different 'flutterings' from those at Saddle
Meadows (26); Pierre will never regain his lost sense of an un-
disturbed moral beauty in the world (65); his crawling under
the Memnon Stone will later hold immense significance for him
(135); in aftertimes with Isabel, Pierre will often recall his first
magnetic night with her (151); Pierre, Isabel, and Delly will
never return to Saddle Meadows once they leave (203). After
the departure from Saddle Meadows the predictions diminish,
as they naturally would past the middle of the book, when predictions are being fulfilled, not made. The pamphlet which
Pierre reads in the coach may influence his conduct (210); he
will later understand the utility of Machiavellian policy though
not have the heart to use it (222); his ties to Glen will involve
in the end the most serious consequences (224); and he will
learn that the world has fire and sword for contemporary
grandeur (264). On reflective scrutiny a few of these predictions seem a trifle misleading, as when the reader may gather
(5) that Pierre's and his mother's lives will divide then continue
apart for longer than actually happens. Still other predictions
(such as those at page 135 and page 151) seem to promise a more
patient following of Pierre's river of mind than occurs after he
arrives at the city and becomes settled at the Apostles'. But the
predictions usually come true in unambiguous fashion. If the
early chapters now stand roughly in order of their composition,
they indicate that Melville had much of the basic plot well outlined from the beginning. The rather thick-strewn predictions
do not, however, prove that no radical new elements were introduced into the plot. Curiously enough, despite all the fulfilled
predictions there is nothing which conclusively proves that Melville intended from the outset to have Pierre become a writer
once he was exiled from his home. In fact, the pattern of predictions makes it seem most likely that if Melville had had any
such plan he would have signalled it at intervals throughout the
Saddle Meadows section. Moreover, Melville may not have
elaborated the city episodes in the ways he had once intended.
These limitations aside, the predictions do furnish at least some
evidence as to the unusual degree of Melville's control over his
material.

Equal care in plotting is revealed in the way much of the book is tied together by cross references such as those to Nature's bounty toward Pierre (13–14, 257); what Pierre and Lucy believe about lovers' secrecies (37, 81, 309); Lucy's easel (39, 318); the will of Pierre's father (55, 179); the first paragraph of Isabel's letter (63, 175); Pierre's promise to protect Isabel (66, 113, 205); the chair portrait in the chintz-covered chest (87, 196); Isabel's one outburst of aggressive enthusiasm (160, 174); Lucy's fainting words (183, 206, 308); Mrs Glendinning's words of banishment (185, 206); the military cloaks which Dates packs (187, 301); the fire at the Black Swan Inn (198, 217, 255–6); Pierre's interest in the pamphlet attributed to Plotinus Plinlimmon (209, 293); Pierre's youthful sonnet 'The Tropical Summer' (245, 263, 306); and Pierre as a toddler (296, 305). The number and aptness of most of the cross references indicate that sometimes Melville was planning ahead for such details with what was, for him, remarkable thorough- ness, while at other times he was making an unusual effort to tie some of what he was writing to particular passages already written; and while writing some passages he may even have gone back to introduce forward-looking references.

Unusual though it was for Melville, control of such details obviously does not of itself lead to great fiction. Indeed the excessive emphasis on predictions early in *Pierre* reflects Mel- ville's satirical playing with one of the routine conventions of popular fiction. His real triumph of control in *Pierre* is the way he leads the reader into fascinated engagement with his remark- able thematic preoccupations. At the outset he risks failing to achieve any such engagement at all, for he strangely idealizes the social rank and superior natures of the characters, who feel extraordinary emotions and speak an extraordinary language. In Book I, 'Pierre Just Emerging from His Teens', the first words of dialogue are ludicrous, by realistic standards, and there seems some fairy-tale quality about the whole situation. The style is often pseudo-Elizabethan bombast, often near the cloying romanticism of female novels of Melville's own time. Yet rapidly the reader begins to feel the tension created between the idealization of the characters and the constant predictions of disaster: the novel is to be a grand experiment in which Fate will take a hand in the life history of a rare specimen of mankind. With daring and often outrageous stylistic improvising Melville is in fact mocking Pierre's adolescent heroics, his unearned sense of security, and his unwillingness to face those dark truths that are to be the burden of the novel. The reader is led to view Pierre with amused, objective condescension and even slight contempt at the same time that he feels concern for the approaching crash of Pierre's illusions. After the early sense of impending calamity, Melville moves into another way of engaging his readers, by giving his hero unbidden inklings of a darker side of life. Events within and without impel Pierre toward maturer thought, yet he is reluctant to become philosophic (which in this novel means to awaken to a tragic sense). At the end of Book II, 'Love, Delight, and Alarm', Grief is still only a 'ghost-story' to Pierre (41). He resists the 'treacherous persuasiveness' (42) of the mournful pine tree and curses his reading in Dante (42), rejecting even imagined, not felt, experience of the darker aspects of reality, thinking, in juvenile pugnaciousness, that deprived of joy he would find cause for deadly feuds with things invisible.

In Book III, 'The Presentiment and the Verification', as Melville begins to develop Pierre's deeper side, his narrative voice becomes more restrained and sombre. He portrays the first stirrings of Pierre's long-dormant Unconscious from which 'bannered armies of hooded phantoms' (49) attack and board his conscious mind. Yet Pierre still shrinks 'abhorringly from the infernal catacombs of thought' when beckoned by a 'fœtal fancy' (51); he fights against his new sensations as a 'sort of unhealthiness' (53) when stirred 'in his deepest moral being' (as he thinks) by the sight of Isabel's face (49). But after receiving Isabel's letter his reluctance to face Truth when he does not know what he is evading changes into overeagerness to face Truth when he does not know what he is inviting (65). Hereafter Melville continues to trace the process of Pierre's mental growth, so that the reader becomes privy to the seemingly 'boundless expansion' (66) of the young hero's life. Previously engrossed and perhaps intermittently baffled by the stylistic virtuosity with which Melville reveals Pierre's absurdities, the reader is now impelled to follow the murky courses of Pierre's mind through all the ambiguous consequences of his absolute behaviour.

Book IV, 'Retrospective', as the title suggests, interrupts Melville's analysis of Pierre's current mental state. Now Melville announces explicitly a major theme present from the beginning but not emphasized before: that of the supersubtle complexity of psychological motivations and indeed of all psychological processes. We had been told (7) that tracing out 'precisely the absolute motives' which prompted Pierre to partake of the Holy Sacraments at the age of sixteen would be needless as well as difficult; merely, Pierre seemed to have inherited his ancestors' religion 'by the same insensible sliding process' that he inherited their other noble personal qualities and their forests and farms. But the stress had been more on Pierre's immaturity than on the subtlety of the processes by which he behaved as he did. Post-adolescent love-extravagancies are associated with 'subterranean sprites and gnomes' (34), but Melville does not then reveal that these quaint monstrosities emerge from the same Unconscious whence hooded phantoms are soon to embark (49). Early in the novel various images of mental processes as gliding and sliding prefigure Melville's full portrayal of the oblique workings of the mind, but not until the first chapter of 'Retrospective' does he confront the theme directly: 'In their precise tracings-out and subtile causations, the strongest and fieriest emotions of life defy all analytical insight. . . . The metaphysical writers confess, that the most impressive, sudden, and overwhelming event, as well as the minutest, is but the product of an infinite series of infinitely involved and untraceable foregoing occurrences. Just so with every motion of the heart' (67). The rest of Book IV uncovers the extremely complex combination of suddenly recalled events and stories and unbidden night-thoughts which leads to Pierre's immediate conviction that Isabel is his father's daughter. Hereafter, treatment of Pierre's inward development is inseparable from the theme of the shadowiness of all human motivation, the 'ever-elastic regions of evanescent invention' through which the mind roams up and down (82).

Moreover, by the end of Book IV Melville has gone beyond the supersubtlety of all human psychology to assert the *autonomy* of those subtler elements of man, as we first see in the description of the adolescent Pierre sometimes standing before the chair portrait of his father, 'unconsciously throwing himself open to all those ineffable hints and ambiguities, and undefined

half-suggestions, which now and then people the soul's atmosphere, as thickly as in a soft, steady snow-storm, the snow-
flakes people the air' (84). The imagery suggests an evanescence
of thought which the individual no more controls than he does
the snow-storm, and Melville distinguishes these 'reveries and
trances' from the 'assured element of consciously bidden and
self-propelled thought' (84). With similar intimations of forces
beyond Pierre's control, Melville refers to the 'streams' of
Pierre's reveries over the chair portrait of his father which did
not seem 'to leave any conscious sediment in his mind; they
were so light and so rapid, that they rolled their own alluvial
along; and seemed to leave all Pierre's thought-channels as
clean and dry as though never any alluvial stream had rolled
there at all' (85). In Book v, 'Misgivings and Preparatives', Fate
irresistibly gives Pierre an 'electric insight' into 'the vital
character of his mother' so that he now sees her as unalterably
dominated by 'hereditary forms and world-usages' (89). As
Melville says, 'in these flashing revelations of grief's wonderful
fire, we see all things as they are' (88). Such use of images of
natural phenomena to suggest the involuntary character of
thought continues with added intensity after Pierre has had
time to reflect on the letter from Isabel, when the thought of
Lucy 'serpent-like . . . overlayingly crawled in upon his other
shuddering imaginings' (104). These other thoughts, we are
told, would often 'upheave' and absorb the thought of Lucy into
themselves, 'so that it would in that way soon disappear from
his cotemporary apprehension' (104). The serpent image and
the image of upheaval imply, once again, an independent vitality
in the thought, free of Pierre's conscious control. Natural
imagery now becomes more complexly elaborated as Melville
portrays an expansion of Pierre's interior dimensions during the
mental turmoil into which his reading of the letter has plunged
him: 'Standing half-befogged upon the mountain of his Fate,
all that part of the wide panorama was wrapped in clouds to him;
but anon those concealings slid aside, or rather, a quick rent
was made in them' (105). Through the 'swift cloud-rent' Pierre
catches one glimpse of Lucy's 'expectant and angelic face', but
'the next instant the stormy pinions of the clouds locked themselves over it again; and all was hidden as before; and all went
confused in whirling rack and vapor as before'. Yet while thus

'for the most part wrapped from his consciousness and vision', the condition of Lucy 'was still more and more disentangling and defining itself from out its nether mist,⁹ and even beneath the general upper fog' (105). This passage portrays a rapidly expanded mental terrain but still a chaotic and uncontrollable one.

What Melville has achieved is an extraordinary conversion of gothic sensationalism into profound psychological exploration. Isabel, Pierre's presumed half-sister, is identified either as his Unconscious or as a product of it, so that his closer involvement with her parallels his gradual opening to incursions from the Unconscious. His after-reveries on her face (41) are associated with his dawning half-admission that Grief may be more than merely a 'ghost-story'. Without 'one word of speech', her face had revealed 'glimpses of some fearful gospel' (43). Within an hour of first seeing Isabel, Pierre felt that 'what he had always before considered the solid land of veritable reality, was now being audaciously encroached upon by bannered armies of hooded phantoms, disembarking in his soul, as from flotillas of specter-boats' (49). After reading Isabel's letter, Pierre 'saw all preceding ambiguities, all mysteries ripped open as if with a keen sword, and forth trooped thickening phantoms of an infinite gloom' (85). Prior to his first interview with her in Book VI, 'Isabel, and the First Part of the Story of Isabel', Pierre gives himself up to 'long wanderings in the primeval woods of Saddle Meadows' (109); formerly sunny and Arcadian, the landscape now mirrors his new sense of the world: in the 'wet and misty eve the scattered, shivering pasture elms seemed standing in a world inhospitable'. The landscape also mirrors the depths and terrors Isabel has opened up in Pierre's psyche:

> On both sides, in the remoter distance, and also far beyond the mild lake's further shore, rose the long, mysterious mountain masses; shaggy with pines and hemlocks, mystical with nameless, vapory exhalations, and in that dim air black with dread and gloom. At their base, profoundest forests lay entranced, and from their far owl-haunted depths of caves and rotted leaves, and unused and un-regarded inland overgrowth of decaying wood – for smallest sticks of which, in other climes many a pauper was that

moment perishing; from out the infinite inhumanities of
those profoundest forests, came a moaning, muttering,
roaring, intermitted, changeful sound: rain-shakings of
the palsied trees, slidings of rocks undermined, final
crashings of long-riven boughs, and devilish gibberish of
the forest-ghosts. (109–110)

When Pierre at last meets Isabel at the red farmhouse, what she
recounts concerns her childhood process of individuation, a
process Pierre is undergoing only now, after first seeing her. She
reveals that her constant psychological state is one in which the
Unconscious impinges upon the Conscious: 'Always in me, the
solidest things melt into dreams, and dreams into solidities'
(117); only now has Pierre's own soul begun to be opened
to the same integrative and disintegrative mental processes. But
Isabel embodies the Unconscious in ways still alien from the
awakening Pierre, even to the point of learning 'new things' from
the thoughts which 'well up' in her and come forth on her tongue
without the intervention of any conscious process, so that the
speech is 'sometimes before the thought' (123). Bursting from
the 'sorceries' of the interview (128), Pierre at the beginning
of Book VII, 'Intermediate between Pierre's Two Interviews
with Isabel at the Farm-house', for 'an instant' almost wishes
for a reversion to his earlier vision of a simpler, unmysterious
world and to ignorance of his own newly-opened, threatening
depths: 'he almost could have prayed Isabel back into the
wonder-world from which she had so slidingly emerged' (129).
Yet the lure of these new depths is more powerful than their
threats, for he again withdraws to a forest where his eye pursues
'its ever-shifting shadowy vistas' and where there come into his
mind 'thoughts and fancies never imbibed within the gates of
towns; but only given forth by the atmosphere of primeval
forests' (139). Formerly the unconscious processes of Pierre's
mind were imaged as a stream; now, indicative of his greater
depths, from the 'thoughtful river' of his mind run 'unending,
ever-flowing', thoughts of Isabel (141). But Pierre's process of
yielding ground in his soul to the invading Unconscious continues to involve occasional checks or reversals. In the interval
after his second interview with Isabel, during which he had
made the most binding pledges, there comes a moment when,
fain to disown his memory and mind, Pierre dashes himself

against a wall and falls 'dabbling in the vomit of his loathed identity' (171). As the narrator warns, the human soul is 'strange and complicate' (176). Pierre's final resolution to champion Isabel by pretending to have married her is arrived at only by 'nameless struggles of the soul' (181).

Moreover, Pierre's 'infinite magnanimities' (177) from the outset are inextricably linked with appalling self-delusion. From the opening pages Melville has set forth, in scenes which initially baffle the reader, the chivalric artifice of Pierre's ideals and intimate relationships – a habit of mind that makes him uniquely vulnerable to the particular appeal Isabel makes. In our first glimpse of Pierre with Lucy he idealizes her as an 'invoking angel' while idealizing himself as a soldier marching under her 'colors'. She participates in the role-playing, crying '"Bravissimo! oh, my only recruit!"' when he fastens her flower to his bosom (4), and both of them speak in what seems an absurdly heightened rhetoric. From this depiction of Pierre as romantic cavalier Melville immediately moves to the depiction of 'romantic filial love', Pierre's benignly presented but ultimately unhealthy habit of treating 'his pedastaled mother' with a 'strange license' under which 'they were wont to call each other brother and sister' (5). Any suitor who might dare to propose marriage to this youthful-appearing widow 'would by some peremptory unrevealed agency immediately disappear from the earth', dispatched by her jealous chivalric protector (5). Pierre's dead father, we learn, had left him a legacy of idealistic maxims, one of which was that no one could claim to be a gentleman unless he 'could also rightfully assume the meek, but kingly style of Christian' (6). Thus at sixteen Pierre, playing the role of young Christian gentleman, partakes of the Holy Sacraments. In Pierre's exalted view 'the complete polished steel of the gentleman' was thereby 'girded with Religion's silken sash' (7). In this atmosphere of ideality he longs for a sister, someone whom he 'might love, and protect, and fight for, if need be' (7). He repeatedly images himself as would-be champion: 'It must be a glorious thing to engage in a mortal quarrel on a sweet sister's behalf!' (7). Predisposed toward such a self-image by both his parents, Pierre finds another source of chivalric notions in Nature herself, who in the beginning did 'bravely' by him (13): 'She lifted her spangled crest of a thickly-starred night, and forth at that glimpse of their divine Captain and Lord, ten thousand mailed thoughts of heroicness started up in Pierre's soul, and glared round for some insulted good cause to defend' (14).

For none of these chivalric impulses is there a normal outlet. There is no real likelihood that Pierre will need to fend off suitors from his mother, despite his playful-earnest role of her knight in waiting. With Lucy, Pierre's chivalric notions must be reduced merely to the courtesies of courtship, since she hardly needs his defence, what with two youthful brothers themselves overeager to fulfil their own chivalric obligations toward her. The first true appeal to his chivalry comes with his earliest glimpse of Isabel's face, on which 'he seemed to see the fair ground where Anguish had contended with Beauty, and neither being conqueror, both had laid down on the field' (47). The narrator's language reveals the intensity of Pierre's chivalric obsession. Beyond the bewildering allure of the beauty and the anguish of the face, Pierre is aware of a special effect, 'the face somehow mystically appealing to his own private and individual affections; and by a silent and tyrannic call, challenging him in his deepest moral being, and summoning Truth, Love, Pity, Conscience, to the stand' (49). Until he receives Isabel's letter, Pierre resists this appeal to his heroism, since his other chivalric obligations, his duty to his mother and his fiancée, forbid any response and since there is no reasonable course of action he can take. Her letter finally gives him the heroic good cause he has been looking for: suddenly he has the sister on whose behalf he can engage in a mortal quarrel. After the first devastating shock, the letter arouses all his would-be heroic, chivalric impulses: he will 'comfort', 'stand by', and 'fight for' Isabel (66).

Yet Pierre is woefully ill-equipped to set out as a Christian Knight-Champion, most obviously because the pattern of chivalric, romantic idealization has developed simultaneously with dangerous sublimation of his sexual feelings. His glide toward physical maturity, we are told at the outset, was accompanied by ambiguous feelings aroused during his reading in 'his father's fastidiously picked and decorous library' (6). There the 'Spenserian nymphs had early led him into many a maze of all-bewildering beauty' that created 'a graceful glow on his limbs,

and soft, imaginative flames in his heart' (6). When first mentioned these nymphs seem to be summoning courtly, aesthetic
impulses, but later it becomes clear that Pierre is unconsciously
responding to them with the stirrings of puberty. For most of
the novel, in fact, Pierre idealizes his sexual impulses, failing to
recognize them for what they are. Latently incestuous, his
courtly 'lover-like adoration' of his mother (16) is deceptively
suffused with religious sentiment: the spell which wheeled
mother and son in one orbit of joy seemed 'almost to realize here
below the sweet dreams of those religious enthusiasts, who paint
to us a Paradise to come, when etherealized from all drosses and
stains, the holiest passion of man shall unite all kindreds and
climes in one circle of pure and unimpairable delight' (16). At
the time the novel opens, Pierre is still unprepared to recognize
his sexual feelings, despite his engagement to Lucy. During
their outing in the phaeton he alternates between mysticalness
and merriment, unaware of the strength of his own sexuality,
for he does not acknowledge the erotic nature of the 'subterranean sprites and gnomes' and 'naiads' that surround him (34).
Lucy instinctively shrinks from him in 'Fear and Wonder' (35)
when he bursts 'forth in some screaming shout of joy', the
'striped tigers of his chestnut eyes' leaping 'in their lashed cages
with a fierce delight'. But even after holding Lucy's hand,
'feeling, softly feeling of its soft tinglingness', Pierre still
idealizes his sexuality, diffusing it into an exalted response to
nature, so that he seems like someone 'in linked correspondence
with the summer lightnings', by 'sweet shock on shock, receiving
intimating foretastes of the etherealest delights of earth' (36).
Later, as he fetches a portfolio from Lucy's chamber, we learn
of more mental contortions which he undergoes in order to
sublimate and generalize the feelings aroused in him:

> He never had entered that chamber but with feelings of a
> wonderful reverentialness. The carpet seemed as holy
> ground. Every chair seemed sanctified by some departed
> saint, there once seated long ago. Here his book of Love
> was all a rubric, and said – Bow now, Pierre, bow. But this
> extreme loyalty to the piety of love, called from him by such
> glimpses of its most secret inner shrine, was not unrelieved
> betimes by such quickenings of all his pulses, that in
> fantasy he pressed the wide beauty of the world in his

embracing arms; for all his world resolved itself into his heart's best love for Lucy. (39)

Thus predisposed, Pierre's mental processes twist themselves anew at the sewing circle in order to let him feel that the mysterious face he has glimpsed is somehow tyrannically challenging him 'in his deepest moral being' (49). Characteristically, he manages to tame and prettify the profound experience, safely Spenserizing it into a 'delicious sadness' so that some 'hazy fairy swam above him in the heavenly ether, and showered down upon him the sweetest pearls of pensiveness' (54).

One immediate aftereffect of reading Isabel's letter is that Pierre suddenly sees his father as morally corrupt, although he had always idolized him to the point of sacrilege (68), and the narrator emphasizes that the extreme of Pierre's idealization was possible only because at the age of nineteen he 'had never yet become so thoroughly initiated into that darker, though truer aspect of things, which an entire residence in the city from the earliest period of life, almost inevitably engraves upon the mind of any keenly observant and reflective youth' (69). To be sure, during the four years that he had possessed the chair portrait of his father, Pierre had felt 'ever new conceits come vaporing up' in him (83), so that the portrait seemed to speak with his father's voice: 'I am thy father, boy. There was once a certain, oh, but too lovely young Frenchwoman, Pierre'. Then, 'starting from these reveries and trances, Pierre would regain the assured element of consciously bidden and self-propelled thought' (84), promising never again to fall into such midnight reveries, suppressing suspicions of his father even as he begins to diffuse his own sexual feelings. In his agonized hours following the reading of Isabel's letter, Pierre feels that 'his whole previous moral being' (87) has been overturned. But though he is no longer free to worship his father, he still does not apply to himself the lesson earlier intimated by the chair portrait and apparently confirmed by Isabel's letter, that 'Youth is hot, and temptation strong', that beneath seeming innocence sexual impulses may be stirring (83). His sense of his own immaculateness is chronic. In sublime delusion he feels Christlike, as if 'deep in him lurked a divine unidentifiableness, that owned no earthly kith or kin' (89). While the narrator offers us 'hell-glimpses' (107), reminding us that Pierre was championing 'womanly beauty, and not womanly ugliness', Pierre himself is asking heaven to confirm him in his 'Christ-like feeling' (106).

More mental contortions follow as the deluded Christian knight begins to respond to Isabel's attractiveness. Accustomed from adolescence to a certain falseness in the relationship of mother-son, and more recently exposed to the new artifice by which Mrs Glendinning had converted Lucy into her little sister, Pierre blames Fate for his bewildered feelings about Isabel: 'Fate had done this thing for them. Fate had separated the brother and the sister, till to each other they somehow seemed so not at all. Sisters shrink not from their brother's kisses' (142). Pierre begins 'to seem to see the mere imaginariness of the so supposed solidest principle of human association' – an incipient discrediting of the taboo against incest – yet feels 'that never, never would he be able to embrace Isabel with the mere brotherly embrace; while the thought of any other caress, which took hold of any domesticness, was entirely vacant from his uncontaminated soul, for it had never consciously intruded there' (142). In this state of mind, and just because his latent incestuous feelings are now stirring, Pierre is compelled, all ignorantly, to sublimate: 'Isabel wholly soared out of the realms of mortalness, and for him became transfigured in the highest heaven of uncorrupted Love' (142). Even as Lucy's bedroom had represented Love's 'secret inner shrine' for Pierre, at his second interview with Isabel the 'deep oaken recess of the double-casement' seems to him the 'vestibule of some awful shrine' (149), though Isabel's power over him is by now more obviously erotic: Pierre feels himself (150) 'surrounded by ten thousand sprites and gnomes, and his whole soul was swayed and tossed by supernatural tides'. (Here the narrator's word 'soul' merely reflects Pierre's own self-protective instinct toward sublimation.) Aware of an 'extraordinary physical magnetism' in Isabel, Pierre nevertheless generalizes his sexual attraction by associating it with a 'Pantheistic master-spell, which eternally locks in mystery and in muteness the universal subject world' (151). Reminiscent of his pledge to Lucy of 'the immutable eternities of joyfulness' (36), Pierre makes extravagant lover-like declarations to Isabel, wishing that his kisses on her hand 'were on the heart itself, and dropt the seeds of

eternal joy and comfort there' (154). In egregious delusion of
immaculate magnanimity, his pledges to Isabel become as
extravagant as his recurrent threats to the gods: 'we will love
with the pure and perfect love of angel to an angel. If ever I fall
from thee, dear Isabel, may Pierre fall from himself; fall back
forever into vacant nothingness and night!' (154). By reinforc-
ing his sense of his own Christlikeness, calling him a 'visible
token' of the 'invisible angel-hoods', and praising the 'gospel' of
his acts (156), Isabel aids Pierre in sublimating the passion
increasingly evident in his words.

Yet both Isabel and Pierre use the licence of their supposed
brother-and-sister, champion-and-damsel, relationship to
indulge in verbal love-making. In language that appeals to
Pierre's religious-chivalric impulses, Isabel describes her
reluctant surrender to him at the sewing circle: 'Once having
met thy fixed regardful glance; once having seen the full
angelicalness in thee, my whole soul was undone by thee . . . till
I knew, that utterly decay and die away I must, unless pride let
me go, and I, with the one little trumpet of a pen, blew my heart's
shrillest blast, and called dear Pierre to me' (159). In his own
imagination Pierre still sees himself as Christlike knight. When
Isabel fears that he might be hurt by any public or secret
relationship with her, he lies – denies what he has so recently
learned about his father – in order to keep his heroic cause from
slipping away: 'Is Love a harm? Can Truth betray to pain?
Sweet Isabel, how can hurt come in the path to God?' (159–60).
He swears by heaven that he 'will crush the disdainful world
down on its knees' to Isabel (160). As she exultingly responds,
her 'long scornful hair' trails out like a 'disheveled banner'
before the would-be knight, who acknowledges 'that irrespec-
tive, darting majesty of humanity, which can be majestical and
menacing in woman as in man' (160). (A part of Isabel's allure
for Pierre is her fleeting resemblance to his mother, whose
'stately beauty had ever somewhat martial in it' [20].) As a
culmination to the emotional self-indulgence which increases
throughout this interview, Pierre and Isabel partake of what
Pierre blasphemously calls 'the real sacrament of the supper'
(162).

Miserably deluded, Pierre thinks, even after his second interview with Isabel, that he is responding to 'the unsuppressible

and unmistakable cry of the godhead through her soul', a cry
which commands him 'to fly to her, and do his highest and most
glorious duty in the world' (174). By the time he has reached his
final resolution his formula, sublimated once again, has become:
'Lucy or God ?' (181), though soon afterward Pierre speciously
claims that he and Isabel will act deceitfully for the 'united good'
of themselves and those they deceive (190). Just after insisting
that he is 'pure' (191) and claiming that he and Isabel reach up
alike to a 'glorious ideal' (192), Pierre whispers his plan as 'his
mouth wet her ear' (192). Then comes an immediate and
appalling descent from the exaltation: 'The girl moved not; was
done with all her tremblings; leaned closer to him, with an
inexpressible strangeness of an intense love, new and inexplicable. Over the face of Pierre there shot a terrible self-revelation;
he imprinted repeated burning kisses upon her; pressed hard her
hand; would not let go her sweet and awful passiveness. Then
they changed; they coiled together, and entangledly stood mute'
(192). For the first time in the book Melville's deluded idealist
acts – and knows that he acts – out of undisguised sexual
passion.

But Pierre's capacity for evading unpleasant self-knowledge
is far from exhausted. Shortly afterwards, at the Black Swan Inn,
he decides that his memorial gold pieces must be spent now 'in
this sacred cause' (196), an obvious denial that Isabel had
'become a thing of intense and fearful love for him' (197) –
fearful precisely because of his terrible self-revelation at the
dairy. Yet that sundown at the Inn Pierre burns the chair
portrait of his father out of an unconscious need to free himself
of the strongest visible reminder that his passion for Isabel,
whatever else it is, is incestuous. In the coach next morning his
'still imperfectly conscious, incipient, new-mingled emotion
toward this mysterious being' (206) appals him, to the point
that he feels 'threatened by the possibility of a sin anomalous
and accursed' – perhaps the unpardonable sin itself. Though he
has learned much about his mother's and his father's character,
he is still in the first stages of reluctantly learning about his own.
Just as he had destroyed the reminder of Isabel's paternity the
night before, now in the coach Pierre refuses to recognize the
applicability of the strange pamphlet on 'Chronometricals and
Horologicals' either to his own situation or to Christianity in

general: he can neither admit that an absolute attempt to obey Christ is apt to involve ordinary mortals 'in strange, *unique* follies and sins, unimagined before' (213) nor that Christianity has flourished for two millennia only by systematically diluting the edicts of its founder, rather than taking them literally, as he has tried to do.

Nowhere in the book, moreover, does Pierre see that for all his efforts to be Christlike he has never been a true Christian. Despite his partaking with his mother of the Holy Sacraments, he has in fact been only nominally a Christian, drawn to the Church as a family responsibility laid down by his father, whose maxim linked gentlemanhood and Christianity. The super-human powers Pierre invokes are ill-sortedly Christian or pagan; consistently he images his relationship with such powers as an antagonistic one: demons or gods, they are to be threatened and, especially, bargained with. The language he uses again and again threatens what he will do 'if' the powers do not act as he wishes. He conjures the 'sovereign powers' that claim all his 'leal worshipings' to lift the veil between him and the mysterious face; if they abandon him to 'an unknown misery', his faith 'may clean depart' and leave him 'a railing atheist' (41). If 'deprived of joy', he feels he would 'find cause for deadly feuds with things invisible' (41). He feels he has a 'choice quarrel' with the Fate which had led him to think the world was one of Joy, if in fact the night which wraps his soul after he reads Isabel's letter is genuine (65). In the interval before his first interview with Isabel he prays that heaven 'new-string' his soul (106), confirming in him 'the Christ-like feeling' he first felt on reading her letter; yet in the same speech he simultaneously invokes and threatens the 'sovereign powers' (106–7) if they betray his faith in them:

> I cast my eternal die this day, ye powers. On my strong faith in ye Invisibles, I stake three whole felicities, and three whole lives this day. If ye forsake me now, – farewell to Faith, farewell to Truth, farewell to God; exiled for aye from God and man, I shall declare myself an equal power with both; free to make war on Night and Day, and all thoughts and things of mind and matter, which the upper and the nether firmaments do clasp! (107)

Pierre's new Christlikeness is a most ambiguous one, since it leads instantly to threats against God. Then, between the two interviews with Isabel, Pierre slides under 'the very brow of the beetlings and the menacings of the Terror Stone', named by him for the temple of Memnon. Not threatening the Stone, he nevertheless promulgates a series of conditions in which the 'Mute Massiveness' is invited to fall on him (134). When the Stone fails to act on the implied challenge, he adolescently assumes a new haughtiness and goes his 'moody way' as though he 'owed thanks to none' (135).

The threats and bargains with the gods culminate in the scene with Pierre and Isabel at the Apostles' the third night after their arrival in the city. Once again Pierre makes pledges, inviting the 'high gods' to join the devils against him if he deceives Isabel (272). Once again he invites instant punishment if he fails in Virtue: 'then close in and crush me, ye stony walls, and into one gulf let all things tumble together!' (273). Once again he warns the gods, this time to 'look after their own combustibles': 'If they have put powder-casks in me – let them look to it! let them look to it!' (273). But in a crucial difference from earlier scenes Pierre now suspects that man himself, instead of the gods, may be a 'vile juggler and cheat' (272). Incapable now in Isabel's presence of denying to himself her erotic appeal, he fears that 'uttermost virtue, after all' may prove 'but a betraying pander to the monstrousest vice', and finally declares that the 'demigods trample on trash, and Virtue and Vice are trash!' (273). Declaring that Virtue and Vice are both nothing, and having already rid himself of the chair portrait, the most tangible reminder of Isabel's link to his father, Pierre is now free to commit incest, though whether or not actual sexual intercourse occurs that night at the Apostles' remains ambiguous but hideously possible.

Up to Pierre's arrival in the city with Isabel and Delly, everything has worked together to enhance the attentive reader's sense that he is in the hands of a profound thinker and innovative craftsman who will convey him through yet more hazardous regions of psychological and aesthetic experience. Melville has not only managed to put sensational gothic plot elements to the service of an acute analysis of a tortuously complex mind; he has also managed to convert analysis into very vivid action, repeatedly portraying Pierre's psychological states and processes in extended metaphors and images, passages that are short, graphic, and frequently intense narratives in themselves.[10] In these highly-charged passages, Melville combines penetrating analysis of his hero's states of mind with the enunciation of general truths, so that the record of Pierre's particular experience is continually expanding to include human experience at large.[11] By the beginning of Book XVI, 'First Night of Their Arrival in the City', the reader wants nothing more than to follow 'the thoughtful river' of Pierre's mind through all the ambiguous consequences of his sublimely absolute and miserably deluded behaviour. Yet despite the brilliance of the scene on the third night at the Apostles', the wish goes mainly unfulfilled. Melville's primary concerns in the first half of the novel only intermittently engage his attention in the second half, and at times he seems lamentably unaware of the direction the first half was taking.

Symptomatic is the flaw in the first paragraph of Book XVII, 'Young America in Literature':

> Among the various conflicting modes of writing history, there would seem to be two grand practical distinctions, under which all the rest must subordinately range. By the one mode, all contemporaneous circumstances, facts, and events must be set down contemporaneously; by the other, they are only to be set down as the general stream of the narrative shall dictate; for matters which are kindred in time, may be very irrelative in themselves. I elect neither of these; I am careless of either; both are well enough in their way; I write precisely as I please. (244)

Earlier Melville had talked bluntly about his demands on the reader: 'This history goes forward and goes backward, as occasion calls. Nimble center, circumference elastic you must have' (54). He had called attention to his apparent disregard of rules in a passage that might strike the reader as 'rather irregular sort of writing' (25), and had announced that he followed 'the flowing river in the cave of man' careless whither he be led, reckless where he land (107). In these instances he had been in superb control, knowing exactly what he was doing with his stylistic absurdities in Books I and II, then knowing that his simultaneous exploration of Pierre's mind and his own might lead him into unknown winding passages (even as he kept to the outline of his plot), but confident that he could bravely follow that flowing river wherever it ran. Not recking where he landed was a way of proclaiming his determination to tell everything 'in this book of sacred truth' (107); he was not abandoning a point of view but asserting his determination to hold to it. The beginning of 'Young America in Literature' marks a drastic change in Melville's authorial purpose, a deep draining off of his control over the relationship between narrator and reader. The change is due to what happened in Melville's life between the last days of 1851 and the first days of 1852, but our concern here is with the effects on the manuscript, not the biographical causes.

After his claim to write precisely as he pleased, Melville continues with this remarkably inexact passage: 'In the earlier chapters of this volume, it has somewhere been passingly intimated, that Pierre was not only a reader of the poets and other fine writers, but likewise – and what is a very different thing from the other – a thorough allegorical understander of them, a profound emotional sympathizer with them' (244). On the contrary, we had been told, by Pierre himself in a moment of insight, that he had *not* been that sort of reader: 'Oh, hitherto I have but piled up words; bought books, and bought some small experiences, and builded me in libraries; now I sit down and read' (91). Furthermore, Melville had also asserted that before Pierre was enlightened by flashing revelations of Grief's wonderful fire, he had *not* been a thorough allegorical understander of the poets:

> Fortunately for the felicity of the Dilletante in Literature, the horrible allegorical meanings of the Inferno, lie not on the surface; but unfortunately for the earnest and youthful piercers into truth and reality, those horrible meanings, when first discovered, infuse their poison into a spot previously unprovided with that sovereign antidote of a sense of uncapitulatable security, which is only the possession of the furthest advanced and profoundest souls. (169)

When he began Book XVII, Melville had simply forgotten this crucial aspect of his characterization of Pierre.[12] But even in the process of crediting Pierre with being 'a thorough allegorical understander' of and 'a profound emotional sympathizer' with poets and other fine writers, Melville seems to have recognized his blunder and attempted an immediate recovery:

> Not that as yet his young and immature soul had been
> accosted by the Wonderful Mutes, and through the vast
> halls of Silent Truth, had been ushered into the full, secret,
> eternally inviolable Sanhedrim, where the Poetic Magi dis-
> cuss, in glorious gibberish, the Alpha and Omega of the
> Universe. But among the beautiful imaginings of the second
> and third degree of poets, he freely and comprehendingly
> ranged. (244–5)

In these rapid second thoughts Melville ends up saying quite
another thing from what he had just said: in fact, he reverts to
saying something very like what he had denied at the outset of
the paragraph, that Pierre was no more than a normally alert
reader. The bitter fun Melville has with his mockery of the
rules of writing comes at the considerable cost of jeopardizing
the reader's trust in the narrative voice.

Deflected into preoccupation with his own literary career,
Melville in Books XVII and XVIII let absurdities intrude upon
what he wrote of Pierre, as in his analysis of the phenomenon of
young writers who win instant success with a book original in
subject matter although not the product of a genuinely original
mind. In this passage (259) Melville plainly has begun to write
about the reception of his own *Typee* six years before, not about
Pierre. From his new vantage point Melville was honest in his
self-assessment, sure that *Typee* was, after all, original – the first
eyewitness account of Polynesian life with the readability of
fiction – although he had unoriginally cannibalized his sourcebooks and employed a second or third hand style. The satire in
Books XVII and XVIII is acute, but only as applied to Melville
and his own critics, not to Pierre, in whose history it is dis-
tractingly out of place. Pierre, of course, has never 'embodied'
any experiences at all in a book, much less 'some rich and
peculiar experience' (259), although the reader is belatedly
apprised of his authorship of 'little sonnets, brief meditative
poems, and moral essays' (248). In suddenly determining to
take satiric revenge upon his own reviewers and his literary
competitors, Melville is indulging in a 'lamentable rearward
aggressiveness' at least as unwarrantable and foolish as Pierre's
toward the Rev. Mr Falsgrave (166). The reader was well prepared for Pierre's folly, but the narrator's own mature wisdom

throughout the Saddle Meadows section, especially his cautious distance from his hero, had left the reader unprepared for authorial recklessness.

Even before the disastrous Books on literature in America ('before' in final placement though not necessarily so in order of composition), Melville had begun dissipating much of the accumulated tension by introducing lengthy narrative and expository passages largely or wholly irrelevant to the central concern of Pierre's commitment to Isabel. Book xv, 'The Cousins', which is devoted to the intense adolescent love-friendship between Pierre and Glen, might be defended as an essential part of this ruthlessly honest history of the soul in which no taboo in Melville's society can be left unviolated, and indeed the analysis of the stages in that relationship are interesting in themselves. However, the Book seems too long and distinctly anticlimactic, coming immediately after the pamphlet: it is not focused on major issues and the analysis does not impel the book forward, does not tell the reader things he needs to know or prepare him for highly significant things to come. Even the most comparable passage in the early part of the novel, the account of Aunt Dorothea's reminiscences, does not seem so relaxed, because there the reader is in suspense, actively putting things together as he absorbs and meditates upon her story rather faster than she tells it. Books xvii and xviii have even less to do with the central issues of the first fourteen Books. By contrast, in Book xix, 'The Church of the Apostles', the history of the building and its inhabitants is potentially relevant, since the Apostles can be seen as versions of Pierre, thwarted idealists, and since the building itself at least casually symbolizes the transfer of power from Christianity to something akin to Transcendentalism. Not enough is made of these points, and the 'gamesome' banter which Melville adopts (267) is distinctly out of keeping with the high seriousness of most of the early part of the novel. The satiric grotesquerie of these pages goes, if not for naught, at least for less than it might have gone in another novel, where other expectations had been set up. Book xx, 'Charlie Millthorpe', seems even more extraneous, since it begins by explaining something which had already been accepted without explanation – Pierre's being at the Apostles'. Now, after the fact, and after the intense scene between Pierre and Isabel which hints at actual physical incest, the reader is told much more than he wants to know about details which are not strictly relevant. Unlike the earlier Books ('Presentiment and Verification' makes a good contrast), Book xx does not significantly add to our knowledge of Pierre's motivation or to our understanding of the main themes. There is considerable verve in the portrait of Charles Millthorpe, just as there had been in the account of the Apostles, but none of the intensity the reader had come to expect. Later, the jocular account of the Apostles' eccentricities (298–301) is jarring, especially when the narrator is led into this commentary upon idealistic behaviour:

> Among all the innate, hyena-like repellants to the reception of any set form of a spiritually-minded and pure arche-typical faith, there is nothing so potent in its skeptical tendencies, as that inevitable perverse ridiculousness, which so often bestreaks some of the essentially finest and noblest aspirations of those men, who disgusted with the common conventional quackeries, strive, in their clogged terrestrial humanities, after some imperfectly discerned, but heavenly ideals: ideals, not only imperfectly discerned in themselves, but the path to them so little traceable, that no two minds will entirely agree upon it.

These observations, offered as if they had just occurred to the narrator, had already formed some of the darkest implications of the pamphlet.[13]

Throughout the second half of the book Melville continues this sort of generalizing tendency, making observations on such subjects as 'boy-love' and the change to love of the opposite sex (216–17), the advisability of converting 'some well-wishers into foes' (221–2), the advantages of simplicity (224–5), the need for 'utter gladiatorianism' in dealing with some reversals of fortune (226–7), the 'dread of tautology' (227), the nature of coach-drivers (232), and 'the *povertiresque* in the social land-scape' (276–7). Earlier in the novel Melville's generalizing commentary had been a major source of power, dealing as it had with the motivation and states of mind of Pierre and the social, moral, and metaphysical problems he exemplified. In the second half the authorial commentary largely creates the impression of improvisation and redundancy, an impression emphasized when the narrator compares himself to one of the 'strolling improvisatores of Italy' (259) and when he carelessly concludes one Book with the mention of something 'by way of bagatelle' (294). The reader who has paid alert attention can only feel cheated by this casualness and laxity in authorial commentary.

Bad as these lapses are, by far the worst failure lies in Melville's altered treatment of Pierre. In the first half of the book, one of the most remarkable features had been the scrupulous and often brilliant presentation of the hero's motives and states of mind. In the last Books, Melville not only fails to provide certain contemplative scenes which were earlier implied if not directly promised (such as scenes in which Pierre thinks about the episode of the Memnon Stone after reaching the city or in which he remembers his first evening with Isabel), he also neglects to analyze sufficiently Pierre's present states of mind, especially as they involve Isabel. Pierre had vowed to cherish and protect her, to treat her as an artisan handles 'the most exquisite, and fragile filagree of Genoa' (189). But he fails to carry out his pledges; instead, in a few days after reaching the city he becomes almost entirely preoccupied with the book he is writing. Isabel is not allowed to participate in his labours (except much later to read aloud proofs to him) and is no longer at the centre of his thoughts. After the arrival in the city, in fact, Isabel is absent from the narrative for long periods. Apart from the scene on the third night at the Apostles' (271-4), she scarcely figures in the story at all until the reintroduction of Lucy. Henry A. Murray aptly comments: 'Pierre, having devoured what Isabel had to give him, is withdrawing libido (interest, love) from her as a person and using it to fold, and warm, and egg round embryoes of thought and to feed a precipitant ambition'.[14] Such an outcome is perhaps credible enough, considering the trauma and the 'widely explosive' mental development Pierre has experienced; even so, Melville appears to have seized upon Pierre's authorship, the pretext for dramatizing his own precarious literary career, as a way to avoid tracing any minute shiftings in the relationship between Pierre and Isabel.[15]

Markedly, what we do learn of Pierre and Isabel – sexual arousal, deceit, insincerity, and unease on his part, suspicion, jealousy, and hysteria on hers – is presented dramatically for

the most part, without the earlier omniscient commentary. We
are told that, on the news of his mother's death and Glen
Stanly's inheritance of Saddle Meadows and rumoured courtship of Lucy, Pierre curses himself for an 'idiot fool' because
'he had himself, as it were, resigned his noble birthright to a
cunning kinsman for a mess of pottage, which now proved all
but ashes in his mouth' (289). We also learn that he feels that
these are 'unworthy pangs' and resolves to hide them from
Isabel (289). But otherwise Pierre's feelings for her are scarcely
explored. His awareness or unawareness of the extent to which
the relationship has deteriorated, his attitude toward that
change, are not examined. Pierre's incestuous passion, once
central to the book, becomes the subject of offhand allusion:
'Not to speak of his being devoured by the all-exacting theme of
his book, there were sinister preoccupations in him of a still
subtler and more fearful sort, of which some inklings have
already been given' (308). When late in the novel we learn of
Pierre that the 'most tremendous displacing and revolutionizing
thoughts were upheaving in him, with reference to Isabel' (353),
the only such thought we actually learn about is the question of
whether she is truly his half-sister. The crucial information
that Pierre's virtuous enthusiasm in behalf of Isabel has declined
comes in an aside; his 'transcendental persuasions' that she was
his sister, we learn, were 'originally born, as he now seemed to
feel, purely of an intense procreative enthusiasm: – an enthusiasm no longer so all-potential with him as of yore' (353). Melville's exploration of Pierre's problems as an author tends to
disguise his failure to explore Pierre's changing attitude toward
Isabel, but the careful reader cannot help but be aware of it.

The more emotionally involved Melville becomes in his
portrayal of Pierre as author, the more he loses his grasp on the
implications of other parts of his narrative. As Pierre's suffering
and degradation in his attempt to be a profound writer worsen,
Melville's rhetoric starts to exalt him: 'In the midst of the
merriments of the mutations of Time, Pierre hath ringed himself in with the grief of Eternity. Pierre is a peak inflexible in the
heart of Time, as the isle-peak, Piko, stands unassaultable in the
midst of waves' (304). Implicitly approving Pierre's commitment, in spite of the self-destructiveness of his attempt to write
a great book, Melville speaks of the 'devouring profundities'

that have opened up in his hero: 'would he, he could not now be entertainingly and profitably shallow in some pellucid and merry romance' (305). In the next passage on Pierre as author, it is in his 'deepest, highest part' that he is 'utterly without sympathy from any thing divine, human, brute, or vegetable' (338). The mental distance between author and character diminishes appreciably: 'the deeper and the deeper' that he dives, Pierre perceives the 'everlasting elusiveness of Truth' (339), an elusiveness that Melville as narrator had postulated earlier (at page 165 and page 285). Pierre's scorn of the critics now is clearly Melville's: 'beforehand he felt the pyramidical scorn of the genuine loftiness for the whole infinite company of infinitesimal critics' (339). As the distance between author and hero narrows, the hero is increasingly exalted, and Melville speaks of Pierre in the same terms as Pierre sees himself. Pierre begins to feel 'that in him, the thews of a Titan were fore-stallingly cut by the scissors of Fate' (339); Melville comments: 'Against the breaking heart, and the bursting head; against all the dismal lassitude, and deathful faintness and sleeplessness, and whirlingness, and craziness, still he like a demigod bore up' (339). Shortly afterwards Melville writes that the 'very blood' in Pierre's body 'had in vain rebelled against his Titanic soul' (341). In focusing on his hero as author, Melville loses sight of Pierre the young man attempting to be Christlike but undone by human flaws. Now he portrays Pierre the embattled demi-god, whose degradation is an inevitable part of his Titanic greatness: 'gifted with loftiness' he is 'dragged down to the mud' (339), even literally (341). Pierre is identified with Enceladus, 'the most potent of all the giants', one with 'un-conquerable front' and 'unabasable face' (345). Melville approves the 'reckless sky-assaulting mood' of both Enceladus and Pierre: 'For it is according to eternal fitness, that the precipitated Titan should still seek to regain his paternal birth-right even by fierce escalade. Wherefore whoso storms the sky gives best proof he came from thither! But whatso crawls contented in the moat before that crystal fort, shows it was born within that slime, and there forever will abide' (347).

But Pierre's increased stature as 'deep-diving' author and admirable 'sky-assaulting' demigod works against the logic of much of the novel's development. For despite Melville's preoccupation with the hardship and misery of Pierre's attempt to write profoundly, the last Books still bring to a climax the disaster entailed in his attempt to be Christlike. A number of events forcefully recall the pamphlet's warnings of calamity for the chronometrical idealist. Lucy writes to Pierre that she intends to join him, that she is commanded by God (311), and that in her 'long swoon' (after Pierre told her he was married) 'heaven' was preparing her for a 'superhuman office', wholly estranging her from 'this earth' and fitting her 'for a celestial mission in terrestrial elements' (310). Pierre is 'sacrificing' himself, she writes, and she is hastening to 're-tie' herself to him (309). Obeying this impulse, she arrives at the Apostles' imitating Pierre's chronometrical self-sacrifice, thereby compounding the possibilities for disaster. In these last Books we are reminded more than once that Pierre is sexually attracted to Isabel, that he may have committed incest with her (308, 337, 351). But after the arrival of Lucy's letter, his relationship with Isabel is seen to deteriorate rapidly and his relationship with Lucy becomes dangerously ambiguous. In the final pages, Pierre bitterly rejects both Isabel and Lucy, and murders Glen; in his prison-cell Lucy dies on hearing Isabel call herself Pierre's sister; Pierre and Isabel commit suicide. Melville does not comment directly on much of the action in the last four Books of the novel, but these events clearly appear to illustrate the pamphlet's lesson that 'strange, *unique* follies and sins' are to be expected from one, like Pierre, attempting 'to live in this world according to the strict letter of the chronometricals' (213).

Yet for all Pierre's status as a profound, deep-diving author, he never consciously understands the relevance of the pamphlet to his life, though he has glimmerings of understanding (and Melville says that unconsciously he understood its application by the end of his life). He does not recognize the danger of Lucy's imitation of his sacrifice of self for another, in spite of his own experience. He reads Lucy's letter and is certain that 'whatever her enigmatical delusion' she 'remained transparently immaculate' in her heart (317), without even recognizing the possibility of a sexual motive in her decision to join him, as in his own deluded resolve to protect Isabel by living with her. He naively admires Lucy as 'an angel' (311), unmindful of the insidious sexual element in his earlier worship of Isabel as 'angel'. He later feels that 'some strange heavenly influence was near him, to keep him from some uttermost harm' (337-8), once Lucy is ensconced at the Apostles', though to Isabel's 'covertly watchful eye' he 'would seem to look upon Lucy with an expression illy befitting their singular and so-supposed merely cousinly relation' (337). Even in the death-cell he sees his predicament as merely the result of his refusal to disown and portion off Isabel (360), just as earlier he tries to accept his grief at the news of his mother's death as a part of the cost at which 'the more exalted virtues are gained' (286). After belatedly recognizing the incestuous nature of his attraction to Isabel, Pierre copes with the knowledge by shutting it out of his consciousness and continuing to deceive himself about his motives. In earlier Books Melville frequently comments on and analyzes Pierre's lack of awareness and his self-deception; now in the last four Books such commentary is notably lacking. Instead, Melville exalts his hero as consumed with devouring profundities, the result of his recent momentous experiences, even while Pierre is revealing a lack of profundity, a lack of perception, and an inability to face the truth of what he has actually experienced – limitations that are as dangerous as ever. While earlier Melville had commented incisively on Pierre's 'strange oversights and inconsistencies', he now fails to recognize a major contradiction in his characterization. He also forgets the origin of Pierre's book. Pierre announces to Isabel that he will 'gospelize the world anew' (273), but his new gospel is delusive, merely the result of his inability to accept himself as anything less than immaculate. Rather than recognizing that he is no longer virtuous, he proclaims that 'Virtue and Vice are trash!' (273). Melville makes no attempt to reconcile Pierre's initial evasion of truth as an author with his later supposed profundity. Nor does he make any attempt to explain the incongruity of Pierre's writing a blasphemous new gospel yet feeling protected by 'some strange heavenly influence' when Lucy joins him, though the incongruity makes Pierre seem more a simpleton than a man of profundity.

Still other parts of the novel are in conflict with the ending. In *Pierre* Melville sets out to demonstrate, among other things, that chronometrical altruism leads inevitably to catastrophe. His self-renouncing hero, as the pamphlet predicts, arrays 'men's earthly time-keepers against him' (212), falls into a 'fatal despair of becoming all good' (215), and works himself 'woe and death' (212). Yet near the end of this progression Melville endorses his hero's 'Titanism'. Thus, in *Pierre* Melville is sceptical of a world-rejecting Christian ethic because it destroys the individual who holds to it, but finally advocates a world-rejecting Titanism equally destructive of the individual who holds to it. Through many Books he prepares the reader to expect a catastrophic ending, a disaster that will be the inevitable result of Pierre's chronometrical sacrifice for Isabel and of his being merely human. But when the disastrous end comes, Pierre's state of mind is a 'reckless sky-assaulting mood' that Melville admires as evidence of demi-godliness. As he goes out to meet Glen and Fred, Pierre proclaims: '"I defy all world's bread and breath. Here I step out before the drawn-up worlds in widest space, and challenge one and all of them to battle!"' (357). In the prison-cell after the murder of Glen, Pierre is like Enceladus with the mountain thrown down upon him: 'The cumbersome stone ceiling almost rested on his brow; so that the long tiers of massive cell-galleries above seemed partly piled on him'; Pierre's 'immortal, immovable, bleached cheek was dry' (360). His defiance in the prison-cell is again Enceladus-like, again implicitly approved, it would seem, by Melville: 'Well, be it hell. I will mold a trumpet of the flames, and, with my breath of flame, breathe back my defiance!' (360). In a sudden reversal, the chivalric posturing ('challenge one and all of them to battle', 'mold a trumpet of the flames', 'breathe back my defiance'), earlier indicative of Pierre's adolescent delusions, is now associated with a 'heaven-aspiring' nobility (347).

These conflicting attitudes toward Pierre's behaviour are not final, meaningful ambiguities Melville has carefully worked towards, but abrupt, confusing contradictions, the ultimate results of his excessively personal sympathy for Pierre's frustrations as an author. The decision to make the hero an author, whenever it was made, led to some powerful writing in the second half of *Pierre*, particularly in the Enceladus vision. It also deprived Melville of a full sense of what he was doing, in the second half and in the novel as a whole. 'Two books are being writ', said Melville (304), referring to the bungled one Pierre is putting on paper to offer to the world's eyes and the 'larger, and the infinitely better' one 'for Pierre's own private shelf', the one being written in his soul as the other is written on paper. In *Pierre* itself two books were also written, the one up through Book XIV (and intermittently thereafter) which examined the growth of a deluded but idealistic soul when confronted with the world's conventionality, and the later one which expressed Melville's sometimes sardonic, sometimes embittered reflections on his own career. There was no successful fusion of the two. As the new obsession drained off Melville's psychic and creative energies, the original purpose was blighted. Under the circumstances, it may be wrong to think of what *Pierre* might have been: behind Melville there was no educated literary milieu, no available models, no shoptalk with other literary masters, no rigorously critical friend, no one to assure him of ultimate glory – nothing, in short, to help him hold to the pervading idea that impelled the first half of the book. Yet he had accomplished so much in this book that one becomes anguished as Melville's genius goes tragically to waste. The great epic of metaphysical whaling came tormentingly close to being succeeded within a few months by a Kraken-book, one of the finest psychological novels in world literature rather than merely the best psychological novel that had yet been written in English.

Notes and References

1. When he wrote this letter to Hawthorne, Melville had just begun work on *Pierre* or else was at the point of beginning it. The fullest timetable of the composition of the book is in Hershel Parker, 'Why *Pierre* Went Wrong', *Studies in the Novel*, vol. 8 (Spring 1976) 7-23.

2. Furthermore, ways of conceiving and organizing passages recur, as in Book IV, where Melville as narrator announces the ultimate futility of 'all analytical insight' (67) and instead resorts to subtler conjurations to convey his meaning, just as he has Ishmael do in 'The Whiteness of the Whale'.

3. 'Melville's *Pierre*', *New England Quarterly*, vol. 3 (April 1930) 195-234.

4. 'Historical Note', p. 407, in *Pierre*, ed. Harrison Hayford, Hershel Parker, and G. Thomas Tanselle (Evanston and Chicago: Northwestern University Press and the Newberry Library 1971). Page references are to this edition. The 'Historical Note' is by Leon Howard (365-79) and Hershel Parker (379-407).

5. See 'Why *Pierre* Went Wrong', cited in footnote one, and Hershel

Parker's 'Contract: *Pierre*, by Herman Melville', *Proof*, vol. 5 (1977). Briefly, after several weeks' intense work on the manuscript, Melville went to New York City in the last days of 1851 to arrange a contract with the Harpers for publication of *Pierre*, then seen as a shortish book of around 360 pages, not the much longer book of some 500 pages which the Harpers eventually published. Not only did the Harpers fail to give Melville an advance, they also insisted upon less favourable terms than ever before. Distressed by his contract negotiations, and further exacerbated by scathing reviews of *Moby-Dick* which were appearing in the January periodicals, Melville immediately began writing his own literary frustrations into the manuscript. Before he left New York City (apparently in the third week of January 1852), Melville had enlarged the book beyond the size he had stipulated to the publisher and had instructed his lawyer-brother Allan Melville to alter the contract accordingly. Allan's letter to the Harpers on 21 January 1852 establishes the rapidity with which Melville's conception of the book changed and locates that change as occurring between the very end of 1851 and the first week or so of 1852.

6. 'Historical Note', pp. 366 and 372.

7. Melville had recently concluded in fact that 'There are some enterprises in which a careful disorderliness is the true method' (*Moby-Dick*, chapter 82, 'The Honor and Glory of Whaling').

8. In 'Retrospective' Pierre may be portrayed as rather more infantile than a lad of twelve or more should be, for instance. Some apparent awkwardnesses, such as the uncertain age of Isabel, may well be deliberate ambiguities.

9. The word 'nether' is Parker's recent emendation for the first edition's 'nearer'. The emendation will be incorporated in subsequent printings of the Northwestern-Newberry edition.

10. Page 65 provides a clear example: 'now, for the first time, Pierre, Truth rolls a black billow through thy soul! Ah, miserable thou, to whom Truth, in her first tides, bears nothing but wrecks!' The passage continues: 'as the mariner, shipwrecked and cast on the beach, has much ado to escape the recoil of the wave that hurled him there; so Pierre long struggled, and struggled, to escape the recoil of that anguish, which had dashed him out of itself, upon the beach of his swoon'. See also the accounts of the 'shrine in the fresh-foliaged heart of Pierre' (68); the 'choice fountain, in the filial breast of a tender-hearted and intellectually appreciative child' (68); the 'charred landscape' within Pierre (86); the 'billow' that had 'so profoundly whelmed Pierre' (104); the things 'fœtally forming' in Pierre (106); the 'electric fluid' in which Isabel seems to swim (151-2); the 'Hyperborean regions' into which strongest minds are led (165); and the 'vulnerable god' and 'self-upbraiding sailor' (180-1).

11. See, for example, the passages explaining that 'From without, no wonderful effect is wrought within ourselves, unless some

interior, responding wonder meets it' (51); that 'in the warm halls of the heart one single, untestified memory's spark shall suffice to enkindle . . . a blaze of evidence' (71); that the 'inestimable compensation of the heavier woes' is 'a saddened truth' (88); that 'when suddenly encountering the shock of new and unanswerable revelations . . . man, at first, ever seeks to shun all conscious definitiveness in his thoughts and purposes' (92); that the soul of man 'can not, and does never intelligently confront the totality of its wretchedness' when 'on all sides assailed by prospects of disaster' (104); that the 'intensest light of reason and revelation combined, can not shed such blazonings upon the deeper truths in man, as will sometimes proceed from his own profoundest gloom' (169); that 'on the threshold of any wholly new and momentous devoted enterprise, the thousand ulterior intricacies and emperilings to which it must conduct . . . are mostly withheld from sight' (175); and that 'There is a dark, mad mystery in some human hearts' (180).

12. Also, the section of 'Young America in Literature' (250-1) on the flirtatious young ladies who entreat Pierre to 'grace their Albums with some nice little song' (and who live within easy walking or riding range, judging by the way his servants deliver the albums back to their owners) seems out of keeping with the portrayal of the maidens of Saddle Meadows in Book III (p. 46, especially). Until Book XVII there is no hint that Pierre has been sought out by any of the local girls, or that he has had social exchanges of any significance with any of them besides Lucy Tartan (who resides only part of the year in Saddle Meadows). Perhaps an even clearer example of Melville's forgetting his earlier characterization is in Book XXI, 'Plinlimmon', where he declares that a 'varied scope of reading, little suspected by his friends, and randomly acquired by a random but lynx-eyed mind' in the course of 'multifarious, incidental, bibliographic encounterings' as an 'inquirer after Truth' had 'poured one considerable contributary stream into that bottomless spring of original thought which the occasion and time had caused to burst out' in Pierre (283). But earlier Pierre's reading was said to have brought him 'into many a maze of all-bewildering beauty', not Truth (6). These examples are conspicuous; probably some other improvised passages are consistent enough with the rest of the book to escape notice.

13. There is always the possibility that this passage was written before the pamphlet and left uncancelled; similar redundancies were created by late additions in *Typee*. However, Melville's forgetting and improvising elsewhere in the second half of *Pierre* tends to cast doubt on this possibility.

14. *Pierre* (New York: Hendricks House, Inc. 1949) p. lxxxiii.

15. Melville's trip to New York probably coincided with his reaching a point beyond which it would have been difficult to proceed with a cautious enough development of the Pierre-Isabel relationship, for the inhibiting sexual mores of the time would hardly have

allowed him to trace all the stages of an incestuous passion and still have his book published. Whatever comments the Harpers may have made on his work-in-progress, for practical purposes he had written himself into an impasse by the time he established Pierre's menage at the Apostles' and made his ambiguous suggestion that incestuous lust may have been consummated. The impasse would have encouraged his urge to explore his new preoccupation with authorship. It would also have encouraged the introduction of another character to facilitate some exploration of Pierre's relationship with Isabel without intensifying the suggestion of its incestuous nature. Melville's choice of Lucy as this agent had the further advantage of providing, through the involvement of Fred Tartan and Glendinning Stanly, the means of a tragic outcome.

Melville:
The 1853–6 Phase

THIS Shakespeare is a queer man. At times . . . he does
not always seem reliable. There appears to be a certain –
what shall I call it ? – hidden sun, say, about him, at once
enlightening and mystifying.   *The Confidence-Man*

The Piazza Tales

Julian Hawthorne wrote in an otherwise percipient reminiscence
of Melville's character and disposition that 'His later writings
are incomprehensible'. This from Hawthorne's son, who had
presumably been initiated into the meaning and method of his
father's work and so should have had some insight at least into
that art which derived from Hawthorne's, suggests how inevitable it was that Melville could find no public for his fiction after
his early phase as a writer of adventure books about voyages by
sea. Even the incomparable *Benito Cereno* made no real impact
in America in Melville's long lifetime.

But to the modern English and American reader, well trained
in practical criticism and knowing with regard to myth, symbol,
allegory and imagery, the writings of the great 1853–6 phase are
of more interest than the earlier novels, evidently more accomplished as art, more varied – written in the short space of three
years and with desperate need of money, they show an astonish-
ing range of subject-matter, attitude, tone and style – and are
noticeably more condensed, controlled and mature than either
Moby-Dick or *Pierre*, the two previous major works; and this in
spite of the discouraging fact that even *Moby-Dick* had not been
a financial success while *Pierre* had been and remained a dead
loss. Yet Melville rallied from the disappointment, though it
seriously affected his health, and triumphantly wound up this
last phase of prose creativeness with an ironic masterpiece, *The
Confidence-Man*. But in order to understand this difficult and
still highly controversial work one must, it seems to me, have

grasped the nature of the tales written while he was gestating the novel. Published mostly in magazines, they were reprinted as *The Piazza Tales* and reveal his interests and preoccupations in these fertile years as well as the kinds of technique he was inventing for these new purposes.

The Encantadas is simply a series of ten sketches which have as unifying theme the horrors of a tropical waterless Nature which sustains only equally infernal forms of animal and human existence. They show how Melville's imagination at this period was haunted by the memory of the histories of the wretched castaways with their inhuman treatment by fellow-men who exceed them in cruelty. This culminates in the history of the poor half-breed woman Hunilla, treacherously deserted with her family by the captain committed to returning for them and, as sole survivor, raped by whaleboatmen to whom she looked for rescue. A pious Catholic, Hunilla had the fortitude to preserve her sanity and faith. Melville concludes her history with Hunilla riding away Christ-like on an ass, eyeing 'the beast's armorial cross', and 'Humanity, thou strong thing, I worship thee, not in the laureled victor, but in this vanquished one' – an affirmation of faith, in humanity at least and in spite of its worst manifestations, which must not be overlooked in any discussion of Melville's attitude to God and man at this period.

The others really are integral tales. They fall into groups, for instance three double tales each consisting of a contrasted pair, a technique that is to be seen in use in *The Confidence-Man*, and these all spring from experiences in England and America that aroused Melville's generous indignation at social conditions – treatment of the poor, class snobbery extending even to religious worship, and surprisingly, in view of the exclusion of women from his previous novels except as ideas in *Pierre* and *Mardi*, to the treatment of women, who are seen as victims of Nature as well as of man and society. Thus in these years Melville was manifesting a considerable degree of emotional and moral involvement in social life on land, both in England and America. In *The Piazza Tales* we are not living in 'The World in a Man-of-War' as in *White-Jacket* or in the world in a whaling-ship as in *Moby-Dick*, but are taken into the full living world of the Anglo-American mid-nineteenth century, a very great step forward for Melville as an artist into the complexities of living, even, into the difficulties of family life for the man and the artist. We remember that Melville was married in 1847 and by now had children, a family to support, and was living in a household that contained also his mother and three of his sisters, a concentration of women with claims on him that inevitably forced on his attention the woman's point of view, and which also obliged him to reconsider the man's role as individual (as in *I and My Chimney*), and as artist tormented by the rival claims of his work and the support of his family.

The tale of *Bartleby the Scrivener* (1853) has received plenty of critical attention and there is no disagreement as to its meaning and the nature of its techniques, which present no difficulty. But recognition has not been given to the fact that it is one of Melville's try-outs and not an adopted position, much less a personal admission of neurosis. This is the only tale of the batch that ends in limbo. Bartleby is posited as the man who adopts a consistently negative response to the demands of unsatisfactory living in the Wall Street society (copying while facing a blank wall). His unshakable 'I would prefer not to' which he persists in until it inevitably leaves him dead of starvation in prison, with 'peering out upon him the eyes of murderers and thieves', is yet felt, like Hunilla's tragedy, to be a triumph of the indomitable spirit: Bartleby, even the lawyer his employer feels, is at rest 'with kings and counselors'. Melville himself concludes with 'Ah, Bartleby! Ah, humanity!' which is unfathomably ambiguous, perhaps a sad recognition of the human condition. Bartleby's suicidal choice is not so much the centre of Melville's attention as the complex reaction to it of his employer, whose mixture of exasperation and pity in his efforts first to save Bartleby and failing this, to wash his hands of him – all too human – are examined not without sympathy. For what could be done for a Bartleby? Can one envisage a society composed of Bartlebies? – Melville examines this question in *The Confidence-Man*. Bartleby's having been a clerk in the Dead Letter Office, and then a mere copyist of other people's compositions, are not very obscure references to the kind of literary non-life Melville saw he himself would be relegated to in all likelihood after the failure of *Pierre* and the destruction by fire in 1853 of the plates of all his novels, and with the increasing weakness of his eyesight (like Bartleby's). Not surprisingly, several tales of this period are discussions of the problem of the artist who has to earn a living in mid-nineteenth-century America – *Cock-a-Doodle-Doo!*, *The Fiddler*, *I and My Chimney*. Only two years before (1851) Melville had praised Hawthorne for as an artist always 'saying No! in thunder' – 'the Devil himself cannot make him say *yes*' – and had since been inclined to castigate all those who do say *yes*, an indication of the line Melville was to explore systematically in *The Confidence-Man*. Characteristically, Melville had proceeded from his ardent endorsement of Hawthorne's apparent attitude to testing its validity by actualizing it in the case of a consistent practitioner, Bartleby, when he recognizes that however heroic it is impracticable; Bartleby's employer, the average citizen, had always been convinced, he says, that 'the easiest way of life is the best', which though ignoble is a means of survival, we see. And a year after *Bartleby* Melville tried out such an alternative to Bartleby's in an odd short sketch *The Fiddler*.

This opens with the despair of the narrator, a poet named Helmstone: 'So my poem is damned, and immortal fame is not for me! Intolerable fate!' But he is 'instantly soothed' by being introduced to the amiable and winning genius Hautboy (presumably meaning 'a high-flier') whose fame has passed and his fortune with it. But he is quite content to drudge for a living by teaching the fiddle: '*With* genius and *without* fame, he is happier than a king', his friend Standard (the average man) assures Helmstone, who feels 'I wish I were Hautboy'. So he tears up his manuscripts and follows this model's example. The tale is merely an annotation of an idea and has none of the convincing detail, the sensitive complexity and the involved technical devices Melville found necessary for the more substantial tales, showing he did not entertain this alternative very seriously. I simply cite it as another proof that his mind worked from theory to posited embodiments in alternative forms of life (like Dickens). For these he drew equally on incidents in his own experience, on documents and historical facts, and on the lives of real people, thus doing his best to keep his theorizing in touch with actuality and to direct his abstract thinking on to the life of the individual and the welfare of society.

Nearly a year before, Melville had published the very

remarkable tale *Cock-a-Doodle-Doo !*. In this case Melville took off from Wordsworth's poem *Resolution and Independence* which must have exasperated him since, starting from reflections of a kind relevant to Melville's own position, on the disastrous fate of poets who from beginning in gladness pass through despondency to madness owing to poverty, Wordsworth apparently found arguments in the fortitude of the Leech-gatherer for reassurance and trust in Providence. To Melville, in debt, and in fear of blindness and possibly also of the madness from which his father died, such optimism was superficial. Accordingly, his tone in this tale is harsh and jeering. He exhibits in refutation of Wordsworth the painful history of Merrymusk (that is, 'Merry Music', creative genius) and his family, the tale being for the most part a rude parody of the poem. The narrator, in financial trouble himself and not finding comfort in Nature like Wordsworth, is cheered by the 'prodigious exulting strains' of a cock which ring through the whole countryside and throw him into a rapturous, buoyant state. It turns out to be owned by a desperately poor but dignified wood-sawyer who proudly declares: 'I raised it'. He calls it Trumpet and it crows only at his command – evidently the voice of his art which, while it can't bring him an income, makes up to him and his sick wife and children for their deprivations in material things. The narrator watches them all die happy in hearing to the last the 'glorious and rejoicing crow' of their unique Trumpet. This part is not satiric: the uncomplaining wife is heroic in her 'long-loving sympathy' with her husband, and as for the four children – listening to the cock 'Their faces shone celestially through grime and dirt. They seemed children of emperors and kings, disguised'. Merrymusk himself insists as he dies that he and all of them are well, 'in a kind of wild ecstacy of triumph over ill'. Last of all Trumpet dies, and the narrator buries them all in one grave with on the gravestone 'a lusty cock in act of crowing' and the possibly unironic inscription 'O death, where is thy sting ? O grave, where is thy victory ?' and – reverting now to the original tone – ends: 'and never since then have I felt the doleful dumps'.

I have never encountered an explanation of why Merrymusk should have named his cock 'Trumpet'. My own conjecture is that Melville had several poems of Wordsworth's, besides *Reso-*

lution and Independence, in his mind when composing this tale, all of them having in common the theme of the poet's creative powers. So Wordsworth's sonnet on The Sonnet was brought in by naming Merrymusk's art after what Wordsworth tells us was the favourite poetic form of great poets, as of Wordsworth himself; and the account culminates in Milton's use of the sonnet, when

> In his hand
> The Thing became a trumpet; whence he blew
> Soul-animating strains – alas, too few!

So in this complex and subtly Wordsworthian tale, which is surprisingly like D.H.Lawrence in tone and content, Melville registers belief in the sustaining and revivifying power of art, and in support of my interpretation we note that the rustic humour and scoffing tone are abandoned whenever the narrator confronts the Merrymusk household. And he is genuinely disturbed by the mighty power of Trumpet: 'the cock frightened me, like some overpowering angel in the Apocalypse' – as well as sincerely humbled by the character of Merrymusk who denies he deserves pity, declaring with superb conviction:

> 'Why call *me* poor? Don't the cock *I* own glorify this otherwise inglorious, lean, lantern-jawed land? Didn't *my* cock encourage *you*? And *I* give you all this glorification away gratis. I am a great philanthropist. I am a rich man – a very rich man, and a very happy one. Crow, Trumpet.'

The narrator admits he 'was not wholly at rest concerning the soundness of Merrymusk's views of things, though full of admiration for him. I was thinking on the matter before my door, when I heard the cock crow again. Enough. Merrymusk is right. Oh, noble cock! oh, noble man!'

Note that New England is envisaged here as a Puritan; that is to say, the land of Puritan settlers was ignorant of art though desperately in need of it. Also, it is unable to appreciate art – no one in the countryside but the narrator and the Merrymusk family is able to hear the cock, a sly touch. An 'inglorious land' indeed! An interpretation that, because the rest can't hear the cock, the voice is imaginary and Melville trying to come to terms with a neurosis; or alternatively, that 'cock' being a sex-term the tale must be understood as a sexual *double-entendre* – are equally instances of perverse critical sophistry. The identification of cocks with poets is made beyond doubt by Melville's parody of Wordsworth's lines (at the end of the seventh stanza of *Resolution and Independence*) on the sad history of poets:

> Of fine mornings,
> We fine lusty cocks begin our crows in gladness;
> But when eve does come we don't crow quite so much,
> For then cometh despondency and madness.

And in his description of the cock's crow we see the characteristics of his own literary voice: 'full of pluck, full of fire, full of fun, full of glee. It plainly says – *"Never say die !"* '

Merrymusk then is Melville's idea of a more convincing model for Wordsworth's Leech-gatherer and he is also, with his inspiring voice Trumpet, Melville the artist (who thought of himself as poet-novelist) – we are told Merrymusk had been first a sailor, then a small farmer, and was now a hired drudge, Melville's own history. The story of the family dying prematurely as they do from harrowing poverty is surely an ironic comment on Wordsworthian trust, carrying on the ridicule with which the tale started. There is also satire in the reiterated fact that the baseless self-confidence the cock's crowing gives the narrator inspires him to reckless financial behaviour and evidently future ruin. Yet there is no doubt that Trumpet is 'the cheerer', and when he perches on the sick children's bed 'All their wasted eyes gazed at him with a wild and spiritual delight. They seemed to sun themselves in the radiant plumage of the cock'. This is sincere and moving. Melville seems to be trying to explain that though the dolours of the poet's life of poverty that Wordsworth brushes aside are inescapable and bear hardest on his family, *yet* they all, and everyone else in the world too, have thereby the consolations of art which can make life blissful and suffering negligible. The artist's support therefore can only be looked for in his sense of achievement, Melville argues.

Wordsworth's 1815 sonnet to the unfortunate painter Haydon is another that Melville seems to me to have drawn on as a help to expressing his theme in *Cock-a-Doodle-Do !*. It is next but one to the 'Trumpet' sonnet in the 1849–50 edition of Wordsworth's poems and is of such importance in elucidating Melville's argument and the conclusion we should extract that I will cite it in full:

High is our calling, Friend! – Creative Art
(Whether the instrument of words she use,
Or pencil pregnant with ethereal hues,)
Demands the service of a mind and heart,
Though sensitive, yet, in their weakest part,
Heroically fashioned – to infuse
Faith in the whispers of the lonely Muse,
While the whole world seems adverse to desert.
And, oh! when Nature sinks, as oft she may,
Through long-lived pressure of obscure distress,
Still to be strenuous for the bright reward
And in the soul admit of no decay,
Brook no continuance of weak-mindedness –
Great is the glory, for the strife is hard!

It is important to note that in these tales Melville shows he is as much concerned as Henry James or Hawthorne with the problems of the life of the artist and the necessity of art for the life of the spirit, because we must also note that these considerations are completely absent from the picture of life in the America of the 1850s drawn for *The Confidence-Man* shortly after. Something he knew to be central and vital has there been deliberately omitted. And these tales, particularly the complex *Cock-a-Doodle-Doo!*, show the kind of difficulty we are faced with in reading these later Melville works. The complexity does not disguise the meaning but it shows that several meanings are intended which, united, provide the means of arriving at a just conclusion. He is in his creative activity exploring all the possibilities in a given human problem, facing and considering them in turn and playing one off against the other, the changes of tone and direction giving us guide-lines. Thus in these tales he developed the method he was to need for *The Confidence-Man*, and one may well feel that tales like *Bartleby*, *Benito Cereno*, *Cock-a-Doodle-Doo!* and *The Tartarus of Maids* are almost inexhaustible.

This last, two years later than the story of Merrymusk, takes up the question of man's relation to woman by contrasting the light-hearted conviviality of bachelors, as Melville had gratefully experienced it in England in the Temple and a London Club (*The Paradise of Bachelors*) with a visit to the representative hell of women, a paper-mill in a New England winter.

Melville actually visited such a mill to buy paper for his writings, in 1851, and the occasion, the uncannily suggestive physical features of the landscape there, and some of the actual names of these features, evidently gave Melville the idea of combining the two aspects of women's hardships – being condemned to drudgery by man and to additional suffering as being designed by Nature for child-bearing.

The mill is owned and managed by a bachelor ('Old Bach') and the only other male is his heartless boy assistant called Cupid. Melville was recurrently foot-loose, and now tied to a household of women and children no doubt looked to the care-free bachelor state as paradisal. There is no need to deduce that Melville was therefore homosexual in feeling. He seems to have formed these associations from the time of Moby-Dick, where the ship 'The Bachelor' encountered by the Pequod represents, Richard Chase thought, 'America sailing off evasively towards an archaic utopia'; Captain Delano's very masculine American ship is named 'The Bachelor's Delight'; and in The Confidence-Man the 'Missouri bachelor' figures ambiguously as a Melville mouthpiece, his bachelor status being part of his refusal on principle to be committed to any human relationship; the name of the paper-mill's boss is therefore consonant with Melville's ideas about bachelorhood after he had married. Before, women don't figure in the novels, but if it is argued that these take place on ships, necessarily a man's world only, it is pertinent to reply that, in Conrad's similarly restricted world of shipboard, women always figure, if not actually then by inhabiting the memories of the sailors – e.g. in Typhoon both officers and men are always thinking what their mothers and wives at home would feel, are writing letters to them, or recalling memories of their homes and shore-leaves, so that their women-folk seem vividly present. This is never so in Melville's ship-worlds. What matrimony and fatherhood did for Melville, it seems, was to give him, as one who then saw bachelorhood as the natural state of man's desir-ing, a sense of guilt and remorse towards his wife and family, and by extension to the corresponding state to bachelor in women, whose lot was comparatively unenviable whether as maid or wife. The implication here is that the bachelor's way of life is only possible because he is selfishly using women as wage-slaves and domestic drudges as well as sexually. And in addition, for Melville in his vocation as writer they toil in the mill to make his paper as well as his children. No wonder *The Tartarus of Maids* carries such weight.

Thus this tale needs, and gets, a dual symbolism, each employed with a devastating effect. The duality is combined in the person of the narrator, who is always of great importance in a Melville tale. He describes himself as a seedsman, one needing paper for his business of distributing seeds to the whole country, thus he represents Melville as both a man and a writer, creative in both aspects, a living pun. This conceit is given a very sombre exposition and we are left with extremely painful impressions: by 'inscrutable nature' woman has been badly treated physiologically compared with man, and by society forced to live by self-destroying and unremitting toil, as the bachelor manager callously and self-righteously explains. The narrator perceives that the physical life of the female is governed by 'unbudging fatality'; horrified, he is overcome with a deadly chill, first brought on by the alarming scenery leading to the mill whose features are described not as erotic but as awe-inspiring, and the women are all consumptive and half-frozen owing to their working conditions. Just as the natural scenery outside is suggestive of the female anatomy in its mechanical aspects, so the machine-tending inside the mill suggests the processes of gestation and parturition. There is neither sniggering nor disgust, but much compassion towards the women, who are described at work 'like so many mares haltered to the rack' ('rack' inevitably suggesting a pun, for they are racked with pain too), and gestation is seen as 'a mere machine, the essence of which is unvarying punctuality and precision' that 'strikes dread into the human heart'. The two levels at which this tale must be apprehended is a technique Melville developed in these tales and later uses consistently in *The Confidence-Man*. To call it 'a game', a device for hoodwinking the reader, is to slight the art of a serious and responsible creative mind.

There are two other tales of this group during which Melville must have been thinking out *The Confidence-Man* which are relevant to it. One is the much-analysed *Benito Cereno*, whose point for this purpose is the ambiguity of the final resolution. The sub-title of *Pierre* was: 'or, the Ambiguities', and this might apply at least as well to nearly all the 1853–6 works which finally, in *The Confidence-Man*, culminate in layer upon layer of ambiguity which has become an all-embracing technique. Captain Delano's disabilities for apprehending the truth – that is, the true state of affairs on board the Spanish slave-ship – are due to his having been indoctrinated with the convenient American theory that the black man is a kind of 'Newfoundland dog', devoted to his master, sub-human in intelligence but amiable and docile. Though Delano has had enough experience as a captain to know the facts of life about white men, this theory prevents him from following up his intuitions of something wrong aboard the *San Dominick*, making him believe, for instance, that the maternal affection shown by the negresses is reassuring, so that there cannot be a conspiracy at work. [This is a preliminary study of the harm done by the Confidence Man, and that novel actually opens with a Negro cripple as the first incarnation of this modern Devil.] Even when the full facts come out in court at the end, the ambiguity of appearances is not resolved by a final manifestation of the truth, for there is still the question that is raised by the introspective Spaniard: Was not the stupidity and blindness of the American what saved him from being murdered by the Negroes ? To have been without illusions would have been fatal. Thus Melville in *Benito Cereno* is not only enquiring why we don't make true judgments but tentatively asks also, Is it always desirable that we should ? The grey sky and sea and the indeterminate horizon give way at the end to blue skies and sunshine and apparent security (the blacks have been subjugated again), but the Spaniard, unlike the American who is untroubled by the experience and has learnt nothing from it – and survives – the Spaniard pines away from the horror of having learnt of what the mind and heart of man are capable. Misjudgment of the Negro due to a belief 'that they were all tractable' was the tragedy of the Spaniards, but, we learn, the salvation of the Americans. White and black as symbols of good and evil, truth and falsehood, are used, but less unambiguously, in *The Confidence-Man*. Delano is therefore cast for the role of an American Candide. His optimism about human nature in general, and black in particular, transcends reality until he sees Babo about to murder Don Benito, when he instantly reassesses the situation and immediately takes all necessary steps to set things right. Melville thus acknowledges the courage and practical virtues of the American extrovert, which he valued, even though he saw its complacency as dangerous.

Another appearance, in person this time, of the con-man in a tale, *The Lightning-Rod Man*, brings us even closer to the novel of the following year. Here he comes as salesman for authoritarian religion, one who 'travels in storm-time and drives a brave trade with the fears of man'. The householder addresses him as Jupiter Tonans, but he is a 'gloomy' figure with melodramatic eyes and a denunciatory style of speech. He claims to be able to protect against lightning by the power of his magic rod which Melville, saying No in thunder, refuses to buy since to do so would be acquiescing in the intruder's pretensions. He is revealed as a combination of witch-doctor, Calvinist minister, Catholic priest, Hell-fire religionist, missionary – in fact, he stands for all domineering advocates of the one-true-religion orthodoxy. Melville's householder's opposition is not atheism but rational and humanistic: he refuses to be afraid of the thunder-storm and when the 'pedlar of indulgences' threatens to stab him to the heart with his trinitarian lightning-rod the dauntless householder breaks it and flings 'the dark lightning-king' out of his house. He has just made to the priest an affirmation of a higher faith, and it is interesting that this comes out in biblical form:

> The hairs of our heads are numbered, and the days of our lives. In thunder as in sunshine, I stand at ease in the hands of my God. False negotiator, away! See, the scroll of the storm is rolled back; the house is unharmed; and in the blue heavens I read in the raingow, that the Deity will not, of purpose, make war on man's earth.

So Melville is not here merely rejecting fear-based religions; his mouthpiece is affirming faith in Renaissance Man and in something symbolized by Noah's covenant with the God of *Genesis*, that was sealed by the rainbow. Like Ahab in *Moby-Dick*, Melville's householder refuses to be 'god-bullied'; but unlike Ahab he is not godless. [Nevertheless, the tale was refused magazine publication.]

In accordance with these views, Melville had in the manuscript dedicated *The Confidence-Man* 'to victims of Auto da Fe';

but he removed this before publication, suggesting that the novel had far transcended the implications of such a dedication, even if he had meant it to be taken widely as referring to the victims of all religious orthodoxies or even all sufferers for intransigence. The earlier parts of the novel do feature religionists – an Episcopal clergyman, a Methodist chaplain and a sanctimonious man in grey, an Evangelical who has mass missionary projects against the heathen to be carried out in 'the Wall Street spirit' – as incarnations or allies of the Confidence Man, but then mid-nineteenth-century Christianity, perhaps the original target, drops out of sight until the last chapter as the writer's intellectual high spirits and fertility of speculation roam over further fields and prospects than Christianity provides.

In none of the tales of this period can I find any justification for Hawthorne's opinion (*English Notebooks*, 20 November 1856) that Melville's 'writings, for a long while past, have indicated a morbid state of mind'. In *I and My Chimney* (published 1855) there is reassuring good-humour in the narrator's recognition that the women of his family suspect the soundness of his home's exceptionally tall and finely-wrought chimney, resent its bulk and mysterious foundations, which they fancy must contain a secret chamber with hidden treasure, and believe that the house would be safer and more comfortable without such a chimney. They torment the old man by getting in 'a master-mason' to test it and arrange if unsound for its removal, but the narrator circumvents them all. He has explained that the chimney 'is my backbone', 'the one grand permanence of this abode' and that 'when all the house shall have crumbled from it, this chimney will still survive'. The tale ends: 'I and my chimney will never surrender'. Thus the chimney is a composite symbol standing, apparently, for his morale, his immortal soul (which he is determined to call his own), the source of his creative power (the chimney's foundations are buried in darkness, deep down), his intellect, his personality, and his inherited traditions (a kinsman named Dacres – that is, 'Sacred' – built the house); the chimney also seems to stand, like the personal tree in European folk-tales, for his life-force, for it is sinking into the ground and crumbling as he himself grows old. This is one of Melville's most intimate and most suggestive tales. It is surely also good proof of its author's mental health. There is much wry amusement at the narrator's situation and some sympathy for the wife, misguided though she is, who has to put up with the disadvantages of living with an obstinately conservative and privacy-loving intellectual, one resigned to old age and death but not to interference with his essential self.

In short, it must be generally recognized that the tales of Melville are some of the finest *contes* and short stories in the language, as well as some of the most original, and that, like D. H. Lawrence and Hawthorne, his claim to stature as an artist is to be based on his tales at least as much as on his novels.

The Confidence-Man

Immediately Melville had got his new novel off his hands he set off for the East, stopping at Liverpool to visit his friend Hawthorne who was consul there. Hawthorne recorded his impressions of Melville in his diary (*English Notebooks*, November 1856) and the passage is so valuable as evidence of Melville's character and preoccupations at the time of writing his last major prose work that I will start by citing it. He notes that Melville on arrival looked 'a little paler, a little sadder' and 'with his characteristic gravity and reserve of manner' 'is much over-shadowed since I saw him last', guessing that Melville 'no doubt suffered from too constant literary occupation, pursued without much success, latterly'. A couple of days later when they had had a long talk he wrote:

> Melville, as he always does, began to reason of Providence and futurity, and of everything that lies beyond human ken, and informed me that he had 'pretty much made up his mind to be annihilated'; but he still does not seem to rest in that anticipation; and, I think, will never rest until he gets hold of a definite belief. It is strange how he persists . . . in wandering to-and-fro over these deserts. . . . He can neither believe, nor be comfortable in his unbelief; and he is too honest and courageous not to try to do one or the other. If he were a religious man, he would be one of the most truly religious and reverential; he has a very high and noble nature, and better worth immortality than most of us.

Before leaving, Melville told Hawthorne that 'he already felt much better than in America'. So writing this group of tales and the novel, and leaving America behind him, had evidently been therapeutic, and the 'annihilation' refers not to suicidal intentions but to his inability to believe in an after-life. And his position as revealed to Hawthorne was not that of the 'village atheist' he has sometimes been labelled but that of a truth-seeker with an open mind. This is what we should have expected from these creative writings, as I've shown. And *The Confidence-Man* itself is speculative, not dogmatic, and diversified by apparently endless, effortless improvisations on the theme he has chosen.

This novel, confidently dismissed by Julian Hawthorne, and declared by later English critics to be 'unreadable', seems to have been rediscovered by Richard Chase in his pioneer book *Herman Melville* (1949), and we now have a consensus of at any rate American literary criticism that it contains Melville's most mature prose writing and some of his most interesting thinking. However, this theoretical agreement has gone along with some ill-judged interpretations of the novel, such as, for instance, that it is entirely or mainly an anti-Christian exercise, or in sum no more than an April Fool jape of an esoteric kind whose object is to reveal God as a heartless joker and life a pointless deceit, one that even adopts for this trivial end an elaborate disguise, the avatars of Hindu mythology, and a Buddhist interpretation of the riddle of the Universe as being a masquerade, or that life is an illusion where black is indistinguishable from white. All these do Melville a considerable injustice for they imply that he was either irresponsible (which we know from his previous creative work and all other evidence of this period that he could not be) or a contemptible thimble-rigger. We know that this was not so, from Hawthorne's testimony at this date to his 'very high and noble nature', nor should any *literary* critic fail to see that Melville is at various points in *The Confidence-Man* deeply involved. We can point to the pugnacious style and strongly presented moral values implicit and explicit. Elizabeth S. Foster who made a careful study of the versions and earlier draft says that 'We see him in his revisions moving always . . . from the loose structure, open clarity, and directness of his earliest versions of passages' into a 'complexity that looks like simplicity', for which he evolved a style that 'desiderates under-

statement, under-emphasis, litotes'; and she shows him 'prun-
ing' and 'groping for the exact word' and 'toning down' – proof
surely of a serious intention.

In fact, readers may well complain of considerable difficulties
that Melville makes by having put excessive ingenuity into
cross-references in the text and into concealing clues, especially
quotations. These are generally from the Bible (a source no
longer commanded by most highbrow readers) but which are
essential for interpreting his meanings. The book therefore
requires – and repays – repeated reading. The main difficulty is
to decide how the multiple ironies, both local and total, which
are generally double-faced anyway, are to be taken. An in-
ordinate amount of misplaced ingenuity has been devoted to
discussion of exactly who the 'avatars' of the Confidence Man
are, and to assigning them to some mythological or theological
system, and to tracking down possible clues to their significance.
But for purposes of literary criticism they do not much matter;
the 'avatars', really disguises of the Devil in contemporary forms
of humbug or cant or dishonesty, serve Melville as excuses for
attacks on aspects of mid-nineteenth-century America, for provoking reactions by the different types of passengers (the
public), and for allowing Melville to activate his sociological
and metaphysical ideas and arguments. A list of the Confidence
Man's appearances may save the reader time and confusion. The
first is Black Guinea the negro cripple. There is disagreement
whether the Episcopal clergyman and the Methodist chaplain
are either or both con-men, but as they seem to be present at the
same time as Black Guinea (perhaps only the former is, though)
they may be confederates but can hardly also be 'avatars'. The
man with the mourning weed in his hat called John Ringman (a
name taken from thieves' cant); the man with a grey coat who
is agent for the Seminole (a Red Indian tribe of particular
malignancy) Widow and Orphan Asylum, who is also an American Evangelical; the proprietor of the Black Rapids Coal Company keeping 'transfer accounts' of speculators thereby destined
for Hell; the dishonest agent of the Philosophical Intelligence
Office; the (Catholic) quack healer who as herb-doctor also
propagands the Romantics' belief in Nature as a cure-all; and
finally the Cosmopolitan calling himself Frank Goodman – all
these are obvious shape-shiftings of the Confidence Man him-

self. But the boat-operator Charles Arnold Noble (another inherently suspicious name like John Truman) is less certain, and may be understood to be an unconscious agent of the Devil, while the boy accomplice of the Cosmopolitan in the last chapter is decidedly an imp of darkness. It has even been suggested that the Cosmopolitan who dominates the second half of the book with his sweet-talking and his ironic line in casuistry is the true Saviour; against this we must remember that he calls himself 'a philanthropist' (a suspect term) and 'ambassador of the human race', is described by the author as 'the mature man of the world, a character the opposite [of] the sincere Christian's', bilks the barber, and finally misleads the pious and confiding old man by stripping him of all sources of belief before quenching the light of the last lamp. Moreover, his sophistry is sardonically criticized by a Melville voice (that of the wide-awake man in the cabin). Melville has only himself to blame for these uncertainties. Another critical controversy centres on the 'lamb-like' non-resistant deaf mute, friendless and without any worldly goods, ironically described as the 'mysterious impostor supposed to have arrived recently from the East; quite an original genius in his vocation' for whose capture a reward is offered, who is clearly Christ – but is he a false or the true Christ? This depends on whether the placard offering the reward is taken straight or as irony, though it seems to me evident that the description of 'impostor' is ironic, since the stranger is vilified by the crowd which consists largely of pickpockets and sharks, the scene suggesting the original Crucifixion. Another theory is that Melville thus implies that the Gospel message is itself a device of the Confidence Man since if followed it leaves its practitioner defenceless against the con-men of this world. No doubt Melville had this last in mind at times, for it is debated in the book. In consequence, it has been alleged that the deaf-mute is the first avatar of the Confidence Man, but this cannot be Melville's intention for the reasons I have already stated.

An edited text with critical appendices and elucidatory footnotes is available in the Norton Critical Edition, edited by Hershel Parker (1971). Melville was a voracious but random reader, and had a better appetite than digestion for some of his reading matter, one feels.

The intellectual fare may be found indigestibly rich; alter-

natively, the absence of life in the round and of sensuous life
may lead some readers to class the book with those characteristic
modern American novels by and for the intelligentsia which
Randall Jarrell has a character in his *Pictures from an Institution*
describe as 'a Barmecide feast given by a fireworks company';
and by many the repetitiveness of the structure is felt to be
monotonous.

This is due to the limitations of the *genre*, the novel of
philosophic speculation, a neo-Classical art form with which
Melville was evidently familiar and found congenial and to
which *Rasselas*, *Candide*, *Gulliver's Travels* and *The Tale of a
Tub*, as well as Peacock's novels, belong, and which type of novel
Melville's chapter-titles deliberately recall. [We find the same
characteristics in modern versions of the *genre*, e.g. Camus's
L'Etranger and Kafka's *The Trial*.] It superseded the romance
of spiritual pilgrimage or quest, with the satisfying progress
towards a solution in a happy ending, that had been nourished
by medieval faith and produced eventually Bunyan's *The
Pilgrim's Progress*. Hawthorne had written an ironical trans-
lation into contemporary terms of this last, a tale called *The
Celestial Railroad*, where the 19th c. pilgrims, on a quick trip by
steam-train over the now safely modernized country of Bunyan's
pilgrims' ordeals, are being driven unawares by devils to the
opposite goal from the Heavenly City. No doubt this was one
source of stimulus for Melville – he makes an allusion to the tale
in *The Confidence-Man* – but its influence is merely marginal, for
Hawthorne's tale is straightforward and single-minded while
Melville's offers evidence only for the difficulty (but not, as
some critics allege, the impossibility) of deciding what *is* right
conduct in such a world as this or how the truth as to evidence
of good and evil can be arrived at. For Melville is enquiring
what alternatives are available which allow one to combine some
kind of social life with self-respect once one has perceived – as is
essential – how fraudulent all relations and institutions generally
are. And though the scenes devised for exhibiting the type
situation are largely dramatic and varied in the novels of this
kind, their method is inevitably repetitive, the progress of plot
and increasing tension in the conventional novel being replaced
by a circular movement that ends with a question-mark or
merely breaks off when sufficient demonstrations seem to have

made the argument carry conviction and exhausted the author's interest – in fact, Melville's seems to have slackened after the middle of his novel.

But these demonstrations need not be abstract, moralistic and didactic, as in *Rasselas*. Melville's lively discussions, like Peacock's, are carried on with versatility of character and language; he deploys rustic idiom as well as polished sentences; like Peacock, he is a master of sardonic humour and makes his points with wit, as in the brilliant dialogues between the Missourian and the miser and the former and the herb-doctor in chapter 21. As Melville says, he passes 'from the comedy of thought to that of action'. The happenings and debates are not predictable, in fact the ironies provide a series of moral and intellectual shocks, the play of ideas is so stimulating as to make a 'plot' unnecessary.

The clue to the book is that, as will be noticed, great use is made of the words 'confidence', 'trust', 'suspicion', 'doubt', and 'belief', which the author examines systematically in dialogue and action. For purposes of the investigation he himself adopts the position of a critically regarded version of himself in an extreme form, who when asked: 'Pray, sir, who or what may you have confidence in ?' replies: 'I have confidence in distrust'. But, Melville enquires, where will this apparently safe guide take us ? The book applies this test to every aspect of life and ends by showing that a state of perpetual distrust is also impracticable; yet the only alternative is to be deceived to *some* extent, and to be deceived at all is liable to be fatal. Nothing will persuade me that Melville was not familiar with, and impressed by, Swift's 'Digression Concerning Madness in a Commonwealth' in *The Tale of a Tub* – Melville is using Swiftian arguments and wit constantly in *The Confidence-Man* – where Swift argues that happiness 'is a perpetual possession of being well deceived' and that 'In the proportion that credulity' is preferable to 'that pretended philosophy which enters into the depths of things and then comes gravely back with informations and discoveries, that in the inside they are good for nothing', 'the sublime and refined point of felicity' is 'called the possession of being well-deceived, the serene peaceful state of being a fool among knaves'. Melville shows likewise that the choice is between being a conscious dupe or a misanthrope, for he cannot be content with 'a state of being well deceived' and accepting that as happiness.

Melville examines the soundness of such solutions as have been advanced to the problem in the form of the realistic scepticism promulgated in the seventeenth and eighteenth centuries by La Rochefoucauld and Chesterfield and Bacon; the theory of Original Sin as held by St Augustine and Calvinists; the views of Greek philosophers and of such contemporary American ones as Emerson and Thoreau (postulated as Mark Winsome and his disciple Egbert in chs 36-8); and numerous other possible strategies of living. One of the leading antagonists of the Confidence Man is described by another character as 'deuced analytical', while the former complains: 'Somehow I meet with the most extraordinary metaphysical scamps today. Some sort of visitation of them'; and the token figure of Emerson is introduced as 'more a metaphysical merman than a feeling man'. One of the disguises of the Confidence Man is as agent of the Philosophical Intelligence Office. One chapter is called: 'The Metaphysics of Indian-Hating', and the metaphysics of misanthropy are likewise examined, as also the relation between goodness and righteousness (ch. 7) where the idea is raised that a good man is one lucky in being born well off enough to get his dirty work done by others (a satire on slave-owners, Emerson's innocence, and upper-class gentry). There is a characteristic discussion on how we are to take Shakespeare's Autolycus because the playwright shows him as both 'wicked and happy', and such practitioners as Talleyrand and Machiavelli come up for reference. Though the action takes place on All Fools Day and the steamer is referred to as a Ship of Fools, this is from association with Pope's *Dunciad*, it seems to me, for the ending shows a 'great Anarch's hand' bringing about 'universal darkness' as one light after another, as in Pope's finale, has been quenched, by doubt, that 'uncreating word'. In fact, in view of Melville's 'metaphysical' pre-occupation here, *The Confidence-Man* would merit the attentions of a professional philosopher. But the main fertiliser after all seems to be Shakespeare. The tragedies of Lear, Timon and Coriolanus are constantly invoked as of types of men who were victims of false confidence (in children, friends, fellow-countrymen and beneficiaries). The deployment of animal imagery is also Shakespearian, especially of the predatory class such as wolf, hyena, fox, rat, leopard; and of course the snake figures constantly as the sign of the con-man, these all being enemies of the Lamb. We know that just before Melville first met Hawthorne, in 1850, he had started on an intensive study of Shakespeare, who provided, it seems to me, a corrective to Melville's intellectualizing tendencies in composition.

I learn from an unpublished piece of research by the Professor of Italian at Belfast University (Professor G. Singh) that it seems that Melville owed some of his disillusioned insights into 'the times and nature of the human soul' to Leopardi: Melville had probably read, for it appeared four years before he published *The Confidence-Man*, the American critic Henry F. Tucker's essay on Leopardi ('The Sceptical Genius') and possibly he knew also of the previous studies of Leopardi by Sainte-Beuve and, in English reviews, by G. H. Lewes and Gladstone, for Melville refers more than once to Leopardi by name in his poem *Clarel*. Professor Singh argues that not only was Leopardi's thought and philosophy, and their expression, of use to Melville in the undertaking represented by *The Confidence-Man* ('some Melvillian themes . . . have an unmistakably Leopardian ring about them') but that Leopardi's prose works, *Operetti morali* and *Pensieri*, provided an example of 'moral irony and satire used as instruments of exposition'. These would associate conveniently with the Swiftian satiric modes which Melville, as I've shown, employs in *The Confidence-Man*, but it seems to me that the novel also contains a satiric strain of thought and mode of expression not present in any previous work of Melville's and not to be found in English eighteenth-century literature, and that Professor Singh's identification of Leopardi as a visible influence accounts for this very satisfactorily.

In the then recently recognized and named 'confidence man' at work in America, operating on society at large, as well as in the Mississippi boats (in addition to the card-sharper), Melville saw a key to and symbol of the corruption he diagnosed in institutions religious, mercantile, financial and charitable, in social life and all personal relations, in the Press, in the claims of quacks of all kinds, in the sentimental cant of Romantic poets, American philosophers, Abolitionists and other instruments of democracy, enlightenment and progress. He saw all these as being operated by or in the interests of the Devil who beguiled our first parents. The devil in various shapes fleeces the public (the *Fidèle*'s passengers, described as the modern equivalents of Chaucer's Canterbury pilgrims) by appealing insidiously to their weaknesses, greed and selfishness to part with money as a sign of acquiescence in the diabolical system. Thus the opposite of such a way of life, Charity, a Christian key-word, comes in for scrutiny in all sorts of connexions, after the bitter ironic drama of the opening chapter. Melville makes plain his disgust for a commercially-minded society whose charity is typified by the passengers throwing coins to the Negro cripple to catch in his mouth for their amusement, making him wince as these hit his teeth 'when certain coins, tossed by more playful almoners . . . proved buttons'. The unpleasantness of this 'game of charity' is increased by his being 'bound to appear cheerfully grateful' and his difficulty in avoiding swallowing the coppers (and pseudo-coins).

Allegory is the inevitable mode of this *genre* which works through a series of parables that culminate in one all-inclusive parable in a key position, generally towards the end, as Kafka's pregnant parable of the man outside the door of the Law Courts is set into the penultimate chapter of *The Trial*. Melville's is placed in the very centre of the book, in the three chapters devoted to considering the case of the Indian-Hater, a parable developed from the exemplary history of a real Colonel More-dock. In this parable Melville is able to bring together several different basic conflicts of American social history: the irrecon-cilable claims of the original owners of the land, a hunting people, and of the colonizing white settlers who must exter-minate the Redskins to survive as farmers (and conversely); the unremitting warfare of the Calvinist against Original Sin, the Red Indians being children of the Devil in the mythology of the Founding Fathers of New England; and the impossibility of living by the code of Charity in a society composed of Cains, Iagos, children like Lear's, wives like Goneril, friends like Timon's, etc., who reveal the malignancy of human nature, the eternal Red Indian in everyone.

To cope with this situation of agonizing problems, which Christianity has not been able to change (and so, alas, Christian-ity must therefore be written off), Melville proposes a technique for self-protection and moral and emotional survival. It might well be called the Philosophy of As If, if that title had not been pre-empted for something different. Melville knows that all wives are not Gonerils, all children not like Lear's, all friends not broken reeds or potential enemies, and so on, but since, he argues, History and Literature and our own experience tell us that they so often and indeed characteristically *are*, it is safer to assume that they *always* are, as in the Greek philosopher's paradox: 'My friends, there are no friends!'. We can thus take precautions as a form of insurance against the worst. Shakespeare has told us that 'Most friendship is feigning, most loving mere folly': Melville says, For practical purposes we had better behave as if *all* are. For not to recognize that the treacherous Red Indian is always potentially active in others is suicidal folly.

But this, he admits, is the ideal. Is it practicable as a mode of existence? This is where the tests of the theory cease to be a matter of the intellect and make the book a novel. Numerous tests are carried out to prove to us that we can trust no one and nothing, certainly not Nature as the Romantic poets and the Transcendentalists allege, or Man living in a state of nature as imagined by Rousseau. The backwoodsman complains that all the boys he has tried as servants are idle and dishonest and compares them unfavourably with machines in a very amusing speech (ch. 22), but he still can't manage his life without them as he hasn't succeeded in inventing a machine that would replace servants; he is persuaded, against all his experience, to believe the agent who argues he can supply a boy who is an exception to the rule, and thus weakening, is of course cheated of his fee. He weakens because, as Melville shows, unfortunately we are dependent on each other. So even the convinced Indian-Hater, devoting his life to exterminating single-handed the Red Indian 'in the forest primeval', will sooner or later feel an over-powering need to trust and love *someone* – just as the Missourian who protects himself by a bachelor and backwoods life and by keeping his 'misanthropic rifle' always at the ready, allowed the con-man 'insensibly to persuade him to waive, in his exceptional case, that general law of distrust systematically applied to the race'. Therefore the Indian-Hater

> after some months of lonely scoutings is suddenly seized with a sort of calenture; hurries openly towards the first

smoke, though he knows it is an Indian's, announces himself as a lost hunter, gives the savage his rifle, throws himself upon his charity, embraces him with much affection, imploring the privilege of living a while in his sweet companionship.

This is a touching recognition of the pathos and tragedy of the need for human relationships, for the passage immediately concludes: 'What is too often the sequel of so distempered a procedure may be best known by those who best know the Indian' – for of course the now defenceless ex-Indian-Hater is invariably scalped. 'No Trust' is a hateful motto, but the barber when talked into suspending it is cheated by the Confidence Man.

The ideal of a wholly consistent Indian-Hater in real life, as Melville thus admits, is impracticable; the best that can be expected is 'the diluted Indian-Hater'. The status of this brilliant parable is indicated by the chapter-title 'The Metaphysics of Indian-Hating'. The parable is then novelized in several dramatic scenes with dialogues illustrating bogus friendship and sham conviviality: 'The Boon Companions', 'The Hypothetical Friends' and the tale of China Aster, ruined through officious 'friendship'. But along with these there is an important appendix representing an alternative to reacting to Timon's situation either by vindictive bitterness and misanthropy, or blindness to being deceived. This is shown in the history of Charlemont, 'a kindly man' but 'not deficient in mind' (that is, though a nice man he is a realist) who, when he falls from prosperity through business losses, cuts dead all his friends in order not to put them to the shame of cold-shouldering him, and disappears, to reappear nine years later having made another fortune abroad. He then reassumes without explanation his convivial habits in his former society but is the prey of a secret melancholy which is at last revealed to an old acquaintance who questions him. Charlemont says only:

If ever, in days to come, you shall see ruin at hand, and, thinking you understand mankind, shall tremble for your friendships, and tremble for your pride; and partly through love for the one and fear for the other, shall resolve to be beforehand with the world, and save it from a sin by prospectively taking that sin to yourself, then you will do as one I now dream of once did, and like him you will suffer.

'Save it from a sin, by prospectively taking that sin to yourself' is surely a Christ-like procedure. But the tale is ironically labelled: 'The Story of the Gentleman-Madman' – 'mad' in the eyes of the average American who could not be expected to appreciate such sensitive forbearance, and who was not a gentleman. This is reinforced by the Cosmopolitan's admission that he invented the story – 'it is what contrasts with real life' he says, ironically challenging his auditor (a hypothetical friend) to say whether in real life friends, himself for instance, would behave as Charlemont assumed his would on hearing he had gone bankrupt. The need to have associates, even such as he knew his friends to be, put Charlemont in the position of the man

> accounting wine so fine a thing, that even the sham article is better than none at all. . . . It is a fable . . . it illustrated, as in a parable, how that a man of disposition ungovernably good-natured might still familiarly associate with men, though, at the same time, he believed the greater part of men false-hearted. . . . And if the Rochefoucaultites urge that, by this course, he will sooner or later be undermined in security, he answers, 'And do you think I don't know that? But security without society I hold a bore; and society, even of the spurious sort, has its price, which I am willing to pay'.

In this way only can one avoid the dilemma of being, as Swift puts it, a fool among knaves or else going mad. But Melville never accepts Swift's brutal alternative, for he implies that there is a sensitive and high-minded man to be considered, who is for Melville the norm. We noted that his objection to Emersonian Man was that that was not 'a feeling man' and was therefore inhuman.

Melville discusses also the alternative to Charity, uncompromising Truth. The wooden-legged man declares: 'Charity is one thing, and truth is another' – being 'charitable' ('Charity thinketh no evil') is easy, but being truthful means exposing dishonesty and false confidence: all the passengers turn on him, especially the Methodist, for declaring the Negro cripple to be a fraud though he is right in his suspicions. Yet truth, Melville also sees, is destructive: 'Truth is like a threshing-machine; tender sensibilities must keep out of the way' says the Missourian, who tells the truth with the relentless incivility that is necessary. He, also, is unpopular, and the Methodist urges him to 'Be not such a Canada thistle', to which he replies, as he broadcasts the seeds of doubt: 'Now, when with my thistles your farms shall be well stocked, why then – you may abandon 'em!', a recognition by Melville of the sterility of perpetual distrust.

The Confidence Man characterizes the wooden-legged man as 'a scoffer who, even truth were on his tongue, his way of speaking it would make truth as offensive as falsehood', a little joke against Melville himself, for there are other ironic references that identify this scoffer with the author. And this is the point at which one must consider Melville's difference from Swift. Melville had also considered it, since he has taken care to dissociate himself from what was for him a morally unacceptable attitude to his fellows, whom Swift in all his writings treats with disgust and contempt. Melville, a morally sensitive man, is unlike him in not being arrogant and in being continuously self-critical. He shows that the Missourian bachelor, who like Swift denigrates the human race in general but objects to being disrespectfully considered himself, is disconcerted when the Cosmopolitan retorts: 'And what race may *you* belong to? Now don't you see in what inconsistencies one involves himself by affecting disesteem for men'. And of the wooden-legged man when he denounces the Negro cripple, the author himself remarks: 'These suspicions came from one who himself on a wooden leg went halt' and that 'cripples, above all men, should at least, refrain from picking a fellow-limper to pieces', a re-phrasing of the axiom that we are all miserable sinners. Melville also declares his possible bias as a satirist: the wooden-legged man is 'a limping, gimlet-eyed, sour-faced person' suffering under a grievance against 'government and humanity' and like 'a criminal judge with a mustard-plaster on his back' – 'In the present case the mustard-plaster might have been the memory of certain recent biting rebuffs and mortifications'. Government had recently failed to give Melville a remunerative consulship and humanity had rebuffed and mortified him as a novelist. Hence he sees that he is liable to take, like the wooden-legged man, a 'one-sided view of humanity'. Humour directed against himself and self-awareness of this kind are unusual in satirical writers, a proof of candour; Melville's irony is not self-protective like that of the Bloomsbury school, on the contrary, his art is profound and courageous.

Melville therefore seems closer to Conrad than to Swift or Samuel Butler, the Conrad who devoted a novel to considering one brought up to be an Indian-Hater – Axel Heyst, warned by his father, the 'destroyer of systems, of hopes, of beliefs', to be scornful of mankind and believe in nothing, and never to become involved with flesh and blood. But Heyst finds a life of moral and physical isolation impracticable, and involvement proves to be both his undoing and his salvation. Melville does not say like Conrad: 'Woe to the man whose heart has not learned while young to hope, to love – and to put its trust in life!' but the constant irony and the sub-title of 'Masquerade', the outbursts of jocosity and jeering, should not mislead us into assuming that there is no depth of feeling in Melville's novel, no *parti pris* or involvement. There is real moral feeling and demand for moral courage in social life visible in Melville's attack on the cowardly who protect themselves by deploring this as 'aggressiveness', when the Missourian condemns the herb-doctor's cant of this kind with: 'Picked and prudent sentiments. You are the moderate man, the invaluable understrapper of the wicked man. You, the moderate man, may be used for wrong, but are useless for right.' Melville is not therefore imprisoned in a moral void like the author of *L'Etranger*, or in contempt and disgust like Swift, or in a neurosis like Kafka, or even in the joylessness of *Rasselas*. He attempts to work out some satisfactory strategy for living because he subscribes to the insight Kafka recorded in his *Reflections*: 'No one should say that we lack faith. The mere fact of our living implies a degree of faith which is inexhaustible' – in spite of Melville's ever-present exasperation at the human dilemma. This he constantly comes back to in different forms, as in making a character say: 'The suspicious man kicks himself with his own foot'. He shows in the novel, though it seems a tissue of ironies, that he thirsts for honesty, courage, honourable conduct, love, integrity, true friendship, true charity, social justice, and that he is agonized because these necessities of life seemed to be victims of the spirit of his age, or even of social life in any age. Thus the Methodist's rant against the 'mad' unbeliever is only partly ironic, for the description of 'the end of suspicion' in a madhouse looks to me to have been taken from the terrifying last plate of Hogarth's 'The Rake's Progress'.

Besides the satiric emanations of himself as the wooden-legged man and the bachelor backwoodsman, there is a much more startling and profoundly serious Melville representative, that of his past self as artist. This is the 'kind of invalid Titan in homespun' who seems to have stepped inexplicably on board the *Fidèle* out of some earlier Melville novel, 'his countenance tawny and shadowy as an iron-ore country in a clouded day', his 'child', of true native American breed, in one hand and a heavy club of swamp-oak in the other; he is a melancholy giant bowed down with suffering and his child (his creative work) is 'a little Cassandra', that is, a prophet of doom; his voice is like 'a great clock bell', it is 'a stunning admonisher'; but though sad and ill and 'bowed over' he is indomitable. Rejecting the salvation cure-all and declaring the healer to be a 'Profane fiddler on heart-strings', a 'Snake', he fells the quack with a blow of his staff and disappears from the book. Melville's self-directed irony again appears in ascribing to his Titan the bias of which he himself was suspected by reviewers – a 'countenance lividly epileptic with hypochondriac mania', and the herb-doctor in the same spirit dismisses him as 'Regardless of decency and lost to humanity!'. But these sardonic jokes don't deprive the 'invalid Titan' of his impressiveness. While invoking thus the author of *Moby-Dick* Melville seems to be recognizing that he is defeated and remote: his 'voice deep and lonesome enough to have come from the bottom of an abandoned coal-shaft', he is offered as a tragic figure.

Again, though there is sardonic treatment of the *organization* and current *practice* of Christianity, of Christianity as represented by churches, priests, the claims of dogmatists and the behaviour of so-called Christians, there is manifest regret at his own inability to accept the religious inheritance of the Bible (which we can see he read closely). Christian practice is examined in the parable of the Indian-Hater, where Melville notes the self-righteous attitude of the New England settler whose devout religious practices did not prevent him from treating the Indians as diabolical enemies. Melville says: '. . . in which the charitable may think he does them some injustice. Certain it is, the Indians themselves think so. . . . The Indians, indeed, protest against the backwoodsman's view of them' etc. And 'the instinct of antipathy against an Indian grows in the backwoodsman with the sense of good and bad, right and wrong. In one breath he learns that a brother is to be loved, and an Indian to be hated.' This is also a satiric parable on the doctrine of Calvinism and Original Sin, the natural man being un-regenerate and the stronghold of the Old Adam, therefore con-veniently identifiable with the Redskin.

But the final chapter seems to admit the need for religion with its account of the passengers' cabin which is lit by 'a solar lamp' that 'the commands of the captain required to be kept burning till the natural light of day should come to relieve it' – though whether this natural light is Reason, or Eternity (when Truth will make all things plain), is not explained. This lamp, we are told by Melville, is the only light left to see by, for the 'other lamps, barren planets, had either gone out from exhaus-tion, or been extinguished by such occupants of berths as the light annoyed, or who wanted to sleep, not see'. This is straight-forward – the extinct lamps are dead religions, and the pas-sengers who had extinguished the lamps are deplored; the 'perverse man, in a berth not remote' who now wanted the last lamp put out is again Melville himself, seen from this point of view as misguided, as no doubt he sometimes feared – for from this berth comes presently the voice of the wide-awake man jeering at the Cosmopolitan.

The Cosmopolitan wins the confidence of the pious old man ('one of those . . . untainted by the world, because ignorant of it') and by sophistry deprives him of *all* his beliefs, so bewilder-ing him that he gives himself over to the guidance of this false Saviour and agrees to let him put out the lamp, leaving them in darkness and with a bad smell on the premises. This last is a Swiftian joke unworthy of the novel, but it does not disguise Melville's recognition of the despair and danger of the outcome which is thus intentionally pictured as degradation. The lamp had on its shade a horned altar (a traditional symbol for the Old Testament) and a robed figure with a halo (representing the New); with the quenching of the light these disappear from view. No doubt Melville, interested like other American writers and academics of his time in Oriental religions, knew that Nirvana means 'to quench the light', not his idea of what humanity should strive for. Thus the book ends on a note of despair. Note that we never see the captain or otherwise hear of him, and his commands are conveyed to the passengers only by a placard outside his office or more directly by the steward; a Kafka-esque situation. Christ is also, as a deaf mute, in keeping with this implied criticism of deity as incommunicado.

Yet Solzhenitsyn's much more dreadful account in *The First Circle* of an evil society (evil beyond Melville's conception and yet an actuality, not a satirist's caricature) does not end in despair, and we must ask why Melville's novel should. We have seen how, shortly before *The Confidence-Man*, Melville had written tales which acknowledged the place of art in the life of mankind and emphasized, and examined, the role of the artist. Why then does he leave out of this book the whole question of the function of the arts, which no primitive society has ever been found without? This omission gives a sense of a hole in the middle of his argument, endorsing the belief of Blake and Hogarth that 'The whole world without Art would be one great wilderness'. If this hole had been filled by representations of the nature of creativeness, which is collaborative, and of its life-enhancing function, the book would not have been open to the charges of aridity and one-sidedness. All that Melville provides in recognition of man's creative achievements as a social being is the racy idiom, rich in exaggeration, picturesque in imagery and delighting in grotesque humour, of the backwoodsman from Missouri, representing the pioneer achievement which Melville backed as the valuable strain in American life – Western as opposed to New England – full of energy and originality because free of restraints and conventions. But the limitations of such a culture are obvious both intellectually and spiritually; the arts were the first loss in a pioneer life. We think of what *The First Circle* would have been if Solzhenitsyn had left out of that novel the representative artist Kondrashov and the account of his work and ideas, and left out too the parts of the novel that testify that literature and music, even the mere remembrance of them, as also of their religious traditions, together with their inherited code of professional ethics, are what combined to sustain the morale of the prisoners as self-respecting human beings capable of disinterestedness, even in an environment designed to reduce them to subordination as starving animals fighting for survival.

But then Solzhenitsyn had Tolstoy as forbear, and alerted by him he asks Melville's questions in a different form. Melville in *The Confidence-Man* asks repeatedly: How can one believe in anything or anyone? Solzhenitsyn proceeds to ask, as Tolstoy had done: What then do men live by? – even in a society that is a cancer ward or the first circle of the Inferno. Thus *The Confidence-Man* seems to take place in something like a prison without the aeration provided by the factors that Solzhenitsyn shows social life provided in the Old World and that George Eliot, writing at the same date as Melville, showed, in *Silas Marner*, English village life had provided. Therefore her discussion of the problem of reintegration into social life of a man who had lost his beliefs is optimistic in conclusion. Poetic in character, it is also witty and full of humour, providing a useful comparison with Melville's satiric, philosophic and negative approach to the same situation. Both use the moral fable and the parable as their art-form – [see my critical introduction and Notes to the Penguin English Library edition of *Silas Marner*.] But of course there was in Russia a great, undying tradition of a literature in general possession and of the poet's importance, which a pioneer society lacked. Melville clearly felt that he and Hawthorne had created great and truly American novels and tales, in defiance of the imitative colonial tradition that they considered was not American but pseudo-English and merely genteel; yet they had been defeated by the indifference of the American public to spiritual values and literary art. So in this last novel the artist and creative thinker appears only as a decrepit Titan. Hence we should not be surprised that *The Piazza Tales* and *The Confidence-Man* are predominantly ironic and painful. What is surprising is that Melville retained his control over satiric impulses and that these works display so much humour, humility, sensitiveness and even, as in *I and My Chimney*, show him accepting without ill-will the odium and misunderstanding that must be incurred by an artist and intellectual in such a society. It is natural that, in his discouragement after the failure of his tremendous expenditure in creative writing between 1853 and 1856, and of the failure to secure a reading public for *Moby-Dick* and *Pierre*, that he should direct his talents in *The Confidence-Man* to isolating the sources of blight and corruption in his age, and write more as a satirical philosopher than as an artist. His death soon after his subsequent twenty years of drudgery as an outdoor Inspector of Customs on the waterfront brought no recognition; he died unknown, and as a prophet unhonoured in his own country, the final irony that confirms the justice of the view of his America expressed in *The Confidence-Man*.

Orpheus and Measured Forms:
Law, Madness and Reticence in Melville

As the 'dark-damasked Chola widow' Hunilla leaves Norfolk
Isle, Melville tells us a seaman working at the windlass, 'un-
warrantedly exhilarated', jumped up on it and in this chance
exuberance which 'high lifted [him] above all others' perceived
the 'otherwise unperceivable'. This 'elevation of his spirits'
showed her white hankerchief waved from an inland rock.[1] But
her endurance has become sacred; she is taboo; her fate may not
be transgressed by narrative; she has become eternally private
in her 'sane despair' or insane hope for survival. This example
of 'nature's pride subduing nature's torture' becomes a myth,
'a heart yearning in a frame of steel. A heart of earthly yearning,
frozen by the frost which falleth from the sky'. Melville, witness
of her narrative, believes it must remain incomplete for us and
remains reticent before 'two unnamed events' which befell her –
'the half shall here remain untold'. The other seamen join in
'silent reverence of respect'. Hunilla moves towards that area
where men make gods, the region which most excited Melville's
lifelong enquiry into the exceptional human life. Hunilla is
carried away from sight on an ass, which by chance law of
nature bears one of the oldest cultural signs, the cross which
binds space and time, intersecting their energies in a design of
natural law. 'In nature, as in law,' Melville writes, 'it may be
libellous to speak some truths.'

Towards the end of his brief life Pierre finds that he has been
corrupted by plots pretending total unravelling, a figure parallel
to Melville's recurrent diver. Alain Robbe-Grillet indicated the
falsity in 'A Future for the Novel'[2] in 1956: 'We had thought
to control [the world around us] by assigning it a meaning, and
the entire art of the novel, in particular, seemed dedicated to
this enterprise. . . . The writer's traditional role consisted in
excavating Nature, in burrowing deeper to reach some ever
more intimate strata, in finally unearthing some fragment of a

disconcerting secret.' The descender into Avernus would return 'triumphant messages describing the mysteries he had actually touched with his own hands. And the sacred vertigo the reader suffered then, far from causing him anguish or nausea, reassured him as to his power of domination over the world'. Melville's scepticism, one hundred years earlier, appears as he speaks, in *Pierre*, of novels' 'inverted attempt at systematizing eternally unsystematizable elements; their audacious, intermeddling impotency, in trying to unravel, and spread out, and classify, the more thin than gossamer threads which make up the complex web of life'.[3] The 'unravellable inscrutableness' which 'all men are agreed to call by the name of *God*' is an absolute. Human intricacies 'hurry to abrupt intermergings with the eternal tides of time and fate'. As Isabel appears as a form of intricacy, Pierre, Melville says, 'determined to pry not at all into this sacred problem', 'the mere imaginariness of the so-supposed solidest principle of human association'. But Pierre surges towards absolutes and solidifies himself into final sterilities of petrification. Like Ahab he is mad in his limitation, imitating the God-Absolute: 'Pierre was now this vulnerable god; this self-upbraiding sailor'. The laws of his scheme must totally include. He is 'an algebraist' who substitutes sign for solution, believing himself self-mastered, 'all the horizon of his dark fate commanded by him'. But again Melville withdraws: 'Some nameless struggles of the soul cannot be painted, and some woes will not be told. Let the ambiguous process of events reveal their own ambiguousness'. The 'endless significances' (Bk 25, ch. 2) of Pierre's tautology can at least force a cry: 'Civilization, Philosophy, Ideal Virtue! behold your victim!' (Bk 22, ch. 2). Pierre's marblized paralysis is a suicide by laws of education thrust into an absurd either/or intrigue: 'chance or God?' Melville's answer is stoic expediency within a social structure radically unimpeded, an oscillation between narcissism and self-violence until forms of death resolve Pierre's Promethean charge against the Absolute. He steals no fire, erotic or intellectual; he is neutered, just as Bartleby is neutered, by absolute consistency, a self-constituted law. As Melville noted in his *Journal Up the Straits*: 'no wonder stones should so largely figure in the Bible'.

Billy Budd is deified not by himself, as might some ancient

Caesar or Tzar, but by his fellow men, and as Hunilla is sainted in her taboo: an ignorant innocent who cannot survive in a society of libidinous evil and rigid formalist law. Ships are necessarily run by law which makes them synechdochic fragments of national structure. Entrusting himself to that law makes a man social. Trust and confidence are therefore essential to the working out of law in American society and fiction which claimed, in the nineteenth century that they had 'all to make'. Beyond the barber's 'No Trust' sign in *The Confidence-Man* lies Mark Twain's lack of confidence that the society of Dawson's Landing or the banks of the Mississippi will change. In Melville's world it is Babo, the regal slave, who breaks laws which supply confidence to white Europe and America on the *San Dominick*, a sham empire turned black republic, and both given as tyrannies. Babo's dead eyes meet without shame in defeat the legal institutions of tyranny: Church and State, or monastery and court. At the conclusion of 'Benito Cereno' the black has destroyed chances of 'salvation' either by institutions or from what Captain Delano calls 'my good nature, compassion and charity'. Among heraldic myths on the stern shield of the *San Dominick* is the Dark God himself, about which Melville is again reticent: 'a dark Satyr in a mask, holding his foot on the prostrate neck of a writhing figure, likewise masked'. Beneath these masks lies the nature of men under nature and law, and their presence makes Delano's overpowering of Babo even less final and more ironically futile: 'his right foot . . . ground the prostrate negro'.

The benevolent dictatorship of the *Bachelor's Delight* and the failed white tyranny of the *San Dominick* are challenged by Senegalese tribal monarchy, against which the white American's 'tranquillizing' thoughts of self-pleasure are a law of sterilization, akin to Pierre's neutering: 'he seemed in some far inland country, prisoner in some deserted château, left to stare at empty grounds, and peer at vague roads, where never wagon or wayfarer passed'. The climax of the story is a knot held mutely by a bachelor. Delano misses the old sailor's invitation to cut the 'gordian knot' he is making 'for some one else to undo', and hands it 'unconsciously' to a black who tosses it overboard. His 'regulated mind' is governed by pride identified with racist and class order, the order of the two ships and *Rover*, his trusty doggy boat plying between them. 'Revelation' breaks when white sailors kill white sailors in battle confusion but with 'deliberate marksman's shots'. Melville's irony peaks as Delano's men board the enemy under the mate's cry of 'Follow your leader!', a slogan already associated with Columbus, the slaver-explorer, the murdered slaver Aranda, and Babo's slave revolt. Delano's slogan, 'all is owing to Providence', cannot extend to the wreckage of Cereno. The Massachusetts Protestant deist believes in his own election as leader, and his confidence is structured from Christian white programmes of superiority. Melville concludes again in deadly sterility after a dialectic in which central ruling codes of the West are violated.

Protestant 'accounting' and confidence in superior benevolence are again defeated in 'Bartleby', the tale of a lawyer reduced to insecurity by a suicidal joker with a Zen passion for aphorism. The 'snug business' of a Wall Street law office is the structure organizing the semantics of the Protestant ethic of salvation by *master*, *work* and *help*. This kingdom is usurped by a mysterious stranger with a single origin – the dead letter office. Melville is reticent about other life for Bartleby, a man beaten by the Emersonian creed of self-reliance in a society which enforces competition. He competes in the only way he can. He is 'pitiably respectable', a member of a group about whom 'nothing . . . has ever been written' – and again, Melville is necessarily reticent. Bartleby copies the law documents of an imprisoning system, but 'no materials' exist for his biography. He ought to be safe but he is not, and the lawyer is 'an eminently safe man' who depends on the 'good opinion' of John Jacob Astor, the unseen pinnacle of capitalism, and on the State's intervention in his appointment as Master in Chancery and the 'life-lease of the profits' from it. Among his employees the sixty-year-old Turkey has grown old in 'submission', Nippers at twenty-five is locked in indigestion and ambitious shadowy transactions of little consequence, and Ginger Nut, a working-class boy sent to the office to work his way out of his class, is caught in the grotesque repetitions his nickname implies.

In this office enclosure of grotesque and law, 'privacy and society were conjoined'. The polar opposite of Bartleby's 'mechanical copying' by sun and candle lights in this autocracy is Byron, 'the mettlesome poet' of discontent with coercive society and its intrusion of privacy. Bartleby's revolt begins with a classic withdrawal of labour but his 'I would prefer not to' has only the force of private choice, even if its second occurence turns the lawyer momentarily 'to a pillar of salt' rather than lava or marble. But the lawyer is as anonymous as his scrivener – who at least has a name – and is both 'touched' and 'disconcerted' at this revolt against working *with* rather than *alone*. Dissent can be accommodated by law provided it remains passive resistance or minority violation of social equilibrium. The lawyer looks forward to 'a delicious self-approval' while, as he says, 'I lay up in my soul what will eventually prove a sweet morsel for my conscience'. In this way his sense of law becomes a characteristic Christian book-keeping which forgets Christ's law: 'Lay not up for yourself treasure in heaven'. In Hawthorne's terms, the lawyer would use the scrivener for the Unpardonable Sin of his own ends in power: 'I burned to be rebelled against again'. He yearns for 'some angry spark' between them through which extra-legality can be made visible and violent. Bartleby is otherwise an exemplary wage-slave, 'a valuable acquisition' in the lawyer's phrase. But the lawyer is not finally in control and this is Melville's issue. He has to remember all his employee's 'peculiarities, privileges, and unheard-of exemptions' against which protest is 'impotent rebellion'.

Melville's key term in all power situations is 'unmanned', and this lawyer is a bachelor unmanned by a bachelor who keeps 'Bachelor's Hall' in his law office, under the benison of Astor and the State on the Petra of Wall Street. The Syrian rock city translated to the sterility of law and finance in 1853 is combined with 'the ruins of Carthage' to suggest the incipient ruin of the American system by the clash of two laws: the right of self-possession and the right of property and master-employee coupling, the confused mainstays of legal liberalism. The lawyer manages a feeling of 'fraternal melancholy' at Bartleby's pathetic endurance but leaves it as 'chimeras of a sick and silly brain'; Bartleby is 'eccentric', beyond help in his 'excessive and organic ill'. The liberal lawyer characteristically has no sense of social cause, and neither has Melville, beyond the scrivener as 'the victim of innate and incurable disorder'. Law cannot cope with disease. The plea of 'I would prefer' invades the office but Bartleby himself remains part of a desert ruin: 'Like the last column of some ruined temple, he remained standing mute and solitary in the middle of the otherwise deserted room'. The original temple was not the temple of the white saintly father in *Pierre* but some dream *polis* where self could exist in utopian anarchism with other selves, a peculiarly American dream of independence within law. But the society of Wall Street *is* the lawyer's office, a society of winning and losing, which Melville identifies with the current election. Withdrawal of labour leads, in the absence of legal, social organization, to a withdrawal to death, to suicidal demonstration of self-possession. Bartleby ends as a foetal-shaped, protesting corpse.

The lawyer's dilemma resolves into violence in his mind, and he recalls a similar case of what appeared to be manslaughter, and we can recall the end of Pierre and of the three heroes of 'Benito Cereno'. But because charity is good self-protective policy, he uses Christ's law: 'A new commandment I give unto you, that ye love one another'. Since charity is the mask liberals place on the face of tyranny, the lawyer now experiences the scrivener's behaviour as tyranny conflicting with 'necessities connected with my business [which] tyrannized over all other considerations'. Like Delano's, his context is the law of 'some mysterious purpose of an all-wise Providence' which has elected him as agent in a 'mission'. Bartleby may be a disguised asset, therefore, but he still threatens 'authority' and 'scandalizes his professional reputation'. Melville's deeper image is therefore out of the Protestant churchgoer's fear of witchcraft: the intruder is an 'apparition', 'an intolerable incubus' of the Dark God, who reappears from the *San Dominick*'s stern. His pallid face masks a black presence which 'haunts the building', and whom with neat irony, the lawyer denies thrice even while he knows he is being 'held to terrible account'. Not surprisingly the lawyer rushes from the building and becomes a victim on the run, 'nothing' fleeing 'something' and paying 'fugitive visits'.

The law's police remove the incubus to the Tombs on an ironic charge of vagrancy. Where Pierre ended a stone between stone walls of a cell, the Petra column of Bartleby solidifies in the prison yard, 'a gentleman forger', as the grub-man rightly believes. Bartleby parodies the isolationist saints of self-reliance in Melville's book of laws. His 'dead-wall reveries' move to a terminus in the law of self-possession. Egyptian masonry encloses him in an imitation of ancient hopelessness, waste and tyranny. The lawyer tries for meaning by injecting the Book of Job, an unfortunate choice since it reinforces arbitrary authoritarianism. Bartleby will not strike through the walls' 'unreasoning mask' even in Ahab's pathetic attempt to be absolute. As C. Wright Mills once observed, when Prometheus 'turns softly inward', the result is sterility. Providence is really John Jacob Astor but the lawyer has to believe that man is 'by nature and misfortune prone to a pallid hopelessness'. The scrivener was therefore reduced by universal law, and it is not one of beneficence and confidence.

Melville once believed that alternative lay in Ishmael's remark after his experience with the Polynesian Queequeg: of a 'mutual, joint-stock world in all meridians. We cannibals must help these Christians'. But the Christians had turned cannibal and consumed self-reliant individuals in the name of the laws of natural selection and competition as Providence. *The Confidence-Man* holds that charity corrupts, as it corrupted the lawyer, since it depends on the law of election to power over other people, the recipient victims. To receive charity, Melville understands, may itself be suicidal to the self and the death of equitable society. As Richard Chase observed on *The Confidence-Man*:[4]

> Intellectually, the liberal preserves himself from self-knowledge by refusing to admit that moral choices have far-reaching consequences and that thought, no matter how ordinary or work-a-day, has its complex resonances of moral, mythical, religious, and cultural meaning . . . liberalism tends to commit suicide by reducing itself to a stance of rectitude, a bondage to the absolute, or a mechanism for denying the necessity to think and feel.

The wall of bone or stone encountered at their end by Melville's primary heroes is for Clarel the city of Jerusalem, 'a stony metropolis of stones'. Mount Zion crumbles to sand; there is no absolute *polis* of eternal law. Absolute communalism, absolute tolerance, absolute self-quest are equally impossible.

It is the sea, the basic proposition or paradigm, of which Melville can say in *Moby-Dick*: 'no power but its own controls it'.[5] Its law of 'universal cannibalism' has an analogy in the land mass, the 'horrible vulturism of earth', explicit in chapter 2 of

Typee and in the figure of Rodondo in *The Encantadas*. Ishmael escapes 'at the axis of that slowly wheeling circle', revolving as a temporary Ixion who is not bound on a wheel of fire in Hades as punishment for transgression of the human limit, the impiety of *hubris*, the curious sin of Ahab, Bartleby, and the bachelors of Melville's fictions. He survives the mad kingdom-ship of Ahab and its sacral allegiance, a system established in chapter 36, 'The Quarterdeck'. Ahab's commanding law submits men to single policy, and as to why they submit, Melville is reticent. The ceremonial drink 'spiralizes' into the crew but in chapter 41, Melville holds back from their possession by 'evil magic'. Ishmael abandons himself to 'the time and the place'. In *White-Jacket* Melville had proposed the condition of man-of-war as an incarceration in which a man is forbidden 'the privilege of dying himself'. In all these ship societies men subserve linear law in single purpose in which a man or a nation becomes a cause for success. The success-seeker is deranged but not as a seer in Rimbaud's sense: 'with what struggling method he can, [he must] dash with all his derangements at his object'.[6] Twenty years after *Moby-Dick* Rimbaud wrote: 'the soul has to be made monstrous'. The theory of noble leaders comes to this in Melville, since they are not artists: Ishmael is rescued by the *Rachel* whose 'masts and yards' are given as 'tall cherry trees, when the boys are cherrying among the boughs'.[7] Her 'retracing' in humane search for the whaleboat redraws the linear as the human map on the surface of the sea, instancing a possible habitable world which combines skills and fertilities away from the tyrannical and suicidal. (One of the 'extracts' prefacing *Moby-Dick* tells the general facts: 'It is generally well known that out of the crews of whaling vessels (American) few ever return in the ships on board of which they departed'.) It is this cherry world which reappears in chapter 135 in the dreams of the doomed mates of the *Pequod*. Ishmael's other experience of fraternity and fertility is, of course, standing hand to hand with his fellow crewmen in the whale sperm and feeling the globules of sperm as 'fully ripe grapes', washing his hands of the 'horrible oath' to Ahab and replacing it with a vision of brotherhood and non-bachelor domesticity. A ship's crew is not necessarily a brotherhood. Ahab will sacrifice any member under his law of allegiance, softening only in recognition of kindred madness in Pip, the unmanned cabin-boy. Even so, Pip is a threat to his purpose: 'Weep so, and I will murder thee! have a care, for Ahab too is mad'. Their master-servant relationship remains a permanence in Melville's stratified model of society. Ahab's monstrousness is that he needs to be masterless, without 'confines', within the competitive 'fair play' of the universe, as he speaks of it in chapter 36. 'Fair play' means competition in a universe of natural selection and divine election under the unapproachable Sun. The Sun is a fact not a god or a state or nation making law, a fact which mad Ahab places in his law of hierarchy: to his challenge of 'Who's over me?' the answer is the Sun. Meanwhile he treats Ocean as Sky, and hunts the sky-god Sun as a mammal in the Zodiac. Chapter 27 may recall the Clootz deputation of world enthusiasm for the French Revolution but there is to be no revolution in Melville's world. In chapter 134 all is reduced to Ahab's riddle which 'might baffle all the lawyers backed by the ghosts of the whole line of judges': how the Parsee will appear before Ahab's death according to linear law of prophecy.

If the 'moving world'[8] of the ship represents western technology, organization and law of government, then ship's time, like factory time – and *Pequod* is a factory – and monastery time, is a division of life-energy into a mechanism of labour for workers and *hubris* for elitist leaders. As a young man Melville experienced a crucial oscillation between Pacific Island desertions for freedom and returns to ship's law. He was ranked a boy at 18 and *Redburn* shows how the ship class structure burned into him. He always wrote from a lower-deck stance – for an origin we have chapter 51 of *Redburn* where cabin passengers are described with contempt and polarized against the condition of crew, steerage and Liverpool slums. As in *The Sea Wolf* and *Two Years Before the Mast* an upper middle-class American is reversed into subordination under codified law and labour-time, exemplified in the master-servant relationship of flogging, D. H. Lawrence's 'state of unstable vital equilibrium'.

'The grotesque young stranger'[9] is renamed Buttons and is ranked 'boy',[10] the target of the 'dictator' Jackson, a broken survivor of world voyages who turns Redburn into an Ishmael. They are so paired in alienation through cleverness and superiority-feeling, cut off from both crew and legalistic captain. But Melville also makes Jackson an example of 'inscrutable curse' in the moral world: Cain, the blighted individualist turned monster, incarcerated now in the 'crowded jail' of the ship. The basic condition is given in chapter 6: 'the motto is "Obey orders, though you break owners" . . . sea-officers never give reasons for anything they order to be done'. In *White-Jacket* this social structure is under military law, and the preface speaks of 'the established laws and usages of the Navy'. The narrator hauls his saturated white jacket aloft 'in accordance with the natural laws',[11] but it is the frigate's system of 'regulations' which prevents the crew from becoming a mutinous mob (Melville refers here to the Gordon Riots of 1780, in which a London mob, instigated by Lord George Gordon, attacked Catholics and those judges and lawyers who supported the recent law of religious tolerance). Captain Claret rules through 'endless subdivision of duties' and the law of his word: 'it is not twelve o'clock till he says so' (ch. 6). His 'high constable' is the master-at-arms, 'a very Vidocq in vigilance'. The 'common seamen' are 'the people', the labour force of the *Neversink*, 'the asylum for the perverse, the home of the unfortunate', 'a lofty, walled, and garrisoned town' in which 'peaceable citizens meet armed sentries at every corner (ch. 18). The men are 'victims' of 'arbitrary government' (ch. 20) and cleanness itself is part of tyranny – even the rusty cannonballs are cleaned (ch. 49). The Fourth of July is a licensed orgy although the crew's theatricals are censored 'to see whether (they) contain anything calculated to breed dis-affection against lawful authority'. To prevent the crew from freezing at one point the captain orders 'all hands skylark!' (ch. 25). But when a storm from the basic proposition loosens the ship's bell under the law of the elements, only disobedience of order by lieutenant 'Mad Jack' saves the ship. Claret of 'the unnecessarily methodical step' arraigns Mad Jack under the Articles of War as part of his 'desire to strike subjection among the crew' (ch. 27). But to Melville the lieutenant is 'a numeral' among 'a long array of cyphers', like Nelson and Wellington: 'one large brain and one large heart have virtue sufficient to magnetize a whole fleet or army'. Mad Jack exemplifies those 'natural capabilities' and 'natural heroism, talent, judgment, and integrity' which Navy law must deny. The contradiction is not examined.

The place of justice is the main-mast, 'the bull-ring' (ch. 32). The main punishment by 'omnipotent authority' is flogging without trial, compared by Melville to the Christian Day of Judgement (chs 33, 34). Claret's Ahab-like reply to the 19-year-old Peter's plea for mercy is 'I would not forgive God Almighty!' The flogged man is 'a slave' punished for crimes created by 'arbitrary laws' which Melville compares to the 160 offences meriting capital punishment under English law. Naval captains simply 'violate the express laws laid down by Congress for the government of the Navy' by their 'license' of interpretation. Melville once again focuses on the sacral centre of endurance of which the scorned body is capable: 'this feeling of innate dignity . . . buried among the holiest privacies of the soul', 'one of the hushed things' around which the silence of the 'sacred' makes the victim taboo. There is no right for legislators to profane this centre by degradation. Melville yields to none of Lawrence's cruel mysticism of blood and electric vitalism. In chapter 35 he repudiates naval illegalities by appeal to 'the genius of the American Constitution' which opposes 'irresponsibility in a judge, unlimited discretionary authority in an executive' and the union of the two. Yet Congress also enacted Article of War 32 which permits naval crimes to be punished 'according to the laws and customs in such cases at sea', thus making a captain 'a legislator, as well as a judge and an executive', with 'an everlasting suspension of the Habeas Corpus'. For the sailor 'our Revolution was in vain . . . our Declaration of Independence is a lie'. Blackstone's *Commentaries* state that 'a law should be "universal", and include in its possible penal operations the very judge himself'. The seed of *Billy Budd, Sailor* lies in Blackstone's 'there is a law, "coeval with mankind, dictated by God himself, superior in obligation to any other, and no human laws are of any validity if contrary to this." That is the Law of Nature . . . "that to every man should be rendered his due"'. That due is the basis of an inviolable preservation of 'the essential dignity of man'. Without it, America reverts to 'the worst times of barbarous feudal aristocracy'; Melville concluded chapter 35: 'It is not a dollar-and-cent question of expediency; it is a matter of *right and wrong*'. Chapter 36 cites the brutal English navy as a prime example of government abuse, and, of course, *Billy Budd*'s context is 'the great mutiny of the Nore' (ch. 74).

The theme resolves into Thoreau's primary question: at what point is disobedience to law and to authoritarian leadership necessary and justifiable? In his Pacific island fictions, Melville recognizes mutiny as a necessity enabling men to 'forever rid themselves of the outrageous inflictions of their officers' (chs 36, 74). His central concern from *Typee* onwards is the relationship of government, leadership and law to the exceptional person – a movement between republican egalitarianism and the developed individual, self-creative to the point of anarchic principle. At the end of chapter 86 of *White-Jacket* he writes: 'The Past is the text-book of tyrants; the Future the Bible of the Free'. Marblization follows, therefore, for rigid traditionalists, and here the employer of Bartleby can be remembered: 'Those who are solely governed by the Past stand like Lot's wife, crystallized in the act of looking backward, and forever incapable of looking before'. Americans are supposed to be 'the peculiar, chosen people – the Israel of our time; we bear the ark of the liberties of the world'; but Americans have also to reckon with the history of law and authority, secular and religious. The arch-codifier of law in nineteenth-century America, David Dudley Field, was associated with the 'Young America' group in New York in the 1840s, whose more important literary pupil, as Perry Miller reminds us in *The Life of the Mind in America*, was Herman Melville. Even this conservative lawyer wrote: 'Why persist in applying here the customs and maxims which belong to Europe?' Common Law to him was a medieval, monkish imposition 'upon the banks of the Hudson and the quiet valley of the Mohawk'. His solution is code against a lawyer class guarding an elite. Coded law would safeguard equality of 'rights and essential attributes'.[12] At this point of time, America collapsed into Civil War over slavery and states' rights. On the *Neversink* the chaplain sermonizes the crew on 'the mystic fountain of Plato' and is once seen with *Biographia Literaria* in hand. Melville comments: 'throne and altar go hand in hand'. Prayer is a law of the ship by the Articles of War, again contradicting the Constitution which says: 'Congress shall make no law respecting the establishment of religion, or the free exercize thereof'.

The devil in this post-lapsarian society is the chaplain's friend, Bland, disguised traditionally as a gentleman, another of Melville's snakey masters-at-arms, a smuggler 'with an angelic conscience', 'an organic and irreclaimable scoundrel'. Melville knows that the naturally depraved yearns to be a policeman, just as a surgeon-doctor yearns to make incision and amputation. So the apex of neurosis and authority on the *Neversink* is Cadwallader Cuticle, a one-eyed grotesque of anti-life. Like William Burroughs' Doctor Benway one hundred years later, 'the department of morbid anatomy was his peculiar love', and his law is the knife, under which the fainting seaman of chapter 63 lies at the hand of a man 'who enacts the part of a Regenerator of life'. His performance parallels the fight between two Negroes which Claret orders for his 'health' – 'whites will not answer'. When the blacks play this game seriously, they are flogged for 'fighting': 'law and gospel, the infallible dispensation and code, whereby I lived, and moved, and had my being on board the United States ship *Neversink*'. By the Articles of War, of 20 penal offences, 13 are punishable by death, or ignominy and death. To replace Poe's Inquisition cell in 'The Pit and the Pendulum' Melville suggests 'a cell, with its walls papered from floor to ceiling with printed copies, in italics, of these Articles of War' (ch. 70). Martial law is a Piranesian entombment or slavery of 'law upon law' without clause for redress. Courage itself, the most private emotion in action for a man of endurance is codified by Article IV and drawn into public law, making death a punishment for surrender, and compelling a man 'to fight, like a hired murderer, for his pay, digging his own grave before his eyes if he hesitates' (ch. 74).

But throughout *White-Jacket*, belief that authority is man-made and not innate or God-granted, conflicts with belief in predestined Fate in various forms – 'a fusion indistinguishable', Melville calls it at end of chapter 75: 'the thing called Fate ever-lastingly sustains an armed neutrality'. But we can vote who will 'rule the worlds': 'I have a voice that helps to shape eternity; my volitions stir the orbits of the furthest suns. In two senses, we are precisely what we worship. Ourselves are Fate'. In the mouth of Ahab that would be madness; for Hunilla an absurdity; to a flogged sailor a cruel denial of his condition. Melville's rhetoric is desperate as he moves to the core of his divided philosophy of law: 'nevertheless', he says, 'we mould the whole world's hereafters'. But this statement of belief is denied by his fictions again and again. The proles do not win. There is no revolution after mutiny. Jack Chase, the aristocratic anarchic individualist, is a dream hero of the lower-deck, a handsome sailor, skilled polyglot, an intellectual who defeats the master-at-arms and Claret-Cuticles by manly sexless nobility, a 'gentleman' to whom Melville gives his 'best love', a tutorial leader but 'a little bit of a dictator' (ch. 4), 'a stickler for the Rights of Man and the liberties of the world' who once 'drew a partisan blade in the civil commotions of Peru' (ch. 5). Chase is an outlaw privileged by skill and noble mind to live a god-like life among officers and seamen. His theatrical role as Percy Royal-Mast is to rescue fifteen fellow sailors from the constable, but the ensuing riot is curtailed by nature in the form of a 'black squall'. Even the weather aids and abets him. In chapter 51 he comes on as sailors' spokesman against the law of precedent but is over-awed, not to say unmanned, by the commodore. He is no rebel against authority, therefore, and is incapable of the murderous rebelliousness of White Jacket in chapter 67. As Melville observes: 'He felt safe enough' – and he does not insist on Chase's hypocrisy, although it is clear in chapter 54: 'I'm your tribune, boys; I'm your Rienzi'. And again in chapter 56: 'we all wear crowns, from our cradles to our graves, and though in *double-darbies* in the brig, the commodore himself can't unking us'. Such crass sentimentality is the price of Chase's 'genius' (ch. 65). Although Melville hints at a further outlawry as 'a sentimental archangel doomed to drag out his eternity in disgrace', he is neither Promethean challenger nor Ishmaelian creative man but a reader and a seaman within the fixed authoritarian state of the *Neversink*.

Billy Budd, Sailor brings Melville's anguish before the nature of law to a final performance, without resolution. Budd, a semi-taboo savage, a law to himself in his god-like beauty, is broken within ship's law under Captain Vere, reader, meditator on law, executor of the Articles of War in time of war. This is Melville's most complex fiction based on four interacting structures. The triangulation of Budd, Vere and Claggart (the naturally depraved master-at-arms constable) is flanked by Paine and *The Rights of Man* (the name of Budd's first ship) and Burke,

Vere's hero of constitutional and legal procedures, and also by Hobbes, Locke and Rousseau, the perpetrators of the Social Contract. Such is, as it were, the political and legal myth of hierarchy on the *Bellipotent*, but the third structure penetrates the ship: the politics of the Nore mutiny, whose main actors are the King, Nelson and British sailors. The fourth structure lies with a loosely Calvinistic sense of nature – innocence, depravity and election by class law exemplified by Budd, Claggart and Vere. Both innocence and depravity threaten rule by law and its viceroy of verity, Starry Vere. Vere is not supposed to veer but to remain firm in his election, and Budd, the Bartleby intruder into ship's time, space and labour organization, is as much a disrupter as Claggart, an intruder, like Ahab, by obsession and the need for total personal allegiances rather than social law.

The action of the stuttering intruder against the 'mystery of iniquity' embodied in Claggart is an instance within a large historical structure, deftly placed by Melville writing at the height of his organizational powers. The Nore mutiny exemplifies the revolts and reformism of the period from 1776 to 1886, the year he began to write the book. Burke and Carlyle penetrate the action with their gradualist beliefs, fascination with leadership, and horror at revolution. The American Union had broken in civil war, and before that Napoleon and Nelson had vied for charismatic dominance of the European imagination of power. Two British Reform Bills in 1831 and 1867 had exemplified the way liberalism could ameliorate by legal franchise and avert that revolution which Marx and Engels were certain would arise from the condition of the British proletariat. The presence of these factors in *Billy Budd*, *Sailor* is placed at the disposal of Melville's need to believe in a natural order which the order of men – state and ship – exemplified, a hierarchy within which his definition of democracy could operate and avert revolution or mutiny in the hands of those whose urgency extended beyond the reformist legal consciousness. Clarel had vanished into the crowded melting-pot of races and creeds of the Via Crucis: 'varied forms of fate . . . cross-bearers all'. His last words echo Bartleby's dead-letter existence in the form of the Atlantic cable which, contrary to Whitman's enthusiasm for it,[13] brings no 'message from beneath the stone'.

Melville returns to stoicism and trust in the feeling heart, the recurring seasons and Providence, in modes characteristic of nineteenth century liberalism and tones similar to those of Arnold and Tennyson. *Billy Budd, Sailor* is a fine organization which demonstrates a decline in confidence that natural law and human law can be brought to single beneficent focus.

It is the sailors who make a god out of a youth sacrificed to the paternalistic authority of law; it is all they have power to do in the face of Vere's system and the dualistic 'necessity' of 'good' and 'evil' instanced in the *Bellipotent*. Law fails its task of mediating 'good' and 'evil', and the instance is not a revolter since Budd, like Chase, to whom the book is dedicated, is content within command authority. Law protects good; evil, in the form of Claggart, is beyond punishment or elimination since it is existential fact incapable of tolerating innocence, comradeship, mutuality and love. The seamen regard Budd as an ideal of uncorrupted manhood, standing apart from coercive force and the touch of women. Law and evil combine to bring him to sacrifice since he is the limitation to any assumption of innate depravity and the need for coercive rule. Law, through Vere, charges mutiny and manslaughter. Evil, through Claggart, recognizes innocence it must oppose. The system permits no prelapsarian Adams.

Inarticulate natural fury under natural speech defect causes Budd to strike Claggart: a non-verbal gesture at a crucial moment of injustice under interrogation. The body fails the head's intelligence, and impatience brings in the process of law. The 'people' treat the ship's mainyard where Budd is hanged as Christians treat the Cross. Budd himself is a white or pale object like Moby Dick and Bartleby, to be coloured by men according to their myth-making needs. The angry breaker of the social contract, recruited from *The Rights of Man*, becomes a martyr; the Handsome Sailor is metamorphosed into a man worshipped by men, after hanging by the Articles of War – the last 'stickler for the Rights of Man'. The dedication to Chase is a measure of Melville's profound nostalgia for human natural power remaining on the lower-deck.

Melville's initial Handsome Sailor is a charismatic black of 'barbaric good humour',[14] a radical extension of Babo's sardonic humour under slavery. He is associated with Anarcharsis

Cloots, the Joachim Murat whom Napoleon made King of Naples, Apollo, Hyperion, Hercules, the Celtic god Beli, Hudd or Budd, the oriental sky-god Budd, and the Bull of Assyrian sun-cult. To Vere he is 'an angel of God'. But his end partakes of that peculiar impotence with which Melville endows his outlaws. The dream of a democratic leader resolves into a harmless, sting-drawn dead Eros recorded in a ballad.

Like Bartleby, Budd is pressed by the system into his master's service. Like Babo, he enters a viceroy's state. He is 'elected' by Lieutenant Ratcliffe, and protest is idle. Captain Graveling is compelled by law to relinquish Budd, the 'fighting peacemaker' whom Ratcliffe dubs Apollo. Graveling may be captain of *The Rights of Man* but he obeys repressive law and is compared to the Philadelphia banker, Girard, who named his ships after such as Voltaire and Diderot. Budd is, fatally, his own regenerative source and family, completely vulnerable in his spontaneity and egoism, and therefore liable to suicidal destruction. He is without 'the wisdom of the serpent' but 'nor yet quite a dove', Eve before 'the urbane serpent' and his success with 'the questionable apple of knowledge' (ch. 2), a cosmic aristocrat of ennobled elements 'prior to Cain's city and citified man'. But the harmony is flawed by 'an organic hesitancy' through which 'the arch interferer' prevents perfection and which, for Melville, is token to the reader that the book is 'no romance' (ch. 2). Budd is himself the interferer into good-natured bachelor Vere's confidence in law and stasis, already shaken by 1797 – Spithead and the Nore, a threat of civil war more important to Melville than the threat of the French because the fleet is 'the right arm of a Power then all but the sole free conservative one of the Old World'. He refers favourably to Nelson's 1805 signal at a time when Napoleon threatened to conquer the civilized world – 'England expects every man to do his duty', but by the rules of *White-Jacket* it is not so much an expectation as an order behind which lies the words of Dibdin's patriotic sailor song: 'And as for my life, 'tis the Kings's!'

Melville is confused because, like Dickens during the same decades (as author, for example, of *A Tale of Two Cities*), he requires both stability and liberty, the self-equilibrating desire of the liberal and authoritarian alike. England is to be free from Napoleon but is not to guarantee freedom under democratic law.

The sailors' mutinies are, for Melville, 'ignited into irrational combustion as by live cinders blown across the Channel from France in flames'. He is with Burke and Vere in stressing constitutional law at all costs. The sailors' obliteration of the union and cross of the national flag signified 'transmuting the flag of founded law and freedom defined, into the enemy's red meteor of unbridled and unbounded revolt'. The cosmic image is appropriate to the panic. Melville roots for the marines, the traditional shipboard constabulary safeguard between officers and sailors, since they enforce 'loyalty'. As Ralph Ellison once observed of Faulkner's emphasis on black allegiance to Southern whites, 'loyalty given where one's humanity is unrecognized seems a bit obscene'.[15] Mutiny for Melville is at this date of his life 'contagious fever in a frame constitutionally sound'. He was quite mistaken. The first Reform Bill, for which Wordsworth and Coleridge worked, was a small beginning to British democratic franchise. The British admirals were exactly what Melville hated in *White-Jacket* thirty-five years earlier. Naval discipline was brutal; pay had remained the same since Charles II; impressment, the most horrible threat to liberty, went unredressed. Yet a seaman's leader could still actually write to the Admiralty: 'we do not wish to adopt the plan of a neighbouring nation, however it may have been suggested'. It was, in fact, the United Irishmen among the sailors who carried a resolution to hand the fleet to the French 'as the only Government that understands the Rights of Man'. No evidence shows engineering from alleged 'English Jacobins'. The British sailors' manifesto of June 6, 1797 is a wholly admirable document:

> Shall we who have endured the toils of a tedious, disgraceful war, be the victims of tyranny and oppression which vile, gilded, pampered knaves, wallowing in the lap of luxury, choose to load us with ? Shall we, who amid the rage of the tempest and the war of jarring elements, undaunted climb the unsteady cordage and totter on the topmasts's dreadful height, suffer ourselves to be treated worse than the dogs of London Streets ? Shall we, who in the battle's sanguinary rage, confound, terrify and subdue your proudest foe, guard your coasts from invasion, your children from slaughter, and your lands from pillage – be the footballs and shuttlecocks of a set of tyrants who derive from us

alone their honours, their titles, and their fortunes ? No, the Age of Reason has at length revolved. Long have we been endeavouring to find ourselves men. We now find ourselves so. We will be treated as such. Far, very far, from us is the idea of subverting the government of our beloved country. . . . You cannot, countrymen, form the most distant idea of the slavery under which we have for many years laboured. . . . Hitherto we have laboured for our sovereign and you. We are now obliged to think for ourselves. . . .[16]

In 1797, 1798 and 1799 acts were passed which suppressed every kind of reformist movement. Melville is happy that the reformed sailors helped Nelson beat Napoleon in the Nile and Trafalgar battles.[17] His central value is like Nelson's, 'duty', a term poised between 'personal prudence' and 'excessive love of glory' but apparently not coloured by coercive law. He believes in Nelson's signal and in Nelson as Tennyson revered him in 1852, as a man of 'priestly motive' fit for heroic, vitalistic epic. He sanctifies both Nelson and Budd as sailors, but he does not focus their actual opposition. Nelson is early removed from the *Captain* to the *Theseus* in order to 'win the sailors by force of his mere presence'; this exactly parallels Budd's removal from *The Rights of Man* to the *Bellipotent*.

Law is the fixed star of the unveering captain of the *Bellipotent* who fears an invasion of 'positive' and 'settled convictions' from 'novel opinion social, political, and otherwise, which carried away as in a torrent no few minds in these days, minds by nature not inferior to his own'. Whether 'lasting institutions' make for majority freedom or not is irrelevant; they are lasting and therefore, for Melville and Vere, endlessly defensible as 'the peace of the world and the true welfare of mankind'. The controllers of institutions are elected by some historical grace as it is 'pendantic', Melville's own term for the captain. Claggart invokes in Vere simply 'a vaguely repellent distaste'; too close an examination of evil power embarrasses the authoritarian personality. Moreover, it is Claggart himself who reminds him of the Nore, only to be rebuffed by his 'immodest presumption' and lack of 'taste'. Vere first notices Budd as a boy 'who in the nude might have passed for a statue of young Adam before the Fall', but such erotic extra-legality is simply applied to 'a capital investment at small outlay or none at all'. Budd, like Bartleby, is cheap labour in a hierarchy not to be disturbed by democracy or the innocent. Vere's cry to what he considers as a 'fated boy' is: 'Defend yourself!' In his world of fixed stars and destiny 'the angel must hang'. Vere has decided for strict obedience to constitutional law, reinforced by wartime stringency, long before his drum-head court. Law is law. There is no reprieve. The rest is 'tragedy', the blanket term for punishment by fixed order, and Vere's unprecedented 'passionate interjections, mere incoherences' which are made on a possible borderline of madness and sanity, in some 'degree of aberration' from his usual 'monastic obedience' (ch. 21). The last phrase relates him to Benito Cereno, but his condition is examined no further than: 'was he unhinged?' (ch. 20).

This question is asked through the surgeon in the brief important chapter 20, together with other questions, which may be partly rhetorical but which express a significant possibility – 'Was Captain Vere suddenly affected in his mind, or was it but a transient excitement, brought about by so strange and extraordinary a tragedy? . . . He recalled the unwonted agitation of Captain Vere and his excited exclamations, so at variance with his normal manner. Was he unhinged? But assuming that he is, it is not susceptible of proof. What then can a surgeon do?' The surgeon is also a subordinate officer under ship's law. To argue with Vere would be 'insolence', 'to resist him would be mutiny'. Therefore he says nothing of his misgivings to the lieutenants and the captain of the marines:

> They fully shared his own surprise and concern. Like him too, they seemed to think that such a matter should be referred to the admiral.

At the beginning of the next chapter Melville makes his own comments. Sanity and insanity blend as violet and orange tints blend in the rainbow. The demarcation of Vere's condition is difficult if not impossible, even if some men might do so for professional pay. Whether the surgeon's 'professional and private' surmise is true or not, Melville leaves to each reader of his narrative. What is certain is that 'in the light of that martial code whereby it was formally judged', the striking of the master at arms by a seaman had caused 'innocence and guilt personified in Claggart and Budd in effect [to] change places'. The officers are perturbed by the privacy of the event, hidden in the quarter-deck cabin, since it resembles events 'in the capital founded by Peter the Barbarian'. But like the monk in a monastery, 'the true military officer' must keep his vows.

Vere is also compared to Tzar Peter of Russia, since Melville has relaxed his criticism of caesarism since *Moby-Dick*, even if his fear of self-confidence manifested as 'mental disturbance' is still alert (ch. 21). Claggart's power hardly penetrates the Vere–Budd ties, and far less so when he is dead; he is simply 'a mystery of iniquity' and 'a matter for psychologic theologians to discuss'. Vere's concern is entirely with the legal conflict between 'nature' and 'allegiance', 'natural justice' and 'innocence before God'. Allegiance to the King is apparently not within Nature, which also excludes Satan, God and Claggart. King and Claggart are both forms of absolute Fate beyond discussion, within which Vere is calcified within his uniform of allegiance. Nature, however, is not law but 'primeval' and 'inviolate' and not evil. An officer is not a 'natural free agent', whatever that might be. So the terms pile in semantic disorder. Vere's legal 'pitilessness' is a head action exactly like Claggart's intellectuality but the relationship cannot be made: 'let not warm hearts betray heads that should be cool'. 'The feminine in man' must submit to male rule or law. 'Natural depravity' is another region. It is not Claggart's death but insubordination in time of war which is Melville's intransigent issue. It is an absurd and cruel situation, since Claggart is both fated and the ship's lawyer-policeman.

The four structures of *Billy Budd, Sailor* map the elements of what Melville needs to understand as an eternal situation, without historical sense: legal order versus the Red Flag, and the human creation of a Handsome Sailor into a Hanged God. He admits that the people have been 'long moulded by arbitrary discipline' and cannot discriminate fine issues, and allows this fact as at least an immediate reason for releasing Budd in the Nore context. In chapter 22 Melville characteristically withdraws from the private interview between Budd and Vere, 'each radically sharing in the rarer qualities of our nature'. What goes on between law and innocence is left blank. But the performance is controlled by mutual allegiance to supreme authority, as the Abraham and Isaac image reinforces at this point. In Ellison's terms, might not there be something obscene in the embraces of

Abraham Vere and Isaac Budd before ritual sacrifice to law which Melville proposes as 'sacrament' between 'two of Nature's noble order', an obscenity which might resist the transcendence (ch. 24) so urgently required at this stage? Melville withdraws:

> There is a privacy at the time, inviolable to the survivor; and holy oblivion, the sequel to each diviner magnanimity, providentially covers all at last.

Surely the rhetoric evades the crucial issues in spite of Melville's plea in chapter 24 for 'something healing in the closeted interview' (ch. 24), a healing which is to be outside *law* and inside *nature*. What can Vere's 'agony' be in the context of absolute belief in allegiance, beyond sado-masochistic feeling? Melville allows Vere to pervert the Orphic myth itself into a political myth of control:

> 'With mankind', he would say, 'forms, measured forms, are everything; and that is the import couched in the story of Orpheus with his lyre spellbinding the wild denizens of the wood'. And this he once applied to the disruption of forms going on across the Channel and the consequences thereof. (ch. 27)

Vere's monomania is hierarchical order, the magical control of animal nature by fixed forms. It follows that the *Bellipotent* captures the French ship *Athée* or *Atheist*, renamed from *St. Louis* – within the plot, the vindication of his allegiance. Claggart's 'monomania' (ch. 17) – 'a peculiar ferretting genius' 'riots in complete exemption' from the law of reason (ch. 11). His 'austere patriotism' (ch. 8) has no outlet in class command, and Melville enters him without reticence, overtly denying 'the Radclyffian romance' of gothic satanism, but actually opting for 'mysterious' theology as motivation for his antipathy for Budd's 'harmlessness'. Law gives way to 'Holy Writ' in order to reach 'certain phenomenal men' and 'depravity according to nature'. Vere's separation of law and nature is therefore mirrored in Claggart, as helpless in his own nature as Vere is helpless within law. Both men yield to the irrational in crises of law, or reason, and nature, or the irrational. Melville is again as psychologically explicit as he needs to be: Claggart's aim has a 'wantonness of atrocity [which] would seem to partake of the insane'. Phenomenal men of natural depravity 'are madmen, and of the most dangerous sort, for their lunacy is not continuous, but occasional, evoked by some special object; it is protectively secret, which is as much as to say it is self-contained ... the aim is never declared – the method and the outward proceeding are always perfectly rational'. Nor has the condition to do with 'vicious training or corrupting books'. It is innate, beyond nurture and culture. Melville's 'romantic agony' trappings only deck out a dogma of need for inexplicable evil to counter inexplicable innocence. Claggart's 'hidden nature' remains so beneath the gothic, but like Vere he sees Budd as a 'moral phenomenon', his platonic opposite, the angelic before fall.

In chapter 64 of *Moby-Dick*, the black cook, Fleece, leans over the side of the *Pequod* and addresses the sharks in the Ocean, telling them to stop smacking their lips in dreadful anticipation but addressing them as 'belubed fellow-critters', creatures capable of change under government:

> Your woraciousness, fellow-critters, I don't blame ye so much for; dat is natur, and can't be helped; but to gobern that wicked natur, dat is de pint. You is sharks, sartin; but if you gobern de shark in you, why den you be angel; for all angel is not'ing more dan de shark well goberned.

To the gruesome Christian mate, Stubb, Fleece's sermon to the big sharks to help the small sharks is Christianity, but Fleece sees that it is useless. Stubb veers and agrees. Fleece's final benediction is:

> Cussed fellow-critters! Kick up de damnest row as ever you can; fill your dam' bellies till dey bust – and den die.

And he decides that Stubb is 'more of shark dan Massa Shark hisself'. Thirty-six years later, Melville believes that Claggart is teleologically, and powerlessly, mad like 'the scorpion for which the Creator is responsible'. His role is 'allotted' (ch. 12). *Billy Budd, Sailor* is an analogue of a cosmic drama between polarized forces within a fixed plan for whose action none of the main actors is responsible: they enact 'The Return of the Same', either to death or to stoic endurance. Claggart's conscience is 'the lawyer to his will' but his will is his Creator's creation in eternal pattern, a structure which includes Melville's further alibis – the Pharisees against Christ and Guy Fawkes against Parliament. The Ocean itself – Vere's 'inviolate Nature primeval' – has its law. Vere believes it is not man's (ch. 21), and yet it contains, it turns out, natural evil as in the sea of human nature. If Budd is 'nearer to unadulterate Nature' (ch. 24), he ought to be as predatory as Ocean, but he is not. Beli is potent in *Bellipotent* as an obedient employee and as a dead piece of nature. Melville's 'pure fiction' (ch. 28) is authoritarian at the end of his life. Budd becomes a divine demi-power, however rejected by British officialdom as a foreign 'alien', and Claggart is a white-washed patriot. Yet the level pitched by the book tells us that Melville needed more transcendence than this. The elements of his fiction remain apart, unified by narrative and the profound urgency of his need for an over-all order in which everything has its measure, and madness is a true aberration. The old Dansker plays Merlin and Chiron to Budd's Arthur and Achilles (ch. 9), aware that 'innocence' is powerless against 'moral emergency'. Budd has two fathers on the *Bellipotent* – Vere and the Dansker, both impotent in 'moral emergency'. As in *The Confidence-Man*, Melville has to lower his sights from the transcendental to the contingent and contemporary. Budd, his last trusting bachelor of dangerous confidence, obeys orders from 'externally' ruling men, but must somehow remain unscathed by 'that promiscuous commerce with mankind where unobstructed free agency on equal terms – equal superficially, at least – soon teaches one that unless upon occasion he exercizes a distrust keen in proportion to the fairness of the appearance, some foul turn may be served him'. Better to be a man of habitual 'ruled undemonstrative distrustfulness', Melville believes. Trust is ignorant innocence. Beyond Vere's blind trust in law lies Budd's sacrifice as 'a condemned vestal priestess in the moment of being buried alive' (ch. 19). His April resurrection from law and the trance in the 'cathedral' of the gun bays is as wilful as Babo's defiant death gaze. The 'superior savage' resists the blandishments of the Christian missionary but is nevertheless consumed by the ship-state. His cross is dismembered. He is 'martyr to martial discipline' (ch. 24). He might just as well have been incarcerated on the *Neversink*.

For Melville, ship or sea are ordered hells of conflict under law and natural law. At crucial moments Vere, Budd and Claggart are paralyzed in 'emotional shock' and then strike out. Melville forgets his fleecy confidence-trickster and the healthy darkness of the extinguished solar lamp of 1857 on the *Fidèle*. Now he gives birth to another solar god, and there appears to be no irony or reminiscence at the end of chapter 27 when he writes: 'the circumambient air in the clearness of its serenity was like smooth white marble in the polished block not yet removed from the marble-dealer's yard'. In terms of Melville's recurrent major image, this is a scene to calcify vitality. Nature itself marblizes and is marbled. The natural sea-birds prey on Budd's body true to their law. 'Moral emergency' has produced a man who proves law by exception, an eccentric of confidence who is returned to the monster-breeding Ocean and its 'wild denizens'. The book is truly 'an inside narrative' – of Melville's search for an end to that costly dualism which haunted Clarel. The great quality of its action lies in its complexity of irresolution, with uneasy assumptions about the terms 'nature' and 'law', and a profound need to maintain order against revolutionary change interpreted as chaos. *Billy Budd, Sailor* is an urgent testimony to Melville's, and our own, concern with those absolutes of religious, moral and governmental controls which were decaying towards relativism in the later nineteenth century, controls which have to be perennially revived or discarded so that sacrificial murder may not be committed in the name of law and order.

Notes and References

1. Herman Melville, *The Piazza Tales*, ed. Egbert S. Oliver (New York: Hendricks House 1948).
2. Alain Robbe-Grillet, *For a New Novel*, trs. Richard Howard (New York: Grove Press 1965) pp. 23-4.
3. Herman Melville, *Pierre*, ed. Henry A. Murray (New York: Hendricks House 1949).
4. Richard Chase, 'Melville's *Confidence-Man*', *Kenyon Review* (Winter 1949).
5. Herman Melville, *Moby-Dick*, Norton Critical Edition, ed. Harrison Hayford and Hershel Parker (New York 1967) chapter 58.
6. Paul Metcalfe, *Genoa*, Jargon 43 (North Carolina 1965) p. 71.
7. *Moby-Dick*, ch. 128.
8. Werner Berthoff, *The Example of Melville* (Princetown 1962).
9. Herman Melville, *Redburn, His First Voyage* (New York: Doubleday 1957) ch. 31.
10. *Redburn*, ch. 12.
11. Herman Melville, *White-Jacket, or The World in a Man-of-War*

(London 1952) ch. 1. All future references in the text are to this edition.

12. Perry Miller, *The Life of the Mind in America* (New York: Harcourt, Brace & World 1965) pp. 261-3.

13. Walt Whitman, 'A Passage to India', sections 1 and 2 (1871).

14. Herman Melville, *Billy Budd, Sailor*, ed. Harrison Hayford and Merton Sealts (Chicago: University of Chicago Press 1962) ch. 1.

15. Ralph Ellison, *Shadow and Act* (New York: Random House 1964).

16. G. D. H. Cole and Raymond Postgate, *The Common People* (London: Methuen 1938) p. 162; R. W. Postgate (ed.), *Revolution from 1789 to 1906* (New York: Harper and Row 1962) pp. 73-4.

17. *Billy Budd, Sailor*, ed. Hayford and Sealts (Chicago 1962) ch. 3. All future references in the text are to this edition.

Melville, Lt Guert Gansevoort and Authority:
An Essay in Biography

When Melville's critics have been interested in Guert Gansevoort (1812–68), it has usually been as a source of information
for Herman Melville about the *Somers* affair, which was at one
point taken to be the 'source' of *Billy Budd*.[1] Critical thought
about *Billy Budd* has moved on, and there has been less interest
in Gansevoort. But the relationship between Melville and his
first cousin, seven years his senior, seems worth reconsidering,
particularly because it may touch some deeper level of relevance
for our consideration of Melville's early fiction.

Guert Gansevoort, second son of Leonard and Mary Ann
Gansevoort of Albany, entered the United States Navy as a
Midshipman in March 1823 at the age of ten. He was assigned
to the *Constitution*, and visited the home of Allan and Maria
Melvill in Bleeker Street, New York City, in 1824 and after.
Allan Melvill, then a prosperous merchant, was solicitous for
young Guert's welfare and went to some expense to buy clothes
and equipment for the young Midshipman's first major cruise
to Africa, which was to last for three years. Writing to Guert's
uncle, Peter Gansevoort, Allan Melvill willingly accepted this
as part of his responsibility to the boy and to the family: the
equipment

> will cost more than you imagine but I thought it my duty
> as it regarded himself, & the name he bears, to put him
> afloat in his country's service as a Gentleman, & with
> GOD's blessing I am proud to anticipate from his general
> deportment that he will be an honour to the family, & to
> the star-spangled banner he is destined to defend.[2]

Writing to Guert on board the *Constitution*, Allan Melvill strikes
something of the same note of piety and patriotism:

> you are now fairly launched at an early age upon the great
> Ocean of life . . . with Honour for a compass, & Glory for
> a watch word, you may in peace or war, become a brave &

accomplished naval Officer . . . but above all, my little
sailor Boy, let me conjure you, *forget not your* Creator in
the dawn of youth . . . neglect not the *Bible*, regard it as
your polar star, its religious precepts & moral doctrines are
alike pure & sublime, & equally inculcate obedience,
patriotism, fortitude & temperance . . .[3]

The 'little sailor Boy' was obviously something of a favourite
with the Melvill family, and when Guert returned to Bleeker
Street at the end of his cruise in 1827 his cousin Herman, by
then eight, was probably looking forward enthusiastically to the
visit. Guert's older brother Peter (1810–32) was also a Midshipman, and the two young Gansevoorts paid visits from the
Brooklyn Navy Yard to their Melvill cousins in lower Manhattan.[4] Guert's next posting was on the *St. Louis* for a cruise to
the Pacific. His letters home reveal a successful, contented
young man:

I have enjoyed excellent health, am growing rapidly, and
in ev'ry respect as happily situated as I could wish. I have
lately been promoted to situation of acting Sailing Master
of this Ship, and am perhaps the youngest person that ever
held the appointment.[5]

Guert returned to his family home in Albany in mid-
December 1831, having been granted leave to attend school after
his three-year cruise.[6] He found the Melvill family no longer
prosperously living in Manhattan, but in Albany; Allan Melvill,
now a bankrupt, presenting to the family 'the melancholy
spectacle of a deranged man'.[7] His death at the end of January
1832 confirmed the disastrous reversal of the Melvill family's
fortunes. Herman, now thirteen, was forced to go to work as a
clerk at the New York State Bank. Guert, having taken leave of
absence from the Navy, was warranted Passed Midshipman in
April 1832.[8] The Melvilles (who petitioned at this time to add
an 'e' to the family name) and the young Gansevoorts were in
frequent and easy contact during most of the 1830s, when Guert
was either on leave of absence, awaiting orders, or stationed at
the Brooklyn Navy Yard. After a series of different employ-
ments in Albany and Pittsfield, Herman moved with his family
to Lansingburgh in May 1838 to a house 'not in the most agree-
able part of the city'.[9] Cousin Guert had in the meanwhile been
promoted to Lieutenant, and assigned to the 74-gun *Ohio* for a

three-year cruise in the Mediterranean (1839–41). Not long after Guert departed, Herman signed on board the *St. Lawrence* in June 1839 as a deck hand for a trip to Liverpool. There were other relatives who had gone to sea, and some even as common seamen, but the family fortunes were at such a low ebb, and with Herman seemingly able to contribute nothing financially, he may have felt it best simply to be out of the way. There was another financial blow when his older brother Gansevoort was declared bankrupt in October 1839. The family was now 'entirely impoverished – mortgages are foreclosing upon her real estate & . . . the furniture is now advertised for sale'.[10]

After a not unsatisfactory experience on the *St. Lawrence*, and a visit to relatives living in Galena, Illinois, Melville shipped out on the whaler *Acushnet* in January 1841. When Guert returned to New York in August, he was reported to 'blame' Herman for going to sea.[11] This, the only recorded comment by Guert on his cousin, is tantalizingly ambiguous. We don't know *why* he blames Herman – was it for leaving the family ? or for going to sea on a whaler, instead of a Navy vessel ? Nor do we know if the family shared Guert's opinion. Augusta Melville was obviously impressed by the force of Guert's denunciation of her brother ('oh how he blames Herman for going to sea'), but too little is known about Guert's character to grasp his full meaning. Guert obviously liked the Navy, and perhaps he felt there was something too unsettled in the life of a seaman on board a whaler to do much good for Melville, or the family. What he felt when word came that Herman had jumped ship in the Marquesas is not recorded – nor, for that matter, do we know what anyone else in the family thought, or even when the news arrived. But in view of the moral and social standards of the Gansevoorts and Melvilles, stiffened, if anything, by financial adversity and Maria's Calvinism, we can suppose that Herman felt he had rather a lot to explain. His father had sent cousin Guert off into the world with a reminder of the need for obedience, patriotism, fortitude and temperance. Maria Melville's letter to her son Allan of 1 May 1841 speaks for itself:

> Remember my beloved Son that you are now arriving at
> an age when the reason with which Your Maker endowed
> you, is to be cultivated, to be called into action . . . you have
> to choose between, respectability, the sure reward, of

virtuous conduct, the approbation of your conscience, & the contrary results arising from an unrestrained indulgence of your unhallowed impulses & wicked passions. Be wise in time & remember you are fatherless, excuse a mother's anxiety & adopt her advice as you would save yourself from unhappiness. . . . Do not go out in the Evening with young men, but stay at home & study, go to bed early, be pure in mind, think purely, and remember that from 'the heart proceeds all evil, & learn to keep your heart with all diligence'.[12]

Melville's explanation of his decision to jump ship in *Typee* is dry, cautious and legalistic. He makes no stirring appeals to universal justice or the rights of man:

The usage on board her was tyrannical; the sick had been inhumanly neglected; the provisions had been doled out in scanty allowance; and her cruizes were unreasonably protracted. The captain was the author of these abuses; it was in vain to think that he would either remedy them, or alter his conduct, which was arbitrary and violent in the extreme. His prompt reply to all complaints and remonstrances was – the butt end of a hand-spike, so convincingly administered as effectually to silence the aggrieved party.

To whom could we apply for redress ? We had left both law and equity on the other side of the Cape; and unfortunately with a very few exceptions, our crew was composed of a parcel of dastardly and mean-spirited wretches, divided among themselves, and only united in enduring without resistance the unmitigated tyranny of the captain. It would have been mere madness for any two or three of the number, unassisted by the rest, to attempt making a stand against his ill-usage. . . . Placed in these circumstances then, with no prospect of matters mending if I remained aboard the Dolly, I at once made up my mind to leave her: to be sure it was rather an inglorious thing to steal away privily from those at whose hands I had received wrongs and outrages that I could not resent; but how was such a course to be avoided when it was the alternative left me ?[13]

In the eyes of Lansingburgh and Albany, was the 'inglorious thing' the failure to seek redress, or the decision itself to decamp ? The last person in the world to be persuaded by Melville's argument in *Typee* was his cousin Guert, by then a Lieutenant in the Navy and thus responsible for the administration of a penal code of draconian severity. Although there were voices raised within and without the Navy in the 1830s at the persistence and radical abuse of flogging, it was not for a recently-commissioned lieutenant publicly to question the accepted wisdom of the Navy itself.[14] There is no evidence that Lt Gansevoort harboured the slightest reservations about flogging and the Articles of War, and considerable indication to the contrary. It is a reasonable assumption that Melville would have known this. But sailing as he had done on a merchant vessel and on a whaler, where discipline was more relaxed, Melville's personal relationship to naval discipline and authority did not become acutely problematic until he was rescued from the Happar valley and sailed on the *Lucy Ann* from Nukuhiva to Tahiti in August 1842.

The disastrous voyage of the *Lucy Ann* is well-documented, especially since the papers of the British Consul in Tahiti were discovered in Sydney.[15] There had been desertions and mutinies before Melville joined the ship. But the first thing which *Omoo* impresses one with is Melville's caution, his instinctive respect for the law. After the death of 'a churlish, unsocial fellow' the crew proposed to rifle the contents of the dead man's chest. Here Melville presents himself as 'endeavouring to dissuade them from this'.[16] Nor does Melville feel any community of interest with the malcontented sailors on board the *Julia* (*Lucy Ann*). When a strong current off the bay of Hannamanoo threatens to drive the ship on to the rocks, the crew 'handled the rope as deliberately as possible, some of them chuckling at the prospect of going ashore', but Melville does not share 'their little plans for swimming ashore from the wreck' (27). Rather, he consciously acts as a restraining influence when the crew, learning that Captain Guy was to be taken off at Tahiti without the ship touching land (for fear of mass desertions), explode in fury:

> The cooper and carpenter volunteered to head a mutiny forthwith; and, while Jermin was below, four or five rushed aft to fasten down the cabin scuttle; others, throwing down the main-braces, called out to the rest to lend a hand, and fill away for the land. All this was done in an instant; and

> things were looking critical, when Doctor Long Ghost and
> myself prevailed upon them to wait a while, and do nothing
> hastily; there was plenty of time, and the ship was com-
> pletely in our power ... had neither the doctor nor myself
> been aboard, there is no telling what they might have
> done. (69–70)

Time and time again Melville and Doctor Long Ghost 'labored
hard to diffuse the right spirit among the crew' (73), and tried
to deflect them from a violent and irretrievable mutiny. They
both wanted to get off the ship, not make principled stands or
foment mutiny. And the best way to achieve this was to act
prudently:

> For my own part, I felt that I was under a foreign flag; that
> an English consul was close at hand, and that sailors seldom
> obtain justice. It was best to be prudent. Still, so much did
> I sympathize with the men, so far, at least, as their real
> grievances were concerned; and so convinced was I of the
> cruelty and injustice of what Captain Guy seemed bent
> upon, that if need were, I stood ready to raise a hand. (73)

But at that moment, when the crew were 'breathing nothing but
downright mutiny', Melville succeeded in 'diverting their
thoughts' by proposing a Round Robin – a petition – to be sent
to the British Consul. The whole scene suggests that Melville's
temperament was conservative, and that even under severe pro-
vocation he found it difficult, if not impossible, to break out of a
consciousness that was still dominated by the pieties of a Maria
Melville. He may have profoundly questioned those pieties, but
their influence was very deeply imbedded within his personality.
The tactic of a petition was successful: the revolutionary ardour
aboard ship calmed down, the Consul visited the *Julia*, and the
disaffected crewmen were taken on shore. Melville during the
whole of his narrative maintains his distance from his fellow
sailors. He had a not unreasonably low opinion of sailors, or at
least of the common sort:

> The crews manning vessels like these are for the most part
> villains of all nations and dyes; picked up in the lawless
> ports of the Spanish Main, and among the savages of the
> islands. Like galley-slaves, they are only to be governed by
> scourges and chains. (14)

Of all the things he detests in the seamen, and the officers for that matter, the worst is their dehumanized, brutal behaviour towards the natives: 'it is a curious fact, that the more ignorant and degraded men are, the more contemptuously they look upon those whom they deem their inferiors' (25). He had devoted *Typee* to this judgment, and to the incongruity and irony behind accepted ideas of 'civilization' and 'barbarity'. He observes sympathetically the refinement and pleasures of native life, comparing it favourably with life in America; but he is not *of* the Typee, any more than he was *of* the crew of the *Julia*. Melville was too much an American of the 1840s, an individualist beginning to discover the tensions between solitude and society. The only 'society' which Melville can conceive of is that of a small group of men, such as that which he found on the main-top in *White-Jacket*; he is chosen, or chooses, to join such a circle. The casual circumstances of life aboard a whaler offer few possibilities beyond what Melville finds in Doctor Long Ghost. So he retains his sense of distance. It is only in *Omoo* that this stance breaks down, when he can no longer evade the dilemmas of tyrannical authority, that he and Long Ghost began to make 'common cause with the sailors' (83). At this point 'neutrality was out of the question'; but so was anything rash or speculative. During the second night off Papeete, the Maori Bembo at the helm tried to let the ship run on the reef. Melville is among those who seize Bembo, and bring the *Julia* into the wind. Despite his courageous and successful attempt to save the ship, when Jermin takes it into harbour Melville finds that he is listed among the mutineers. Subjectively, Melville feels innocent, his role has been one of continually advocating restraint; but objectively (despite his inner conviction that his 'contract' with the sick Captain Guy was at an end) Melville was as guilty as any of the mutineers under maritime law. This was something cousin Guert could have told him; but Melville's attitude is consistent in its avoidance of the obligations to the general 'society' of men around him. He is an isolate individual whose personal agreement with authority is legally at an end, and he wants out.

When he sat down to write *Redburn* and *White-Jacket* in 1849, there was a new spirit of confidence and aggression in the way he denounces the evils before him. Yet it seems particularly striking that the deservedly famous description of Launcelott's-Hey in

Redburn is set up with considerable care to ensure that young Wellingborough Redburn is unable to do anything about what he has seen. Like the young reformers, crusaders for temperance, abolitionists, whose protest grew stronger through the 1840s, Melville writes with increasing grasp of the *specific* grievances everywhere around him. It was an emotion of intense frustration which we see at the moment when it finally breaks through the surface of his rhetoric:

> The pestilent lanes and alleys which . . . go by the names of Rotten-row, Gibraltar-place, and Booble-alley, are putrid with vice and crime; to which, perhaps, the round globe does not furnish a parallel. The sooty and begrimed bricks of the very houses have a reeking, Sodom-like, and murderous look; and well may the shroud of coal-smoke, which hangs over this part of the town . . . attempt to hide the enormities here practiced. These are the haunts from which sailors sometimes disappear forever; or issue in the morning, robbed naked, from the broken door-ways. . . . Propriety forbids that I should enter into details; but kidnappers, burkers, and resurrectionists are almost saints and angels to them. They seem leagued together, a company of miscreant misanthropes, bent upon doing all the malice to mankind in their power. With sulphur and brimstone they ought to be burned out of their arches like vermin.[17]

This reminds us that Melville was a contemporary of William Lloyd Garrison and John Brown; but Emerson had a reply:

> What boots thy zeal
> O glowing friend,
> That would indignant rend
> The northland from the south ?
> Wherefore ? to what good end ?
> Boston Bay and Bunker Hill
> Would serve things still;—
> Things are of the snake.[18]

But there were no republican pieties to which Melville could appeal in *White-Jacket*. The book is an effective, intelligent polemic against the customary practices of the navy, as Melville saw them on board the frigate *United States* in 1843 and 1844, and in particular the operation of the Articles of War, and the prevalence of flogging. Melville dismissed *Redburn* and *White-*

Jacket in a letter to his father-in-law, Judge Lemuel Shaw, on 6 October 1849: '. . . no reputation that is gratifying to me, can possibly be achieved by either of these books. They are two *jobs*, which I have done for money – being forced to it, as other men are to sawing wood'.[19] But the impression given by the text contradicts his own opinion. Melville's purchase on the issue of flogging was timely (Congress voted to abolish the practice later in the year *White-Jacket* was published, 1850), and cogent; no less than three rear-admirals of the United States Navy responded to the book.[20] Despite the overwhelming presence of Melville's polemic, within the book we find that same process of dissociating himself from the life of the sailors on board the *United States*, and also, perhaps, from his own advocacy:

> I feel persuaded in my inmost soul, that it is to the fact of my having been a main-top-man; and especially my particular post being on the loftiest yard of the frigate, the main-royal-yard; that I am now enabled to give such a free, broad, off-hand, bird's-eye, and, more than all, impartial account of our man-of-war world; withholding nothing; inventing nothing; nor flattering, nor scandalising any; but meting out to all – commodore and messenger-boy alike – their precise descriptions and deserts.[21]

One does not feel that Melville is 'impartial' about flogging, nor towards the Articles of War. Nor can his claim to withhold nothing, invent nothing, sustain more than a cursory glance at the way Melville acquiesced at the bowdlerising of the American texts of his novels, or the way he deliberately censored his own journal entry written in London on 20 November 1849.[22] He wrote to Evert Duyckinck on 14 December 1849: 'What a madness & anguish it is, that an author can never – under no conceivable circumstances – be at all frank with his readers. – Could I, for one, be frank with them – how would they cease their railing'.[23] The stance which he presents in this passage from *White-Jacket* is one deliberately designed to mask the real tensions which Melville was living with at this time. He frequently complains of conditions on board ship, of the frequent abuse of authority, the floggings, and petty abuses designed to inconvenience and humiliate ordinary sailors; but when he comes to write of his own response to these facts he either minimises the implications of his actions (as in *Typee*), presents his behaviour as subjectively legal and principled (in *Omoo*), or indicates his own powerlessness to do anything but denounce (in *Redburn*). In other words, he had to find a way to avoid the implications of what he has seen and done. In *White-Jacket*, where he seems so buoyed up by the sheer force of his denunciation, the book ends with a plea for what is tantamount to a Christian Stoicism:

> Oh, shipmates and world-mates, all round! we the people suffer many abuses. Our gun-deck is full of complaints. In vain from Lieutenants do we appeal to the Captain; in vain – while on board our world-frigate – to the indefinite Navy Commissioners, so far out of sight aloft. Yet the worst of our evils we blindly inflict upon ourselves; our officers can not remove them, even if they would. From the last ills no being can save another; therein each man must be his own saviour. For the rest, whatever befall us, let us never train our murderous guns in board; *let us not mutiny with bloody pikes in our hands*. Our Lord High Admiral will yet interpose; and though long ages should elapse, and leave our wrongs unredressed, yet, shipmates and world-mates! let us never forget, that
>
> > Whoever afflict us, whatever surround,
> > Life is a voyage that's homeward-bound.
>
> (399–400, my italics)

This is not at all what Redburn had in mind ('With sulphur and brimstone they ought to be burned out of their arches like vermin.'), but suggests how radical are the inner divisions in Melville's consciousness before authority.

His attitude was complex, divided, perhaps even crippled by a constraint which bit deep, and which was part of his Calvinist heritage. The question of authority was certainly before him, on his return to America aboard the *United States* in 1844, perhaps most immediately in the *Somers* affair, and the role played by his cousin Lt Guert Gansevoort.[24] In November 1842 the *Somers*, cruising off Africa, was affected by what we would regard today as a seizure of collective hysteria. Lt Gansevoort was informed that there was a mutiny planned, and he immediately told Commander Alexander Slidell Mackenzie (1803–48). The ringleader of the mutiny was alleged to be Midshipman Philip Spencer, nineteen years old, and the son of

John C. Spencer (1788–1855), Secretary of War in Tyler's cabinet. Spencer and two others were arrested. An informal court of inquiry was conducted by First Lieutenant Guert Gansevoort and the other officers, but they reported to the Commander that the evidence did not appear conclusive. The only concrete evidence was a list drawn up by Spencer in Greek, dividing the crew into probables, possibles, and those who would be allowed to survive because they possessed special skills. It may all have been a prank; there had been no overtly mutinous act. But Commander Mackenzie told the officers through Lt Gansevoort

> that it was evident these young men [the junior officers] had wholly misapprehended the nature of the evidence ... and that there would be no security for the lives of officers or protection to commerce if an example was not made in a case so flagrant as this. It was my duty, he urged, to impress these views upon the court. I returned and did, by impressing these considerations, obtain a reluctant conviction of the accused.[25]

Midshipman Spencer and two others were hanged at the yardarm on December 1. The *Somers* returned to New York on the 14th, and the 'mutiny' soon became a *cause célèbre*. Those elements in American society which saw in authority, hierarchy and social discipline a necessary corrective to the abuses of democracy came to the defence of Mackenzie. The 'judicial murder' of Spencer became the rallying cry for democrats; in their eyes the actions of Mackenzie and the response of the Navy was an example of the Federalist and Whig traditions perverting the course of justice for their own interests. The fate of Philip Spencer became one of the symbolic expressions of the very real political struggle in the United States. Inevitably, the family and friends of the Spencers launched an attack upon Mackenzie. At one level, it was one famous New York political family against another, for Mackenzie's father was president of the Tradesman's Insurance Company and was a merchant banker. Slidell Mackenzie's elder brother, John, had left New York for New Orleans in 1819, where he became prominent politically. He served as Commissioner to Mexico in 1845, in an attempt to adjust the Texas border, and to buy New Mexico and California. The failure of his mission helped prepare the way for the war with Mexico. John Slidell was elected to the Senate from Louisiana in 1853, and after the succession was appointed Confederate ambassador to France. He was seized and taken from the British ship *Trent* while on his way to France, and a diplomatic outcry was needed to secure his release. He remained in Europe until his death in 1871. Slidell Mackenzie's wife, Catherine, came from a prominent New York family. His sister married Commodore Matthew C. Perry, who was to 'open' Japan in 1852.

Slidell Mackenzie combined a successful career in the U.S. Navy with an equally successful career as an author. After a cruise as lieutenant on board the *Terrier* suppressing piracy in the West Indies, he travelled to Spain in 1826. He met Washington Irving, an acquaintance of Slidell Mackenzie's father, in Madrid. Irving, then forty-three, was in the midst of writing his biography of Columbus, and Slidell Mackenzie was able to provide expert assistance on the route of Columbus's first voyage. 'The author of this work', wrote Irving, 'is indebted for this able examination of the route of Columbus to an officer of the navy of the United States, whose name he regrets the not being at liberty to mention.' Slidell Mackenzie's *A Year in Spain, by a Young American* (2 vols., Boston 1829) was a considerable success, going through five editions. Irving arranged for John Murray to publish *A Year in Spain* in London in 1831, and wrote a favourable review of it for the *London Quarterly*. Slidell Mackenzie served on board the *Brandywine* for a cruise in the Mediterranean, and then returned to America to publish a collection of essays on naval subjects (which he had contributed to the *Encyclopedia Americana*), and two further travel books: *The American in England* (1835), and *Spain Revisited* (1836). He published biographies of Oliver Hazard Perry in 1840, and John Paul Jones a year later. He tried his hand at a naval adventure novel, but Longfellow persuaded him to leave it unpublished. Slidell Mackenzie attracted the obloquy of James Fenimore Cooper over his treatment of the battle of Lake Erie in the Perry biography (Cooper's *The Battle of Lake Erie: Or, Answers to Messrs Burges, Duer, and Mackenzie* appeared in 1843). But Slidell Mackenzie maintained a wide acquaintance among men of letters. He remained a favourite of Washington Irving. He had met Longfellow while in Spain in 1827, and they travelled together to Segovia and the Escorial. Their friendship survived the *Somers* affair. Longfellow described him in 1846 as 'a very good fellow, with sound sense and great love of literature'.[26] Their correspondence, through the 1830s and 1840s, suggests a strong friendship. Richard Henry Dana, one of Slidell Mackenzie's most enthusiastic supporters, described him in 1843:

> Commander A. S. Mackensie [sic] called with Lieut. Davis. His appearance & manners are very prepossessing. He is quiet, unassuming, free fr. all military display in manner, self possessed, & with every mark of a humane, conscientious man, with sound judgment & moral courage. He is unusually interesting, & creates a feeling of personal affection towards him in those whom he meets.[27]

In addition to being Commodore Matthew C. Perry's brother-in-law, he was something of his protégé as well. Slidell Mackenzie was given command of the *Somers*, on which one of Perry's sons served. The crew consisted mainly of boys and Midshipmen specifically selected to test some of Perry's ideas about naval education. It was hardly surprising that the Navy hierarchy supported Slidell Mackenzie when a Court of Inquiry sat between 28 December 1842 and 19 January 1843. The verdict, that the commander has simply done his duty, did not satisfy public opinion. To avoid a civilian trial, Slidell Mackenzie requested a court martial and was duly acquitted in April 1843. Fenimore Cooper had initially accepted the account of the mutiny which Slidell Mackenzie gave at the Court of Inquiry, but he became restless with the manner of the defence, which he described as 'a medley of folly, conceit, illegality, feebleness and fanaticism'.[28] Partisans on both sides were pleased to find their views widely shared. 'The better opinion', writes Cooper, 'is everywhere against him'. Dana was sure that 'the prevailing opinion (I have not met an exception) is that Mackensie [sic] will justify himself. I have little doubt of it'.[29] By the autumn of 1843 Cooper's 'Elaborate Review' of the *Proceedings of the Naval Court Martial in the Case of Alexander Slidell Mackenzie* was under active preparation. He felt that the *Somers* affair was 'one of the darkest spots on the national escutcheon', and that the Court of Enquiry was 'a mere mockery of justice'.[30] The debate about the affair quickly spread across the country. News reached the Pacific Squadron as early as 13 March 1843.[31]

Lt Gansevoort returned to his family immediately after the *Somers* docked:

> He was then in such a situation from fatigue & exposure; that I sca[r]cely knew him – he had a violent cold; coughing constantly; very hoarse his limbs so contracted; that he walked like an infirm man of seventy; his eyes were red & swollen, & his whole face very much bloated – his back & sides were so sore, from the strap & weight of the huge & heavy ships Pistols; that he could not raise himself erect – Having imprisoned so many of the crew; they were short of hands & he, poor fellow, did more than double duty – the eve^g of which I speak, his first visit to us; he had not even his coat off in four days.[32]

It would have taken a Hawthorne to do justice to Guert Gansevoort at this moment. The family were given a simple, pious, coherent and reassuring explanation of his behaviour:

> I *feel*, that we did our duty; & the consciousness of having *done my duty*; shall ever sustain me – It was not only the public property, the Flag of my country; & my own life that was in the utmost jeopardy; but the lives of the crew, (those that were true); but of those apprentices, those *children* entrusted to the care of the Officers; for whose safety we were responsible, – to God, to their country, & to their *parents*; to many of whom, before we sailed; I had pledged myself, to extend parental care & advice – Tell him [Guert's uncle Peter], that nothing was done in 'fear or haste' – & I believe it was *approved* of God; & I have faith to trust it will be by my fellow man.[33]

It is not known when Melville first learned of the *Somers* affair. The *United States* called at Callao, Peru, in December 1843, where it is quite likely that the story of the mutiny, and the hanging of Midshipman Spencer and two other sailors, was an obsessive topic of conversation. When Melville was discharged along with the crew of the *United States* in Boston in October 1844, Lt Guert Gansevoort was stationed on board the receiving ship in the Port of Boston. Leon Howard suggests that it was Gansevoort who announced Herman's return to America.[34] It seems quite likely that he heard of the *Somers* affair at first hand at this point, but then again the family as a whole tended towards reticence, and Herman may have felt unwilling to raise such a painful subject with his cousin. But it seems remarkable that Melville says nothing about the affair in his surviving letters, nor is it mentioned in other family papers. Melville mentions the affair twice in *White-Jacket*, in chapters 71 and 72, both times suggesting that the *Somers* mutiny was a good example of the severity of the Articles of War. Spencer had not received a trial in any legal sense. 'Three men, in time of peace, were then hung at the yardarm, merely because in the Captain's judgment, it became necessary to hang them' (303). Gansevoort's role is not mentioned. Whatever reservations Melville felt about his cousin's part (Cooper referred to Gansevoort as a 'wonder-monger' and held him partly responsible),[35] he refrained from putting anything down on paper. It may have been family loyalty which kept him silent; more likely, he may have felt that any questioning of Guert's behaviour could not be done within the family. In 1862 Melville received a letter from his brother Thomas which had been passed on to him by Guert – an interesting detail, since the letter was initially addressed to Herman's mother, who sent it to Guert. This suggests that Guert, being older than the children of Maria Melville, was close to his aunt. That would have added further weight to Herman's reticence. In a reply to his brother, Melville proudly announced that cousin Guert had been given the command of a sloop, the *Roanoke*: 'I am rejoiced to hear it. It will do him good in more ways than one. He is brave as a lion, a good seaman, a natural-born officer, & I hope he will yet turn out the hero of a brilliant victory'.[36] In 1847 Guert had been on board the *John Adams* and commanded a cutter during the amphibious landing at Vera Cruz: it was an episode which clearly belonged to the mythology of the family.[37] Melville recalled it in 'Bridegroom Dick', written in 1876, his first published reference to his cousin, who had died eight years earlier:

> But where's Guert Gan ? Still heads he the van ?
> As before Vera-Cruz, when he dashed splashing through
> The blue rollers sunned, in his brave gold-and-blue,
> And, ere his cutter in keel took the strand,
> Aloft waved his sword on the hostile land![38]

There are disguised references to Gansevoort in the same poem, as 'Dainty Dave' and 'Tom Tight':

> Tom was lieutenant in the brig-o'-war famed
> When an officer was hung for an arch-mutineer,
> But a mystery cleaved, and the captain was blamed,
> And a rumpus too raised, though his honor it was clear.
> And Tom he would say, when the mousers would try him,
> And with cup after cup o' Burgundy ply him:
> 'Gentlemen, in vain with your wassail you beset,
> For the more I tipple, the tighter do I get'.
> No blabber, no, not even with the can –
> True to himself and loyal to his clan.

And there is a reference to the *Somers* affair in *Billy Budd*. When the sailing master asks Captain Vere if the penalty for killing Claggart may not be mitigated, Vere, sounding very much like Commander Mackenzie, argues that the circumstances of the voyage and naval usage, duty and law, only admit of one verdict. Vere is given a humanitarianism singularly lacking in Mackenzie, noted to be a strict disciplinarian and flogger, but the effect of his speech on the assembled officers is no less decisive than Mackenzie's message to Lt Gansevoort:

> Loyal lieges, plain and practical, though at bottom they dissented from some points Captain Vere had put to them, they were without the faculty, hardly had the inclination, to gainsay one whom they felt to be an earnest man, one too not less their superior in mind than in naval rank.[39]

Among these 'plain and practical' men, without the instinct or willpower to controvert a superior, Melville includes his cousin Guert Gansevoort. The judgment is not unkind. He had himself, however grudgingly, jumped ship and taken part in a mutiny. He had opposed authority and the law, and written four novels to explain and justify himself. Cousin Guert was a Starbuck, a type of the essentially good man without the moral courage to oppose authority. By the time of Gansevoort's death in 1868, it may be that Melville saw something finer in the limitations of his cousin's virtues, of a morally simple man crushed by tragic necessity, than in his own wavering and opportunism before authority when he was a young sailor.

Notes and References

1. Charles R. Anderson, 'The Genesis of *Billy Budd*', *American Literature*, 12 (November 1940) 329-46. There is a summary of critical interpretations of *Billy Budd* in the Hayford-Sealts edition (see note 39, pp. 182-3), and in Milton R. Stern's introduction to his edition of *Billy Budd* (Indianapolis: The Bobbs-Merrill Company 1975).

2. Allan Melvill to Peter Gansevoort, 25 October 1824, quoted by William H. Gilman, *Melville's Early Life and 'Redburn'* (New York: New York University Press 1951) p. 36.

3. Jay Leyda, *The Melville Log: A Documentary Life of Herman Melville 1819-1891* (New York: Harcourt, Brace & Co. 1951) p. 19.

4. Allan Melvill to Peter Gansevoort, 3 December 1828, quoted in Gilman, p. 37.

5. Guert Gansevoort to Peter Gansevoort, 13 March 1831, quoted *Melville Log*, p. 47.

6. Charles R. Anderson, *Melville in the South Seas* (New York: Columbia University Press 1939; rev. ed. New York: Dover Publications, Inc. 1966) p. 17. Anderson suggests that Guert Gansevoort 'could at least have brought the romance of the seas and of distant lands to Melville's eager ears', and briefly sketches his career to 1838.

7. Peter Gansevoort to Thomas Melville, Jr., 10 January 1832, quoted *Melville Log*, p. 51.

8. *Register of the Commissioned and Warrant Officers of the Navy of the United States . . . for the year 1833*. Printed by order of the Secretary of the Navy, Washington, 1833.

9. Journal of Allan Melville, 9 May 1838, quoted *Melville Log*, p. 79.

10. Peter Gansevoort to Lemuel Shaw, 4 October 1839, quoted *Melville Log*, p. 96.

11. Augusta Melville to Allan Melville, 11 August 1841, quoted *Melville Log*, p. 120. The passage reads 'Guert was here yesterday, he started for Clarendon Springs this morning, he looks very much like Herman, we all noticed it, oh how he blames Herman for going to sea. . . .'

12. Maria Melville to Allan Melville, 1 May 1841, quoted in Eleanor Melville Metcalf, *Herman Melville: Cycle and Epicycle* (Cambridge, Mass.: Harvard University Press 1953) p. 25.

13. *Typee: A Peep at Polynesian Life*, ed. Harrison Hayford, Hershel Parker and G. Thomas Tanselle (Evanston and Chicago: Northwestern University Press and the Newberry Library 1968) pp. 21-3.

14. See Harold D. Langley, *Social Reform in the United States Navy 1798-1832* (Urbana: University of Illinois Press 1967) *passim*.

15. Ida Leeson, 'The Mutiny on the *Lucy Ann*', *Philological Quarterly*, 19 (October 1940) 370-9.

16. *Omoo: A Narrative of Adventures in the South Seas*, ed. Harrison Hayford, Hershel Parker and G. Thomas Tanselle (Evanston and

Chicago: Northwestern University Press and the Newberry Library 1968) p. 45. Further references to this edition of *Omoo* will be included in the text.

17. *Redburn: His First Voyage*, ed. Harrison Hayford, Hershel Parker and G. Thomas Tanselle (Evanston and Chicago: Northwestern University Press and the Newberry Library 1969) p. 191.

18. R. W. Emerson, 'Ode Inscribed to W. H. Channing'.

19. Herman Melville to Lemuel Shaw, 6 October 1849, quoted *Melville Log*, p. 316.

20. See Charles R. Anderson, 'A Reply to Herman Melville's *White-Jacket* by Rear-Admiral Thomas O. Selfridge, Sr.', *American Literature*, 7 (1935-6) 123-44; and Langley, pp. 194-5. In the first flush of scholarly enthusiasm for Melville the importance of *White-Jacket* in the struggle to abolish flogging was exaggerated. Recent scholarship, as in Langley, tends if anything to undervalue Melville's contribution.

21. *White-Jacket, or, The World in a Man-of-War*, ed. Harrison Hayford, Hershel Parker and G. Thomas Tanselle (Evanston and Chicago: Northwestern University Press and the Newberry Library 1970) p. 47.

22. *Journal of a Visit to London and the Continent by Herman Melville 1849-1850*, ed. Eleanor Melville Metcalf (Cambridge, Mass.: Harvard University Press 1948) p. 40 and facing illustration.

23. Herman Melville to Evert Duyckinck, 14 December 1849, quoted in Metcalf, *Herman Melville*, p. 71.

24. See *The Somers Mutiny Affair: A Book of Primary Source Material*, ed. Harrison Hayford (Englewood Cliffs, N.J.: Prentice-Hall 1959). Frederic F. Van de Water in *The Captain Called it Mutiny* (New York: Ives Washburn 1954) follows Cooper in his hostility to Slidell Mackenzie. There is a novel by Henry Carlisle, *Voyage to the First of December* (London: Gollancz 1973) based on the *Somers* affair.

25. *Melville Log*, p. 158.

26. Longfellow's doubts about the novel by Slidell Mackenzie appear in a letter of 31 May 1840, *The Letters of Henry Wadsworth Longfellow*, ed. Andrew Hilen (Cambridge, Mass.: The Belknap Press of Harvard University Press 1966) II, pp. 232-3. For Longfellow's reaction to *A Year in Spain*, see the letter to Slidell Mackenzie, 15 October 1829, in Lawrence Thompson, *Young Longfellow (1807-1843)* (1939; New York: Octagon Books 1969) pp. 150-1. Slidell Mackenzie describes his trip with Longfellow ('He was just from college, full of all the ardent feeling excited by classical pursuits, with health unbroken, hope that was a stranger to disappointment, curiosity which had never yet been fed to satiety.') in *A Year in Spain* (London: John Murray 1831) I, 355ff. Longfellow's reflections are recorded in a letter to his mother of 13 May 1827. The visit in 1846 was recorded in Longfellow's diary, 11 December, *Life of Henry Wadsworth Longfellow*, ed. Samuel Longfellow (London: Kegan Paul, Trench & Co. 1886) II,

pp. 66-7. See also Longfellow's letter to Slidell Mackenzie's widow, 30 October 1848, *Letters*, ed. Hilen, II, p. 184.

27. *The Journal of Richard Henry Dana, Jr.*, ed. Robert F. Lucid (Cambridge, Mass.: The Belknap Press of Harvard University Press 1968) I, p. 218.

28. Letter to Mrs Cooper, 4 January 1843, *The Letters and Journals of James Fenimore Cooper*, ed. James Franklin Beard (Cambridge, Mass.: The Belknap Press of Harvard University Press 1964) IV, p. 337.

29. Cooper to Paul Fenimore Cooper, 28 January 1843, *Letters and Journals*, IV, p. 349; Dana, journal entry, 29 December 1842, *Journal*, I, p. 112. Longfellow, an old friend, wrote to Slidell Mackenzie that 'The voice of all upright men – the common consent of all the good – is with you', July 1843, *Letters*, ed. Hilen, II, p. 546.

30. Cooper to William Sturgis, 17 September 1843, *Letters and Journals*, IV, p. 405; see Dana, *Journal*, ed. Lucid, I, p. 160n.52.

31. Anderson, 'The Genesis of *Billy Budd*', p. 336.

32. Mary Ann Gansevoort to Peter Gansevoort, 2 January 1843, quoted *Melville Log*, p. 159.

33. *Melville Log*, p. 161.

34. *Melville Log*, p. 185.

35. Cooper to William Branford Shubick, 9 December 1843, *Letters and Journals*, IV, p. 429.

36. Herman Melville to Thomas Melville, 1862, quoted *Melville Log*, p. 652.

37. Leyda quotes an account in the *Daily Wisconsin* describing Lt Guert Gansevoort as 'one of the first to plant the American standard on the beach of Vera Cruz', in *Melville Log*, p. 238. But Gansevoort is not mentioned in other contemporary accounts. The landing was made by 65 boats, carrying 4,500 soldiers, and was unopposed. The Commodore of the United States fleet mentions 'a number of officers of the squadron' who took part in the landing, in *Taylor and His Generals: A Biography of Major-General Zachary Taylor* . . . (Philadelphia 1847) p. 293. George B. McClellan captures a particularly haunting moment: '. . . when the first boats struck the shore those behind, in the fleet, raised [a cheer] . . . Our company and the 3rd Artillery ascended the sand hills and saw – nothing'. *The Mexican War Diary of George B. McClellan*, ed. William Starr Myers (Princeton: Princeton University Press 1917) p. 54.

38. *Collected Poems of Herman Melville*, ed. Howard P. Vincent (Chicago: Packard & Co. 1947) pp. 169-70. 'Bridegroom Dick' was first published in *John Marr and Other Sailors*, 1888.

39. *Billy Budd, Sailor (An Inside Narrative)*, ed. Harrison Hayford and Merton M. Sealts (Chicago: University of Chicago Press 1962) p. 113. The description of Slidell Mackenzie as a strict disciplinarian and flogger is that which his enemies sought to use to discredit him before the public. In the absence of further

evidence, it should be allowed to stand. There is a description of a hanging in *A Year in Spain* which is graphic and moving. He ends the passage with a note of the strongest possible disapproval, but it remains unclear whether it is directed at the public nature of the occasion, or the particular method of capital punishment employed. *A Year in Spain* recounts the observations of a young man of 24. He was 39 when he hanged Spencer and the others on the *Somers*.

An Organic Hesitancy:
Theme and Style in *Billy Budd*

Despite the fact that its dilated style is the most immediately striking feature of *Billy Budd*, criticism of the story has tended to deal only with its possible themes. Here I shall try to put forward what I consider to be Melville's main purpose and then suggest ways in which that purpose is realized through the form and language he uses.

The central theme in this story may be put as the relation of nature and civilization. The larger context of the narrative is, first, the war against revolutionary France, a revolution which, however tyrannical its eventual outcome, expressed the rebellion of human nature against despotic custom, energy against order, flux against conservative stasis; and, second, within this background, the ever-present fear of mutiny in the British navy since the rebellions at Spithead and the Nore in the same year of 1797. In this sense civilization is at war with nature in the form of the rights of man: and it is from a merchant ship of just that latter name that Melville has Billy Budd pressed aboard the warship *Bellipotent*. On the *Bellipotent*, Billy, who is presented as primally innocent, accidentally kills the evil master-at-arms Claggart when the latter provokes him in front of Vere, the captain, with a false accusation of mutinous plotting. The slaying of a superior officer is, formally, an act of mutiny:[1] with the spectres of the Nore and Spithead before him, Vere feels he must take unhesitating action and convenes an instant drumhead court. The trial of Billy is conducted by Vere in terms of the warfare of civilization with nature: he acknowledges to his fellow-officers the claims of natural sympathy for the innocent Billy, while asserting that those claims must be overridden:

> 'But your scruples: do they move as in a dusk? Challenge them. Make them advance and declare themselves. Come now; do they import something like this: If, mindless of palliating circumstances, we are bound to regard the death

of the master-at-arms as the prisoner's deed, then does that deed constitute a capital crime whereof the penalty is a mortal one. But in natural justice is nothing but the prisoner's overt act to be considered? How can we adjudge to summary and shameful death a fellow creature innocent before God, and whom we feel to be so? – Does that state it aright? You sign sad assent. Well, I too feel that, the full force of that. It is Nature. But do these buttons that we wear attest that our allegiance is to Nature? No, to the King. Though the ocean, which is inviolate Nature primeval, though this be the element where we move and have our being as sailors, yet as the King's officers lies our duty in a sphere correspondingly natural? So little is that true, that in receiving our commissions we in the most important regards ceased to be natural free agents. When war is declared are we the commissioned fighters previously consulted? We fight at command. If our judgments approve the war, that is but coincidence. So in other particulars. So now. For suppose condemnation to follow these present proceedings. Would it be so much we ourselves that would condemn as it would be martial law operating through us? For that law and the rigor of it, we are not responsible. Our vowed responsibility is in this: That however pitilessly that law may operate in any instances, we nevertheless adhere to it and administer it.

But the exceptional in the matter moves the hearts within you. Even so too is mine moved. But let not warm hearts betray heads that should be cool. Ashore in a criminal case, will an upright judge allow himself off the bench to be waylaid by some tender kinswoman of the accused seeking to touch him with her tearful plea? Well, the heart here, sometimes the feminine in man, is as that piteous woman, and hard though it be, she must here be ruled out.'[2] (110–111)

Some particular points emerge from this. One is that Vere argues that the existence of law removes moral responsibility from its agents: he partly tempts his officers with a means of smothering their consciences. Secondly, the maintenance and operation of law are shown as depending not infrequently on neglect of the basic principles of right and wrong on which they are ostensibly founded. Third, Vere is stating here a code of conduct which of itself would not be sufficient justification – and is not, to his fellow-officers – for so summary a trial and execution as he is bent on carrying out. Behind the totem of the maintenance of law lies in fact a simple fear that if Billy is not hung as an example, the omnipresent threat of mutiny may be fomented into acts aboard the *Bellipotent*: and it is this monition, as no other, that finally sways Vere's fellow-officers in the court (113–14). That is, principles are here a mask for self-preservation. Fourth, the analogy between Billy's case and that of the tearful kinswoman of the accused is inapposite, for in the latter case the prisoner may well be a guilty man in motive as well as in act: by thus dividing Billy's innocence from his act Vere perpetrates something not far removed from a lie.[3] Lastly, we notice from the passage that Vere associates Nature with the sea: indeed just previously we have seen him pacing the cabin to and fro athwart, 'in the returning ascent to windward climbing the slant deck in the ship's lee roll, without knowing it symbolizing thus in his action a mind resolute to surmount difficulties even if against primitive instincts strong as the wind and the sea' (109). Elsewhere he describes revolution as a roaring flood tide (62). It is clear that the struggle in this story is in one way that of land with sea – the rigid, the static and the conscious with the mobile and the unconscious. In terms of Billy's fate we have the impact of a voluntaristic view of all human behaviour – if he killed Claggart, then he must be treated as having intended to – on an involuntary, instinctual mode of life.

Melville has made much of his story a test-case of civilization: in the pure and irresistible form of Billy Budd and his unintended deed, he sets out the rights of a man essentially innocent, opposed and destroyed by a human law which demands inhuman allegiance. Civilization is shown as ultimately a juggernaut, and the foundation of law and duty, apparently made by men for their happier society, becomes revealed as destructive of human nature, whether that which is reluctant to enforce the law, or that which suffers its rigour. Melville later extends the point to the role of the ship's chaplain aboard the *Bellipotent*:

> Marvel not that having been made acquainted with the young sailor's essential innocence the worthy man lifted not a finger to avert the doom of such a martyr to martial

discipline. So to do would not only have been as idle as invoking the desert, but would also have been an audacious transgression of the bounds of his function, one as exactly prescribed to him by military law as that of the boatswain or any other naval officer. Bluntly put, a chaplain is the minister of the Prince of Peace serving in the host of the God of War – Mars. As such, he is as incongruous as a musket would be on the altar at Christmas. Why, then, is he there? Because he indirectly subserves the purpose attested by the cannon; because too he lends the sanction of the religion of the meek to that which practically is the abrogation of everything but brute Force.[4] (121–2)

Religion and morality, twin bastions of civilization, are seen in the crucible of war as stemming in the final analysis not from any absolute sense of good and evil or of justice, but from motives of self-interest and the preservation of the *status quo*. To the plea that Billy 'purposed neither mutiny nor homicide', Vere replies:

'Surely not. . . . And before a court less arbitrary and more merciful than a martial one, that plea would largely extenuate. At the Last Assizes it shall acquit. But how here? We proceed under the law of the Mutiny Act. In feature no child can resemble his father more than that Act resembles in spirit the thing from which it derives – War.' (111–12)

The unnatural usage of the closing natural analogy could not be more pointed. War is not the exception, but the exception that must prove the rule. The trial we are given here is not only of Billy, but of civilization itself: if when tested it is found wanting, then whatever justice and charity may prevail on land in time of peace are rendered nebulous. In this analysis Melville not only prognosticates some of the special inhumanities of modern civilization, but demonstrates to his own satisfaction the primal roots of all civility in that savage impulse of self-protection and survival evident in naked form not only in the first man, but throughout the animal kingdom since the beginnings of life. In short, he postulates the view that civilization and the darker aspects of nature are not in this sense finally opposed. In a context like this, Vere's and Billy's 'father-son' relationship subsequent to the trial and sentence can be seen only as a frail holiday, a merely 'licensed' expression of humanity within the grip of iron and ironic law.

Vere is no monster, but within Melville's Manichean world the choices are absolute, white or black, sheep or goat. It is precisely from some of the best and most 'civilized' of intentions that the captain has Billy condemned. Vere is an exception among sailors of his time in that he is an intellectual, a man of literary taste, particularly for books of history, biography and philosophy which deal with real people and practical principles. His reading has confirmed and strengthened his 'more reserved thoughts' to the point where these have become convictions on which to act. These convictions harmonize conveniently with the national purpose he serves; he is a beneficiary of that infrequent coincidence of personal motives and patriotic duty which he described to his fellow-officers in the drumhead court: and Melville is at first dry on the subject, 'In view of the troubled period in which his lot was cast, this was well for him' (62). However the account he gives of Vere's motives is such as to disengage him personally from the promptings of self-interest or fear:

> His settled convictions were as a dike against those invading waters of novel opinion social, political, and otherwise, which carried away as in a torrent no few minds in those days, minds by nature not inferior to his own. While other members of that aristocracy to which by birth he belonged were incensed at the innovators mainly because their theories were inimical to the privileged classes, Captain Vere disinterestedly opposed them not alone because they seemed to him insusceptible of embodiment in lasting institutions, but at war with the peace of the world and the true welfare of mankind. (62–3)

To such a man the Mutiny Act finds correlation in his own mind, whatever the purpose that framed it, and from almost the best of principles. But the word is 'almost': the dryness will not be forgotten. Vere acts on disinterested motives – well and good, but is there not something a trifle austere, even cold, in that? So it is that Melville portrays him as slightly disengaged from life, not fully 'salted' as a captain, but looking more like a civilian than a sailor, and inclined to occasional dreamy moods, at the interruption of which by some minor matter requiring his attention 'he would show more or less irascibility; but instantly he would control it' (61). We are told, of his tendency to make literary references above the heads of his officers, that 'considerateness in such matters is not easy to natures constituted like Captain Vere's. Their honesty prescribes to them directness, sometimes far-reaching like that of a migratory fowl that in its flight never heeds when it crosses a frontier' (63). The Olympian view, the habit of thinking in terms of large issues, of seeing the particular in terms only of the general, is what makes Vere carry out a manifest injustice on an individual for the supposed benefit of a larger common weal – an act which so far as the crew of the *Bellipotent*, who are certain of Billy's innocence (131), are concerned, provokes those very mutinous thoughts it was intended to silence (122–8). We begin drily with Vere, and similarly end, as the incipient rebelliousness of the sailors at the burial of Billy is dissipated by a call to familiar disciplines and tasks:

> 'With mankind,' he would say, 'forms, measured forms, are everything; and that is the import couched in the story of Orpheus with his lyre spellbinding the wild denizens of the wood.' And this he once applied to the disruption of forms going on across the Channel and the consequences thereof.[5] (128)

But there is a further and deeper consideration. When all is said of Vere's character and motives, his remark before proceeding to judgment on Billy Budd must reflect ironically on himself, reducing the significance even of the better of his impulses – '" intent or non-intent is nothing to the purpose"' (112): the repulsive act is everything; what worthy or innocent motives lie behind it, nothing. By his unveracious refusal of Budd's intentions Vere must in the last analysis forfeit consideration of his own. In this sense we must judge him by his acts alone.

Had Vere not been captain, had one of his more 'salted' officers been in his place, Billy's trial would have been deferred – with possibly happier outcome. But Melville himself insists on the exceptional natures of his characters. He makes Vere as he does because he wants as both judge and accused a man who is at once an exemplar of the best in 'landed' civilization and one actively engaged in its defence at sea. He pushes this civilization into a tight corner by having Billy's crime set within the contexts both of the lonely struggle of Britain against the forces of revolution abroad, and of the fear of mutiny at home. At the same time, however, he makes this crime one committed in total innocence, and on someone whose evil was primal and whose death was a positive good. Melville's aim is thus to sharpen the conflict to an extreme; thereby to show, first, how the survival of civilization is founded ultimately on the rejection of the individual and of truth, and second, that such rejection involves alignment with Claggart and the forces of darkness. On this latter point, the debased newspaper report of the episode, which Melville outlines at the end of his story, and in which Vere is seen as the righteous defender of order and the Claggarts of this world, has ironic truth.

It is fitting therefore that while we are told that Billy Budd and Claggart are respectively natural innocence and depravity, the latter is described as being able to use civilization for his own ends, where the former is not. We are made constantly aware of the gulf between Billy's nature and that of the city. On his transference aborad the *Bellipotent* we are told, 'As the Handsome Sailor, Billy Budd's position aboard the seventy-four was something analogous to that of a rustic beauty transplanted from the provinces and brought into competition with the highborn dames of the court' (50–1). He is 'a sort of upright barbarian, much such perhaps as Adam presumably might have been ere the urbane Serpent wriggled himself into his company' (52). Civilization, which Melville goes on tentatively to propose as the correlative of man's Fall (52–3), has no part in his 'primitive qualities' (53):

> . . . it is observable that where certain virtues pristine and unadulterate peculiarly characterize anybody in the external uniform of civilization, they will upon scrutiny seem not to be derived from custom or convention, but rather to be out of keeping with these, as if indeed exceptionally transmitted from a period prior to Cain's city and citified man. The character marked by such qualities has to an unvitiated taste an untampered-with flavor like that of berries, while the man thoroughly civilized, even in a fair specimen of the breed, has to the same moral palate a questionable smack as of a compounded wine. (52–3)

And that fair specimen of the civilized breed, Captain Vere, is described by his fellow-officers in just such 'compounded' terms (63). Faced by the suggestion of his joining a mutinous plot, Billy recoils from the evil 'like a young horse fresh from the pasture suddenly inhaling a vile whiff from some chemical factory' (84). He has the straightforwardness (ironically contrasting with Vere's directness), and the honesty of sailors, who are incapable of the indirections, crookednesses and duplicities of landsmen – and in his case in the highest degree (52, 86–7). Yet his very virtues make him a helpless victim of this duplicity, just as his fellows are, to a large extent, the unthinking, unquestioning victims of naval discipline (87). Again, in his case, it is an extreme: he has as much self-consciousness 'as we may reasonably impute to a dog of Saint Bernard's breed' (52). He has no idea that Claggart hates him, and is baffled by the sage Dansker's assertion that '"*Jemmy Legs* . . . is down on you"' (71). Trusting Vere, he accepts almost as contentedly as the rest of his life the decision to end it. Naturally incapable of understanding or embracing evil, he remains unaltered by his experiences. His only defect – his stutter – is a natural, not a moral one (Melville carefully leaves us to reconcile his statement that Billy was 'one to whom not yet has been proffered the questionable apple of knowledge' (52) with his comment that in his stutter 'Billy was a striking instance that the arch-interferer, the envious marplot of Eden, still has more or less to do with every human consignment to this planet of Earth' (53)). But Billy's very defect is one whereby nature makes him more surely her own. Speech is the fabric of civilization, and of this when deeply stirred Billy becomes incapable. His stutter thus precisely delineates his remoteness from citified man.

Not so Claggart, who discourses to Vere of Billy's supposed crime 'in the language of no uneducated man' (92). He is the 'urbane Serpent' (52): raising his corpse was 'like handling a dead snake' (99). Like Billy's innocence, his evil is primal, '"Natural Depravity: a depravity according to nature"' (75): it stems from no experience in Claggart's life, nor is it transmitted by his forbears, but is absolutely islanded; it is 'the mania of an evil nature, not engendered by vicious training or corrupting books or licentious living, but born with him and innate' (76). But natural evil is able, unlike natural goodness as Melville portrays it, to find a place for itself in the offices of 'Civilization [which] especially if of the austerer sort, is auspicious to it. It folds itself in the mantle of respectability' (75). It is 'invariably . . . dominated by intellectuality' (ib.); it is able to use the foundation of civilization, reason, for its demonic purposes, 'Toward the accomplishment of an aim which in wantonness of atrocity would seem to partake of the insane,. . .[it] will direct a cool judgment sagacious and sound,' . . . 'the method and the outward proceeding are always perfectly rational' (76). Claggart can understand the 'moral phenomenon' that is Billy Budd, even if he cannot share it (78, 87–8), where Billy cannot comprehend him (86, 88–9).

If Melville turns away from civilization, hospitable as it is to primal evil and not to good, one would not readily expect him to turn instead towards a natural order which can as readily throw up a Claggart as a Billy Budd. There is a sense however in which the conflict of Claggart with Billy is more real to him than the debate on acts and motives in which Vere is involved; we may recall that Billy, and then Claggart, were the first characters present as Melville developed his story. This lies in his ulti-mately greater interest in, and sense of the greater reality of, the mysteriously instinctual rather than the consciously reasoned. (To what end the apparently careful reasoning of the narrator of the story is directed we have yet to debate.) Reasoned causes and motives in this story become, like the dismissal of Billy's own motives by Vere, mere pretexts or irrelevancies. Claggart succeeds in convincing himself that he has a case to present against Billy to Vere, yet what drives him has nothing whatever to do with justification. The corporal who feeds him with mutinous epithets falsely attributed to Billy, the episode in the mess of the accidental spillage of soup by Billy as Claggart is passing – these trifles are used, as any might have been, by Claggart to give himself supposed cause for a hatred of Billy which has no part in causality:

> Claggart's conscience being but the lawyer to his will, made ogres of trifles . . . nay, justified animosity into a sort of retributive righteousness. The Pharisee is the Guy Fawkes prowling in the hid chambers underlying some natures like Claggart's. And they can really form no con-ception of an unreciprocated malice. Probably the master-at-arms' clandestine persecution of Billy was started to try the temper of the man; but it had not developed any quality in him that enmity could make official use of or even pervert into plausible self-justification; so that the

occurrence at the mess, petty if it were, was a welcome one
to that peculiar conscience assigned to be the private
mentor of Claggart. (80)

Even Vere's decision to have Billy so summarily executed
emerges not so much from his reasoned defence of the Mutiny
Act as from what is to him an immediate practical threat aboard
his own ship. The case is analogous to that of Ulysses' lengthy
speech on 'degree' in Shakespeare's *Troilus and Cressida*, where
a highly theoretic statement of the foundations of order, dis-
connected from any practical solution to the condition of the
Greek army during the Trojan war, descends into a cynical, and
ultimately ineffective, plot to coax Achilles out of his tent. That
is, Vere's act is finally the instinctual one of self-protection – and
this even if we allow him the benefit of motives which he so
coldly disallows in Billy's case. In this sense Vere, too, acts
primitively.

The schema of the story here gives way to certain large images
that run through it, making a symbolic narrative of their own:
the sailor-cynosure astride the yardarm-end in a gale, 'A superb
figure, tossed up as by the horns of Taurus against the thunder-
ous sky, cheerily hallooing to the strenuous file along the spar'
(44); the ironic gaze of the delphic Dansker (70–1); Claggart's
changing features as he watches Billy Budd (88); Claggart
emerging from 'his cavernous sphere' for his interview with
Vere (91); Claggart's eyes 'protruding like the alien eyes of
certain uncatalogued creatures of the deep' as he accuses Billy
to his face (98); Billy on the night before his execution lying
white amid the black-painted cannon and the darkness of the
upper gun deck (118–19); the silent muster of the crew at dawn
(122); Billy's motionless ascent to the yard-end, taking as he
does so 'the full rose of the dawn' (124); the gathering of the
large preying sea-birds at his burial, approaching so near to the
ship that 'the stridor or bony creak of their gaunt double-
jointed pinions was audible' (127). These images amass to
themselves a power of their own, so that we seem to be witness-
ing a pre-ordained drama through a series of 'stills', as on Keats'
urn; the nature of each actor, as we are told of Claggart, must
'act out to the end the part allotted it' (78). At this level the story
takes on the quality of myth.

And like all myth, it invites, indeed here is encouraged by

Melville to invite, allegorical interpretation by the 'civilized' mind of the reader or literary critic. Yet every such reading proves in some way defective or limiting. If we say that Billy is a type of Adam – with a stutter? – Vere God, Claggart the tempter, and mutiny the prohibition, we are forced to leave the mystery no further plumbed: for a God who destroys his own creation (Vere's father relationship to Billy would have to do service here) for an act, both inevitable and committed in total innocence, is one open to no small question; and Vere as we have seen specifically distinguishes between his brand of justice and that which would be meted out by God at 'the Last Assizes' (111).[6] Certainly Melville draws parallels between Billy's nature and Adam's, or Claggart's and Satan's, but the precise character of the *action* described in no way offers any acceptable account of man's Fall. Nor can Billy's history be likened to Christ's, though his aspect during Claggart's accusation is 'as a crucifixion to behold' (99), and though we are told that to the sailors afterwards a chip of the spar from which he was hung is 'as a piece of the Cross' (131). He lives as the witness of no new faith; he is born out of nature's order, not by any supernatural infusion; his death is seen not as endured for the sake of all men or the remission of their sins, nor is it the perfection of his life, even if he forgives Vere as Christ did Pilate; and the ascent of his dead body into the dawn, though this might be seen as paralleling the Resurrection, is starkly qualified by the subsequent descent of that same corpse into the alien deeps of which his adversary Claggart seemed to have so much a part. Nor, to go wider, are we encouraged, as in *White-Jacket* or *The Confidence-Man*, to read the society of the *Bellipotent* as a microcosm of the world outside – quite apart from the simple fact that the ship has no women aboard. Although the impressed numbers of the crew come from a cross-section of mainly the lower order of society on land, the remainder are confirmed sailors, and sailors, Melville frequently tells us, are of quite a different nature – simpler, happier and more honest – from landsmen (52, 86–7).

Indeed it would be better to see the enclosed realm of the ship, like the oracular remarks of the Dansker, as imaging the ultimately enclosed and mysterious nature of the myth Melville has touched, which mystery he has encouraged us to fathom so that our bafflement may make us more fully aware of it.

Nevertheless it is sufficiently clear where Melville's sym-
pathies – nostalgically, even sentimentally – come home in this
his last story. He is reaffirming his delight in the characters and
high deeds of true sailors and in that fatal natural element the
sea, to whose changes all mariners, however skilled, are subject,
and to whose temper the spirits of men afloat are attuned, as to
nothing natural on land (52). Indeed, as we have observed, the
indictment of civilization which he makes in the story is in one
way a derogation of the land by the sea. He prefers heart to
head,[7] or unthinking, even joyous acceptance of one's experience
to any intellectual detachment from it. Of such a character was
Nelson. Some 'martial utilitarians' accuse him of 'foolhardiness
and vanity' in his emblazoning and exposing to danger of his
person at Trafalgar, but Melville disputes their claims of how
much more of the fleet might have been saved from the storm
which followed the battle had Nelson been alive to direct
matters (57); and he goes on, 'Personal prudence, even when
dictated by quite other than selfish considerations, surely is no
special virtue in a military man; while an excessive love of glory,
impassioning a less burning impulse, the honest sense of duty,
is the first' (58). The statement is clear and unequivocal. We
cannot but contrast Vere's later behaviour with this – as too with
the way Nelson's glowing personal presence could turn the
former mutineers of Spithead and the Nore to the heroes of the
Nile and Trafalgar (55–6, 59). Melville's enthusiasm becomes
oratorical:

> At Trafalgar Nelson on the brink of opening the fight sat
> down and wrote his last brief will and testament. If under
> the presentiment of the most magnificent of all victories to
> be crowned by his own glorious death, a sort of priestly
> motive led him to dress his person in the jewelled vouchers
> of his own shining deeds; if thus to have adorned himself
> for the altar and the sacrifice were indeed vainglory, then
> affectation and fustian is each more heroic line in the great
> epics and dramas, since in such lines the poet but embodies
> in verse those exaltations of sentiment that a nature like
> Nelson, the opportunity being given, vitalizes into acts.
> (58)

Nelson is fully 'salted': he is elemental, and on the sea in his
element, where Vere and civilized men generally have a 'com-

pounded' moral and personal character. (Melville may even be hinting that since life evolved originally from the sea, it can never be fully at home on land.) In this sense, as in many, Nelson and Billy are alike: they are open to experience, even naive, but they know joy and are ready to risk all in pure delight; they are sailor-cynosures, the expression to the full of an open-heartedness and vitality which is for Melville the native character of all mariners:

> Habitually living with the elements and knowing little more of the land than as a beach, or, rather, that portion of the terraqueous globe providentially set apart for dance-houses, doxies, and tapsters, in short what sailors call a 'fiddlers' green', his [Billy Budd's] simple nature remained unsophisticated by those moral obliquities which are not in every case incompatible with that manufacturable thing known as respectability. But are sailors, frequenters of fiddlers' greens, without vices? No; but less often than with landsmen do their vices, so called, partake of crookedness of heart, seeming less to proceed from viciousness than exuberance of vitality after long constraint: frank manifestations in accordance with natural law. (52; see also 86–7)

We may speculate that this starkness of sympathy with sailors arose from the fact that Melville was both old and long removed from direct experience of the sea when he wrote the story; when he was near to that experience he produced the far more ambiguous heroism of a Captain Ahab. Thirty years of 'civilian' employ and existence ashore could well have brought one of his wandering spirit to pine acutely, especially if, like Nelson, he had a presentiment of his own final voyage out of life: for thus he would in two senses be committing himself to the deeps.[8] But whatever the explanation, the clarity with which Melville's emotional engagement comes through here at once explains the directness of and underscores the attack on the values of civilization which is at the centre of his story. Or to put the latter point in other terms, it makes more certain the reading we have advanced of *Billy Budd* as just such an attack.

Our next main consideration with this story must be with its style and form, and the extent to which these express its theme. Melville disdains artistic form as untrue to life:

The symmetry of form attainable in pure fiction cannot so readily be achieved in a narration essentially having less to do with fable than with fact. Truth uncompromisingly told will always have its ragged edges; hence the conclusion of such a narration is apt to be less finished than an architectural finial.[9] (128)

We may feel that in the forms of the innocent Billy and the demonic Claggart we have characters belonging to 'fable' rather than to 'fact'; and that Melville's claim that Billy's stutter is 'evidence . . . that the story in which he is the main figure is no romance' (53) is insufficient: but Melville believes in the real existence of such extreme natures as he has portrayed, and wants us to do so too. To this end he must make his story feel like reality. At a formal level this involves destructuring the narrative constantly, filling it with digressions and blind alleys which imitate the random character of life itself – and perhaps particularly of the sea on which the story is set. The object of those 'literary sin[s]', (56) will be that we should thus apprehend facts directly, rather than facts translated and moulded into form. (The obvious irony, namely, that such careful destructuring could be argued to involve no less art than is employed on the most highly-wrought imaginative creations, does not affect the outcome.)

That at least may be the theory, but whether the practice expresses it is another matter. Certainly this question is a very real one in relation to Melville's use of words; as for example in this typical passage:

If in some cases a bit of a nautical Murat in setting forth his person ashore, the Handsome Sailor of the period in question evinced nothing of the dandified Billy-be-Dam, an amusing character all but extinct now, but occasionally to be encountered, and in a form yet more amusing than the original, at the tiller of the boats on the tempestuous Erie Canal or, more likely, vaporing in the groggeries along the towpath. Invariably a proficient in his perilous calling, he was also more or less of a mighty boxer or wrestler. It was strength and beauty. Tales of his prowess were recited. Ashore he was the champion; afloat the spokesman; on every suitable occasion always foremost. (44)

The whole of the first long sentence contributes almost nothing to our understanding of the Handsome Sailor, even while it has the air of offering most careful definition. 'A bit of a' removes almost all force from 'Murat', even if we knew what was meant by the name here; as for the 'dandified Billy-be-Dam', we know nothing more of him than that he is dandified, or rather, *was*, since Melville says he is now almost extinct; but he then brings him back momentarily to life on the Erie Canal, which hardly any of his readers have visited (unless in chapter 54 of *Moby-Dick*), before once more stifling him in the *more* amusing character of the personages to be found there. We feel uneasily that we ought to know what Melville means, since he seems so diligent in trying to be clear, but the whole sentence does not even tell us clearly what the Handsome Sailor was not: at most we have a vague sense of vanity which we have been told (43) is not his portion. The syntax drifts off, pursuing the undefined sailor, in a series of subordinate clauses which increasingly lose connection with their subject; then contorts itself into terse simplicity, 'It was strength and beauty. Tales of his prowess were recited', destroying the sense of rhythm or forward movement. Slang jostles with latinate diction – 'a bit of a', 'Invariably a proficient in his perilous calling'. Qualifiers seem not to aid but to obscure definition – 'in some cases', 'a bit of a', 'nothing of the', 'all but', 'occasionally', 'in a form yet more', 'more likely', 'more or less', 'on every suitable occasion always' (this dissipates itself into vagueness and contradiction). At the same time there is a certain unevenness in the combinations of words, so that the reader pauses subliminally: the first twelve words, for instance, have six short 'i' sounds, and there is a choking repetitiveness in 'a bit of a nautical Murat in setting'; or again the recurrence of sound in 'dandified Billy-be-Dam' is confusing. The syntax in the first sentence pushes us to a dead end, after which we have to look back to find our bearings: for the 'If' seems at first to relate to 'the Handsome Sailor', after whose clause we would expect a sense along the lines of 'he nonetheless, did the following. . . .' Meanings are slightly twisted also: 'vaporing in the groggeries along the towpath', coming as it does in the midst of concrete reference to people and scenes, makes us want to feel 'vaporing' as an exhalation as of mist, rather than as speech issuing from a particular moral nature; 'more or less of a mighty boxer or wrestler' confuses also because the two 'or's are in parallel, and because the sense of 'mighty' seems to have little to do with a qualifier like 'more or less'.

There are thus several effects. The first, obviously, is that a reader interested in what is going to happen in the story is frustrated by the existence of such a passage; and perhaps begins to wonder why Melville could not have embodied all these reflections within action and character, rather than leaving them as a penumbra offered *ex cathedra* by the author. Then, the reader is meant to feel the passage essential to an understanding of the hero, and yet finds it totally inessential, except as giving the sense that the type of the Handsome Sailor is a real one, and one having a social context of near-likes. Further, the passage encourages a critical, discriminating response through the sense of attempted precision in its continual qualifiers, yet just this response is turned in effect into total obscurity and confusion. Finally, the passage is the reverse of an aesthetic pleasure to read.

Other, larger issues are raised. Apart from the irrelevance, many aspects of the passage – its detached, Olympian objectivity of approach, its convoluted syntax, its recondite reference – are close to the idiom of Captain Vere, whom Melville condemns partly for those very qualities. More generally, the scientific or intellectual approach that Melville is using here ostensibly to define the Handsome Sailor's character, is precisely that hall-mark of civilization which he in effect attacks in his story. And this stylistic mode is recurrent throughout *Billy Budd*.

Nevertheless the style is not always like this: and we may better understand its obscurities by looking at some of its clarities. When Melville deals with what limited narrative acts his story contains he can become precise:

> The ship at noon, going large before the wind, was rolling on her course, and he [Billy Budd] below at dinner and engaged in some sportful talk with the members of his mess, chanced in a sudden lurch to spill the entire contents of his soup pan upon the new-scrubbed deck. Claggart, the master-at-arms, official rattan in hand, happened to be passing along the battery in a bay of which the mess was lodged, and the greasy liquid streamed just across his path. Stepping over it, he was proceeding on his way without

comment, since the matter was nothing to take notice of
under the circumstances, when he happened to observe
who it was that had done the spilling. His countenance
changed. (72)

There seems nothing problematic here: even the slightly unnecessary 'the master-at-arms' has some justification in view of
the official rattan. There is a certain disjunction in the first
sentence: the 'and he below at dinner' seems to follow from
'The ship . . . was rolling,' but in fact is quite separate, being the
subject of the later 'chanced . . . to spill'; it seems not unjustifi-
able here to see this as a brilliant grammatical imitation of the
ship rolling, and of the way in which the movement of the ship is
communicated to Billy and thence to the soup pan. In the first
three sentences there is a suspension of central information until
the end, which has the effect of increasing narrative tension.
This parallel mode in the first three sentences also imparts a
certain security which is torn away by the abrupt 'His countenance changed'. At the same time there is sufficient clarity of
expression for another series of parallels: Billy 'chanced' to spill
his soup, Claggart 'happened' to be passing by the mess bay,
Claggart 'happened' at the last moment to see who had done the
spilling: and all this refers us back to that initial impulse of
chance, that element to which chance is as it were native: the
sea. The precision here suggests that the lack of it in other
passages could be deliberate.

Nevertheless, Melville's purpose is often to obscure the
dynamic aspect of his narrative, and to portray rather a series of
tableaux. There can be little dramatic conflict: even Vere, who
suffers under the burden of condemning Billy, nonetheless feels
instinctively that he must hang him from the first instant of his
knowledge that Claggart is dead – '"Struck dead by an angel of
God! Yet the angel must hang!"' (101); and Billy unhesitatingly
accepts his sentence. Billy's function is simply to *be*, as is
Claggart's, so that the two may explode like opposed chemicals
when brought together. His striking of Claggart comes from
nowhere: it is instant repugnance combined with incapacity to
express it otherwise, and the blow and Claggart's collapse are
over in two sentences. Billy's execution is an ascension: we are
asked to pay attention more to this aspect of it than the fact that
he is being hung. In the sense that there is little real sequence of

motive and act, and every deed is spontaneous and instinctive, emerging from what the characters are rather than what they do, description of the acts is finally of minor importance.

Melville is extremely fulsome in his descriptions of settings, painting a series of 'still lifes'. His purpose here seems not only to turn the story into a series of images, but to make his characters more credible by anchoring them to the objects and people about them.

> Life in the foretop well agreed with Billy Budd. There, when not actually engaged on the yards yet higher aloft, the topmen, who as such had been picked out for youth and activity, constituted an aerial club lounging at ease against the smaller stun'sails rolled up into cushions, spinning yarns like the lazy gods, and frequently amused with what was going on in the busy world of the decks below. (68)

The constant inversions and suspensions – 'well agreed' and the material separating 'There . . . the topmen . . . constituted' slow the account. The loosely-connected participial phrases at the end, whose relation is diffused between the plural 'topmen' and the singular 'club', imitates the easy detachment described. After 'Billy Budd' in the first sentence one would expect 'he' to follow 'There' in the second, and is brought up short by 'the topmen'; and 'spinning yarns', coming after such an account of cloth and cushion, gives further pause till we dispose of the pun. In this passage again Melville's style is singularly fitted to its purpose; and similar appositeness can be seen, for example, in the chiaroscuro portrait of Billy on the upper gun-deck on the eve of his execution (118–19).

The equivalent 'painting' of the central characters is carried out in a much more diffusive manner. Part of Melville's purpose here seems to be to isolate the natures of his characters by contrasting them with a range of social figures with which they might be thought to have a certain kinship – just as he sets off Billy's figure from his surroundings in the upper gun-deck description, and exploits there the contrast of light and dark. Indeed the technique of contrast can be argued as central to Melville's descriptive method.[10] The purpose may also be seen as one of setting his figures in a fabric of reality. It would be easy to say, simply, 'Claggart is natural depravity, Billy natural innocence, and Vere an intellectual sailor'. But Melville's detachment, the way he treats each character almost as a case history, is here essential to the sense of reality with which we apprehend his central figures. Further, the characters become more credible the more they are compared with other people: Vere with Nelson and his fellow-officers, sailors with landsmen, Claggart with criminals (or attitudes to him aboard ship with those which might be evinced by clerics, lawyers or psychologists), Billy with other types of sailor-cynosure, with Adam, or Christ, or even dogs and horses. It is precisely such comparisons which at once make the exceptional in Melville's characters seem rooted in life, and as in some of the analogies with our world used by writers of fantasy to make their strange realms more credible, heighten their sheer unlikeness to anything in our economy. Unlikeness, C.S. Lewis once remarked, is never more evident than when two near-likes are brought together.[11]

Nevertheless, rather more than this is often happening. Just as with Billy, Melville does not so much draw comparisons as suggest them while rejecting them (the portrait of the Billy-be-Dam), so with Claggart, he offers a lengthy series of surmises and possibilities concerning his character, before abandoning them all. He tells us first that 'His portrait I essay, but shall never hit it' (64). He describes the duties of a master-at-arms, gives some physical description of Claggart, and mentions how his pallor, his separation from manual toil and his intellect marked him off from the other sailors; and proceeds to tell us that his manner and bearing so suggested an 'education and career incongruous with his naval function that when not actively engaged in it he looked like a man of high quality, social and moral, who for reasons of his own was keeping incog.' (64). A long account now follows of the sailors' speculation that Claggart is an aristocrat who was haled to trial for some crime and volunteered for the navy as a substitute for punishment. Melville then proceeds to give some foundation for this view, in an even longer account of how it was the practice of the time, when the navy was short of men, to secure adequate crews by drafting direct from the jails; nor does he fail to diverge to draw the ironic point of jailbirds fighting, in the form of the previous inhabitants of the Bastille, other jailbirds, before digressing further into the apocalyptic horror that then seemed presented by the French Revolution all over the world. After this, he turns to say that the sailors' speculations concerning Claggart deserved very limited credit, emanating as they did from the usual detestation of a person in Claggart's rank aboard a man-of-war. Melville ends this, his first section on Claggart, with the statement that the sailors knew no more of the master-at-arms' behaviour before he joined the navy than 'an astronomer knows about a comet's travels prior to its first observable appearance in the sky' (67); and that the entire foregoing material has been designed only to show how sailors were constitutionally incapable of understanding the 'moral phenomenon' of Claggart in terms other than those of mere 'vulgar rascality' (ibid.). He concludes by giving us the definite facts of the master-at-arms having started in the lowest position in the crew, before his bearing, his assiduity, his toadying and his apparent patriotism ensured his promotion. And there, apart from certain analogies drawn between the shape of Claggart's chin and that of Titus Oates, and the statement that his complexion 'seemed to hint of something defective or abnormal in the constitution and blood' (64), we are left for the time.

Clearly there is no accounting for this by any of the stylistic objectives we have so far outlined. When we return to Claggart, after two chapters, the method is continued (ch. 11), and here more directly. Melville raises the possibility that Claggart's hatred of Billy could have been the result of some past incident in which he had met him, only to dismiss such a resolution of 'whatever of enigma may appear to lurk in the case'. Then he tells us:

> And yet the cause necessarily to be assumed as the sole one assignable is in its very realism as much charged with that prime element of Radcliffian romance, the mysterious, as any that the ingenuity of the author of *The Mysteries of Udolpho* could devise. For what can more partake of the mysterious than an antipathy spontaneous and profound such as is evoked in certain exceptional mortals by the mere aspect of some other mortal, however harmless he may be, if not called forth by this very harmlessness itself? (74)

Simply we could say that this tells us that Claggart's hatred of Billy arose from the strong antipathy of bad to good. Yet the whole account effects a blurring of so naked a statement. In relation to the material immediately preceding, Melville is saying that the resolution of the enigma produces an enigma, or, that the removal of the mystery of Claggart's motivation reveals a purpose which is the quintessence of mystery. And why? – because what drives him is in a sense no drive, an impulse without efficient cause. Therefore, it may be, Melville mystifies us through his style, in order that we should lose touch with certainty. Instead of saying, 'And yet the cause is . . .', he describes the cause as 'necessarily to be assumed as the sole one assignable' – which leaves open other possibilities: thus he at once informs us that this is the sole cause, and that we are making it so. This mode of 'advance and retire' seems fundamental to his style throughout. At the same time, the orotund mode of expression has been such as to fog the issue further even as it presents itself as clarification. The phrase 'in its very realism' is also obscure, or at best the deadening of experience by concepts: the realism could be 'its actuality within life' or 'what it is found actually to be through analysis', but we cannot be sure. Nor can we be certain of whether Melville is then going on to say that its mystery is in direct proportion to this realism: all we can be sure of is that Claggart's motives are at once 'real' and 'mysterious'. Then, to proceed to say that these motives are 'as much charged with that prime element of Radcliffian romance, the mysterious, as any that the ingenuity of *The Mysteries of Udolpho* could devise', quite apart from losing us in a literary reference, is to say the same thing twice (and we may recall that Mrs Radcliffe's mysteries were most of them explained away in quite 'natural' or 'realistic' terms). The last sentence continues the fogging – 'partake of' instead of 'be'; the placing of two (abstract) adjectives after an (abstract) noun; 'such as' followed by 'certain' and then 'some other'; the constantly tumid and general language ('antipathy', 'evoked', 'mortals', 'aspect', 'called forth', 'this very', combined in the heaviness of the rhetorical question); and the last phrase of the sentence, tacked on as it is, seems momentarily an answer to the opening words of the question 'For what can more partake . . . ?' than a modification of the two clauses immediately before it.

Melville now proceeds to point out how such antipathy would be exacerbated in the confined world of a ship, where there is of necessity constant contact between the opposite natures of one like Billy Budd and a 'peculiar human creature the direct reverse of a saint' (74). He then decides that the 'hints' he has so far given the reader concerning Claggart's nature are insufficient for ordinary people, 'To pass from a normal nature to him one must cross "the deadly space between." And this is best done by indirection' (ibid.). We recall here that in his story as a whole Melville characterises evil in terms of crookedness, and contrasts sailors and landsmen as the direct and the more or less corruptedly indirect: here again we see him practising, perhaps for a purpose, the very methods he disdains in his story.

The indirection followed is one of giving fictive examples of other 'Claggart' types in the past who have taxed the understandings of those in contact with them. The functions of this method might seem, first, that the particular Claggart Melville is describing should gain in credibility from other seemingly authenticated cases, and second, that the precise nature of the imaginative leap required to comprehend his nature should be more fully grasped. Yet the labour expended on this 'de-mythologizing' of Claggart, rather than serving to clarify, seems both unnecessarily lengthy and confusing. For example:

> Long ago an honest scholar, my senior, said to me in reference to one who like himself is now no more, a man so unimpeachably respectable that against him nothing was ever openly said though among the few something was whispered, 'Yes, X — is a nut not to be cracked by the tap of a lady's fan. You are aware that I . . .'. (74)

This may be a masterpiece in the art of losing the reader. The 'Long ago', 'my senior' and 'one who like himself is now no more' are quite irrelevant information, the purpose of which seems only to tangle the thread of discourse to the point where 'a man so unimpeachably respectable' seems for a moment to refer to the honest scholar, since the other person has so far been mentioned only as 'one'. The definiteness of 'nothing was ever openly said' blurs into 'though among the few something was whispered'; and by the time the speech is opened we have so lost the scholar that for the time we take the utterance as that of 'the few' until jerked short by the 'you' and 'I'.

So the account continues, orotund, repetitive and confusing. In any objective sense the labour expended on making Claggart credible appears unnecessary – the whole could have been rendered in a quarter of the space. Even if we were to argue that Melville's purpose was at once to make Claggart 'real' by setting him in a social context, while at the same time putting over the 'mysterious' in his nature by the device of confusing the reader, this does not seem sufficient: Shakespeare, for example, realises the reality and the 'mystery of iniquity' of his Iago by means quite different and terse, and without authorial comment. Here something further is the object.

Nor, we may add, is the obfuscating style confined to those characters, Billy Budd and Claggart, who could be said peculiarly to embody the mysterious in the story; it is recurrent. Now clear, now dim, the tale, the characters and the scenes themselves appear to slip in and out of focus continually. Definition and certainty seem no sooner proffered than they are withdrawn.

> To the British Empire the Nore Mutiny was what a strike in the fire brigade would be to London threatened by general arson. In a crisis when the kingdom might well have anticipated the famous signal that some years later published along the naval line of battle what it was that upon occasion England expected of Englishmen; *that* was the time when at the mastheads of the three-deckers and seventy-fours moored in her own roadstead – a fleet the right arm of a Power then all but the sole free conservative one of the Old World – the bluejackets, to be numbered by thousands, ran up with huzzas the British colours with the union and cross wiped out; by that cancellation transmuting the flag of founded law and freedom defined, into the enemy's red meteor of unbridled and unbounded revolt. (54)

After putting the desperate nature of the situation very succinctly in his first sentence, Melville glosses it, and with his very oblique reference to Nelson's Trafalgar injunction, simultaneously begins to lose us: the subordinate clauses, 'In a crisis when . . .' 'that . . .', 'what it was . . .', '*that* was the time . . .', and the jerk to a different time and back again loosen our grip not only on the particular moment but the sense. The parenthesis on the fleet finally dislocates the sentence; the juxtaposed word-orders of 'founded law and freedom defined' blur the very clarity they purport to describe; and the shrill 'red meteor' amasses more attention than the more abstract and yet precise 'unbridled and unbounded' which would otherwise have gained force from their contrast with the previous 'founded' and 'defined' natures of law and freedom.

'There are some enterprises in which a careful disorderliness is the true method' (*Moby-Dick*, ch. 82). By now we may have some of the materials with which to provide a justification of the suitability of Melville's style to his theme in this story. Most basically we can suggest that here he evinces the extent to which he would take realism: his quarrel may have been not only with artistic form, but with words themselves, for words and sentences make patterns and forms of what for Melville is ultimately formless – the random nature of life, the finally instinctual, uncivilized nature of all humanity, and the sea itself, on which dark abyss the frail shells of human rationality pass in ignorance of the depths beneath. Here the nautical setting has symbolic aptness. Here, too, Billy's stutter is central, for it images that incapacity of speech which Melville could be seen as trying to portray in his own style.

The method, if method it is, is one of paradox. In the theme of his story Melville condemns omniscience, indeed all detachment from the heart of experience and of man, and yet writes his tale as an omniscient narrator: but the paradox is removed when his omniscience is seen to be but fumbling ignorance, and when his civilized, careful diction reveals itself as uncertain, empty, or irrelevant. Thus, in a kind of 'evaporation of wit', or on the principle that 'One fire drives out one fire; one nail, one nail,'[12] civilization would be being used to explode civilization. (Perhaps this is figured in the recurrent use of double negatives in the story.) Melville's civilized, Vere-like mode of discourse could be seen as a means of engaging precisely the qualities in his reader which it is his purpose to undermine – intellectuality, sophisticated reflectiveness, comfortable distance, and the sense of dealing with life, like the lawyer in 'Bartleby' with his opaque scrivener, as a gallery of interesting case-histories. In this sense, if the sense be true, Melville is a dramatized narrator.

We know that by the time of writing *The Confidence-Man* (1857), Melville had finally turned his back on 'the tribe of "general readers"' or 'superficial skimmers', leaving out even the pretence of a gripping narrative and forcing his reader's attention much more directly and continuously on the complex and less flowing mode in which this work was written;[13] and we may surmise that the long years of isolation and doubt before he wrote *Billy Budd* pushed the process further. The form of his last story is really a series of glosses on a small and constantly broken thread of narrative; its successive manuscripts follow a process of elaboration or dilation. It is quite likely that, as in *The Confidence-Man*, where as has been shown he uses a debased and corrupt style as an imitation of and comment on the nature of the central detestable figure,[14] so in *Billy Budd* Melville uses the idiom of civilization to expose it. Thus, while he may be writing for those 'of head-piece extraordinary', he is arguably doing so not to please them but to torture them rarely. If so, Melville has moved in *Billy Budd* to the point where he wants no mere *readers*, and where his style becomes a satire on the condition of reading. Billy Budd, his prime character for the story, is, we may add, illiterate. If *The Confidence-Man* is caviar to the general, it may well be that in his last story Melville intended his caviar-eaters themselves to choke on their own delicacy.

Notes and References

1. At least, this fact is not questioned in the story. C. B. Ives, '*Billy Budd* and the Articles of War', *American Literature*, 34 (1962-3) 31-9, has shown that in point of legal fact an act of mutiny required a combination of two or more persons, and that the Mutiny Act applied only to the army and not to the navy. But without help from the author the reader is unlikely to know this; it is probable that Melville was either ignorant of the facts or had forgotten them.

2. References throughout are to Herman Melville, *Billy Budd, Sailor*, ed. Harrison Hayford and Merton M. Sealts, Jr. (Chicago: University of Chicago Press 1962).

3. Vere's position here is very close to that of Shakespeare's Angelo in *Measure for Measure*: resolved to crush the burgeoning vices of his time Angelo revives an over-harsh law which he uses to sentence Claudio for an act essentially committed in innocence; and he is waylaid by a 'tearful kinswoman of the accused' in the form of Isabella. Melville may have had this situation at least faintly in mind.

4. Hayford and Sealts, pp. 185-6, cite parallel passages from *White-Jacket* (1850) and *Clarel* (1876).

5. We may note that this is ironically followed by Melville's disclaimer of form in his story (128).

6. Lawrance Thompson, *Melville's Quarrel with God* (New Jersey:

Princeton University Press 1952) 355-414, argues that Melville is here recording his view of God's authorship of evil, and that his 'early and deeply-rooted Calvinist belief' (361) made him, when more critical, both endorse and lament a view of evil as necessitated by God. But this is to read declarations made in Melville's earlier work (e.g. *Moby-Dick*) too readily into the story: without the reader's knowing the Calvinist view of the Fall, or Melville's bitter acceptance of it as a universal truth, he is given no other incentive in this story than to try to fit the narrative facts into the orthodox account based on the concept of human free will. To back up his claim Thompson has to term the teller of the tale Melville's 'stupid narrator' (377), from whose supposed bland acceptance of the disciplinarian line we are to be ironically distanced; but this in fact involves postulating not so much a stupid narrator as a supersubtle reader.

7. Compare his letter of June 1851 to Hawthorne, 'I stand for the heart. To the dogs with the head!' (*The Letters of Herman Melville*, ed. Merrell R. Davis and William H. Gilman (New Haven: Yale University Press 1960) 129).

8. Compare Melville, *Moby-Dick*, ed. Luther S. Mansfield and Howard P. Vincent (New York: Hendricks House 1952) ch. 112, p. 481.

9. Compare *Moby-Dick*, ch. 32, p. 142.

10. In *Moby-Dick* Ishmael says, 'there is no quality in this world that is not what it is merely by contrast. Nothing exists in itself' (ch. 11, p. 53).

11. C. S. Lewis, *Surprised by Joy: The Shape of My Early Life* (London: Geoffrey Bles 1955) p. 170.

12. Shakespeare, *Coriolanus*, IV, vii, 54.

13. Cecilia Tichi, 'Melville's Craft and the Theme of Language Debased in *The Confidence-Man*', *ELH*, 39 (1972) 643-4.

14. Tichi, op. cit.

INDEX